Springer Series on Social Work

Albert R. Roberts, D.S.W., Series Editor

Mary Joy Quinn, R.N., M.A., is a Court Investigator for the California Superior Court, City and County of San Francisco. She is a public health nurse and since 1973 has focused exclusively on frail elders. She formerly directed a geropsychiatric day treatment center and has published in the field. She is on the faculty of the San Francisco State University Gerontology Certificate Program.

Susan K. Tomita, M.S.W., is an Assistant Director of Social Work at Harborview Medical Center, Seattle, Washington. As a social worker in the Senior Care Program, she pioneered the development of an elder abuse protocol which has been published and distributed nationally. She is a Clinical Assistant Professor of Social Work at the University of Washington.

ELDER ABUSE
AND NEGLECT

Causes, Diagnosis, and Intervention Strategies

Mary Joy Quinn, R.N., M.A.
Susan K. Tomita, M.S.W.

Springer Publishing Company
New York

Springer Publishing Company, Inc.
536 Broadway
New York, NY 10012

86 87 88 89 90 / 5 4 3 2 1

Library of Congress Cataloging-in-Publication Data

Quinn, Mary Joy.
　Elder abuse and neglect.

　(Springer series on social work; v. 8)
　Bibliography: p.
　Includes index.
　1. Abused aged—United States.　2.　Social work
with the aged—United States.　3.　Abused aged—Services
for—United States.　I.　Tomita, Susan K.　II.　Title.
III.　Series.
HV6626.Q56　1986　　　362.6'042　　　86—6696
ISBN 0—8261—5120—5

Printed in the United States of America

To our parents,
E. Joy Stine and Walter T. Stine
and
Hiroko Miura Tomita and Susumu Tomita,
whose caring has taught us to care for others

Contents

Foreword

Congressman Claude Pepper

Elder abuse. The phrase still sends shock waves among the majority of Americans. Most find it hard to believe how widespread and frequent this problem is. Most would prefer not to acknowledge that elder abuse, which flies in the face of traditional American ideals, exists.

Eight years ago the Select Committee on Aging began an investigation into the problem of elder abuse. A series of field hearings and considerable research revealed the sad truth—elder abuse was far from an isolated and localized problem involving a few frail elderly and their pathological off-spring. The problem was a full-scale, national epidemic which existed with a frequency few dared imagine. In fact, abuse of the elderly by loved ones and caregivers existed with a frequency and rate only slightly less than child abuse. Subsequent work in this area has shown that the problem has increased dramatically through the years. Our latest figures show that 1.1 million, or one out of every 25 elderly persons, is the victim of abuse each year.

I think Ms. Quinn and Ms. Tomita are to be congratulated for their very comprehensive work on elder abuse. A recurring observation in the Committee's 1985 survey of state adult protective service workers was the dearth of information on elder abuse—particularly how to spot victims and provide appropriate intervention. I feel *Elder Abuse and Neglect: Causes, Diagnosis, and Intervention Strategies* will prove useful to anyone concerned with elder abuse—social worker, scholar, legislator, caregiver, or ordinary citizen.

We have a long way to go if we are to eliminate elder abuse in this nation. In the meantime, proper detection and intervention can ease the pain. I welcome the appearance of this important and timely book.

CLAUDE PEPPER

*Chairman, Subcommittee on Health and
   Long-Term Care
U.S. House Select Committee on Aging*

Preface

This book was written for anyone who works with elders and is concerned about their well-being. It is intended to serve both as an introduction to the subject of elder abuse and neglect and as a guide to effective intervention. It is our hope that the book will contribute to the information, sustenance, and energy that are needed to work with these challenging situations.

Although most research indicates that the typical victim of elder abuse and neglect is a woman, we have alternated the feminine and masculine pronouns throughout the book in an effort to simplify matters and to acknowledge both sexes. We also alternated the use of the pronouns when speaking of practitioners and abusers for the same reasons.

The case examples cited throughout the book are real. For the most part, they have been drawn from the authors' clinical experience, although a few cases came from newspaper accounts and from examples shared with the authors by other practitioners.

So many people gave generously of their time, experience, support, and wisdom in the preparation of this book that it is not possible to name them all. We wish to thank those known and anonymous who have contributed their ideas, insights, and knowledge.

We wish to thank Albert R. Roberts for his encouragement and suggestions regarding the submission of the proposal for this book. We also wish to thank Barbara Watkins for her support and concrete suggestions with regard to the preparation of the manuscript. Our appreciation goes to Ursula Springer for her abiding interest in the field of gerontology.

Many practitioners, particularly Donald Lachman, Nan Grayston, and the participants in workshops in elder abuse and neglect which were conducted by the authors, shared information and treatment suggestions that are incorporated in this book. We are grateful to Barbara Wertheimer for her advice regarding the chapter on legal issues and to Dennis Gustafson for his insights into the workings of a law enforcement agency and how practitioners and officers can learn to work together. Thanks also go to Betty Wood for her assistance and insights into the issues surrounding child abuse and neglect. Nikki King shared her materials on counseling and psychotherapy techniques. We thank Daniel Sonkin for his helpful words on batterers, and Cecelia London for her information on family systems and the elderly. Veronica Rodriguez and Maureen Kelly are appreciated for sharing their innovative casework techniques.

Our gratitude goes to Erica Goode, who edited portions of the manuscript and brought clarity to the book, and to Sarah Dana, who meticulously prepared the references. Thanks also go to Helen Friedman for her attention to detail in the preparation of portions of the final draft of the manuscript and the references. Our special thanks go to Myrna Anderson and David Redick, who typed numerous drafts of the manuscript efficiently and with great expertise.

Ms. Quinn would like to thank Judge Jay Pfotenhauer for his sensitivity toward the problems of older adults, Judge John A. Ertola for his energy, enthusiasm, and commitment to the administration of justice for frail elders, and Judge Raymond J. Arata, Jr., for his continuing support and willingness to help practitioners understand the workings of the court system. She would also like to thank Frederick J. Whisman, Executive Officer of San Francisco Superior Court, for his encouragement, advice, and practical suggestions. Ms. Quinn is especially grateful to her colleagues Catherine Gibbons, Felton J. Williams, and Angela Buscovich for their unfailing support during the writing of this book, and especially for their contributions to the section on financial abuse.

Special thanks go to Priscilla Ebersole for her concrete advice and sustaining support, and for her illuminating insights regarding elders, as well as for her expert suggestions with regard to portions of the manuscript. Jack McKay has made numerous helpful contributions, but more importantly, he has been a mentor and a valued colleague in the field of gerontology for over a decade, and much of the philosophy that is found in this book originated with him.

Family and friends are especially helpful in an endeavor such as developing a book. They contribute ideas and act as sounding boards. They also forego the companionship of the author. Frank A. Quinn, husband extraordinaire, not only took over all the household duties during the preparation of this manuscript, he early on recognized that the cases his wife was seeing in her work were unique and virtually unknown to the general population. He read portions of the manuscript and offered encouragement, enthusiasm, and tangible support at every step of the way.

The earliest portions of the book appeared in 1981 and were in part the result of exciting exchanges of ideas among several individuals at Harborview Medical Center. Shirley Anderson, M.D., formerly of the Sexual Assault Center, and Karil Klingbeil, M.S.W., Assistant Administrator, and Director of the Social Work Department, served as Ms. Tomita's mentors. Their teachings and encouragement sustained Ms. Tomita in her efforts to develop new tools to detect and treat elder abuse and neglect. Michael Copass, M.D., Chief of Emergency Services, saw the importance of training the emergency room staff to recognize elder abuse and neglect. His commitment to the development and use of uniform procedures to detect and treat all forms of domestic violence in the Emergency Trauma Center cannot be matched by others. Hugh Clark, M.D., formerly of Harborview Medical Center, collaborated on the development of the written protocol that is presented in this book. He too was a leader in promoting the training of practitioners to detect elder abuse and neglect.

Ms. Tomita's Senior Care Program colleagues, particularly Richard Uhlmann, M.D., and Itamar Abrass, M.D., never grumbled about her work overflowing into their office areas and monopolizing the office staff and equipment. Her social work colleagues Sue Oskam and Sandra Sanchez Burga helped with lightening her work load so she could write. Last, Ms. Tomita wishes to express special gratitude to Wendy Lustbader for her weekly supportive contacts over coffee and to her son Jason, who exhibited great patience as his mother spent hours on the telephone collaborating with Ms. Quinn.

Introduction

The plight of abused children and victims of battering spouses has received wide publicity. More recently, another aspect of hidden abuse has come to public attention in the form of elder abuse and neglect. The first research studies to document the abuse and neglect that older adults are experiencing in their own homes in the United States began appearing in professional journals and monographs in 1978. Most studies were exploratory and based on mail surveys, case studies, and a combination of personal interviews and secondary data analysis (Douglass & Hickey, 1983).

The methods employed by the studies vary, and so do the definitions of elder abuse and neglect. For instance, lack of personal care and supervision is, in one study (Block & Sinnott 1979) termed "physical abuse" and in another (Douglass, Hickey, & Noel 1980) termed "active neglect." The authors of one study (Douglass et al., 1980) did not ask the respondents to list incidents of financial abuse because they were focusing on other types of elder abuse and neglect. Despite this, the respondents to the survey listed incidents of financial abuse anyway, writing them into the questionnaire.

Although these studies are embryonic in nature and do not share the same terminology, there are common threads that give us some idea of the exact nature of elder abuse and neglect. It seems fairly clear, for example, that the typical victim of elder abuse is a woman over the age of 75 who is physically and perhaps mentally dependent. Typically, the abuser is a relative, and frequently the adult child of the victim. Pillemer and Finkelhor (1985) state that the abuser is often dependent on the victim for financial support and housing. The abuse is often ongoing (not limited to a single incident) and it may take several forms: financial, physical, or psychological. Abuse may include the violation of basic rights such as the right to worship as one chooses, the right to assembly, the freedom to be left alone, and the right to handle one's personal and financial affairs unless declared incapable of doing so by due process of law (Block & Sinnott 1979; Douglass et al., 1980; Lau & Kosberg 1978; O'Malley, Segars, Perez, Mitchell, & Knuepel, 1979).

To date there has been no sophisticated, full-scale randomized study of abused elders, of their caregivers, or of specific interventions that can produce favorable outcomes for the elder. In fact, each new study has served to draw attention to further gaps in our knowledge and to questions not yet answered. Each study also points to the need for further research and inquiry.

In response to these germinal studies, the Select Committee on Aging of the U.S. House of Representatives held extensive hearings and in 1981, published a report entitled *Elder Abuse: An Examination of a Hidden Problem*. In that report, the committee concluded:

> . . . elder abuse is far from an isolated and localized problem involving a few frail elderly and their pathological offspring. The problem is a full-scale national problem which exists with a frequency that few have dared to imagine. In fact, abuse of the elderly by their loved ones and caretakers exists with a frequency and rate only slightly less than child abuse on the basis of data supplied by the States. (U.S. House Select Committee on Aging, 1981)

In addition, the committee concluded that the abuse of older people is far less likely to be reported than the abuse of children, and that victims of elder abuse make up at least 4% of the elderly population. In 1981, this meant that one out of every 25 older Americans, or 1,000,000 people, suffered from some form of elder abuse. The committee estimated that one out of every three child abuse cases is reported (despite the fact that every state in the Union has laws mandating the reporting of child abuse). The Committee found that elder abuse only occasionally (one out of six cases) comes to the attention of authorities. In 1985, the committee found that elder abuse is increasing nationally, and that there was an increase of 100,000 moderate to severe abuse cases annually over 1981. The committee also found that 82% of all adult abuse cases reported annually involve elderly victims (Pepper, 1985).

Federal legislation to establish a National Center on Elder Abuse has been introduced unsuccessfully into the House of Representatives a number of times since 1980 by Congresswoman Mary Rose Oakar and Congressman Claude Pepper. The center would have a range of functions. It would serve as a clearinghouse for information and research on elder abuse, neglect, and exploitation. Technical assistance would be made available to a variety of agencies to assist them in planning, improving, developing, and implementing programs relating to elder abuse. The center would also conduct research and could make a comprehensive study of the incidence of elder abuse, neglect, and exploitation, including whether or not the incidence and severity are increasing. In the future, this legislation will probably be reintroduced until it gains the support needed to pass.

Federal legislation addressing some of the issues involved in elder abuse and neglect was signed into law in the fall of 1984. That legislation, contained in the Child Abuse Amendments of 1984, provides for the establishment of a National Clearinghouse on Family Violence, which will collect statistics and compile information on all types of family violence including elder abuse and neglect. The Secretary of the U.S. Department of Health and Human Services (HHS) was directed to make a report within 18 months (Spring 1986) on legislation to address family violence and to work with the National Institute on Aging with regard to elder abuse and neglect. In addition, federal funds were allotted to states for demonstration projects such as respite care.

The executive branch of the federal government has also tackled the problem of elder abuse and neglect. In the fall of 1983, Attorney General William French Smith announced the formation of a Task Force on Family Violence to study problems such as spouse abuse and child abuse and the mistreatment of the elderly. Smith noted that family violence is a "serious and complex crime problem" which has "for too long been viewed as a private matter best resolved by the parties themselves." The Task Force held hearings across the country and spent time with professionals concerned about elder abuse, including legislators, nurses, researchers, social work practitioners, and physicians. They also interviewed victims of abuse who bravely gave personal accounts of what it is like to experience abuse. A unique and hopeful aspect of the Task Force's work was that former abusers also came forth and gave testimony.

In September 1984, the Task Force published its findings (Attorney General's Task Force on Family Violence, 1984). The Chairman of the Task Force, Detroit Police Chief William L. Hart, concluded: "Family violence permeates all levels of our society. It is not unique to any particular social or economic group nor is it restricted to any one sex or age group." Chief Hart also noted that a victim of family violence is just as much a victim as someone who is abused by strangers.

The Task Force made recommendations to the various levels of government including the justice system: law enforcement, prosecutors, and judges. Among other things it recommended that prosecutors cease requiring victims of family violence to sign a formal complaint to initiate prosecution. Recommendations were also drawn up for other areas of concern including violence in the media, pornography, violence in military families, grandparents' rights, and victim assistance. Additional areas of concern were the gathering and reporting of family violence statistics, research, education, and training of professionals who must deal with both victims and abusers. Last, the Task Force had several recommendations for enhancing public and professional awareness of family violence.

Prior to 1978, the subject of elder abuse and neglect received scant attention aside from periodic anecdotal reports of abuse and neglect of the elderly, published in American and British medical and social services journals. Occasionally, an article on the subject also appeared in the print media, usually describing a particularly dreadful case of abuse or the discovery of an older person living in self-imposed filth and squalor.

Professionals who work with older adults have always known that elder abuse and neglect exist. But the problem has been difficult to grasp and define. It has been hard to understand the full import of elder abuse because so much of it has been hidden and denied. Often the elder is reluctant to admit that abuse by a son or daughter is occurring out of shame and humiliation at having raised a child who would do such things, or out of fear of being placed in a nursing home. The abuser is likely to hide the problem out of self-interest, and even when it is discovered often denies it or rationalizes it away by blaming the victim or the pressure of circumstances. Even practitioners who work with elder abuse and neglect every day encounter their own disbelief on a regular basis. They often cannot believe what they are seeing. The whole notion of middle-aged children physically or emotionally abusing their parents or taking financial advantage of them is alien to the American ideal and runs counter to the precepts of major religious faiths and, indeed, a sense of common decency. Practitioners are most likely to believe accounts of elder abuse and neglect when there is an extremely pathological caregiver doing the abusing, or when the abuse is so serious as to be life-threatening.

Not only has the problem of elder abuse and neglect been difficult to detect and comprehend, but concrete strategies for thoughtful and successful interventions have until now been nonexistent. Practitioners have had few guidelines to draw on when dealing with elder abuse and neglect, even in situations which endanger elder life. Community resources have also been sparse. Shelters for battered women have been reluctant to take in abused old women because their health problems and needs for physical and emotional care are beyond the capacity of most shelters.

There has always been elder abuse and neglect, just as there has always been child abuse and neglect and spouse abuse. What is new is the willingness of our society to confront these hidden issues and search for solutions. Suzanne Steinmetz, an acknowledged authority on family violence, has noted that the 1960s were the time for the discovery of child abuse, the 1970s brought new realizations about spouse abuse, and the 1980s will be the decade in which elder abuse is uncovered and brought into the consciousness of Americans (Steinmetz, 1978). While this country has been slow to admit that family violence exists, child abuse and spouse abuse are now commonly acknowledged. Even if their causes and solutions are not perfectly known, at least the public has been exposed to the issues, and some remedial steps have been taken. These include restraining orders preventing abusers from having continued contact with their abused spouses, mandatory reporting laws with regard to child abuse, and an infusion of funds from federal government to support programs such as shelters for battered women, telephone hotlines, resource centers, and training of professionals who encounter family violence.

Eventually, there will be federal governmental support for the detection and treatment of elder abuse and neglect as well. In the meantime, many communities have formed coalitions to combat elder abuse occurring in their locales, and most states have some type of mandatory reporting law regarding elder abuse and neglect. Research will continue, but we cannot wait until the research is complete to take action—the need is far too great. The publication of new research findings and theoretical formulations, increased government funding, and the development of practitioner techniques undoubtedly will move forward together. Professionals working in the field need to be continually aware of those research findings and need to talk to their colleagues and share ideas.

Since the emergence of elder abuse as an acknowledged problem, a number of papers have appeared in journals and a textbook has been published which includes contributions from researchers and theoreticians in the field. No textbook, however, has been published outlining in detail what practitioners dealing with elder abuse need to know. Anyone who works with the elderly and encounters elder abuse needs to be aware of the characteristics of elder abuse, the sociological background against which it occurs, its causes, how cases of elder abuse and neglect actually "look," and the methods of detection and strategies for intervention and treatment. There has been no book, so far, which combines current theory with clinical practice. That is the purpose of this book. Our intent is to combine theory with practice so that the practitioner—be it social worker, public health nurse, psychologist, police officer, attorney, or judge—can recognize and act effectively in situations where elder abuse and neglect are suspected. It is our belief that elder abuse and neglect can happen to any older person and that they can be treated using clinically developed protocols that are specific and have been validated by professionals who have dealt extensively with the problem.

Dealing with elder abuse and neglect can be complex and emotionally taxing. Inevitably, the practitioner must deal with his or her own outrage as well as a myriad of problems that affect the abused elder including housing, legal assistance, case management, counseling and protective services, in-home care, respite care, and emergency shelters. A case may go on for a period of months and, at times, seem to defy solution. For those reasons, we have included material on the practitioner's reactions to elder abuse and neglect and ways of coping constructively with the strong feelings that are sometimes engendered.

We must take steps now to address elder abuse and neglect in all their insidious forms. The incidence of elder abuse will increase given the rapidly growing numbers of frail old people in our society. This increase will be exacerbated by the pressures associated with inflation, the high rate of divorce, shifting of family roles, geographical mobility, and the threat of nuclear annihilation. There are more and more older people and they are living longer and longer. The 75-plus group is currently the fastest growing segment of the population. In 1900, there were 895,000 people age 75 and older, but by 1980, those numbers had increased to 9,967,000. In 1982, the population 75 and older constituted approximately 5% of the population, but by the year 2030, it is conservatively estimated that the number will increase to 10% of the total population (U.S. Senate Special Committee on Aging, 1984). It is the elders in this group who are most likely to become victims of abuse and neglect; they are a particularly vulnerable group of people. For the most part, they are frail and cannot speak for themselves or act on their own behalf. Unless there is widespread understanding of the phenomenon of elder abuse and neglect and society makes a commitment to a wide range of reform and assistance in both government and the private sector, the abuse, exploitation, and suffering will continue.

The Phenomenon of Elder Abuse and Neglect

Part One examines the emerging phenomenon of elder abuse and neglect including the nature and types of abuse and neglect, the profile of the typical victim and her abuser, and the various hypotheses as to why older adults, frequently impaired and dependent, are being abused and neglected in our society.

Chapter One explores the hidden nature of elder abuse and neglect. Other forms of domestic abuse such as child abuse and neglect and spouse abuse have been recognized for approximately 25 years, but it is only within the last 8 years that the abuse and neglect of elderly family members has come to the attention of the public and professional groups.

Chapter Two focuses on the victim of elder abuse and neglect and the dynamics of an abusive situation. It demonstrates the complexities of this type of abuse, the time and effort needed to resolve a case, and the frustrations typically encountered by practitioners.

In Chapter Three, the various types of abuse and neglect are described and case examples are given. Most people, even those who work with other forms of domestic violence, have difficulty visualizing exactly how elder abuse and neglect are manifested. In some instances, they closely resemble child abuse and neglect and spouse abuse. However, there are some unique aspects to elder abuse and neglect, such as financial abuse. Children and women typically do not own real estate or have other assets. Elders usually do, and this can make them a target for abuse and neglect.

Chapter Four focuses on the hypothesized causes of elder abuse and neglect including societal attitudes such as ageism and sexism, which create a climate for the maltreatment of older people. As yet, no specific theories have been proved or disproved by methodical research, but these various hypotheses offer a framework which practitioners will be able to utilize in their practice.

1 Elder Abuse and Aging

Although some preliminary steps have been taken in addressing the problem of elder abuse and neglect, they have as yet not received the same attention as other forms of domestic violence. In fact, doubt and skepticism are still widely expressed as to whether older people living in their own homes or with relatives are abused in any way. When the subject of elder abuse is mentioned, the general public usually thinks of nursing home abuses or of crime in the streets or fraudulent insurance schemes. It seems inconceivable that older people, perhaps frail, vulnerable, and unable to protect themselves, are being abused on a regular basis by those they trust the most: their families, their caregivers, sometimes even their nurses, doctors, or attorneys. There is some awareness that domestic violence affects women and children; but our society has yet to admit that it also touches the elderly.

A HIDDEN PROBLEM

Why have elder abuse and neglect remained such a secret, so hidden and unacknowledged? Some of the reasons are rooted deeply in the traditional nature of the family; others can be traced to the dynamics at work between domestic abusers and their victims. Still others flow from the ambivalent feelings society holds about growing old. On the practitioner's part, there has been a lack of information and a lack of support services for elders. In addition, agencies have had difficulty in trying to create procedures and policies that address elder abuse and neglect effectively.

Professionals who have worked in the field of family violence know that it is one of the toughest societal problems there is and that, even after 25 years of awareness, there is still a great deal of work to be done in bringing child abuse and spouse abuse fully into consciousness in this country. Until recently, both types of abuse have been sanctioned as proper behavior. Children and wives were viewed as chattel, the rightful property of the male head of the household, and it was his duty to discipline them if they "went astray." There was very little interference from the state. Harsh treatment was rarely viewed with concern, but rather as a righteous effort to discipline a disobedient child or a wayward wife.

Violence in the family and the neglect of helpless family members are emotionally charged issues. The home is traditionally the place where people feel the most secure. To think that one would not be safe there is nearly incomprehensible. This is one reason why it seems to take a great deal of knocking at the door of society's conscience in order for there to be recognition that abuse means something is wrong in an individual's private life, and that society has the responsibility to do something about it. The private home has been traditionally looked upon as a sanctuary from governmental interference of any kind. Indeed, this country was founded on this principle (among others), and many of those who left their homelands to come here did so to escape governmental interference in their private lives. Straus (1979) notes that the norms of American society make behavior inside the home a private affair, and that even after violence occurs, the rule of family privacy is so strong that it works to prevent victims from seeking help. This view is termed the "traditional position" in the *Final Report* of the Attorney General's Task Force on Family Violence (1984), which notes that until this century, wife battering and child abuse were viewed as private matters exempt from public scrutiny or jurisdiction. The Task Force also notes that this traditional view is still widely held by the public as well as by some law enforcement officers, prosecutors, and judges.

Why Elder Abuse Victims Don't Tell

Many older people are concerned about their family's privacy and the privacy of their relationships, and that is why they do not report the abuse and neglect they are suffering or why they tell practitioners they do not want to take any action against the abuser. They fear public exposure, the embarrassment and humiliation they are sure it will bring. They feel shame at having raised a child who would hurt them in any way (U.S. House of Representatives, 1981). They do not want others to know that their lives have come to such a pass. Some victims prefer to suffer in silence rather than break the family code of solidarity (Jacobs, 1984). Linked to these feelings of shame and embarrassment is the anxiety about what will happen if an "outsider" finds out about the abuse. The older person may fear realistically that the perpetrator will retaliate with still more mistreatment if the abuse is reported. There is also often concern that the abuser, who is usually a family member or a caregiver the older person has come to rely upon, will be put in jail and that as part of that process, the older person will have to testify in court against the abuser. This means still more public exposure and possible rupturing of intimate relationships. Victims of elder abuse and neglect also worry that reporting means incarceration for the perpetrator, who may be the only caretaker or even the only relationship the elder has. This in turn raises the specter of placement in a nursing home, a fate most people view with horror:

> Almost all older people view the move to a home for the aged or to a nursing home with fear and hostility. . . . All old people—without exception—believe that the move to an institution is the prelude to death. . . . [The old person] sees the move to an institution as a decisive change in living arrangements, the last change he will experience before he dies. . . . Finally, no matter what the extenuating circumstances, the older person who has children interprets the move to an institution as rejection by his children. (Shanas, 1962)

Other family ties may also prevent the older person from reporting abuse. He may resist out of parental love, or the sense that a parent should protect and nurture a child no matter what the child has done. Some victims minimize the abuse out of family loyalty or for fear they will alienate whatever family they have.

> One man who lived in a nursing home was aware that his son had taken $90,000 from his bank account. He told the state ombudsman, however, that he did not want his son prosecuted and he did not want to take any steps to recover the money. "The money isn't important," he said. "My son is. After all, some family is better than none. He's all I got." The son rarely visited his father in the nursing home.

Child abuse victims fear losing parental affection and battered women fear losing the affection of their batterers; both fear the disruption of the status quo (Walker, 1984). Elder abuse and neglect victims are no different; they too fear rejection and disruption of their lives, even though they may be badly abused.

Some older people feel they deserve the abuse and accept it fatalistically. There may be a religious justification or a belief that suffering in the present will bring rewards in the future. The older person may feel that God means for him to suffer and that the suffering has a purpose that will be revealed in due time. Sometimes the female elder abuse victim will not report the abuse or prosecute because she has never been very assertive or effective in getting what she wants out of life; she has passively accepted whatever has come her way. Possibly she has learned that nothing she does will affect her circumstances. If she is abused in late life, that too is accepted. It may also be that she is a repeat victim of violence. Walker (1984) studied battered women and reported that early and repeated sexual molestation and assault in childhood make a woman more susceptible to being battered in later life. Almost one-half of the battered women in Walker's study reported that they repeatedly had been sexually molested as children. This dramatic pattern of victimization raises the question as to whether the elder abuse victim, who is usually a woman, may have been abused previously as a wife and as a child.

Some older people accept or do not acknowledge abuse because the way they lived their lives or their dependence on others makes them failures in their own eyes. It is only with great reluctance that older people resign themselves to being dependent on someone who once depended upon them for physical survival.

Some older people do not report the abuse and neglect because they are not aware of the abuse or they are incapable of realizing that they are being abused. Financial abuse can be well hidden, sometimes for years. Some victims are too impaired mentally or physically to be aware of abuse. The old-old, elders who are 75 and older, the most frequent victims of elder abuse and neglect, are more likely to be impaired, often disoriented in regard to time, place, and person, and incapable of physically taking care of themselves. They simply do not know what's going on around them.

Finally, elder abuse victims do not report that they are being abused because there is always the hope that the abuse will somehow stop—just as children hope abuse will stop; just as battered spouses hope that battering incidents will stop.

Role of the Abuser

Abusers, too, refrain from reporting abuse. This may occur out of conscious self-interest. But generally speaking, abusers tend to rationalize or minimize their actions and to deny that they have inflicted damage on the victim. An abuser may feel justified in his or her actions, alleging that the victim provoked the abuse and therefore got "what he deserved." They often excuse their behavior. If they are repentant and remorseful after a battering incident, this period is short-lived, and the abuse begins anew, escalating in frequency and intensity (Attorney General's Task Force, 1984; Sonkin & Durphy, 1982). Elder abusers commonly try to blame elder victims for their injuries by saying that they fell, but the astute practitioner can determine whether the injuries are the result of an accident or are intentionally inflicted.

Some elder abusers literally may not know that they are abusing, particularly if they themselves are demented or suffer from a mental illness. However, this type of abuser is likely in the minority.

A stressed caregiver, who suddenly and impulsively strikes out, may feel too ashamed to ask for help or may feel that no help will be forthcoming if he asks for it. He may also ask for assistance in a way that precludes receiving help. For example, he may request that a practitioner help him with one service when, in fact, elder abuse and neglect are on the hidden agenda. One study (Block & Sinnott 1979) reported that 95% of abuse cases were reported to some authority but no help was obtained. The agency most likely to be contacted was a public social service agency. Second was a private social service agency. A friend was the third most likely resource to be contacted; family and hospital/clinic were listed fourth, with courts and physicians the fifth most likely contacts. Help may not have been forthcoming for a variety of reasons. In some cases, the request for help may have been veiled or indirect or it may have been impossible for the agency to fulfill. In other cases, the request may not have been recognized as a call for help—the study is unclear in this regard. Traditionally, practitioners have not been trained to recognize and deal with elder abuse and neglect, and because of financial constraints, public adult protective service agencies have been unable to arrange for the amount of practitioner time needed to cope with the complex issues of elder abuse. Some practitioners do not intervene in cases of elder abuse and neglect because they continue to feel that domestic violence is a family matter and they should not intrude.

Another study (O'Malley et al., 1979) indicates that families and victims seldom *directly* report abuse, and that in 70% of the cases, it takes the active involvement of a third person before the issue comes to the attention of a professional or paraprofessional. In that study 24% of the abuse citings were brought to the professional's attention by the victim, and 5% of the cases were reported by a member of the victim's family. The rest of the citings came from personal observation of practitioners and their co-workers, from a variety of agencies, and from medical practitioners, the police, and others.

These two studies seem to contradict each other. The first study notes that the great bulk of cases have been directly reported, while the other indicates that it takes a third party to discover the case. The seeming contradictions in these studies may be due to the inability of the reporting family member or victim to report the abuse as *abuse* in a way that is unmistakable to the person receiving the report.

Growing Old

Some of the reasons that we do not recognize elder abuse and neglect have to do with the isolation of the aged and how we think and feel about growing old ourselves.

The elderly, especially the frail elderly, are more invisible than other age-groups. They are not visibly on the streets, and unlike children, they do not go to school every day where abuse and neglect are frequently detected by an observant teacher or school nurse. Frail elders do not go out of the house much; they tend to be more isolated than abused spouses, who may at least get to the supermarket and theoretically can walk away from an abusive situation. If the elder is bed-bound, the isolation may be complete. That elder may seldom if ever be seen by anyone other than family members or his caregiver.

Many people tend to shy away from the old, especially the elderly who are mentally and/or physically impaired. These elders may seem other-worldly, and many people do not feel comfortable being around them. Going into a nursing home for the first time can be traumatic, and many people come to believe the myth that all elderly people end up in nursing homes. It *can* be overwhelming to see large numbers of extremely impaired dependent elders living in one place. The thought, "Is this what my old age will be like?" is inescapable and frightening. These frail elders are literally unknown to the general public. Many people find it difficult to know how to act in the presence of an elderly individual who is obviously impaired; how much help to give, how to hold a conversation. Often there is a feeling of wanting to get away quickly.

The elderly constitute the only minority we all hope to join, no matter how ambivalent we may feel personally about the aging process. But old age is rarely seen as the triumph of survival that it really represents. The myths and stereotypes about aging infect everyone.

EMERGENCE OF ELDER ABUSE

Even though elder abuse and neglect traditionally have been concealed, they are now emerging as issues our society is willing to consider. The initial research and the congressional hearings in the late '70s and early '80s (where abused elders told their stories) sounded warning of this "new" form of domestic abuse. That call fell on fertile soil because groundwork already had been laid by dedicated researchers and clinicians working with other forms of domestic violence, i.e., spouse abuse and child abuse and neglect. So, even though the discovery that old people also suffer domestic violence has been met with shock, revulsion, and some denial, it is not as unbelievable as it might have been had it emerged before the discovery of other forms of private abuse.

There has been a fair amount of response on the state and local level. As of Spring 1985, 37 states had passed mandatory reporting laws requiring that elder abuse and neglect be reported to the authorities (Thobaben & Anderson, 1985). These state laws vary widely in their definitions of abuse and neglect. They also differ in who is required to report abuse, to whom the abuse is reported, and the penalties for not reporting. But despite these caveats, it is safe to say that in the long run, state laws will result in even more cases of elder abuse and neglect being uncovered. In one California county, caseloads increased by 49% in six months after a state mandatory reporting law was passed and publicized. This increase in cases has certainly been the experience with mandatory reporting laws for child abuse and neglect. For instance, in California, the annual number of reported child abuse and neglect cases jumped from 4,000 in 1968 to 80,000 in 1978 at which time the mandatory reporting law was well in place (Davidson, 1981).

Still another reason for the emergence of the detection of elder abuse and neglect is that there is a climate of concern that is at once new and genuine. Basically, this society is more compassionate than it once was, and most people are aware that all is not well with old people or with the way they live out their lives. There is also concern at many governmental levels about the enormous costs involved in seeing to the needs of the frail elderly. Medicare funding is always under siege and Social Security—the single most important source of income for the elderly—is preserved only because older people ceaselessly advocate for it (U.S. Bureau of the Census, 1984).

In a way, the awareness of elder abuse and neglect has been thrust upon society because of the unprecedented growth in the number of older people, particularly those 75 and older, the age-group that seems to be most vulnerable to abuse and neglect. This increase means enormous shifts in family roles, in public policy, and for elders as well.

GRAYING OF AMERICA

Never before in this country have so many middle-aged and young-old (aged 65–75) adult children had surviving parents or found themselves having to take care of their aging parents in the old-old age range (75 and over). Put simply, there are more elderly people than ever before, they are living longer, and their disabilities and dependencies increase in severity with their age. For example, a person born in 1900 could expect to live an average of 49 years. The person born in 1981, however, can expect on the average to live to nearly 74—a gain of approximately 25 years (U.S. Bureau of the Census, 1983; see Figure 1-1). According to government statistics, life expectancy increases nearly every year. In addition, those who are already old have had years added to their lives by advances in medical technology. Figures for 1980 indicate that a person who turned 65 that year could expect to live another 16.4 years, a person who was 75 could look forward to another 10.4 years, and a person who was 80, an astonishing 8.2 years (U.S. Bureau of the Census, 1984).

The fastest growing segment of the population is the group 75 and older, which means that more and more middle-aged adult children will have old-old parents, and four-generational families will become commonplace.

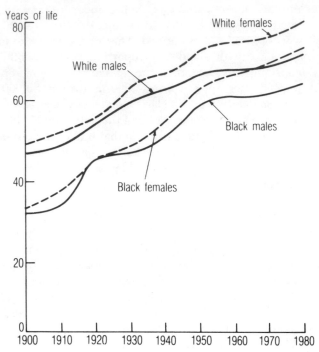

FIGURE 1-1 Expectation of life at birth, by race and sex: 1900–1980. (*Source:* National Center for Health Statistics, Vital Statistics Division, U.S. Department of Commerce, Bureau of the Census, *Historical Statistics of the United States,* 1975, and National Center for Health Statistics, *Monthly Vital Statistics,* Vol. 29, No. 13, September 1981, as it appears in U.S. Bureau of the Census, Current Population Reports, Series P-23, No. 128, *America in Transition: An Aging Society,* U.S. Government Printing Office, Washington, D.C., 1983, p. 5.)

The 85 and over group is growing particularly rapidly, up 165% from 1960–1982 (U.S. Bureau of the Census, 1983; see Table 1-1).

Clearly, dramatic shifts are taking place. There is every reason to expect that this "graying of America" will continue well into the next century. In 1982, Americans 75 and older constituted approximately 5% of the country's population. But by 2030, that number will rise to 10%, and by the year 2050, it will be 12%. It is this group that has the greatest needs for "social, income maintenance, housing, and health services" (U.S. Senate Special Committee on Aging, 1984). There is the strong possibility that even these figures are conservative because they cannot take into account continuing medical advances and voluntary changes in health habits such as diet modification and cessation of cigarette-smoking (Ostrovski-Quinn, 1985). For those concerned about elder abuse and neglect, these figures are particularly impor-

Table 1-1 Growth of the Older Population, Actual and Projected: 1900–2050

Year	Total population all ages	55 to 64 years		65 to 74 years		75 to 84 years		85 years and over		65 years and over	
		Number	Percent	Number	Percent	Number	Percent	Number	Percent	Number	Percent
1900	76,303	4,009	5.3	2,189	2.9	772	1.0	123	0.2	3,084	4.0
1910	91,972	5,054	5.5	2,793	3.0	989	1.1	167	0.2	3,950	4.3
1920	105,711	6,532	6.2	3,464	3.3	1,259	1.2	210	0.2	4,933	4.7
1930	122,775	8,397	6.8	4,721	3.8	1,641	1.3	272	0.2	6,634	5.4
1940	131,669	10,572	8.0	6,375	4.8	2,278	1.7	365	0.3	9,019	6.8
1950	150,697	13,295	8.8	8,415	5.6	3,278	2.2	577	0.4	12,270	8.1
1960	179,323	15,572	8.7	10,997	6.1	4,633	2.6	929	0.5	16,560	9.2
1970	203,302	18,608	9.2	12,447	6.1	6,124	3.0	1,409	0.7	19,980	9.8
1980	226,505	21,700	9.6	15,578	6.9	7,727	3.4	2,240	1.0	25,544	11.3
1990	249,731	21,090	8.4	18,054	7.2	10,284	4.1	3,461	1.4	31,799	12.7
2000	267,990	23,779	8.9	17,693	6.6	12,207	4.6	5,136	1.9	35,036	13.1
2010	283,141	34,828	12.3	20,279	7.2	12,172	4.3	6,818	2.4	39,269	13.9
2020	296,339	40,243	13.6	29,769	10.0	14,280	4.8	7,337	2.5	51,386	17.3
2030	304,330	33,965	11.2	34,416	11.3	21,128	6.9	8,801	2.9	64,345	21.1
2040	307,952	34,664	11.3	29,168	9.5	24,529	8.0	12,946	4.2	66,643	21.6
2050	308,856	37,276	12.1	30,022	9.7	20,976	6.8	16,063	5.2	67,061	21.7

Source: U.S. Department of Commerce, Bureau of the Census, Censuses of Population, 1900 to 1980, and Current Population Reports, Series P-25, No. 922, *Projections of the Population of the United States: 1982–2050 (Advance Report),* middle series projections, as it appears in U.S. Bureau of the Census, Current Population Reports, Series P-23, No. 128, *America in Transition: An Aging Society,* U.S. Government Printing Office, Washington, D.C., 1983, p. 3.

tant because all known evidence indicates that the person most likely to be a victim is over the age of 75.

Impact on Families

Families, traditionally looked upon as the caregivers of frail elderly kin, are facing many changes because their old-old members live so long, especially if the elder becomes dependent in any way. The term "generational inversion" has been coined to describe the phenomenon whereby responsibilities, status, control, and dependency for survival are permanently inverted, and adult children assume the roles previously held by their parents (Steinmetz, 1983). It is an unforeseen, and not always welcome, situation for both parent and child; no one envisioned that the parent would live to such an advanced age. More and more Americans are finding themselves in this position. The old-old often express amazement that they are still alive. During the course of a social service interview, one 94-year-old woman turned to her 92-year-old husband and said, "John, why on earth have we lasted so long?"

One very concrete result of longevity is that it becomes impossible to pass on an inheritance. The elder wants to give it and most likely the adult child needs it. But the impaired elder ends up using the money to purchase a variety of services, many of them health-related. Elders use medical services more than younger people: people 65 and over average six physician visits for every five of the general population. Older adults are also hospitalized approximately twice as frequently as younger people and stay twice as long. The elderly use twice as many prescription drugs (U.S. Bureau of the Census, 1983). Length of hospitalization appears to be directly correlated to age. For those 55 to 64, the average hospital stay in 1982 was 1.9 days, while for those 65 to 74, the average stay was 3.2 days. On the average, those 75 and over were hospitalized the longest—6.0 days (Brotman, 1982). Thus, needed services for the very old may consume the inheritance.

Dependency and Disability

Most people understand that older adults may need some assistance. But being largely dependent over long periods of time, perhaps years, is not looked upon favorably by either old people or by those who must care for them. On the contrary, such dependency is often viewed with fear, dread, disrespect, shame, and disapproval. Needing others is not the American way. There is still a strong ethic in this country that says the most admirable people are those who are able to suffer without complaining and who can take care of themselves without the aid of others. Rugged individualism, no matter the cost or the circumstances, is more valued than dependency or even interdependency. We accept dependency in children because we understand that children need their parents for survival. But children grow up and gradually become less dependent. This is not true for some old adults, who become dependent because of physical and/or mental impairments. These impairments are likely to worsen over time, given the nature of chronic illness. The older adult becomes progressively more dependent, and therefore more vulnerable to actions of others.

Types of dependence encountered in the process of aging can include economic dependence, as the individual moves from a producer to a consumer; physical dependence arising from waning physical strength and energy and diminishing ability to perform daily tasks; social dependence occurring if mobility becomes problematical and/or contemporaries die; and mental dependence, often an outcome of the other forms of dependence (Blenkner, 1969).

The kinds of dependence that come normally and gradually to many of the aged can be exaggerated by the mental and physical conditions that frequently accompany old age. As we age, the incidence of acute illnesses greatly decreases, but the incidence of chronic physical and mental disease increases, leading to permanent impairments which take their toll on functional abilities. In 1982, Butler and Lewis reported that 86% of older adults have at least one chronic health problem, and many have more than one. Most chronic health conditions are not disabling. But with increasing age, however, they are much more likely to be associated with disability (Blake, 1984). The old-old, that is, those over 75, generally need more care and assistance than those under 75. For instance, 40% of nursing home residents are over 85 years of age (Butler & Lewis, 1982). In the age range 65 to 74, only 6.7% of persons need assistance in essential personal care and home management activities. That figure doubles to 15.7% for people in the 75- to 84-year age-group and increases to 39.3% in the 85-year-and-older age-group (U.S. Senate Special Committee on Aging, 1984).

Although the likelihood of spending one's life in a nursing home increases with age, most older adults, contrary to popular belief, continue to live in the community whether or not they are impaired; only 4.7% of those over the age of 65 live in nursing homes at any given time (U.S. Senate Special Committee on Aging, 1984). This means that the great bulk of impaired and dependent older people are living in the community and are dependent on others for assistance.

Reactions to Dependency

Most families respond in caring and helpful ways to the dependence of elder members and do not abuse or neglect them in any way. And there are many families who exhibit amazing creativity, compassion, and heroism in their dealings with aged dependent family members. The reactions of the dependent elder are also a factor; some older adults are able to accept dependency with more grace and style than others. But for most people, it is a very difficult time, and not all families have the capacity to react to dependency in a constructive manner.

Some families react in ways that exacerbate the difficulties of dependence. Adult children may deny the dependency because it is too painful to confront and to acknowledge that a beloved parent is losing strength and may no longer be the authority in the family; it means "growing up" and is a hint of their own mortality (Kirkpatrick, 1955). It is also a forceful reminder that the parent will leave by dying, placing the adult child in the position of being in the "lead generation," next in line to face the terrors of old age and death.

Other adult children fail to acknowledge an aging parent's dependency because it frightens them and they do not know what to do about it. They become paralyzed. Still others deny that their aged parent is failing because they do not wish to know and do not wish to help, sometimes for understandable reasons but other times due to selfishness and cruelty. Some adult children rush their parents into complete dependency out of ignorance, because it means gaining control, or because it is easier than coping with someone who is partially independent (Kirkpatrick, 1955).

Older people may deal with dependency in ways that make it even more problematical. Some embrace it prematurely, even when they are still capable. This can anger adult children, who are busy with their own lives and feel their parent could cope if only he tried. Other old people resist dependency, denying it verbally and struggling to maintain their former position of power, all the while having to accept more and more assistance from their adult children (Kirkpatrick, 1955).

Losing Control

Any one impairment increases the possibility (and in many instances, the probability) that the elder will lose the capacity to handle his or her own personal and financial affairs. With that profound loss comes an inevitable decrease in personal control, including loss in decision-making power. Other people may be given the legal authority to decide such critical matters as who the attending physician will be or whether a lifelong home should be sold.

The elder may lose the ability to reciprocate when a caregiver performs a service. As a group, elderly people have diminished social and economic power with which to make exchanges with younger persons (Dowd, 1975). People who are physically and/or mentally impaired usually receive more in goods and services than they can return. Generally speaking, there is a loss of power when one cannot reciprocate in kind. The balance of power shifts. Those (caregivers) with the most goods (money), services, and capacities become the ones with the most power and are in a position to wield control over those (elders) with fewer goods, services, and capacities. Sometimes older people try to reciprocate by using what resources they have left as payment to the caregiver, or by leaving real or personal property to the caregiver in a will. The agreement, usually unwritten, goes like this: "You take care of me until I die. In return, I will leave you everything I have including my house." Older people, alone and lonely, have been coerced into signing their homes over to a caregiver as a condition of being taken care of. This places the older person in an untenable situation because he can be removed from the house at any time the caregiver chooses—the house no longer belongs to the older person.

It frequently happens that people in a position of trust, handling other people's resources (real property, bank accounts, stock portfolios) come to think of those resources as their own. This seems to occur particularly if the rightful owner of the resources is impaired and incapable of understanding how the resources are being used, and if the impairment has extended over a long period of time. It is a cruel reality that there always has been maltreatment of those less able to take care of themselves, of those who have lost the power of personality, and of those who cannot fight back effectively. The more vulnerable and impaired an individual is, the more tendency there is for others to objectify that person, to "thingify" and to attribute fewer and fewer human characteristics to the person until, in fact, the frail dependent elder may not be seen as human at all but is perceived as an object of frustration and stress.

Through the multiple losses of power that can come in old age, elders can come to feel that they are a burden—sometimes an accurate perception. Some older people react by becoming more compliant and obsequious, which in turn may be a stimulus for even more abuse, particularly with a cruel or indifferent caregiver. Many older people come to believe that events are beyond their control, and feelings of impotence take root. The elder feels helpless to do anything to change the way he is being treated, stops trying to do anything, and accepts whatever treatment is offered. This phenomenon was described by Seligman (1975), who termed it "learned helplessness." Seligman postulated that helplessness produces emotional disturbances. The motivation to respond to a situation is sapped if the individual feels that he can do nothing to affect the outcome. Another person may perceive that a particular reaction will make a difference in a given situation. But the person afflicted with "learned helplessness" will not think of that solution. There is also a decreased ability to perceive success. The elder may do something that does indeed change the situation for the better, but may not be aware of the success or fully comprehend that it was his action that made the difference. The individual cannot recognize success even when it is publicly acknowledged. In this way, even success begets failure. According to Seligman, perceived helplessness produces fear as long as the person is uncertain of being able to influence events, and then it produces depression.

Still other older people react to losses of personal power by becoming resistive and verbally combative, as they try desperately to hang on to what little power they may still have. This, too, may bring on abuse and neglect as the caregiver becomes frustrated with an uncooperative elder.

SUMMARY

Over the last several years, elder abuse and neglect have emerged as still another facet of domestic abuse. In part, this is due to the rapidly increasing number of old people, especially those who are 75 and over and in need of assistance in daily living. This reality is affecting large numbers of people, especially families, who have traditionally furnished the caregiving for elder members. It is also a dilemma for the elderly.

No one wants to be a burden; most people want to live to a healthy old age until they come to the end of their days. Then, they want to die quickly, painlessly, and effortlessly with no fuss or trouble to those around them. Because of increased longevity, and the frequency of health impairment and disability in late old age, fewer and fewer are being granted that wish.

2 The Abused Elder

When I was a laddie
I lived with my granny
And many a hiding ma granny di'ed me
Now I am a man
And I live with my granny
And do to ma granny
What she did to me.

—Traditional rhyme, *anonymous*

This folk poem speaks to the issue of family violence as it crosses genera-tions. Not a great deal is known about how elders fit into this theory, but it was thought to be a factor in the following case history, which was taken from official court records. The case illustrates much of what is known about elder abuse and neglect. Several forms of abuse are present, the profiles of the abuser and the victim are fairly typical, and the abuse is recurring. The case also describes the frustrations of the case practitioners, the complexity of the issues relating to abuse and neglect, and finally, the resolution of the situation through the tenancity, competency, and compassion of the prac-titioners.

She was 76 years old and totally helpless. Four years earlier, she had fallen and struck the back of her head. The blow was so hard that her brain had slammed into the front of her skull; it was badly bruised and bled profusely. Although surgery helped and the blood clots were removed, part of her shattered skull bone could never be replaced. To protect the brain, a plastic disk now sat where once there had been bone.

Though she was alive, she was confined to her bed. With effort, she could turn over. She had difficulty swallowing and had to be fed. She ate very slowly. A tube carried away her liquid body waste. She was fragile and thin. She could not care for herself in any way; she was totally dependent on others for all her needs.

She spoke in a whisper and tended to drift off into a dreamlike state after a few sentences, which were usually not related to the subject at hand. She could not hold a real conversation. In fact, her brain had been so badly damaged that she was incapable of asking for anything—even a glass of water. Most likely, she didn't know where she was. She had lost her ability to think, to dream, to imagine, to reason. She smiled sweetly and often. She was helpless, mentally and physically.

She and her son Harry lived in a two-bedroom apartment in a "nice" part of town. The apartment itself was dirty, dank, and dark and cluttered to an extreme degree. There was no place to sit in the living room because papers and materials, probably articles of clothing, were piled several feet high on chairs and tables. Harry said that he was doing research and that the clutter was temporary. It looked very permanent to even the most casual observer.

Harry had dismissed all the household help and was taking care of the apartment and his mother by himself. He was 50 years old and unemployed. He said he had been a postal worker but had developed hypertension and resigned on doctor's orders. When he tried to qualify for disability payments, he had been found to be able-bodied.

Harry had been appointed, by the superior court, to handle all of his mother's affairs when she became disabled. He had done this on the advice of the doctor, who had told him that his mother would never be able to handle her own affairs again. Thus, Harry was his mother's conservator of person and estate and as such was empowered legally to handle her money and to determine the kind of care she would receive. Income to the household was $900 per month and came from his mother's pension and social security checks. Harry had no income of his own; he depended on his mother for food, clothing, and shelter. He was an only child and had never married. There were no close relatives.

A visiting nurse was still coming to the house because Medicare paid for the service. While visiting nurses had been involved since the original injury, they were growing discouraged and feeling impotent. Despite their best efforts to teach Harry techniques of caring for his mother, he did not follow through. Worse, his mother was hospitalized every time she was eligible for Medicare hospital benefits. The diagnoses were always the same: dehydration and malnutrition. Often, bruises about the face were noticed. On one admission, the mother had a split lip that was swollen and bleeding.

Other patients in the hospital saw Harry strike his mother on the side of the face when he thought she didn't swallow fast enough. He admitted hitting her. "I have to," he said. "She is deliberately not paying attention to her swallowing. I have to get her attention. Otherwise, it would take forever to feed her. It has to be done."

The hospitalizations always coincided with Harry's trips to southern California to see his "spiritual counselor." Inevitably, his mother would do well in the hospital. She would brighten considerably and regain physical functioning through rehabilitation. Just as inevitably, she would be discharged home to her son. He refused to place her in a nursing home even though a doctor had recommended that he do so. He said that she had cared for him in his youth and now it was his turn to pay her back.

Harry was always cheerful and affable. A tall man with a large protuberant stomach, he tended to intimidate people because of his bulk and his tendency to stand very close when holding a conversation. He became "too close for comfort."

One day the visiting nurse noticed that the mother's arm was swollen, bruised, and misaligned. She spoke to Harry about it and he told her what had happened. He had been feeding his mother a hamburger, he said, and she was eating very slowly. Out of frustration, he left the room. When he returned, he found that she had made a mess with the food. He reached over her to clean up the mess. It was then, he said, that she raised her arm to protect her face. In the following confusion, he lost his balance and fell on her. As he fell, he pushed her arm "out of the way" and he heard a distinct "popping noise" come from the arm. Harry called the doctor, who told him to wrap the arm but he refused to treat the arm more than that. The visiting nurse finally convinced the doctor to permit a portable X-ray machine to come to the house. He was reluctant to do so because "she's old and it wouldn't be worth the effort to treat her." The X-rays revealed a broken arm and elbow. The doctor still refused to treat the arm, even though this was the mother's functioning arm, the one that had been the center of much rehabilitation attention in the hospital. Now all use of the arm was lost.

The nurse was horrified. She began to feel that the doctor was in collusion with the son. She called a practitioner from the adult protection agency, who went to the home and tried to work with Harry. The practitioner offered to assist Harry in getting household help to care for his mother and the house. Harry refused. The practitioner then offered to help Harry get vocational training; Harry refused that too.

At all times, Harry spoke with affection for his mother and denied that he was under undue stress in caring for her. Yet even as he spoke, his smiling eyes seemed to belie hidden hostility. Practitioners who knew the case observed coyness and flirtation between the mother and son. One practitioner said it gave her the creeps; another said, "There's something unnatural about that relationship."

Harry continued to disregard rehabilitation suggestions. He refused to stop smoking in his mother's room even though he knew it increased her respiratory distress and aggravated her swallowing problems. He smoked incessantly while feeding her. He did not follow through on any of the treatment plans that had been devised by the rehabilitation team at the hospital. He would not help her turn in bed or reposition her. He never even sat her up in her chair. Her condition continued to deteriorate. The same doctor who was "sure" that Harry had had nothing to do with his mother's original fall was also now sure that Harry "pushed and pinched his mother." He was positive, too, that Harry caused the bruises and lacerations about the mother's face, but he had a hard time accounting for her multiple hospitalizations for dehydration and malnutrition. He said he felt Harry did the best he could but that it must be very frustrating to deal with someone as helpless and dependent as Harry's mother. Yet, though he questioned Harry's ability to care for his mother, he declined to actively help place the mother in a good nursing home. "Harry just won't pay for it," he said.

Then Harry said he wanted to visit his "spiritual counselor" in southern California; the doctor would cooperate by placing mother in the hospital, Harry explained. That was when a fresh bruise appeared on the mother's chin. Harry said, "Maybe I had to help her close her mouth."

In sheer desperation, the practitioner from the geriatric home visiting team called the local superior court and asked the court investigator for the court's help in protecting the mother. Much to the practitioner's surprise, the investigator discovered that Harry was indeed his mother's legal conservator and thus responsible to the court for his mother's care and the administration of her finances. What had been a care issue now became an official legal concern. A judge, upon learning the preliminary facts of the case, ordered a full-scale investigation and set a courtroom hearing in five days.

The court investigator who conducted the investigation talked to everyone involved in the case, reviewed all the medical records, and made several determinations. First, she concluded that the case properly belonged in the court, both because the court had appointed the son legal conservator and because community workers had already exhausted all other approaches. Second, she concluded that the mother was in need of 24-hour skilled nursing care. She said that the son could not possibly provide it, and that he was actually harming his mother. Finally, she recommended that the son be removed from his position as conservator of person and estate of his mother.

The hearing was held as scheduled. Testimony was taken from the doctor, the visiting nurse, and the practitioners from the adult protective service agency and the geriatric home visiting team, from Harry, and from the court investigator. The judge rendered his decision from the bench at the end of the hearing. Harry's legal powers over his mother were terminated and, on the order of the judge, she was immediately removed from the apartment and placed in a nursing home known to have especially kind, loving, and competent staff. It was the feeling of the judge and all the workers that the mother would be in jeopardy if she were in the apartment when her son returned from the court hearing. If her arm could be broken "accidentally," maybe she could suffer a more serious "accident." Maybe she could die "accidentally." It would not take much. She would not be able to fight off a pillow over her head. In fact, maybe the original fall was not an accident.

Today, the mother continues to live in the nursing home. She has gained weight, she speaks more clearly, and enjoys a vastly improved mental state. She no longer cringes when her son comes at mealtimes to feed her. He is carefully watched by the nursing staff whenever he spends time with his mother. He has never admitted any wrongdoing and continues to believe that he is doing "what is best for mom."

Upon the judge's referral, the district attorney is now investigating the case; there is the possibility that Harry will be prosecuted for the physical and financial abuse of his mother.

Discussion of Case History

This case history illustrates many facets of elder abuse and neglect. Several forms of abuse were present: physical, psychological, and financial. The physical abuse was obvious and ongoing; it escalated from bruises about the mouth to a broken arm and included compromising the mother's respiratory and swallowing mechanisms by the son's incessant cigarette smoking in her room. There were strong indications that the son was deliberately withholding food and liquid from his mother in order to make her eligible for periodic Medicare-reimbursed hospitalizations, which in turn afforded him respite from caring for her. His failure to follow through on rehabilitation recommendations or to get his mother up in the chair can be seen as neglect which may or may not have been intentional on his part. Although no evidence of sexual abuse was found, the coyness and flirtatiousness between mother and son suggested that theirs was an unusual mother–son relationship; one worker speculated that there may have been sexual contact between the two when the son was a child. Certainly their attachment was very strong; the son had never married and the two had lived together for a number of years.

The mother was incapable of speaking more than a few phrases of social amenities, so it was not possible to determine whether she *felt* psychologically abused. But psychological abuse can be inferred from the fact that the mother frequently cringed and cowered whenever her son was in the room, as was observed by the nurses and hospital patients both in the acute care setting and in the nursing home. This behavior gradually stopped after the woman was placed in the nursing home where the nursing staff could closely observe the son whenever he visited his mother.

The financial abuse was clear; the son used his mother's money to support himself instead of purchasing homemaker and health aide services that would have benefited his mother. As her legal conservator, he was bound to use her money only for her. In essence, he refused to work and support himself.

This case illustrates the complexity of the issues when elder abuse and neglect are involved. It can take several months for practitioners to be certain that elder abuse and neglect are occurring, and then it may take just as long to find successful interventions. This can be very frustrating. There may be other practitioners involved in the case whose actions are questionable. In this instance, the physician appeared to be colluding with the abuser. The case was finally resolved only because the practitioners never stopped looking for solutions and refused to give up.

In this case example, the profile of the "typical" abused elder is much as it is described in the four germinal research studies. (Block & Sinnott, 1979; Douglass, et al., 1980; Lau & Kosberg, 1978; O'Malley et al., 1979). She is a widow over the age of 75, poor or of limited means, who has significant mental and physical impairments and is dependent on an adult child with whom she resides. Although there are subtle differences among the studies, and the data was gathered using different methods, the profile of the abused elder is consistent across studies.

THE GERMINAL STUDIES

First Wave of Research

The first public knowledge of elder abuse and neglect cases came in 1978 when Dr. Suzanne Steinmetz, a noted researcher in family violence, startled a congressional committee with her descriptions of "battered parents." She described elderly persons who reside with their relatives, are dependent on them, and are battered by them. Dr. Steinmetz based her information on case studies and information gathered from social services, hospital social workers, and emergency rooms. At the same time, Rathbone-McCuan (1978, 1980) was also conducting case studies. The information obtained by these groundbreaking studies formed the first works published on elder abuse and neglect and led to further research.

Lau and Kosberg (1978) gathered data from 404 new cases of patients over 60 who were accepted during a 12-month period into the Cleveland, Ohio, Chronic Illness Center. Agency staff were asked to identify cases of abuse or neglect from case documentation and their recollections of individual patients. These elders lived in the community and were dependent upon family or others for services to keep them in the community. Lau and Kosberg found that 30 of the 39 abused elders were women and of that number, 58% were widows. More than half (51%) of the elders could not walk without the assistance of another person or required a wheelchair, and 18% were partially or totally incontinent. Ten percent had hearing difficulties, and almost half (41%) were either partially or totally confused or "senile." Collectively, more than three-fourths of the abused elderly had at least one major physical or mental impairment. Twenty-seven of the 39 abused lived with a spouse, a daughter, or another relative. Most of the abused elders were white (29); 10 were black.

The study done by Block and Sinnott (1979) reflects data obtained from solicited case reports from health and human service agencies and from elderly persons living in the metropolitan Washington, D.C., area as to their knowledge or experience with domestic neglect or abuse of the elderly. The researchers also mailed out questionnaires to three practitioner groups thought to have contact with abused elderly: members of the American Psychological Association, emergency room physicians, and members of the Gerontological Society who live in Maryland. The total number of cases obtained was 26. The researchers found that the abused elder tends to be a woman (81%) who is over 75; the mean age in their study was 84. Impairment levels were significant: 94% of the abused elders were physically impaired (62% could not prepare their own food and 54% could not take their own medication), and 47% were moderately to severely mentally impaired. Other factors measured in the Block and Sinnott study were race, religion, and socioeconomic status. The majority of abused elders were Caucasian (88%); 12% were Afro-American. Most of the abused group were Protestant (61%), 8% were Catholic, 4% were Jewish, and in 27% of the cases, the religion was unknown. Economically, the abused elder was most likely to be middle class (58%), although 27% were retired on pensions. The great bulk of the abused elders lived with their children (46%) while 23% lived with their spouses and 39% lived with other relatives.

O'Malley et al. (1979) surveyed 1,044 medical, legal, police, and social work professionals and paraprofessionals in Massachusetts in March and April 1979; they received a total of 355 (34%) responses, which reported 183 citings of elder abuse occurring over an 18-month period. The findings generally agree with the other studies as to the profile of the abused elder, although some of the numbers differ. In this study, the abused elder also tended to be a very old person (36% were over 80; 19% were aged 75–79) with a significant physical or mental disability that prevented the elder from meeting daily needs. Of the 183 citings of elder abuse, 80% involved female victims. The researchers noted that national census figures indicate that women account for only 58% of the population 60 years and older; therefore, women may represent a proportionately larger share of the abused elders than their numbers in the general population would suggest. The point is made by the researchers that women may seek assistance or report abusive behavior more often than men and that the client population of the professions surveyed may be composed largely of women and/or "very old" elderly. In three-fourths of the citings, the victim lived with the abuser, and in 84% of the citings, the abuser was a relative of the victim.

Ethnically, the abused elders in this survey were Caucasian (85%), Afro-American (4%), native American (7%), Latino/Latina (1%) with the remaining percentage not reported. As to religion, this study found that 37% were Catholic, 25% were Protestant, 3% were Jewish, and the rest were identified "none" or "other" or "not applicable." Economic figures in the survey indicated that 27% of the households where elder abuse occurred received incomes of less than $5,200 annually. This last question appeared to be difficult for practitioners to answer—37% of those surveyed left this question blank. The average income of elderly women in the survey was markedly lower than that of men, leading the researchers to speculate that old women may be more financially dependent on their families, possibly one reason why there are more abused women than abused men.

Douglass et al. (1980) conducted 228 semistructured interviews with a variety of practitioners: lawyers, doctors, social service and mental health workers, police, coroners, and clergy in Michigan. They also included personal interviews with a small sample of nursing home staff and carried out a secondary analysis of both Detroit police data on crimes against the elderly and nursing home admission data. Authors of this study emphasize three issues: Do neglect and abuse of the elderly exist in the community? What are their characteristics? Why do they occur? They found that there was a significant level of abuse and neglect of the elderly, that most of the mistreatment was passive and neglectful, rather than active and abusive. The study provided additional support for the findings of earlier studies regarding the profile of the abused elder; the typical victim is an older woman who is highly dependent and frail.

Second Wave of Research

Other studies have followed the first wave, some using more detailed investigative techniques and others addressing the shortcomings of the initial studies. Some of the second wave studies had control groups and others conducted interviews with the victims themselves. According to Pillemer and Finkelhor (1985), three studies in this group stand out.

Researchers at Wayne State University focused on identifying factors that put the elder most at risk to become abused (Hwalek, Sengstock, & Lawrence, 1984; Sengstock & Hwalek, 1983a, 1983b). A set of over 100 risk indicators was developed and applied to 50 services agencies (Hwalek et al., 1984). Control cases were also used. Nine risk factors were identified which were 94% accurate in classifying cases into either the control group or the abused group. Some of the factors were whether the victim was a source of stress to others, whether threats had been made to the elder, and whether the caregiver was dependent on the elder for financial support.

Another study (Phillips, 1983) also used control groups. Again, both the control group and the abuse group were taken from social services agencies. One of the most interesting findings from this study is that abused elders were *not* more likely to be impaired than the control group. However, they had less social support and were more likely to be depressed.

The third study was conducted by Pillemer (1985a, 1985b) and was based on 42 cases taken from the caseloads of three Model Projects, a research study funded by the Massachusetts Department of Elder Affairs and the Administration on Aging (Wolf, Godkin, & Pillemer, 1984). Control groups were used and the emphasis was on physical abuse. All the victims were interviewed by the same person. Pillemer also found that the abused group was not necessarily more impaired than the control group. In fact, he found that the control group was more likely to require help with the activities of daily living. A rather fascinating finding of this study is that 64% of the *abusers* were dependent on the victim for financial support and 55% were dependent on the victim for housing.

In summary, there can be little doubt that elder abuse and neglect exist. The population most at risk appears to be women over 75 years of age who are widows and, in most instances, reside with relatives, one of whom is the abuser. The elderly woman is most often white, is of poor to modest financial means, and is a Protestant. She is frail and vulnerable. Unlike abused children, who grow stronger with time, the abused elder will grow more dependent—with the abuse becoming even more likely. The typical abuser is presumably a caregiver because most victims clearly suffer from a range of physical and mental impairments. For victims of elder abuse and neglect, the abuser who also does caregiving may be all that stands between them and nursing home placement. The abuser is most frequently an adult child. It is not yet clear whether the usual abuser is a son or a daughter; the studies vary on this, although most tend to implicate the son and other males more heavily. The abuser is middle-aged unless he is a spouse or a grandchild. The abuse incidents are ongoing and can be expected to continue (Block & Sinnott, 1979; Douglass & Hickey, 1983; Lau & Kosberg, 1979; O'Malley et al., 1979; Wolf et al., 1984)

EXCEPTIONS TO THE TYPICAL PROFILE

Having outlined a "typical" picture of the elder abused person, it is important to realize that we must not think solely in terms of a profile. For a variety of reasons, the picture is far from clear.

First, the currently available research raises many questions. The studies can be best viewed as descriptive and as the first and second wave of research. Most of the studies do not use comparison groups, making it difficult to distinguish between the characteristics of abused elderly and those who are not abused. For instance, it is probably true that the majority of all elderly are widowed women who are somewhat dependent on others and have chronic health problems (Douglass & Hickey, 1983). The studies just described can be considered exploratory—no full-scale randomized sample study has been done regarding the abused elder and the circumstances surrounding elder abuse and neglect. In fact, the populations that were studied may be very select—they were people who had fallen into the social service system or who had been reported by other practitioners in the "helping professions." Large numbers of impaired elderly never seek social services and, in fact, view them as being suitable only for the poor, "those who don't have good families," and members of racial and ethnic minorities. An added complication is the fact that the abuse may not be recognized as such by the practitioner. Block and Sinnott (1979) found that 95% of the cases cited in their study had been reported to some authority, but help had not been obtained. It may be that the abuse goes unrecognized, that agencies do not support practitioners who try to work with abuse, or that practitioners are too busy trying to solve the problem to worry about what caused it.

Second, the studies note that there are significant numbers of older people who do not fit the profile of the "typical" abused elder. Practitioners working with frail elders know there are elderly impaired women who are not abused and that there are elderly men who are abused. The following case example illustrates this point.

> An elderly couple lived near the edge of town. The neighbors became concerned when they did not see the couple for several weeks; they knew the wife was "strange" and that the man was bed-bound due to a severe arthritic condition. They called the police to go over and check on the couple. The police found the man in bed with the covers pulled up to his chin. He said everything was fine and so did his wife. There was a foul odor in the house and the police thought it was because the man needed a bath. When they asked him if he would like to have a nurse come in and bathe him, he agreed. The geriatric nurse went out with a practitioner from the social service agency; the odor in the house was even more foul than the police had indicated. After setting up her materials and establishing rapport with the man, the nurse proceeded. When she pulled back the covers of the bed, she found that the man had multiple pressure sores that were large and infected. His wife, who was schizophrenic, had stuffed paper into them thinking that would help. As the nurse began to bathe him, he wept and said, "I'm so glad you've come."

Nor are all abused people poor; on the contrary, some are very wealthy and it is their wealth that targets them for abuse. For elderly wealthy people who are "alone in the world," financial abuse is an ever present danger. If there has been any alienation from the family, if the family lives elsewhere, or if there is no family, a void can be created that is filled by "new friends" as in the following example.

> The husband and wife lived in a downtown hotel, where they moved after selling the house that had become too large for them to maintain; they were financially "comfortable"; their estate was over $200,000. After the husband died, the woman found herself entirely alone; her friends were either far away or had died. Her only contact was her hairdresser across the street. She confided in him and he in turn began spending more time with her to the point of helping her bathe and dress when she became too confused to do those things herself. She would go to his shop every day to chat and he began charging her estate for a manicure or a hair set, sometimes up to 4 manicures per week and several hair sets. He also started taking her out to dinner at

expensive restaurants together with a large group of his friends. She always paid. He said, "Well, she is so confused. I wouldn't enjoy myself at all if I didn't have some of my own company."

Being in good health does not necessarily exempt the elderly from being abused, as can be seen in the following case example.

At one time, he had been a scriptwriter for a famous comedian. Now he had grown old and lonely. He lived in a large city and dreamed of becoming active in show business again. He also wanted to pass his knowledge on to a younger person, to "help someone get started." One day when he was standing in line at a bank, he met a young man who said he was trying to break into show business. This is what the former scriptwriter had been waiting for, and he invited the young man to his room where they "hit it off" and had several drinks. Soon after, the old man decided that he could best help the young man by giving him money; he offered to share his $20,000 bank account with him and as proof of his offer, he signed a power of attorney with the bank, which gave the young man equal access to his bank account. The money soon disappeared. Amazingly enough, the young man did not; he continued to visit the old man, who said he "didn't blame" the younger man. "He needed the money," he said.

SUMMARY

This chapter has described both the "typical" abused older person and the older person who is abused and does not fit the profile of an abused elder. Since the research is not complete as to the exact nature of elder abuse, practitioners should maintain a high index of suspicion for elder abuse when working in any situation where older people are involved; it is likely that any one of them could be suffering from some type of abuse.

3 Types of Elder Abuse and Neglect

One of the first hurdles practitioners face when dealing with elder abuse and neglect is deciding exactly what constitutes abuse and neglect. The terms *abuse* and *neglect* have been defined differently in the preliminary studies, and the two terms have been run together, leading to a great deal of imprecision and confusion. Generally speaking, neglect has been viewed as being less serious than abuse with regard to the *intent* of the caregiver. Neglect is seen as an act of omission, of not doing something, of withholding goods or services, perhaps due to ignorance or stress on the part of the caregiver. This type of neglect has been referred to as "passive neglect." Some observers have concluded that this means it may not be deliberate and that supportive services and education for the caregiver would alleviate the problems. Other clinicians have noted that neglect can be deliberate and malicious, resulting in no less damage to the elder than outright abuse on the part of a perpetrator who knows full well that he is being neglectful. This type of neglect is often referred to as "active neglect."

Abuse is generally viewed as being more serious. This is seen as a deliberate act of the caregiver, an intentional act, an act of commission. The caregiver means to inflict injury (Douglass & Hickey, 1983).

The intent of the caregiver is a critical subject when dealing with interventions and trying to decide how to approach a case. For instance, a practitioner may choose to arrange for respite care if she has assessed that the abuser struck an impaired elderly person once out of extreme fatigue and is remorseful and frightened by his actions. A different intervention will be indicated when an abuser admits hitting a dependent elder, has inflicted substantial damage, blames the victim for the abuse, and says nothing can stop him from hitting the elder again. In the end, however, when defining the *effects* of the abuse or neglect, it does not matter whether or not the act was deliberate—the elder is injured in some way. It may never be clear to anyone, not even the abuser, whether or not the elder was injured intentionally.

O'Malley, Everett, O'Malley, and Campion (1983) have suggested another approach to definitions which is nonjudgmental and is aimed at eliminating any sense of the caregiver being blamed for the symptoms of abuse or neglect. They suggest that the terms *neglect* and *abuse* have accusatory implications and lead to lack of cooperation on the part of the caregiver, who may decline to answer questions or permit further interviews if she feels blamed and threatened. They propose that definitions be based on the *needs* of the elder for physical and financial support and suggest that the abuse or neglect stems from an abnormal expression of the caregiving role. They propose to define neglect as the failure of a caregiver to act to resolve a significant need of the elder despite an awareness of available resources. Abuse is seen as an active intervention by a caregiver "such that unmet needs are created or sustained with resulting physical, psychological, or financial injury." In this model, the practitioner focuses on the *unmet needs* of the elder and aims to resolve them regardless of what might be causing them. The label "abuse" is used only where a non-caregiving family member exhibiting pathological behavior is involved. It is the sense of O'Malley et al. (1983) that defining abuse and neglect in terms of unmet needs enables practitioners, specifically those who work in the medical arena, to remain nonjudgmental and focus on treating the abused person without labeling the caregiver.

A nonjudgmental attitude is imperative when investigating cases of suspected elder abuse and neglect. A great deal of time and effort must be expended before it can be determined that mistreatment of an elder has occurred. If prejudgments are made and acted upon by the practitioner, the treatment plan may be aborted or subterfuged by the client, the caregiver, or both. Both could decide to collude to keep the worker out of their sphere. Of course, in emergency situations such as are described in Chapter 7, the practitioner must quickly judge and act.

What are we to do then about definitions? Fortunately, there is some agreement among the studies and articles in journals as to the types of abuse: physical, psychological, financial, violation of rights, and self-neglect. The types of abuse and neglect may be defined a bit differently or measured in varying ways, but there is some commonly held ground. As research proceeds, investigators will have to decide whether they are measuring the *intent* of the caregiver or the *effects* of the abuse and/or neglect. Decisions will have to be made as to whether the maltreatment will be measured by acts of omission or commission. For the purposes of this text, the terms *abuse* and *neglect* will be used as they specifically relate to the *effects* on the elder, how the elder looks and acts as a result of actions by others or, in the case of self-neglect, by self. Often an elder is the victim of several forms of abuse and neglect at the same time and they are ongoing, that is, not limited to a single incident (Block & Sinnott, 1979; Lau & Kosberg, 1979; O'Malley et al., 1979). Most likely, some professionals see one type of abuse more often than another. Medically trained practitioners, police, social workers, and mental health workers are more likely to see physical abuse and neglect, whereas lawyers and judges are more familiar with financial abuse and neglect (Douglass et al., 1980).

PHYSICAL ABUSE AND NEGLECT

The outcome of physical abuse and/or neglect is bodily harm, which can range from bruises and scratches to death. Figure 3–1 shows the range of conditions, many of which can be observed by practitioners in any setting. These conditions are not in themselves diagnostic of inflicted abuse or

```
                                                          Death
                                                          Murder

                                                Paralysis
                                                Injuries from
                                                    attempted
                                                    murder

                                    Detached retina
                                    Hematoma
                                    Pressure sores
                                    Fractures
                                    Choke marks
                                    Dislocation

                        Hypothermia
                        Abnormal
                            chemistry
                            values
                        Malnourishment
                        Dehydration
                        Contractures

                Sprains
                Punctures
                Pain on
                    touching
        Welts
        Scalp injury
        Gag marks

    Cigarette burns
    Rope burns

Scratches
Cuts
Bruises
```

FIGURE 3-1 Indicators of physical abuse and neglect. (*Source:* Tomita & Quinn, 1984.)

neglect. Rather, they are clues and thus helpful in assessing the client's total situation. (The reader should refer to Chapter 6 for more information on physical assessment of the elder.)

Bruises over soft tissue areas are frequently signs that an elder has been grabbed or hit. Many older adults have fragile skin, which bruises easily and may even tear with the slightest trauma. If there are healing bruises and new bruises at the same time, the practitioner should be alert to the possibility that abuse is occurring and is repetitious (Tomita, 1982). Abusers will frequently say that the elder fell as an explanation for the bruises, but the aware practitioner who is familiar with patterns of bruising will be able to assess whether or not the sustained bruises could be due to an accidental fall. Scratches, cuts, and burns can also be recurring and appear in various stages of healing. Rope burns and bruises or pressure sores about the ankles and wrists and under the armpit area may indicate that the elder is being confined to a bed or a chair for long periods of time.

Failure to Thrive

Dehydration and malnutrition are widespread among the elderly for various reasons. When they are accompanied by abnormal blood chemistry values and pressure sores, a diagnosis of "failure to thrive syndrome" may be made. Practitioners familiar with child abuse and neglect will recognize the term and recall that it is usually applied to infants who fail to gain weight and grow normally due to lack of proper nutrition (Cantwell, 1978). In elders it can occur in both dependent living and in independent living. The following cases illustrate home situations that have been discovered by practitioners.

> An elderly woman was mute and unresponsive when admitted to an acute hospital. She had been living in subsidized senior housing and had a full-time attendant, who was being paid by the county Department of Social Services. When the woman became more disabled, the attendant took her to her own home with the permission of the social work practitioner, who had no reason to doubt that the woman would receive good care. The attendant was the elderly woman's representative payee for her Social Security and she continued to receive a salary from the Department of Social Services—the total income was $1,200. Visiting nurses were coming regularly and over a period of time, they noticed that the elderly woman was always tied to the bedside commode. She was becoming more and more lethargic and pressure sores were developing on her buttocks. Finally, the nurse and the social worker called an ambulance and, over the protestations of the attendant and her very large, threatening boyfriend, had the woman taken to the hospital. On admission, the woman was found to be filthy and unkempt. There was evidence that she had been left lying on one side at all times because there was a great deal of swelling over the entire left side of her body. She was diagnosed as having acute dehydra-

tion and malnutrition with profound elevation of her blood sodium and her blood sugar. The attendant lobbied to have the woman returned to her care and was outraged when this was not permitted. The woman was placed in a county chronic care hospital which enjoyed a reputation for providing excellent nursing care.

Two sisters, one 85 years old and the other 92, were being cared for by the son of the younger woman. The son, a former priest with no known income, removed his mother from a convalescent hospital in order to save money, took possession of the women's bank accounts, and refused to hire adequate help in the home. Both women were bed-bound and incontinent of bowel and bladder. The son seemed incapable of understanding what must be done to care for the women. Over a period of six months, they were repeatedly hospitalized with pneumonia, pressure sores, severe dehydration and malnutrition, and abnormal blood chemistries due to the malnourishment. On one admission, the mother's temperature was 92 degrees and she was covered with human excrement. Adult protective service workers removed the women from the abuser's care after determining that he was incapable of properly caring for them or accepting assistance. Application was made to the Public Guardian's Office for joint conservatorships so that the women's funds could be used for their care.

In dependent living, malnutrition and dehydration occur when an elder is incapable of preparing food for himself or even reaching for a glass of water and a caregiver neglects to encourage fluids or spend the time necessary to feed him. Some impaired elders can take up to an hour to eat when they are being fed. Few caregivers think to keep track of how much an elder eats and drinks, although more and more nursing homes are now doing so. If the intake of food and liquid is not monitored, no one knows whether the elder is taking in adequate amounts of nutrients. Elders may fail to eat properly because caregivers do not individualize meals to preferences or culture or because the food is not the right consistency. Supplements such as vitamins and commercially prepared liquid nutrients may not be utilized when elders do not have proper intake, leading to still further malnourishment (Anastasio, 1981). Some caregivers withhold liquids when the elder is incontinent of bladder so that they do not have to change the clothing or the bedding as frequently.

Elders who live independently are also subject to malnutrition and dehydration, sometimes to the point of actually starving themselves. There may be an acute and chronic decrease in the quantity and quality of food, or alcohol intake may be replacing meals and/or causing nutritional deficiencies. Common causes of nutritional neglect and abuse in independent living are diminished appetite secondary to depression, isolation, or decreased taste acuity. Bereavement is a frequent cause of a poor appetite in the aged and can be traced to the death of a loved one or the onset or increasing severity of a chronic illness. Financial constraints impel some elderly to purchase and eat less food. Sometimes, the actual process of eating may be difficult. As elders grow older, their gums tend to shrink—hence the term "long in the tooth," which is a shorthand way of saying that someone is old. Those who have dentures must have them relined periodically to make them fit properly. As a result, many older people have dentures that do not fit and they are unable to chew their food well. Eating becomes a problem. Elders who have mobility or transportation problems may find it difficult to get to the grocery store and thus may take their nutritional needs less seriously. Medical conditions, therapies, and medication may affect the appetite or the ability to prepare and eat foods. Some medications have unpleasant side effects such as nausea (Anastasio, 1981). Elders who are demented may simply forget to eat or they are unable to keep track of when or if they ate.

Signs and symptoms of malnutrition and dehydration include sunken eyes and cheeks, extreme thirst, loss of weight unrelated to an illness, and a gaunt appearance such as is seen with victims of starvation or concentration camps, although it should be noted that obese people can also be malnourished. Practitioners may be able to determine whether an elder is malnourished simply by putting an arm around the elder's shoulders; in the malnourished elder, the bones may be so prominent that the skin seems like thin tissue paper stretched over a frame. Elders who are malnourished may also be confused and apathetic and suffer from hallucinations.

One elderly woman who was seeing black and white faces coming at her from the television set and hearing her upstairs neighbor's voice talking to her through her radio lived alone and was found to be suffering from malnutrition. A homemaker was hired to purchase food and prepare meals for her. Once the elderly woman was eating properly, both the visual and auditory hallucinations vanished.

Pressure sores, frequently termed decubitus ulcers or bedsores, are another symptom of the failure to thrive syndrome. They are due to sustained pressure on soft tissues which deprives them of proper blood supply. The blood is squeezed out when the skin is under heavy pressure and the soft tissues in between a bone and a surface do not receive the nourishment that a good blood supply furnishes. Pressure sores usually occur over bony parts of the body such as the sacrum ("tailbone"), elbows, heels, and hips. The most common site for a pressure sore is under the sacrum because most bed-bound people spend a great deal of time lying on their backs. Many conditions predispose an elder to pressure sores; diabetes, circulation problems (common in the elderly), anemia, nutritional inadequacy, certain drugs, and breakdown of the skin caused by lying in urine and feces. The first sign of a pressure sore is a reddened area. If the pressure continues, the skin blisters and opens, exposing tissues underneath the skin. In the next stage, the open wound widens and deepens and the bone underneath becomes visible. Surgery to remove dead tissue may be required, and it may become necessary to graft skin over the wound. Pressure sores are notoriously difficult to heal and call for exemplary nursing care (Kennedy, Graham, Miller, & Davis, 1977). The cost of pressure sores in human suffering and dollars is enormous. Expenditures for the treatment of one pressure sore can range from $5,000 to $34,000 (Blom, 1985).

Other Conditions Encountered in Physical Abuse and Neglect

Deprivation of appliances such as glasses, hearing aids, and walkers can be abusive. In one case, an attorney reported that his client was being abusive.

> The Court Investigation Unit received a call from a concerned attorney, who stated that a nursing home was telephoning him continually about a patient who was being deprived of a wheelchair by her conservator, who was the attorney's client. The patient was an elderly woman who suffered from diabetes; both of her legs had been amputated as a result of poor circulation. Her conservator was an old friend. The investigator contacted the conservator, who admitted that she was not supplying the wheelchair. She said, "If I supply a wheelchair, she'll only go out and sit in the hall like all those other old goofy people. That's no life." The conservator also refused to purchase powders and lotions for the woman saying they weren't necessary, and she declined to buy the woman a television set saying "There's never anything good on anyway." The conservator was also delinquent in paying the pharmacy and nursing home bill. The investigator interceded; all items were purchased and the bills were brought up to date. It was later learned that the conservator was the sole beneficiary of her longtime friend's will, and the question arose as to whether she had been saving her friend's money for herself.

Permanent damage can result from elder abuse and neglect. In the following case, the elder suffered the loss of an eye.

> An 89-year-old woman was both physically and financially abused by her grandnephew, who had lived in her home for approximately 14 years. The house was literally falling down around the occupants, but the grandnephew said that it wasn't bothering him, that he had no plans to do anything about it, and that it was "just a matter of lifestyle." He had no income and had never held a job. He paid the bills out of his aunt's savings, but the house taxes were delinquent and there was no insurance. When her savings got low, he planned to get a power of attorney from his aunt and begin cashing her bonds. He fancied himself a scientist or an artist who could "make a million if I wanted to." The appointment of a conservator prevented further financial abuse and deterioration of the property.

The grandnephew admitted to hitting his aunt to "get her to shut up." When her eye injury was mentioned by the practitioner, he expressed amazement that her eye had been surgically removed as a result of an injury in the home. According to him, she fell off a stool and hit the side of her head, injuring her eye. She did not receive medical treatment for over a week. The elderly woman either did not recall how the injury happened or was covering up for her grandnephew. She said that "something flew in the window and got in my eye." All professional staff involved in the case felt, but could not prove, that the grandnephew was responsible for the eye injury. Explanations given for the injury were suspicious and implausible. He did not visit his aunt when she was hospitalized and did not want her to return to the home following the hospitalization. He relented only when reminded by staff that it was legally her house. A week after the woman was discharged from the hospital, when no one answered the phone or the doorbell, concerned practitioners called the fire department and forced entry into the house. They found the woman lying in a bed of human excrement. Her grandnephew had not cared for her in any way, although she was frail and disabled, and he had not permitted in-home attendants into the house. She was rehospitalized and placed in a board and care home. She continues to think of her grandnephew as a wonderful scientist and wants to return to her home. It was impossible to return her to her home because she did not have enough money to make the house fit for human habitation. The grandnephew occasionally visits his aunt and has been found sleeping in vacant rooms or closets of the facility.

As noted in the previous case, physical abuse often accompanies financial abuse. In some cases, sexual abuse is also involved.

A 78-year-old widow, severely mentally impaired from dementia, had always lived with her adult son. He was described as being a "Charles Manson type" in appearance. Her two daughters, both capable women, had tried to encourage their mother to live with them for years because they frequently noticed bruises on their mother's arms and legs and because the mother and son lived in squalor. The mother refused to move, saying, "I want to be with Jimmy." The son never held a formal job or filed an income tax return. He dissipated a trust that had been left to his mother, lived on her Social Security, and induced her to put his name in joint tenancy on her home.

One daughter finally took action and filed a petition to become the conservator after the mother was hospitalized with serious injuries. She was brought to the emergency room by the son, who said she had fallen. Her injuries were inconsistent with the type of fall he described. She had a head injury that was so severe as to cause massive blood clots on the left side of her brain. Her head and body were covered with contusions, and there were wounds on her neck resembling human teeth marks. Severe bruises were noted about the lower part of her abdomen. Surgery was performed to remove the blood clots. The son's behavior toward his mother after the surgery was such that he was never permitted to be alone with her. He had been discovered trying to get into bed with her on one occasion and on another occasion he was observed with his hands under the sheets manipulating his mother's genitals. The mother, whose mental status was confused under the best of circumstances, frequently referred to her son as her husband.

The mother was well enough to attend the hearing for the conservatorship, at which time she reviled the daughter for seeking the conservatorship and said, "I gave her life. Isn't that enough? What more does she want?" She spoke in glowing terms about her son. At the conclusion of the hearing, the son came up to the mother and it was apparent to observers that he physically yearned to be with her. There was a feeling of "unnaturalness" in the air. The mother did not recognize her son because he had changed his appearance in order to come to court. His shoulder-length hair, which apparently hadn't been cut for years, was now shorn and he had put on a suit. The daughter was appointed to serve as conservator of the person and estate of her mother.

In some instances, death can occur from elder abuse and neglect.

A petition was filed in Superior Court by the daughter of an elderly woman, who had been struck on the head by her 37-year-old son. Before the petition could be investigated, the woman died. The son was later held on murder charges.

In another case that made newspaper headlines, a New York socialite was found guilty of first degree murder for having persuaded her teenage son to murder her millionaire father. She was quoted as being absolutely obsessed with the fear that her father would cut her out of his will.

In still another case, a 20-year-old woman was arrested by homicide officers for arson and murder stemming from a fire which killed an 85-year-old invalid. The young woman had visited the elder and argued with the bedridden cancer victim over money. As she left the apartment, she contemptuously flicked a lighted cigarette into an open closet. The smoldering butt apparently later burst into flames and the elderly man died from smoke inhalation.

Two elderly sisters slowly starved to death while living in a board and care home that was under the supervision of the Department of Social Services, Adult Protective Services division. The operator had given good care for a number of years, but after her divorce from the nephew of the women, she locked them in a room and stopped giving adequate care. At one point, an ambulance was called to the home and both women were taken to a university medical center. Although the ambulance personnel made efforts to let all concerned know that the women lived in squalor and were found in their own excrement, no one, including the doctors who examined the two women, made a diagnosis of elder abuse and neglect. The women, who were severely demented, died from malnutrition and dehydration. They weighed less than 80 pounds each at the time of death.

PSYCHOLOGICAL ABUSE AND NEGLECT

Manifestations of psychological abuse and neglect are seen in the actual behavior of the elder and can range from shame and passivity to severe anxiety, "nervous breakdown," and, theoretically, suicide. The disturbance can include confusion and disorientation, fearfulness, trembling and fidgeting when talking about certain subjects, changing the subject frequently, cowering in the presence of the caregiver, and referring all questions to the caregiver, even basic ones. Figure 3-2 details the range of behaviors. Psychological abuse is also difficult to prove, and the practitioner is cautioned to proceed slowly. Wolf et al. (1984) found that victims of psychological abuse were functionally and cognitively intact, but they were more likely to be emotionally ill and so were their abusers. However, some families have always spoken in loud voices or even yelled at each other as a matter of

Suicide

"Nervous
breakdown"

Fearfulness
Depression
Helplessness
Hopelessness
Severe anxiety

Disorientation
Confusion
Anger
Agitation
Hypervigilance

Cowering
Lack of eye
contact

Evasiveness
Isolation
Trembling
Clinging

Passivity
Denial
Mild anxiety
Non-
    responsiveness
Implausible
    stories

Ambivalence
Deference
Obsequiousness
Shame

FIGURE 3-2 Indicators of psychological abuse and neglect. (*Source:* Tomita & Quinn, 1984.)

course, and they may consider it normal behavior. In addition, some behaviors commonly occur with the various types of dementia, or other chronic diseases such as Parkinsonism.

Most likely, psychological abuse is an integral part of the other types of abuse. Victims often report being threatened with nursing home placement if they protest physical abuse or if they threaten to tell someone outside the family or if they refuse to hand over money. Living with constant threats can be very debilitating.

Some elderly find themselves physically impaired, living alone with no one to help them. They may become dependent on attendants who are hired from agencies. The attendant may exploit the situation by playing on the fears of the elder.

An 83-year-old woman who was alert and oriented lived alone and was confined to a wheelchair. She had been a waitress, she said and a "damn good one." Her hair was dyed bright red but was growing out gray from her center part. She had recently been hospitalized. When she came home from the hospital, she contacted a reputable home health agency, and a housekeeper was sent out to clean her house, do the cooking and shopping, and help the elderly woman with bathing.

At first, the housekeeper was attentive and did a good job. Then, she began eating at the elderly woman's house pleading hunger and citing the poor wages she was receiving. She began bringing her granddaughter to the elderly woman's house, and she too began eating the elderly woman's food. The elder felt trapped. She was angry and knew she was being taken advantage of, but she felt weak and sick and she was afraid of being alone.

The subject of finances came up. The housekeeper suggested that the elder change her will and make her (housekeeper) the main beneficiary. When the woman demurred, the housekeeper insisted and said, "You know you need me. You can't do by yourself. You help me and I'll do for you. Otherwise, I'll have to leave you. What would you do then?" The elderly woman became desperate. She had no close relatives and her son was a "no-good" who hadn't contacted her in years. She signed a new will that was drawn up by the housekeeper's attorney. Over the next weekend, she decided that it just was not right. She called the home health agency on Monday morning and told the supervisor what had happened and said she "never wanted that woman in my house again." She contacted an attorney and eventually changed her will back to its original form. The housekeeper came to the house to pick up her things. She screamed at the elderly woman, gave her a hand gesture, and told her to "go do it to yourself." She slammed the door and took some of the woman's new clothing and $200 in cash. The woman was terrified that the housekeeper would come back "with some of her people" and kill her. "It's just not right," she said. "People like me are fair game. There's other people just waiting to move in on us. Now I know what old people mean when they say they don't want to go on. I'm a fighter but I'm getting tired. I'm sick and I'll never be well again."

Clinging behavior may be a sign that affection is missing from the elder's life or that it is being deliberately withheld. Prejudice against the aged who are impaired can lead others to deny that they have emotional needs.

The court visitor interviewed a 90-year-old woman who was living in a nursing home in a three-bed ward. Her estate was worth well over $300,000, so the visitor talked with her about luxuries such as having her own room. At that point, the woman began crying and said, "If I didn't have these other two women for companionship and if I couldn't visit with their company, I would be totally alone. All my friends are dead and I've outlived most of my relatives. I have no children and what relatives I do have live on the East Coast. Please don't have me moved." As the court visitor prepared to leave, the woman grasped her arm and said, "Please say you'll come back soon. I need people."

In reviewing the court file, the court visitor learned that the woman's longtime attorney was her conservator. She wrote a report describing what she had seen and related that according to nursing staff, the woman had no visitors. She also said that she was aware that the attorney was very busy and that she knew of compassionate gerontologists who could provide the personal attention and care the woman needed and craved. She offered to help the attorney/conservator make the arrangements.

No sooner had the attorney received the report than he was on the phone to the court visitor. He was furious. He said, "Why, I go there every month for a few minutes just to make sure she is all right. I never bother to talk with the nurses at the desk. If someone was hired, it would mean that it would cost money and her apartment house might have to be sold." The court visitor knew there were enough liquid assets to cover the cost of a gerontologist and she wondered why the attorney raised the question of selling the apartment house. She also thought to herself, Even if the apartment house has to be sold, so what? It belongs to the woman, it is her money, and why shouldn't it be used to bring her happiness? She speculated that the attorney might be a beneficiary of the woman's will.

Sometimes, a nursing home can be a haven, especially if being in one's own home means being abused. In the following case, an elder chose to leave her home.

An attorney went to the judge complaining that an 84-year-old woman was being held in a nursing home. The judge ordered an investigation. It was discovered that the elderly woman had been placed in the nursing home when her attendant, who was also her conservator of person, went on vacation. She was very happy in the nursing home and did not want to return to her own home and the care of the attendant, who she said was abusing her psychologically by cursing at her and insulting her on a regular basis because she was unable to walk. She said she was kept in one room all the time and was not permitted to use the rest of her house. The woman was alert, drug-free, and oriented. She had made friends at the nursing home and wished to remain there. The judge honored her wishes and removed the attendant as the conservator. It was later learned that the attendant had induced the woman to sign over stocks and to give the attendant and her family "gifts" of over $80,000.

Unlike physical abuse, psychological abuse is difficult to measure. Nevertheless, the damage is real. Battered women in one study reported that psychological abuse caused them the most pain, anguish, and humiliation (Walker, 1984).

Psychological abuse includes social and financial isolation and, in some instances, will fit the definitions of psychological torture which were devised by Amnesty International to assist in understanding the mental states of prisoners of war and hostages (Walker, 1984).

Depression and Suicide

Depression, found throughout the life cycle, is the most common emotional illness in old age (Butler & Lewis, 1982). It can resemble dementia and, in fact, is often confused with it. Compounding that fact is the reality that in the beginning stages of dementia, depression is frequently present, particularly if the elder is aware of the dementia (Heston & White, 1983). Burnside (1976) has noted that depression in the elderly may go unnoticed because it differs from depression in the young. The main characteristic is apathy. Irritability, common with depression at any age, may be dismissed as "cantankerousness" in the old. Biological signs of depression in the old are common and may be the presenting complaint to the physician. Such signs can include constipation, slow movements, and insomnia (Burnside, 1976). When depression is obvious, it can include feelings of helplessness and hopelessness, frequent feelings of guilt, loneliness, and despair, fear of death, sexual disinterest, and loss of appetite which can result in weight loss. Hypochondriasis and somatic symptoms are frequently evident. Depression may follow the diagnosis of a chronic illness or the death of a loved one. It can occur as a side effect of medication or result from a loss in status in the community such as retirement, which brings with it a fixed income (Butler & Lewis, 1982; Heston & White, 1983). Suicide is common among the old although its relationship to elder abuse and neglect is still unknown. The highest rate of suicide occurs in white men in their 80s. Suicide is still one of the ten leading causes of death in this country and is probably underreported because of religious taboos. People over 65 are extremely "successful" at suicide; attempts rarely fail, especially with men, although rates for women are rising around the world, especially for older women (Butler & Lewis, 1982; U.S. Senate Special Committee on Aging, 1984).

FINANCIAL ABUSE

Financial abuse means that the assets of the elder are misappropriated. It can range from stealing small amounts of cash from an impaired elder or shortchanging him at the grocery store to inducing him to deed over his house. Elders who are financially abused may complain of not understanding recent changes in their financial status, such as checks bouncing. An elder may state that he is giving large gifts of cash to housekeepers or newspaper boys or simply be very confused about his financial status. There are several indicators of financial abuse.

- There is unusual activity in bank accounts. Accounts may be changed from one branch of a bank to another or there are several withdrawals in one day for large amounts of money.
- Bank statements and canceled checks no longer come to the elder's home.
- There is activity in bank accounts that is inappropriate to the older adult, i.e., drastic changes in types and amounts of withdrawals or withdrawals from automated banking machines when the elder cannot walk or get to the bank.
- Documents are drawn up for the elder's signature but the elder cannot understand what they mean. These documents might include a power of attorney, a will, joint tenancy on a bank account, or a deed to his house. The elder may say that he has been signing "papers" but doesn't remember what they were.
- The care of the elder is not commensurate with the size of the estate or the caregiver refuses to spend money on the care of the elder or there are numerous unpaid bills such as overdue rent, utilities, taxes, when someone is supposed to be in charge of the elder's money.
- There is a lack of amenities, i.e., television set, personal grooming items, or appropriate clothing when the estate can well afford it.
- The caregiver expresses unusual interest in the amount of money being expended on the care of the elder and asks only financial questions of the practitioner, not questions about the care of the elder.
- Recent acquaintances express gushy, undying affection for a wealthy older person.
- Personal belongings such as art, silverware, jewelry, or furs are missing.
- A housekeeper tries to isolate the elder from his family by telling him that his family does not care about him. She then tells the family that the elder does not want to see them and later induces the elder to sign over assets by telling him that she is the only one who cares for him. After all, she says, I am the one who takes care of you.
- A caregiver or a recent acquaintance makes promises of lifelong care for

- the elder ("I'll keep you out of a nursing home") in exchange for deeding all property and/or bank accounts over to the caregiver.
- The signatures on checks and other documents do not resemble the older person's signature.
- The older person cannot write but there are "signatures" on documents.
- There is a lack of solid arrangements for financial management of the elder. The caregiver is evasive about the sources of income.
- There are implausible explanations about the finances of the elder by the caregiver and/or the elder.
- An eviction notice arrives when the elder thought he owned the house.

Financial abuse can be difficult to detect, investigate, and prove. Practitioners may not be accustomed to asking clients questions about money. An elder may be reluctant to divulge the location of his bank accounts or may swear that the $20,000 he gave a person he just met was a "gift." It can be difficult to check the nature of bank accounts because banks have strict confidentiality guidelines which prohibit them from sharing information with practitioners. Forgery can be very hard to prove. Accurate statistics regarding financial exploitation may be hard to come by because the abuse is reported to the police but not to the agency mandated to receive elder abuse reports or because banks, lawyers, and judges, who traditionally are aware of it, are not mandated to report it (Salend, Kane, Satz, & Pynoos, 1984).

The following case examples illustrate situations practitioners can encounter in working with financial abuse.

An 84-year-old woman and her 81-year-old brother were the victims of two separate incidents of financial abuse. The abusers were a corner grocer, who systematically robbed the woman of thousands of dollars, and a bank official who withheld trust money to which the brother and sister were legally entitled. The woman was severely demented and was persuaded to give the grocer power of attorney over her finances and to name him as sole beneficiary in her will. He subsequently transferred $220,000 of her savings to a bank account in another county. When the fraud was discovered, there was some evidence that the grocer was acting with others who planned to defraud the elderly woman entirely and then murder her and her brother. During the same time period, a bank officer—who visited the elderly pair in their home—refused to release money from a $573,226 trust fund held in their names because he thought the brother was "funny." The brother was receiving Social Security and Supplemental Security Income because he had no other resources. The court ordered a conservatorship established for the sister and brother and the trust fund was eventually distributed to them with the conservator acting as the fiduciary.

A 90-year-old widow who had lived in her neat-as-a-pin home for more than 50 years was induced to deed her home, worth $120,000 at the time, over to a bogus contractor. He was eventually forced by authorities to deed the home back to the woman, but by that time, it carried a $70,000 lien from a loan the "contractor" had taken out. Cash and stocks worth approximately $92,000 vanished after the elderly woman met the "contractor," leaving her to get by on $200 a month in Social Security and her $8,000 savings. The district attorney felt she was too mentally impaired to testify against her abuser so charges were not brought against him. A conservator was appointed and he filed a civil suit against the abuser, seeking to recover the $70,000 plus punitive damages. Several other elderly people, most of them unable to testify because of mental impairments, were defrauded by the same man and/or his partners.

An 84-year-old widow was bilked out of approximately $50,000 by her sister and brother-in-law, who arrived from the Midwest two months after her husband died. The elderly woman had assets totaling nearly $500,000 in investments and income property. She suffered from dementia and was confused and disoriented. Aided by his wife, the brother-in-law put pressure on the elderly woman to give him money, to sell her property, and to make out a will naming him and his wife as sole beneficiaries. His actions raised the suspicions of the woman's tenants, friends, and bank officials, who alerted authorities. The court established a conservatorship and ordered the brother-in-law to return the $20,000 they could prove he had taken. He is believed to have taken an additional $30,000. On the witness stand, the man denied wrongdoing and said, "I'm just a country boy."

An elderly woman who lived in a pleasant residential home for seniors wanted very much to live in a private home. She made friends with one of the employees of the home and asked her to get an apartment so the two could live more comfortably. After a few months in the apartment, the former employee began to talk about getting a house and bringing her family to the United States. A house was rented and gradually the entire family of the former employee was brought into the country. Initially, the woman was being charged $1,000 for the care she received, but when other family members were brought into the household, the charge skyrocketed to $2,000 in one month's time. The elderly woman was paying one-third of the utilities, rent, and food even though the household consisted of six adults and one two-week-old baby. By this time, the elderly woman was significantly impaired because of her Parkinsonism. A conservator was appointed to protect her after her accountant became alarmed over the money that was going out. The conservator bargained with the caregiver, keeping in mind that there was a relationship between the caregiver and the impaired elderly woman and that the only alternative for the elderly woman would be a nursing home. On the recommendation of the court investigator, the judge reduced the monthly charges to a sum which was consistent with community standards and included all personal care, food, and utilities.

A 20-year-old legal secretary in a small town called the District Attorney's Office when she became aware that her boss, an attorney, was embezzling funds from an elderly client. An investigator went down to the seedy hotel where the elderly woman lived in order to see if she was all right and if she needed anything. The investigator never saw the woman because she would not answer the door, but she could be heard talking to herself in the room using many different voices. Neighbors reported that the woman looked well-nourished and that she carried groceries into her room, apparently cooking against hotel regulations. Whenever the woman left her room, she nailed it shut with very large nails.

The investigator telephoned the attorney, who told her that the woman originally had $60,000 but that her fund was now down to $800 after only a few years. The investigator feigned confusion and said, "Well, I know you've been sending her $600 per month for expenses and that includes a $200 Social Security check. At current interest rates, her funds should have lasted much longer, in fact, several years." The attorney acknowledged that the investigator might be right. The following day, the legal secretary telephoned the district attorney's office and reported that the attorney had deposited $52,000 into an account with the elderly woman's name on it.

VIOLATION OF RIGHTS

The Select Committee on Aging of the U.S. House of Representatives noted in their 1981 report entitled *Elder Abuse: An Examination of a Hidden Problem* that all Americans have certain inalienable rights under the Constitution as well as federal and state laws. Some of these rights are the right to personal liberty, the right to adequate appropriate medical treatment, the right not to have one's property taken without due process of law, the right to freedom of assembly, speech, and religion, the right to freedom from forced labor, the right to freedom from sexual abuse, the right to freedom from verbal abuse, the right to privacy, the right to a clean, safe living environment, the right not to be declared incompetent and committed to a mental institution without due process of law, the right to complain and seek redress of grievances, the right to vote and exercise all the rights of citizens, the right to be treated with courtesy, dignity, and respect.

An examination of the case examples throughout this text will reveal that these basic rights have been violated in almost every instance of elder abuse and neglect. Violations of rights can range from not being permitted to open one's personal mail to being totally divested of all civil rights. Some observers have noted that convicted criminals have many more due process protections in this country than do elders facing incompetency hearings. Chief among the protections not accorded to most elders in these situations is the right to have an attorney represent them. In some states, merely being old is reason enough to have a conservatorship or guardianship imposed.

A client whose rights are being violated may complain of not being permitted to vote or go to church. In one instance, a conservator/son directed the board and care operator not to permit his elderly father to receive visits from church members because he feared that the father would change his will and leave his considerable estate to the church. In another instance, an elderly woman was deprived of her personal liberty and her right to assembly by her housekeeper.

> A retired schoolteacher had a bank acting as her conservator of estate but no one checking on her physical well-being. The bank had contacted a home health agency, which provided an attendant. The attendant forced the woman to stay in her bedroom by saying that she was weak and needed to rest. She removed the television from the bedroom and put it in the living room so she could watch it without the interference of the elderly woman. She pinned all the curtains shut saying that the woman "didn't need to look outside." She took all the pictures off the walls and substituted her own pictures. She refused to give the woman her mail, instead telling her that there was no mail. When friends would call, she would tell them that the elderly woman was not well enough for them to stop by or she would make an appointment for them to visit, but when they arrived she would tell them that the woman was too sick to have company. She also refused to bathe the woman. The elderly woman was rescued from this situation only because the attendant dropped dead from a heart attack. A new attendant arrived and the first thing she did was to bathe the woman and give her a permanent. She also threw open the curtains, and put the woman's pictures back on the wall. She found the address book and called all the woman's friends and urged them to come over and visit. She reinstated all magazine subscriptions and made sure that the woman got her mail. She took her to the doctor and initiated a medical regimen. In effect, she saved the woman's life.

> In another instance, a son who lived out of state was appointed to be his father's conservator of person at the father's request. The son refused to hire in-home care and immediately proceeded to confine his wealthy 86-year-old father to a nursing home, despite the fact that the father was alert, oriented, and complained that he was "going crazy" in the nursing home. The son said, "Well, we all have to put up with things in life that we don't like." In effect, he violated his father's right to personal liberty and his right to privacy. The court carefully monitored the situation because the son lived out of state and because he did not seem interested in his father's care. The father was returned to his own home only after he threatened to change his will and disinherit his son.

In some cases, the professionals who are placed in charge of the care of a helpless elder may be abusive. In the following case, a woman thought she had done everything possible to protect her older sister and could not bring herself to believe that there had been any abuse. She violated her sister's right to adequate appropriate medical treatment until the court stepped in.

A woman in her mid-80s and in the end stages of dementia could not care for herself in any way. She was alert but disoriented as to time, place, and person. She was not capable of complaining of inadequate care; she seldom spoke. She was living in an apartment of a multilevel care facility run by a church group. She had private-duty nurses around the clock, which were costing her estate $6,000 per month. Over a period of time, the nurses refused to permit anyone from the facility to see the woman and, in fact, developed an adversarial relationship with all facility staff. A doctor would visit occasionally, but he never examined the woman completely because the nurses always told him that she was "the same" and he trusted their opinion. Finally, the administrator of the facility instructed the director of nurses to go into the apartment and examine the woman. The director of nurses found 13 pressure sores, some of them far advanced with necrotic tissue, others so deep that bone was exposed. The conservator could not bring herself to believe that the nurses she had hired could possibly be mistreating her sister, and she refused to permit her sister to be hospitalized until the administrator called in an investigator from the court, who threatened to get a judicial order if the conservator did not hospitalize her sister. It was later determined that in addition to the pressure sores, some of which required surgery, the nurses had been oversedating the elderly woman.

SELF-NEGLECT AND SELF-ABUSE

There is some question as to whether self-neglect and self-abuse should be included when considering elder abuse and neglect. Salend et al. (1984) surveyed 16 states that had mandatory reporting laws in 1981 and found that the highest percentage of reported cases within neglect categories were those classified as self-neglect. In child neglect, parents benignly or malevolently withhold care and services that the child needs for survival. The situation is somewhat different with older adults, who are considered to be responsible for themselves unless they are declared incapable or incompetent by a court of law. Therefore, if they choose to neglect themselves, it may be a matter of free will. Salend et al. point out that "one man's self-neglect may be another's exercise of free judgment." This does not mean that adult protective services should not be investigating situations where individuals are putting themselves at risk. However, it does raise the question as to whether self-neglect and self-abuse should be classified as one of the several types of elder abuse and neglect. Certainly, many state laws requiring reporting of elder abuse and neglect include that classification, and although the definitions may vary widely, as a practical matter, practitioners are having to consider self-neglect and -abuse as one of the types of elder abuse and neglect.

Self abuse and -neglect mean that an individual is failing to provide the necessities of life for himself such as food, clothing, shelter, adequate medical care, and reasonable management of financial resources. It ranges from poor grooming and eating habits to disintegration of the body through ignored medical care. The financial assets of the individual may be wasted. With the elderly, it is usually associated with the increasing severity of mental and/or physical impairments, but it can also be part of a life style such as is frequently seen with alcoholism or drug abuse. It can include a filthy and unhealthy living environment with animal droppings in the house or dissipation of bank accounts or other assets. Some elders in this category isolate themselves from those who would care for them. They show physical signs of self-neglect such as dirty matted hair, layers of clothing inappropriately arranged, clothing inappropriate to weather conditions, lack of food in the refrigerator, or food that is decayed and moldy. Some older people who cannot cope are abandoned by their families or live too far away for the families to be of assistance. Some simply have no family; they are the last to survive. In one case, the Public Guardian petitioned the court to become the conservator of an elderly woman whose daughter lived nearby but had become alienated from her for unknown reasons.

The referral for conservatorship had been received by the Public Guardian's Office from the Geriatric Home Visiting Team, who in turn had been contacted by the gas and electric company when the woman had failed to pay her bill for several months. The team made several visits to the woman, explaining that the bill needed to be paid. Initially, she said that she was unaware that the bill was past due and then began to fabricate excuses such as, "A man hit me over the head and that's why I forgot to pay." She would always agree to pay but never did, and the team became increasingly concerned about her because winter was setting in. Her mental impairment was obvious. She thought the year was 1941 (it was 1981), and that her mother was still living, although she herself was in her mid-80s. Her ankles were grossly swollen, but she denied that there were any problems and said that they had always been that way and that she would go to a doctor if she really needed to. She was always very pleasant. She had a dog whose hair was falling out because he was truly flea bitten. Large areas of his pink skin were showing through his meager hair, and there were large bumps on his skin. He scratched himself incessantly. This did not seem to disturb the woman, who said there were not any problems with the dog, that sometimes he had hair and other times he didn't. There was also a scruffy cat. She never took the animals outside, and as a result, the upholstered furniture had semi-circles on the legs where the animals had relieved themselves. Her house was neat but it was permeated by an extremely foul, dank odor. The practitioner found herself retching if she breathed through her nose. The kitchen floor was covered with animal feces, and when the woman was asked about it, she said, "Why, my goodness, someone must have come in and put that there when I was out shopping." The ceiling of the kitchen had been severely rain-damaged and was collapsing. When that was pointed out, the woman said, "Oh, that must be new." The kitchen sink was backed up with smelly dirty water and the woman seemed surprised about it. She seemed genuinely concerned about the sink but could not think what must be done about it or how to go about getting it fixed. It was very apparent that she could not mobilize to get anyone into her house to repair it.

In some instances, self-neglect and -abuse can lead to death.

A disabled elderly woman, believed to be in her 80s, was trapped inside her burning home and died. Firefighters found a foot and a half of paper debris, consisting of junk mail, newspapers, and other paper stacked throughout the residence. Cardboard boxes which were stacked up on top of a floor heater apparently caught fire and started the blaze. The firefighters noted that the cluttered living room ignited like a ready campfire. A passerby saw the blaze in its early stages and contacted the Fire Department, which quickly put out the blaze and rushed the woman to the hospital, but she died from extreme third-degree burns. A fireman said, "I suppose she hated to live that way, with all that junk in her house, but she just couldn't help herself. For years, everything went into that house and nothing came out."

INDICATORS OF ABUSE OR NEGLECT FROM THE FAMILY OR THE CAREGIVER

Frequently, practitioners sense when something is "not quite right" in the life of an elder, but it may be difficult to pinpoint the exact nature of the problem. Often, there are clues in the behavior of the family or the caregiver which are suspicious or unsettling. Detecting elder abuse and neglect is frequently a matter of "putting all the pieces together" and coming up with a definite diagnosis. In those tragic cases where death has resulted from abuse or neglect, hindsight may reveal that a practitioner missed clues or did not follow up on "gut feelings." Practitioners who are alert to the following indicators of abuse and neglect will be in a better position to detect maltreatment.

- The elder is not given the opportunity to speak for himself or see others without the caregiver being present.
- The family members or the caregiver has attitudes of indifference or anger toward the elder.
- The caregiver fails to provide the proper assistance or necessary mechanical devices for the frail elder.
- There are too many "explained" injuries, or explanations are inconsistent over a period of time.
- A physical examination reveals that the client has injuries that the caregiver has not divulged.

- The client or caregiver has a history of "doctor shopping" and utilizing several different medical practitioners over a period of time.
- There is a prolonged interval between the trauma or illness and presentation for medical care.
- The caregiver or family withholds security and affection from the elder or teases him in cruel ways or threatens him with nursing home placement.
- There are conflicting or implausible accounts regarding injuries or incidents. The physical findings are either better or worse than the accounts would lead the practitioner to believe.
- There is flirtation or coyness between the elder and the caregiver, which may indicate a possible inappropriate sexual relationship.

HIGH-RISK SITUATIONS

There are some situations that seem to be particularly dangerous for elders. This is when the practitioner should be especially alert and monitor the case carefully, remembering that some elders have been permanently injured and others have died while under the care of others.

A caregiver may have unrealistic expectations of an older person or an ill person and consequently feel that he should be punished if he does not do what the caregiver thinks he is capable of doing. Some caregivers feel elders are incontinent on purpose or are faking when they say that they cannot walk. Others are overconcerned about correcting what they see as "bad behavior" in the elder. Families with a history of domestic abuse or with a family member who has trouble controlling his temper are potentially unsafe for dependent elder members. In those families, hitting each other on a regular basis may be acceptable as a way of "correcting" unwanted behavior.

Some caregivers are incapable of taking care of dependent elders because of their own problems. Some are young and immature and have dependency needs of their own. They cannot possibly take care of a frail elder, particularly if the elder is demanding or needs a great deal of personal supervision. The risk for abuse and neglect of elder members is also high if the caregiver is mentally ill or has problems with alcohol or drug abuse.

Other high-risk situations include those where the caregiver is forced by circumstances to take care of the elder or where the care needs of the elder exceed or soon will exceed the ability of the caregiver to meet those needs. A caregiver who is ill himself may be under further stress and be unable to adequately care for an elder. In those instances, the caregiver may be unwilling or reluctant to plan for or to implement the care of a dependent elder. He may refuse services, thus placing further stress on himself and, inevitably, the elder.

Situations where the caregiver is dependent on the elder for financial support are high-risk for the elder. Frequently, these are situations where the middle-aged adult child never left home. Clinicians have noted that these caregivers tend to be evasive about financial and care arrangements for the elder and frequently are angry and resentful if they have to take care of the elder. There may be contempt toward the elder, who was formerly powerful and in charge of the household but now is less able to defend himself verbally and physically.

Sometimes, an elder unknowingly creates a high-risk situation by taunting his heirs with money or possessions either through gifts while he is living or through his will. He may change his will regularly, according to whim and depending on the behavior of his heirs. This erratic behavior has the effect of breeding resentment and bringing out the greed in everyone associated with the elder. Shakespeare notes this phenomenon in his play *King Lear*. In his old age, Lear decides to relinquish his vast holdings to his three daughters prior to his death. He is mistakenly certain of their affections and demands that they publicly declare their love for him. The elder daughters, Goneril and Regan, give obviously insincere protestations of love for their father, which he believes, and they are rewarded handsomely with lands and money. The youngest daughter, Cordelia, gives a simple forthright statement of love which her father misinterprets to mean that she does not love him. She receives nothing. Thereafter, the two greedy older daughters turn their frail elderly father out of what is now their property and effectively deprive him of food, clothing, and shelter. They gain revenge for all the taunting they received from their father over the years. The play is a classic study of elder abuse and neglect in which the elder had a role.

SUMMARY

There are several types of elder abuse and neglect, each with indicators. Additionally, there are certain situations that should raise the suspicions of the practitioner. At this stage of knowledge about the phenomenon, practitioners must be investigators, carefully searching for clues and answers to puzzling situations. Detecting elder abuse and neglect requires that the practitioner realize that they exist and know the forms they take. If the practitioner is not alert to the indications and clues, she will not be able to "see" the abuse and neglect.

4 Why Elder Abuse and Neglect Occur

What causes elder abuse? What causes neglect? Do they represent a random striking out by the abuser? A way of venting anger or frustration? Or are they deliberate, part of an unending chain of maltreatment that extends over months or sometimes years? Are there families who have always, as a matter of course, settled conflicts and arguments by hitting each other or by abusing each other verbally? Is abuse a way of "getting even" with an elderly parent for real or imagined wrongs that happened decades earlier?

And what about financial abuse? Is it motivated by opportunism and greed? Is the caregiver suddenly given access to a frail elder's bank accounts, and knowing the older person is too impaired to realize that funds are being misused, act impulsively? How much plotting goes into deciding to defraud an elderly relative out of her home or valuables?

Are large numbers of old people really being placed in nursing homes against their will? Are families abandoning their elders to the care of strangers when they no longer wish to be bothered?

Self-neglect and self-destructiveness raise other, slightly different questions. The issue here is whether the abuse and neglect are long standing, part of a life style, or whether they are evidence that physical and perhaps mental impairments have overtaken the older person's ability to reason and to make sound judgments.

All of these questions and more come to mind in trying to understand elder abuse and neglect, and some tentative answers will be explored in this chapter. To date, there have been no studies involving in-depth interviewing of abused older people and their abusers, so we cannot be certain why elder abuse and neglect occur. Existing studies do offer, however, a place to begin and can help us consider general theories of causation.

O'Malley et al. (1983) reviewed case reports and research studies of elder abuse and neglect and developed some preliminary hypotheses regarding the causes. They grouped the hypotheses into four categories:

1. Those focusing on physical and mental impairment of an older adult.
2. Those emphasizing the effect of stress on the caregiver.
3. Those concerned with the influence of families which have learned to solve problems by being violent with one another.
4. Those theories which focus on the individual problems of the abuser.

To these four categories can be added a fifth: the effects of a society which casts older adults in the role of nonpersons through ageism, sexism, and destructive attitudes toward the disabled and toward those who are perceived to be unattractive. Greed is also a part of this category and cannot be discounted where financial abuse is present.

THE PHYSICALLY AND MENTALLY DEPENDENT ELDER

Several researchers have noted that the majority of victims of elder abuse and neglect are impaired—physically, mentally, or both (Block & Sinnott, 1979; Douglass et al., 1980; Lau & Kosberg, 1979; O'Malley et al., 1979; Rathbone-McCuan, 1978, 1980; Steinmetz, 1978; Steuer & Austin, 1980). The inability of impaired older people to carry out the tasks of daily life such as personal grooming, dressing, toileting, food shopping and preparation, money handling, and other vital activities make them vulnerable and dependent on caregivers' actions and, perhaps literally, "at their mercy" (O'Malley et al., 1979; Hickey & Douglass, 1981).

Conditions Causing Dependency

Many conditions, both physical and mental, bring on dependency and disability. Often it is the interplay between the two that proves disastrous to the functioning of the elder. Sometimes conditions are viewed as being either primarily physical in origin or primarily psychological. In reality, of course, there is a great deal of crossover between body and mind. People are holistic beings and tend to respond in a total fashion when one system is damaged.

Physical Conditions

The most common physical problems limiting the activity of the elderly include arthritis and rheumatism, heart conditions, hypertension with heart involvement, impairments of the lower extremities and hips, and impairments of the back and spine. Arthritis, rheumatism, and heart conditions account for *half* of all conditions placing limitations on the activity of older adults (U.S. Bureau of the Census, 1983). Older people themselves are well aware of the prevalence of arthritis—it is the most frequent physical complaint reported by those over 65 who live outside of institutions (Brotman, 1982). Physical illness has been unequivocally linked to psychiatric complaints and to hospitalization. Retirement and widowhood seem easier to bear than poor health (Pfeiffer & Busse, 1973).

Types of Assistance Needed In 1980, 40% of the elderly population living in the community said one of their major activities had been limited by health problems, while half of those over 85 reported being unable to carry on a major activity because of a chronic illness (U.S. Bureau of the Census, 1983). These figures are compelling when we realize that the great bulk of older people live outside of institutions and thus may be dependent on those around them for assistance (see Figure 4-1).

In 1979, a nationwide survey was conducted which measured specific types of assistance that older people might need, including physical help with activities of daily living, home management assistance, and nursing or medical care (National Center for Health Statistics, 1983). The survey was conducted by household interview and sampled 42,000 households, with a total of 111,000 people. The types and amounts of assistance needed increased markedly with advancing age.

Out of 1,000 people aged 65 to 74, 52.6 needed help with at least one basic physical activity such as walking, going outside, bathing, dressing, using the toilet, getting into or out of bed (or a chair), or eating. This figure rose to 114.0 per 1,000 for people who were aged 75 to 84 and more than tripled for people over 85 years of age—348.4 per 1,000.

The same trends were seen in the need for assistance with home management, which included such things as shopping for personal items, doing routine household chores, preparing meals, or handling money. For people aged 65 to 74, 57.3 per 1,000 needed such assistance, while for those 75 to 84, the frequency rate was 141.8 in every 1,000. Those 85 and over needed the most assistance; 399.0 people out of 1,000 needed help.

Of those adults who lived in private homes and were bed-bound from chronic health problems, the rate was higher for older people. For people aged 18 to 44, 1.4 persons in every 1,000 needed assistance, while 51.2 in every 1,000 of those 85 and over needed it.

The number of individuals needing assistance among those elder adults who required nursing or medical care in the home was also greater and increased for people 65 and over, who frequently needed services such as dressings and injections, the survey found.

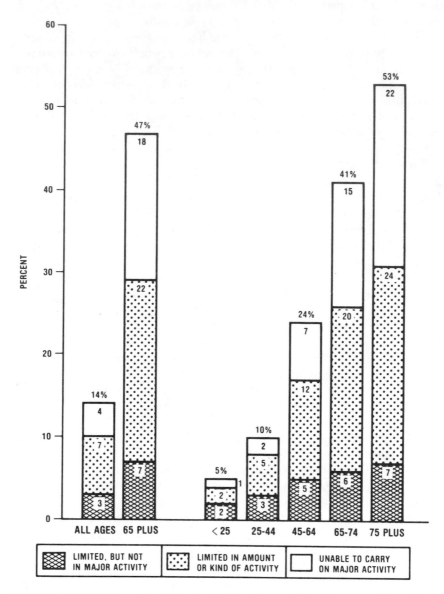

FIGURE 4-1 Limitation of activity due to chronic conditions by type of limitations and age, 1981. (*Source:* National Center for Health Statistics, 1981, Health Interview Survey, unpublished, as it appears in U.S. Senate Special Committee on Aging in conjunction with the American Association of Retired Persons. *Aging America: Trends and Projections* (2nd ed.). Washington, D.C., 1984, p. 61.)

Mental Impairment

Depression In addition to physical problems, the functioning of older people is often hampered by depression. It is estimated that 30 to 68% of the population over 65 will have a serious episode of depression which will interfere with the activities of daily living (Ban, 1978). Depression in older people often goes unrecognized, sometimes because the elder does not confide the feelings for fear of being thought abnormal or because she believes "feeling blue" is a natural part of growing old. Frequently, the depression is associated with the onset or worsening of a chronic illness.

Organic Brain Syndromes Besides depression, two other serious mental disorders frequently afflict the aged, often leading to dependency. These are organic brain syndromes, specifically, delirium and dementia.

Delirium Delirium is an acute condition which is temporary and reversible if properly diagnosed and treated. It can be caused by malnutrition and dehydration, systemic disease, subdural hematomas (blood clots on the brain), ingestion of toxic substances or drugs, cerebrovascular accidents as in transient ischemic attacks (TIAs), or head trauma. Delirium is often confused with dementia because the mental symptoms can be similar: disorientation, memory deficits, and disturbance of the sleep–waking cycle. Other symptoms can include hallucinations and a dazed and confused state of mind. Many of the reversible deliriums are now being recognized and treated so that they do not cause permanent damage or consign the elderly person to a nursing home; it is also less likely that they will lead to death from misdiagnosis or from an undiagnosed cause. If the underlying cause is diagnosed rapidly and treated, the older adult can return to the community—usually within a matter of weeks. Of course, the person with a disabling dementia can also have episodes of delirium (Butler & Lewis, 1982; Mace & Rabins, 1981).

Dementia Unfortunately, dementia does not carry the same optimistic prognosis. There are several types of dementia, and they are a major source of permanent, continually deteriorating and global disability in older people. One-third of those afflicted with a dementia are so impaired in their daily lives that they cannot manage even routine activities such as bathing, grooming, dressing, or eating by themselves (Aronson, 1984). There are two major types of dementia: Alzheimer's disease, thought to account for at least half of the dementias, and multi-infarct dementia, which is associated with damage to cerebral blood vessels through arteriosclerosis ("hardening of the arteries") and accounts for another 10 to 15% of the dementias. Approximately 20% of those afflicted with dementia suffer from a combination of the two major forms while the remaining dementias are caused by conditions that are more rare (Butler & Lewis, 1982; Heston & White, 1983; Jarvik & Kumar, 1984; Mace & Rabins, 1981).

Alzheimer's disease is a major killer and has been called "the disease of the century." It afflicts 1.5 to 2 million Americans, and at least 100,000 people die from it every year (Wurtman, 1985). Alzheimer's is a disease of the old-old: the longer we live, the more likely we are to contract it. Heston and White (1983) report that 20 to 30% of those who reach their mid-80s are likely to contract the disease. This means that it affects more women than men because women tend to live longer.

In its early stages, Alzheimer's disease is characterized by memory deficits and slight declines in many areas of intellectual and physical functioning. The disease may take 7 to 10 years or longer to run its course, and it is typically characterized by increasing incapacity. In later stages, assistance from others becomes necessary in order for the victim to make it through a day. Alzheimer victims eventually forget the names of even close relatives and spouses. Urinary and fecal incontinence set in and, with time, become total. Finally, all verbal abilities are lost, and the victim is totally incapable of toileting, eating, or bathing alone and loses the ability to walk. In the last stages, Alzheimer victims cannot even recognize themselves in the mirror (Butler & Lewis, 1982; Mace & Rabins, 1981; U.S. Department of Health and Human Services, 1984). The personality fades and dies long before the death of the body. The period of total care can go on for years and, contrary to popular myth, most demented people are not placed in nursing homes. They are cared for at home by their families, in spite of the tremendous hardships that are involved (Aronson, 1984).

Currently the cause of Alzheimer's disease is unknown, there is no known treatment, and there is no way to prevent it. It remains very difficult to diagnose (definitive diagnosis is possible only on autopsy), mysterious, and frightening. Therefore, practitioners should be extremely careful about casually labeling older people as "Alzheimer's." The term *senility*—used in a cavalier fashion by the general public and the medical profession alike for years—has just as cavalierly been replaced by the term *Alzheimer's disease*, and the label is frequently applied without the benefit of an adequate diagnostic work-up. Granted the disease is difficult to diagnose; but it is a disservice and possibly a misdiagnosis to consign anyone to the label of Alzheimer's disease without proper medical investigation. It can be seen as ageist and as still another sign of the basic disregard for aging and old people in this country.

Dependency and Elder Abuse and Neglect

Not all older dependent people are abused. The question then becomes, Why some and not others? There are probably two factors other than dependency that must come into play before abuse and neglect occur. First, there must be an individual who, for some reason, abuses or neglects to take a necessary action. Second, there must be a triggering event—a crisis of some sort which precipitates the incident of abuse (O'Malley et al., 1983). It may be that the elder's beginning impairment or the worsening of her impairment creates a crisis leading to abuse or neglect, or the abuse may occur when the need for assistance with activities of daily living increases (Blenkner, 1965, 1969; Steinmetz, 1980). The elder may have been fairly independent but then her need increases and she turns to her adult child for help. Some parents expect that their adult children will take them in, perhaps in spite of the fact that they have never had an amiable relationship. The elder may see it as the child's obligation to do so, and the child may see it in the same way or capitulate out of guilt or fear of being judged harshly by friends or family. Some adult children take their elderly impaired parents into their homes too quickly, without considering other viable alternatives or planning how they will go on with their own lives (Burston, 1978). The elderly parent and the adult child may have had a good relationship up until the impairment and dependency began, but the parent's dependency changes the relationship by shifting the balance of power.

Web of Dependencies

In some instances, the *abuser* may be dependent on the *elder*. Wolf and Pillemer (1984) call attention to the many cases they found in their research which indicate that a large number of abusers are dependent on their victims financially, emotionally, and for housing. They termed this phenomenon "web of dependencies."

Pillemer (1985a, 1985b) focused on 42 physical abuse cases from the above-named research and found that 64% of the abusers were financially dependent on their victims, and 55% were dependent on their victims for housing. In general, Pillemer found that physical abusers were frequently heavily dependent people. This may be true in particular of some sons who seem to feel that their parents are being lazy if they don't fulfill former roles although they have developed physical and/or mental impairments. The truth may be that the son cannot bear to face the fact that his parents are failing and can no longer take care of him. Hwalek, Sengstock, and Lawrence (1984) have also called attention to the dependencies of the abuser and view it as a high-risk factor.

Finkelhor (1983) attempted to identify common causes of family abuse and noted that abusers of women and children frequently *perceive* themselves as being powerless and that the acts of abuse serve to compensate for those feelings. This may be true also of elder abuse and neglect, especially because the adult child who is dependent and abusive knows in some way that he is not fulfilling the expectations of society by remaining dependent on his parent(s). Striking out or abusing in some fashion becomes an equalizing act by which the abuser again feels potent.

THE STRESSED CAREGIVER

The notion of an exhausted caregiver suddenly and impulsively striking out at an impaired elder after years of frustration is probably the most understandable of the theories as to why elder abuse and neglect occur. It is important to realize, however, that although this theory of causation is the easiest to identify with, it is not necessarily the right one. Nearly everyone has, at one time or another, experienced the *feeling*, however fleeting, of wanting to strike out at a dependent person who needs a great deal of help with activities of daily living. Most of us have at times felt impatient or intolerant of an older person who walked slowly in our fast-moving world, had trouble assimilating new information, told the same stories over and over, or incessantly ruminated over lost opportunities.

The hypothesis of the stressed caregiver has received a great deal of attention from researchers and clinicians, not only because it is the most readily acceptable explanation, but also because it fits with interventions that have been pioneered by those working in the field of domestic violence, particularly in child abuse and neglect. Those intervention models include peer groups which provide emotional support and information about resources and normal growth and development, respite care enabling a caregiver to have time for herself, telephone hot lines to help in times of crisis, and in-home services to lighten the load of the caregiver.

Families and Caregiving

The family has traditionally been expected to provide care and support for impaired elderly family members. Fewer than 5% of people over the age of 65 live in nursing homes, so it is obvious that the great bulk of impaired older people are in the community and are dependent on their family, friends, or others for assistance with daily living (Aronson, 1984; U.S. Bureau of the Census, 1983; U.S. Senate Special Committee on Aging, 1984).

For a variety of reasons, nursing home placement is usually a last resort for families and elders. The public image of the nursing home industry, which grows more corporate every day, has not been generally favorable. Although new laws regulating the operation of nursing homes go into effect each year, there are still "bad" nursing homes which give substandard care. For many people, the existence of such homes makes placing an aging parent an unattractive proposition. Nursing homes which do give competent, kind attention seldom receive public notice. In addition, nursing homes can be expensive. In 1985, the average cost of a nursing home in an urban area was $63 per day excluding doctor bills, medication, or special treatment such as physical therapy. At this rate, even a frugal elder's resources would be rapidly dissipated. There also may be community or family pressure for adult children or spouses to care for the elder in her own home or take her to live with them. An adult child may have promised her parents that she would never put them in a nursing home. Often spouses make a similar promise to one another, a promise which is kept even when circumstances have drastically altered.

A 71-year-old woman, described as a "sweet little old thing" by police, pleaded guilty to voluntary manslaughter in the death of her 92-year-old husband. Her husband's pajama-clad body was found on the couple's bed when the coroner arrived. He had been called by the crematorium society, who in turn had been called by the woman. The woman told the coroner's investigator that her husband had died in his sleep. But the investigator was immediately struck by the line around the dead man's neck. From the line down, the body was the color of a normal dead body. But above the line, the face was reddish-purple. When the investigator told the woman that something was not right, she showed him to the telephone and he called the police.

Neighbors indicated that the couple was very close but that the husband's memory had begun failing about eight years before. He had also suffered several strokes and was afflicted with arteriosclerosis, emphysema, and severe hearing loss. He would be found wandering the neighborhood and got lost even on the way to the bathroom in his own home. After their eldest son committed suicide, the husband became much worse. The wife refused to hire any help because she had been a nurse and had reared three children. She refused to place him in a nursing home because the couple had promised one another that neither would put the other in a nursing home. She kept thinking she would be able to handle it. Two weeks before the death, she broke down in the arms of a friend and said, "I just can't take this."

Some families take their elders in because they fear what others will say if they do not at least attempt to care for the elder in a home setting. Other families traditionally cared for their impaired elderly in their homes. For some adult children, taking care of an impaired elder relative in the home is perceived as the last chance to resolve negative feelings left over from the past. Few anticipate that the care of the elder will impose further stresses which may make it impossible to do the healing work (Hayes, 1984b). Further, the role of caregiving is not satisfying to everyone and may not fulfill the adult child's fantasies of what it would be like.

Caring for an elderly parent is rapidly becoming a "normative" adulthood life event (Brody, 1985). Older persons themselves prefer care from family and friends first and then second from friends and neighbors, and finally, as a last resort, from formal agencies and organizations (Ory, 1985). Although it may be reassuring to learn that elders are not being abandoned in institutions, family care should not be idealized or romanticized. Some families care for their elders out of their own pathology and inabilities to take advantage of formal and informal support. Others are psychologically unable to place a severely impaired elder in a nursing home even though the entire family is severely deprived by the caregiving. And in some instances, caring for the elder involves a search for parental affection and approval, a search that by this time is fruitless. This type of caregiving can be termed excessive caregiving and may be due to pathology, not heroism or love (Brody, 1985; Brody & Spark, 1966).

Pressure of Caregiving

There are undeniable pressures on middle-aged children to care for their frail elders at home, even though the burdens can be enormous and extend over long periods of time. Dementia, which is the most common cause of mental impairment among older people, has a long course, sometimes 7 to 10 years, and the period of total physical care (feeding, bathing, coping with bladder and bowel incontinence) may extend over several years (Aronson, 1984). One study noted that the *average* length of time for caregiving was 9.5 years (Streib, 1972). With time, many physical and mental conditions become even more disabling, requiring increased levels of care. The result is increasing isolation for the caregiver, who must focus more and more on meeting the survival needs of the elder and forgo time for herself. Vacations, a career, education, and friendships may go by the wayside. In a study of support groups for relatives of functionally disabled older adults, feelings of severe isolation and entrapment were reported as the foremost concern (Hayes, 1984b). Zarit, Reever, and Bach-Peterson (1980) studied 29 caregivers who were responsible for the care of demented persons and found that the level of burden experienced by the caregivers was directly related to the number of visits from other family members to the household. The more visits, the less the caregiver felt burdened. Surprisingly, the level of burden was not related to the level of physical or mental impairment of the elder or the duration of the illness or behavior problems of the elder.

Caregivers are under other stresses too. Frequently, the caregiver or "family" is one person—usually a middle-aged woman—who does the caregiving with no respite and very little understanding either from her spouse or her children or from her family of origin (Steinmetz, 1983). In fact, her immediate family members may subtly increase their demands on her in order to balance out the attention she is giving to the impaired elder, especially if they do not like the elder (Schmidt, 1980).

Sommers (1985) estimates that 85% of caregivers are women. Until the advent of the women's rights movement, it was assumed that women would stay in the home and care for all dependent members, including the frail elderly. However, that has changed in recent years and just as women with small children are juggling careers and family, so too are women who have elder family members in need of assistance. The phenomenon of "Superwoman," who has a career and a family and "does it all," crosses generational barriers and creates pressure and conflict for women of all ages. If there is disharmony in the caregiver's family of origin, those members may feel free to criticize the primary caregiver for the type of help she gives the elder, and/or for the amount of time and money being spent on the elder's care. Old patterns of sibling rivalry can flare up when a parent becomes dependent. Some clinicians have observed a direct relationship between the amount of complaining done by siblings or primary caregivers and the level of contribution they make to the care of the elder: the more complaining, the less contribution. It often happens that the adult child who is doing the most work gets the least credit or is even blamed by the elder, while the sibling who does virtually nothing receives praise from the aged person for the slightest contribution. This seems to be true particularly when the daughter is the primary caregiver and the aged parent favors a son. Generally speaking, caregivers receive little or no recognition for the unrelenting work they do. There may be a Mother's Day but there is no Caregiver's Day.

People who are taking care of their impaired spouses face, in addition, having to take on household duties that the spouse used to perform. The prospect of a life happily shared in old age dissolves as the work load increases. If the spouse is demented, there are personality changes which irrevocably alter and diminish the couple's relationship. Some spouse caregivers have noted that they feel as if they are in a state of perpetual mourning for a "lost spouse," who is still living.

Fitting and Rabins (1985) report that there are differences between men and women when it comes to caregiving. They base their findings on spouse caregivers and note that no research is available on caregiving sons. In a study of 28 male and 28 female caregivers (55 caregivers were spouses and 1 was a sister), Fitting, Rabins, and Lucas (1984) found that there were minimal differences between the men and women as to feelings of burden, family environment, psychological adjustment, and social contacts. However, the women had significantly more symptoms of depression than the men. Traditionally, women, who have had less societal power, have internalized anger and rage whereas men have had more permission to act it out. This may account for the high numbers of male abusers despite the fact that most caregivers are women.

Interestingly enough, the men tended to hire help more than the women did, possibly as a result of having been in the work world and learning the value of delegating tasks and knowing that one person cannot do it all. Younger caregivers were found to resent the caregiving role more than older caregivers, possibly because of other family and career obligations (Fitting et al., 1984).

There is some evidence to indicate that caregiving is different depending on whether the caregiver is a spouse or an adult child. Spouse caregivers often appear to be suffering from greater objective burdens, but adult children have greater perceptions of burden, possibly because their caregiving to an elder parent means more disruption in their lives (Ory, 1985). Adult children may be more likely to seek physical and emotional distance from the impaired elder as time goes on. Spouses, who may be more emotionally involved with the elder and more distressed by the changes wrought by disease, may find themselves becoming more enmeshed in the relationship as the dependency deepens (Johnson & Catalano, 1983; Zarit, 1985). The couple may increasingly withdraw from social involvement as the caregiving needs compound, especially if there is no one to help. If the spouse caregiver's health collapses, immediate institutionalization may result for the impaired spouse. In many instances, adult children will insist on placing the impaired spouse in an institution when the caregiver's health has broken down.

Unknowns in Caregiving as Contributors to Stress

The generation which came to adulthood in the 1930s and 1940s is the first generation of adult children to face caring for elderly parents on such a wide scale. There are many unknowns. Information about normal aging and the diseases associated with aging is not generally available. Indeed, recent discoveries showing that much of what has been considered normal aging is in fact disease have not been widely publicized. This lack of information can result in confusion as to whether a given condition is treatable or whether it will worsen and become chronic.

Techniques for dealing with disabilities, particularly with the behaviors associated with dementia, are not widely known. Some caregivers feel that if they physically discipline the impaired elder, it will resolve the problem.

They simply do not know what to expect, or do not believe that the elder is really impaired.

> An elderly stroke victim was living alone and recovering well. The van came every day and took her to a rehabilitation center. Her son was divorced, allegedly because his wife could no longer stand the beatings he administered. After the divorce, he came home to live with his mother. He immediately began interfering with her treatment plan, first by forbidding her to go to the rehabilitation center and then by telling her that the only therapy she needed was to go out into the back yard and pull the weeds, which were nearly four feet high.

Obstacles to Caregiving

A caregiver faces many obstacles in trying to care for an impaired elder responsibly. Doctors and other medical practitioners are often consulted by caregivers, but they may not offer the desired assistance or information. Caregivers may be too intimidated by physicians to press their concerns. Physicians may not take the time to explain medical conditions adequately, leaving the caregiver with an imperfect understanding of the situation. Community resources such as respite care or in-home services are sparse.

A further difficulty is the lack of adequate role models or mentors for caregivers. It is not uncommon for stressed caregivers to express bewilderment at the quantity and quality of work entailed in taking care of a frail elder and to wonder aloud, "Why didn't someone tell me?" Of course, no one could tell them, because previous generations have not had to cope with these issues. Few families have had dealings with the old-old (over 75), and they often seem like unknown and almost exotic creatures.

Elder as Source of Stress

The elder herself can be a source of stress for the caregiver. In one study, 63% of elder abusers reported that the elder was a source of stress because of the high level of physical and emotional care required (O'Malley et al., 1979). With demented elders, there are a number of behaviors that can be worrisome and disconcerting for caregivers such as wandering, primitive eating habits, leaving stove burners on, insomnia, and disrobing in public. There is the fear that the elder will hurt herself or others. It is this emotional burden rather than the physical work that seems to put the greatest strain on caregivers. Doing household tasks, grooming, and transporting an impaired elder are reported by caregivers to be time-consuming but not stress-producing, whereas the strain of dealing with elders who have emotional problems or are demented creates tension for the caregiver (Steinmetz, 1983).

Other Stressors

Other stressors have to do with the relative maturity of the caregiver and the elder. Old battles can come back to life when elder and adult child are thrown together. Conflicting ideas about such things as politics, love relationships, raising children, or the conduct of one's work life can haunt the caregiver, resulting in renewed anger and resentment. Character traits which the parent always disliked in the child may provoke "guilt trips." Not all caregivers can always control their anger, modulating it, channeling it, and understanding it. In addition, some parents do not learn to let go of their adult children and never perceive them as adults with rights and responsibilities. The parent may berate the adult child for what she is not or for what she could have been, or may compare her unfavorably with other siblings. With the onset of dementia, the elderly parent may only be disapproving and be unable to give the warmth, tenderness, and support that is critical to successful parenting, or indeed to any relationship. Paranoia may set in, leaving suspicion where once there was respect and regard. The demented elder may become accusatory, putting extra stress on a caregiver already chronically fatigued and doing everything possible to keep the elder comfortable.

Steinmetz (1981) studied 60 adult children who were caring for a dependent elderly parent and found strong evidence that parent and child tried to control one another. She termed this "double-direction violence." The most common form of control was screaming and yelling, but hitting and slapping also occurred. Caregivers who slapped an elder often gave the same reasons for their behavior that child-abusing parents do, saying that the slapping or hitting was done to discipline the elder and to ensure her safety (see Tables 4-1 and 4-2).

A parent who in the past has always wielded control over her children may be left open to abuse by strangers when her family does not recognize that she is failing. Family members are so accustomed to being bullied by the elder or so fearful of crossing her (perhaps for fear that she may change her will) that a void is created into which an opportunistic stranger may step and take advantage. The adult children are too intimidated to notice that a hairdresser or doctor or newspaper boy or corner grocer or housekeeper has engaged their parent's affections and is moving to gain control of the elder's entire estate, at the same time pleading undying affection for the elder and fueling the elder's own paranoia about his family.

The role of external stressors in precipitating abuse has yet to be well defined. The effects on the abuser of variables such as overcrowding, finan-

Table 4-1 Methods Used by Adult Children to Control Their Elderly Parents

Methods	Percent
Scream and yell	40
Use physical restraint	6
Force feeding or medication	6
Threaten to send to nursing home	6
Threaten with physical force	4
Hit or slap	3

Source: Reprinted from S. K. Steinmetz, "Elder Abuse." *Aging, 315–316* (Jan.–Feb. 1981), p. 7.

Table 4-2 Methods Used by Elderly to Control Their Adult Children

Methods	Percent
Scream and yell	43
Pout or withdraw	47
Refuse food or medication	16
Manipulate, cry, or use physical or emotional disability	32
Hit, slap, throw objects	22
Call police or others for imagined threats	10

Source: Reprinted from S. K. Steinmetz, "Elder Abuse." *Aging,* 315–316, Jan.–Feb. 1981, p. 9.

cial problems, unemployment, alcohol and drug abuse, and long-term medical problems have been investigated to some extent in three of the exploratory studies (Block & Sinnott, 1979; Douglass et al., 1980; O'Malley et al., 1979). One study found that almost 75% of abusers were experiencing some form of stress (O'Malley et al., 1979). Another study found that frequently either the abuser or the elder abused alcohol (Douglass et al., 1980). No doubt these factors will receive further attention in future research.

LEARNED VIOLENCE

This theory of how elder abuse and neglect occur draws on research and clinical work that has been done in recent decades regarding child abuse and neglect as well as spouse abuse. Although it remains for future researchers to draw specific relationships between these types of domestic abuse and elder abuse and neglect, a brief review of the issues relating to domestic violence is important to the understanding of this contributor.

Domestic Violence

Child abuse and neglect have been defined as such only within this century. Historically, children were viewed as the possession of the male head of the household and were considered his to do with as he chose. It was thought that children needed to be trained and that it was the parent or guardian's responsibility to see that the child learned his duties. Some young noblemen had whipping boys so that they could escape being punished personally (Radbill, 1968). This harsh treatment of children has been controversial, with an increasing number of voices objecting and drawing attention to the rights of children. The current wave of concern is the result of advances in X-ray technology. In 1946, Caffey published findings that called attention to the common association of subdural hematomas with abnormal X-ray changes in the long bones of children (Caffey, 1946). Later observers corroborated these findings, and it was gradually realized that these injuries had been willfully inflicted. In 1961, the American Academy of Pediatrics held a symposium on the subject, which by then had been termed by Kempe as "the battered child syndrome" (Radbill, 1968). Gradually, government agencies became interested and funding was supplied for research grants. Currently all of the 50 states have mandatory reporting laws and services for both parents and children are widespread. Nevertheless, practitioners in the field point to the need for more understanding and programs. Just recently, in the mid 1980s, the hitherto taboo subject of sexual abuse of children has begun receiving national attention for the first time.

Concern about spouse abuse has arisen only within the last two decades, stimulated by the book *Scream Quietly or the Neighbors Will Hear*, which was published in 1974 by English author Erin Pizzey. That book was followed in 1976 by Del Martin's pioneering book, *Battered Wives*. Women too have been historically viewed as the property of the male head of the household and therefore subject to his control. Wife beating has been condoned for centuries and encouraged as a way of preserving control. It has been sanctioned by church authorities as a form of instructional discipline for actions on the part of women which their husbands found unacceptable. Martin (1976) notes that at least one society issued instructions detailing the circumstances under which a man might most effectively beat his wife. Actual murder or femicide has not always been viewed with concern. There are still many societies that look upon women as second-class citizens or as the legal possessions of the head of the household. Wife battering remains common. Walker (1979) estimates that 50% of all women will be victims of battering at some point in their lives.

Very little evidence is available to describe what happens when the battered woman grows old. However, one descriptive study verifies some of the observations seen in younger battered women. Gesino, Smith, and

Keckich (1982) studied two older women who had been admitted to an adult psychiatric ward with diagnoses of depression. Both women were described by their children as having been physically and psychologically abused for most of their married lives. One woman, age 73 and married for 37 years, was physically assaulted in the early years of her marriage but as the couple aged, the physical abuse tapered off. However, the threatening verbal abuse continued until the husband's death two years before the hospital admission.

The other woman, age 76 and married for 47 years, experienced physical assaults up until five years prior to admission and verbal threats were still going on. Although she suffered numerous injuries, she never sought medical attention. The physical abuse declined as the husband's physical health deteriorated. She had become his caregiver and had to assume many of the roles he could no longer fulfill.

Gesino et al. (1982) note that both women "became depressed as a result of the loss of the familiar pattern of relating, and the shift from a submissive role to a dominant one."

Neither woman would discuss the abuse she had received and according to both, it was not a problem. The women did not feel it was proper to share the intimate details of their marriages with others. Divorce was not an option for either one of them and both felt that their husbands could not control their behaviors; neither man was held accountable for his actions. Both women accepted the man as the authority in the house and had no social life other than what the men permitted. In fact, they had no friends of their own. Both women demonstrated a strong sense of loyalty to their husbands.

The women had different reasons for staying in the marriage besides the stigma of divorce. One felt that it was her responsibility to stay and make the marriage work, and the other felt that her primary role in the marriage was to fulfill her husband's demands. The latter also felt that she was not a good person, and the abuse served to confirm her feelings.

Both women had low self-esteem, understandably limited social skills, and a passive interpersonal style, which was probably adaptational. Both showed vegetative signs of depression such as declines in personal care and sleep and eating disturbances. Both responded to long-term inpatient treatment which included individual and group psychotherapy, socialization, medication, and electroconvulsive treatments.

Incidence of Domestic Violence

The first nationwide study of domestic violence, *Behind Closed Doors: Violence in the American Family* (Straus, Gelles, & Steinmetz, 1980), was published in 1980. The researchers studied 2,143 intact, mentally healthy families who were selected randomly. Children under the age of three were not included. Neither were elders. Violence, defined as "any act carried out with the intention or perceived intention of causing pain or injury to another person" was found to be widespread in the United States. Most incidents were minor assaults such as pushing, slapping, or shoving. But more severe violence—including kicking, biting, or hitting with a fist, battering or trying to batter with an object, threatening the other with a knife or gun, or actually using a knife or a gun—were quite common. Approximately 6 out of every 100 married couples admitted to being involved in one of these acts. On a national level, this means that severe violence takes place in three million American homes every year. Twenty-eight percent of the spouses also reported having engaged in at least one act of violence during their marriage. The incidence of wife beating was 3.8% while the incidence for husband beating was 4.6% (Straus, 1979; Straus, Gelles, & Steinmetz, 1980). The higher rate for husband beating probably represents retaliation on the part of the wife or violence by both parties. Other studies have noted that men engage in more violent actions than do women, and they inflict more serious damage. Walker (1984) found that women may strike back at the men who batter them, but their efforts to stop the abuse are usually futile and the harm they inflict on the men is minimal, although the net effect may be that the severity of their own injuries is lessened. The women in Walker's study tended to be less violent when they were not living with a violent man.

For children, the violence figures are higher; 14 out of 100 children are the victims of severe violence in a given year, which means that 6.5 million children are victims of child abuse each year. Because many people consider hitting a child with a belt or a hairbrush to be acceptable, the researchers separated that action out from the severe violence category. They then found that 4 out of every 100 children are victimized each year or 1.7 million children face being kicked, bitten, punched, beaten up, or being threatened or actually attacked by a parent with a knife or a gun. Straus (1979) notes that the family is where most people learn to act in violent ways and that there is a greater chance of being assaulted in one's own home than on even the most dangerous of city streets.

Transgenerational Violence

Many observers have concluded that domestic violence such as child abuse and neglect and spouse abuse is learned in the home and passed from one generation to the next (Ackley, 1977; Kempe & Kempe, 1978; Martin, 1976; Pizzey, 1974; Roy, 1982; Sonkin & Durphy, 1982; Straus, 1979; Straus et al., 1980; Walker, 1979, 1984). Walker (1984) interviewed 435 women who volunteered to talk about the physical violence they had suffered at the hands of their men and found that the men tended to be generally violent people with a high incidence of other violent activity. Men who abused their partners tended to have more arrests and convictions and to be involved in more child abuse incidents than nonbattering men. Sonkin and Durphy

(1982), who have treated battering men, found that 65% of male abusers came from homes in which they saw their father abuse their mother or where they themselves were abused. These men have learned that physical violence against others is a legitimate way to deal with anger, stress, interpersonal conflict, and frustration, according to Sonkin and Durphy. The best indicators as to whether a man will be violent in a relationship seem to be past incidents of violence either in his home or toward pets, a previous criminal record, or longer time spent in military service where specific training for violence takes place (Walker, 1984). Straus et al. (1980) found that men who have seen their parents attack each other are three times as likely to hit their wives than others, and the statistics are roughly the same for women. On the other hand, those people whose parents were never violent toward them had the lowest rate of spouse abuse—2%, the researchers found. Of the one-third of parents with teenagers who reported hitting them, 37.3% were almost universally hit by their own parents when they were teenagers. Adults who had received most punishment as teenagers had a rate of spouse beating four times greater than those whose parents did not hit them. Age was also a factor in spouse abuse. People under 30 were more active in every form of domestic violence. A low income was found to be correlated with spouse abuse (Straus et al., 1980).

Walker (1984) found in her study that most wife batterers had always lived in homes filled with violence: in 81% of their childhood homes, spouse or child abuse occurred, as compared with 24% of the nonviolent men's homes. The majority of the abusive men (63%) saw their fathers beat their mothers. In 61% of the homes, the men were battered by their fathers and in 44% they were battered by their mothers; in some cases both parents battered. Victims of spouse battering also report battering in their backgrounds. In one study, over 66% of battered women came from homes where battering occurred (Walker, 1984), and another study reported the figure of 35% (Roy, 1982). Walker (1984) found more than one-half of spouse abusers also beat their children, and that battered women were more likely to discipline their children physically when living with their batterers.

The death of children from child abuse may be directly related to incidents of spouse abuse. Weston (1968) reported on a study of 23 children who came to a hospital or medical doctor in a terminal or postmortem condition. The average age of the children was 24 months. In cases where the mother was the assailant, several mothers said they were beaten in childhood and also in the weeks and months prior to the death of the child.

Abusers

Most research has shown that abuse cuts across all racial, religious, education, and socioeconomic lines (Ganley, 1981; Kempe & Kempe, 1978; Sonkin & Durphy, 1982; Steele & Pollock, 1968; Straus et al., 1980; Walker,

1979, 1984). Straus et al. (1980) point to external stressors as playing a part. In their study, families with low incomes or in which the man was employed part time or unemployed had higher rates of violence, as did families in which the parents were under the age of 30. The latter finding also may be applicable in elder abuse and neglect, when grandchildren or even great-grandchildren under 30 years of age do the caregiving.

Most research indicates that the characteristic most abusers have in common is having learned to use violence to deal with their feelings, that the violence was learned in the home, and that it has been transmitted from one generation to the next.

Patterns of Abuse

Elder abuse and neglect, spouse abuse, and child abuse and neglect seem to follow patterns that are somewhat clear. To date, these patterns are less clear with elder abuse and neglect, although we do know that the victim is likely to experience repeated incidents (Block & Sinnott, 1979; Lau & Kosberg, 1979; O'Malley et al., 1979). Child abuse usually occurs most frequently during the first three years of life, probably in response to intractable crying which cannot be stopped by the parent. In frustration, the parent strikes the child, causing head injuries—the most common inflicted injuries in infants (Kempe & Kempe, 1978). Parents may see the crying as an accusation and their comforting efforts as ineffective. Child abuse is not constant and seems to occur in response to a crisis, which could be anything from a spilled glass of milk to intractable crying to a major event such as divorce or death. Some children can sense when a parent is becoming upset and may be able to anticipate danger. The child may even try to comfort the parent. One clinician reported observing an 18-month-old soothe her mother, who was in tears. The child was sucking a bottle when she observed that her mother was upset and weeping. She put the bottle down, went over to her mother, and touched her, effectively calming her down, something the social worker had been unable to do (Davoren, 1968).

Further research into elder abuse and neglect may reveal that there are specific irritants which trigger elder abuse episodes.

One adult son could not tolerate his widowed mother's alleged incessant talking when she was in the midst of a psychotic episode. He hit her repeatedly about the eyes and dislodged a lens in one eye, which left her in constant pain despite surgery. He maintained that he had a right to hit her, that he "stood in the place" of his dead father and that he would hit her again if "she needed it" and told the investigator, "No judge can keep me from doing my duty." This same son refused to permit his mother to receive the psychiatric treatment that she badly needed.

Certainly many elderly who are dependent must be fed and are incontinent. The reader will recall from Chapter 2 that abuse episodes often center around feeding issues. Caregivers of dependent elderly report that some aspects of caregiving are more irritating than others. Incontinence and interrupted sleep night after night are reported to be the most stressful conditions for caregivers to deal with (Crossman, London, & Barry, 1981). It may be these stresses which precipitate abusive episodes. Also, many demented people have characteristic vocalizations that are repeated over and again, no matter what the circumstances are. For example, the elder may cry out "Help me, help me" or "She's killing me. She's killing me." Such behavior may be analogous to the intractable crying seen in infants.

Spouse abuse may have more clearly delineated stages for each episode of abuse. Walker (1979, 1984) has suggested that there are three stages. In the first stage, there is a tension building, a "gathering before the storm" in which the man expresses dissatisfaction and may engage in verbal abuse. The woman tries to placate him and keep from doing anything she thinks will antagonize him. This anger and frustration, however, continue to grow and finally erupt into the second stage—the acute battering episode. The acute episode acts as a tension-reliever for the man and in that sense, is an effective and reinforcing way for him to deal with internal conflict. The third phase then ensues and is marked by loving, contrite behavior; the man apologizes and swears he will never do it again and the woman wants to believe him. The warmth and attention the woman receives in the third phase serve to make her feel it is worth-while to stay in the relationship, and she feels hopeful that things will change. But according to Walker (1984) and Sonkin and Durphy (1982) the battering will reoccur.

Domestic violence always escalates in frequency and severity over time; the need for medical attention increases and the use of weapons becomes more common (Kempe & Kempe, 1978; Sonkin & Durphy, 1982; Walker, 1984; Weston, 1968). There seem to be certain times when abuse is more likely to happen. With spouse abuse, it occurs more frequently during pregnancy, when there are infants and small children in the house, and when children are adolescents (Walker, 1984). Child abuse and neglect seem more likely to occur in times of external crisis such as the loss of a job or a fight with a supervisor, or when an infant's crying interrupts the parents' sexual intercourse. A study of 4,000 partners in violence in the late 1970s revealed several contributing factors or catalysts to spouse violence, the first of which was arguments over money. Next was jealousy and then sexual problems, with alcohol and drugs coming fourth (Roy, 1982). Most domestic violence studies mention the involvement of alcohol (and other drugs). Alcohol appears to be involved in more than half of the cases, but it is still unclear whether alcohol is the stimulus, the effect, or the frequent companion to domestic violence.

Comparison Between the Various Types of Domestic Abuse

The theory that violence is learned behavior, taught in families and perpetuated through generations, is convincing. It is a wonder that elderly people have for the most part been exempted from the major studies on domestic violence. It is almost as if domestic violence vanishes when a family member turns 65, no matter how violent the elder may have been all her life or how much she may have been victimized. This is, of course, highly unlikely. The evidence with regard to learned violence is overwhelming and should be a red flag to geriatric practitioners. Questions about family violence should be woven into every interview situation with older adults and their caregivers. This includes caregivers who are not family members. Given the high rate of family violence, it is obvious that many non-family caregivers have grown up in violent homes and may look upon violence as a way of shutting up a complaining elder. Added to this is the reality that many non-family caregivers and their elderly charges form family-like relationships and may transfer old family patterns of interacting onto any intimate situation.

There are similarities between the various types of abuse and neglect. For instance, elders are noted to suffer from a similar "failure to thrive syndrome" as do infants. In elders, it is manifested in malnutrition and dehydration, frequently accompanied by pressure sores. It is not uncommon to observe an emaciated elder enter a nursing home and proceed rapidly to gain weight. Dependent elders and children both rely on others to see to their basic needs and may be incapable of asking for what they must have for survival.

Spouse abuse and elder abuse and neglect have one main commonality—their victims are both adults who are legally able to make their own decisions until a court of law decides otherwise and appoints a guardian or conservator. These decisions can be silly or wasteful or dangerous, but the adult has the right to make any of them until judged incapable of doing so.

The problems confronting practitioners are greater with elder abuse and neglect because of the complexity of the needs of elders, especially their physical needs. Leaving the home where the abuser is the sole caregiver presents many dilemmas, especially if the elder owns the home. The question of who should leave becomes an issue and so does the problem of who should do the caregiving. Currently, nursing home placement is the most widely used and probably the most feared alternative. Shelters for abused women have traditionally shied away from taking in older women because they do not feel they have the necessary resources for their care. Even if they did take female victims of elder abuse, they could not take male victims. In addition, shelters for battered women are already overcrowded.

There is one aspect of elder abuse and neglect which is different from other forms of domestic violence. Elderly people are more likely than children or younger women to have money and to own property. In 1979, three out of four households maintained by an older adult were owner-occupied, and half of those houses were owned free and clear. More than one-third (37%) of the owner-occupied elderly households were inhabited by elderly men or women living alone. Two-thirds of all homes owned free and clear were maintained by an elder person (U.S. Bureau of the Census, 1983). In 1980, 72% of all elderly owned their own homes (U.S. Senate Special Committee on Aging, 1984). These homes were acquired at a time when home ownership was economically feasible and expected; many older people have lived their entire adult lives in the same house. Over the years, the homes have increased greatly in value, and they represent security and safety to their elderly owners, who may not be aware of their market value. The inflated value of the homes make them a target for fraudulent practices on the part of unscrupulous strangers, "friends," and family.

THE PATHOLOGICAL CAREGIVER

The theories in this category focus on the role of the abuser as the sole factor in elder abuse and neglect. The abusers are seen as having profound disabling conditions: addiction to alcohol or other drugs, sociopathic personalities, serious psychiatric disturbances, dementia, mental retardation, or chronic inability to make appropriate judgments where the care of a dependent elder is concerned. With time and further research, it is likely that this category will be smaller than the others, but there will always be situations where it applies. Wolf, Strugnell, and Godkin (1982) found that 31% of abusers had a history of psychiatric illness and 43% had substance-abuse problems.

These abusers can be the most difficult for practitioners to work with. They may not respond to traditional or even to innovative interventions. They may be cavalier in their treatment of a frail elder and blithely ignore the elder's basic needs such as food, clothing, shelter, and medical care, despite repeated interventions by the practitioner. Often they fail to see any connection between their actions and an injured elder. They cannot or will not exercise judgment, even if given new information and followed over a long period of time by an experienced and sympathetic practitioner. Some give elaborate and preposterous explanations for their abusive behavior. Frequently, the practitioner is hard put to find genuine concern for the elder in the abuser's attitude.

The abusers in this category who have sociopathic tendencies or personalities may totally disregard conventional mores and may offend or even violate cultural standards—for example, they may have served time in prison. They are unable to form meaningful relationships or identify with others, and they exhibit a remarkable lack of conflict, guilt, anxiety, and insecurity. They do not seem to profit by experience and seem unable to control their impulses (Brantley & Sutker, 1984). Often they appear intellectually intact, even bright, but they are incapable of following through with practitioner recommendations even when they promise to do so. This can be very confusing for the practitioner, who is accustomed to associating intellectual functioning with appropriate physical actions. Some abusers in this category have extremely charming and magnetic personalities, while at the same time demonstrating emotional immaturity and a callousness that can be shocking. People with sociopathic tendencies or personalities often cheat, lie, or steal, even when there seems to be no particular advantage to doing so (Manfreda & Krampitz, 1977). Some clinicians have noted that the most damaging physical abuse cases, which also feature sexual abuse, are frequently associated with sociopathic-like sons and their elderly mothers. The adult sons live at home, either because they never achieved the maturity necessary to leave or because they came home to live with a widowed mother after a failed marriage (which may have been marred by spouse battering) or because they couldn't function in a competitive society. Some of the sons have sustained severe and permanent brain damage from indiscriminate and prolonged use of street drugs or alcohol. These sons, who seem outside the mainstream of society, and oddly different from their peers, may have failed to complete an earlier stage of psychosocial development (Ostrovski, 1979).

Some adult children may be actively abusing chemical substances. On one geropsychiatric unit, the staff noticed that the daughter of a severely demented man visited her father an average of once a month. Gradually, the staff realized that the daughter, an obvious heroin addict, was coming to the unit the first week of every month and bringing her father's Social Security check so that he could sign it over to her. She would then cash the check and keep the money to support her habit. The staff remedied the situation by finding a responsible party to serve as the representative payee for the checks. In another drug-related situation, an elderly woman who was mentally impaired was found sleeping on municipal buses night after night. A bus driver finally reported the situation to his supervisor, who called social services. It was discovered that her son, a drug addict, had gained title to her house and had sold it to an innocent third party. The mother literally had no place to go until she was placed in a board and care home and public benefits were instated. She was not only demented; she was psychologically in shock.

Some caregivers were once institutionalized themselves. Beginning in the early 1960s, the treatment and custodial care of developmentally disabled people and chronically ill psychiatric people began shifting from large rural facilities to "the community"—a euphemistic term for urban board and care homes where the staff is usually untrained. Typically, there were (and still are) few community resources for these emotionally and cognitively impaired people. Some went to live with their aging parents. Others always lived with their parents because their parents fought to keep them out of an institution or because they were unable to separate themselves from the impaired child. There may be no other siblings, or if there are, they leave the family home and go on to their own careers, perhaps relocating in other states. This leaves the impaired sibling to do the caregiving should the parent become dependent.

When the caregiver is demented, it is most likely a spouse. The elderly couple lives together and has become isolated. The demented spouse is physically healthy, while the physically fragile spouse is mentally intact. Together, they make "one whole person." As the demented spouse's illness progresses, so does the mate's physical incapacities, until there is a severely demented caregiver and a bed-bound invalid. Abuse becomes a possibility. Often both individuals need a protected setting, and they may consent to being placed in the same facility and sharing the same room. It should be noted, however, that not all aged married.couples want to live in the same room or even in the same facility. A physical illness or mental impairment may bring about a separation that the couple has long desired but did not know how to initiate.

Sometimes, those in the position of handling the affairs of others become incapable themselves.

An 81-year-old woman who had been a yeomanette in World War I became emotionally depressed and unable to function in the 1950s, when her job was phased out in a corporate merger. She admitted herself to a Veteran's Hospital and took up residence there. She was ambulatory, alert, and oriented. She had her hair done weekly, attended luncheon parties, and engaged in other social activities associated with a leisurely life style. She also visited her brother in a convalescent hospital. He had been her guardian until he became incapacitated and turned her affairs over to his law partner. The law partner, an elderly man, was for several years very faithful in sending her $200 monthly allowance, but gradually he began to forget to do it or sent it so late that the woman was greatly inconvenienced. From conversations with other parties, the woman ascertained that the law partner was "slipping" and she came to believe that he was "senile." She asked the court's help in terminating the guardianship. A public defender was appointed to represent her, and she was restored to capacity after it was learned that her pension checks could be sent directly to Patient Accounts at the VA hospital; she would then have direct access to her funds, and the accounting department would have a supervisory role. The retired yeomanette gained a great deal of self-confidence and felt even more independent once she was able to have control of her funds.

SOCIETAL ATTITUDES AS CONTRIBUTORS
TO ELDER ABUSE AND NEGLECT

There are several societal attitudes which contribute to elder abuse and neglect. While not causes in themselves, these attitudes create an atmosphere that paves the way for maltreatment of the elderly. Among these attitudes are ageism, sexism, attitudes toward the disabled, and plain old-fashioned greed.

Ageism

Myths and stereotypes about the old and the process of aging are widespread and contribute to a pervasive prejudice against elders. This prejudice has been termed ageism and is defined as:

> . . . a process of systematic stereotyping of and discrimination against people because they are old, just as racism and sexism accomplish this with skin color and gender. Old people are categorized as senile, rigid in thought and manner, old-fashioned in morality and skills. . . . Ageism allows the younger generations to see older people as different from themselves; thus they subtly cease to identify with their elders as human beings. (Butler & Lewis, 1973).

In our fast-moving technological society, older people are often seen as having nothing to offer, as being in the way of "progress," or as having no future. In fact, they are shunned and avoided, especially if they are impaired. The old are frequently removed from the mainstream by placement in segregated institutions such as nursing homes and retirement communities. Aging or infirmity has become a stigma. The unique set of personality characteristics, the yearnings, triumphs, and strengths which make up a life, the knowledge gained from overcoming personal handicaps and surviving tragedies and fears, the growth achieved through loving others and one's own imperfect self—these have little value when measured against the visual reality of graying hair, joints gone arthritic, facial wrinkles, and minor memory losses. Old age has become synonymous with loss of personal power, disability, and lack of control over one's own life. Seen in that light, it is little wonder that there is so much ambivalence about growing old, and it is understandable that ageism has arisen as a way of distancing ourselves from and fending off old age. Ageism serves to protect younger generations against thoughts of growing old and impaired, and especially against death. But the respite is temporary. With each advancing year, and particularly in late middle-age, the realities of physical aging become apparent. Ageism is a time bomb of the most personal nature because most people also hope to live long lives and will end up as part of a minority group against which they have always harbored prejudice. They become targets of their own internalized myths and stereotypes about aging. Ageism is alive and well, and living in everyone.

There are many false beliefs about growing old. They include the following: Everyone ages at the same rate. Normal aging lowers productivity and leads to a desire to disengage from life. All older people are inflexible and less adaptable to change than younger people. And, perhaps the most damaging myth of all, old age inevitably brings "senility" (Butler, 1975). The older people become, the more likely they are to remark that they "must be getting old" if they forget something or, more recently, that "Alzheimer's disease must be setting in." While some forgetting is common in aging, and pathological memory loss is a hallmark of Alzheimer's disease, forgetting occurs at other points in life too. We are likely to forget things which are too unpleasant to remember, for example, the pain involved in giving birth to a child or the details of a traumatic event such as a divorce. We also forget if we don't make a conscious effort to remember, or if we were not really paying attention to details or if we had too many other things to think about. And yet, after a certain age the explanation most people seize on for minor losses of memory is that it must be due to a chronic, debilitating, and terminal disease.

For some people, anxiety about forgetting prompts even more memory lapses, until they lose all confidence in their power to remember. They may feel that this is the normal course of events. After all, "Doesn't everyone become 'senile' with age?" This, then, is the danger of stereotyping; the victim comes to believe the myths and to act accordingly. The myths get reinforced by others who believe them. Synder (1982), who has investigated self-fulfilling stereotyping, noted that when prejudiced people deal with the objects of their biases, they often elicit the behavior they expect. In fact, they tend to selectively notice and remember the ways in which the person reinforces the biases and to resist evidence contradicting the stereotypes. Thus, those who harbor negative attitudes toward the aged may actually cause the elder to act in a negative or powerless way, or in a way which reinforces myths and stereotypes about aging. Prejudice is learned at an early age and is deeply held, perhaps sometimes at an unconscious level. It is difficult to dislodge.

Ageism shows up in the use of language. Most of the adjectives or adverbs used to describe aging are negative. Aged wine, cheese, or lace may be looked on with respect and value, but this is rarely true with aged people. Nuessel (1982) notes that positive, age-specific attributes descriptive for aging—mature, mellow, sage, veteran—are sparse. He lists 75 terms he considers ageist including battle ax, decrepit, fogy, goat, old-fashioned, obsolete, over-the-hill, second childhood, toothless, and wizened. Many of these terms become even more denigrating if the word *old* is placed in front of them. Medical professionals reveal their negative attitudes in the terms they often use to describe the elderly, referring to old people as crocks, codgers, hypochondriacs or, for women, douche bags (Brown, 1978).

Ageism is also apparent in social policy and government funding patterns. For instance, there has always been more funding for public child protective services than for adult protective services, clear evidence that children are more valued than elders and that there is more interest in the future than in the past. Studies of family violence, though well-researched and docu-mented, have always excluded the elderly for reasons not entirely clear at the present time. It may have been inconceivable that elderly parents would ever be abused because of the religious imperative found in many faiths which instructs children to honor their parents. Or perhaps it was just too painful to contemplate.

Many people, even lawyers and physicians, still assume that all impaired older people belong in nursing homes and should be under conservator-ships. In fact, in many states just being old is reason enough to have a guardianship or conservatorship imposed, regardless of functioning abilities. Ageist attitudes are as common in the legal system as anywhere else. One lawyer, referring to a severely mentally impaired woman, called her a "fruitcake," a "vegetable," and a "slab of meat." Social workers dealing with the case were puzzled by the attorney's use of food images to describe the patient, but it was clear to them that he did not regard the elderly woman as human.

Medical practices tend to be ageist in part because medical students receive little, if any, training in gerontology. Conditions which produce temporary symptoms of confusion and disorientation are often misdiagnosed as dementia. Thoughtful and meticulous assessment of the complex medical problems of the elderly is only now beginning to take place. Ageism can show up in subtle ways. One nursing home house physician routinely places all residents on salt-free diets saying, "Well, it can't hurt them." In fact, those who do not need a salt-free diet are deprived of more tasty food and may not eat nutritionally as a result.

What does ageism have to do with elder abuse and neglect? Are the two related and, if so, how? Again, specific research is lacking but speculations can be offered.

Through myths and stereotyping about the old, they come to be seen as nonpersons, as less than human. They are taken less seriously than are younger people and are less valued as human beings by themselves and by others. As a result, mistreatment of the elderly may be viewed as less important or of less consequence than mistreatment of younger people. Certainly, little attention has been paid to it until recently. Jensen and Oakley (1980) believe that there is sufficient evidence to suggest that the appearance and behavior of old people was at one time a deterrent to physical attack by others. But appearance is no longer effective and, in fact, may be a stimulus for aggressive behavior on the part of others. They urge older adults to become more assertive, and to take an active "mastery" approach to their problems whether political or personal.

Block and Sinnott (1979) note that attitudes, misperceptions, and distortions may be heavily implicated in abuse and call for more research into the role of ageism. They suggest that the old may view abusive treatment as deserved or as unavoidable because they internalize society's negative stereotypes.

Attitudes Toward the Disabled

Negative attitudes toward the disabled may also play a part in elder abuse and neglect. Many older adults are disabled, and our society has traditionally viewed disabled people as nonproductive and as not contributing to the economy. They are seen as a drain on society and as undesirable. According to studies by English, nearly half of the nondisabled population holds primarily negative attitudes toward the disabled (English, 1977, 1980). Other studies have indicated that children's stories and comic books often portray evil characters as having some type of physical abnormality or disability or as being very unattractive. Butler (1982) has noted that there seems to be a human propensity for hostility toward the handicapped based perhaps on aversion and revulsion, but possibly also on the fear of becoming disabled. Many primitive societies do not permit disabled people to live and put them to death at birth or as soon as disability becomes obvious. This is also true for the aged.

As with other stigmatized groups, the disabled must fight stereotyping by others as well as their own internalized prejudices against their disabled state. The disabled are seen as dependent on the charity of others, and they come to view themselves that way (Johnson, 1983). Thus, there is a self-image that facilitates feelings of helplessness, hopelessness, and vulnerability in disabled people of all ages.

Sexism

A disproportionate number of elder abuse and neglect victims are women. This suggests that sexism may play a part in the maltreatment of elderly women. Over the past two decades, the women's rights movement has documented the ways in which all women lack the power to control their lives. Where older women are concerned, the issue of powerlessness is clear and dramatic, surfacing in such basic areas as low income, poor health, and negative societal attitudes toward older women.

All women suffer from sexism, whether or not they acknowledge it. Most women (80%) continue to be clustered in a small range of low-paying employment categories, working in jobs which have no promotion potential and pay only 65% of what most men make (Commission on the Status of Women, 1984). Low wages mean that women cannot make significant contributions to pension plans or to Social Security or to build up private savings for their old age.

With advancing age, sexism and ageism link and work together to create a poisonous climate for many women. The traditional emphasis on physical beauty as a way to attract a man and to "hold" him screens out the old. Divorce is becoming more and more common after 30 and 40 years of marriage, not always because it is desired by the woman. Older women, particularly the old-old (over 75), are rarely described as attractive or vital or sexually appealing. On the contrary, they are termed "hags," "old bags," or worse. Many authors have called attention to the imprisoning roles of adult women: first as partners to men, then as child-bearers, and finally as nurses to their ailing husbands in their final illnesses (Brown, 1978; Butler & Lewis, 1982; Pedrin & Brown, 1980; Rathbone-McCuan, 1982). Widowhood, a common condition for old women, who tend to outlive their husbands, contains no ready-made roles for women, although being a grandparent might. But the latter role can become attenuated in a world where the nuclear family is often impermanent and people move around the country.

Elderly women are frequently viewed as being in the way or as problems if they are dependent because of their disabilities. With few exceptions, older women are not taken seriously and, in fact, are encouraged to remain passive and invisible. Many older women internalize these negative attitudes and refer to themselves as "useless," especially when they become impaired. It is not uncommon to hear an older woman say, "I have nothing to contribute," or, "I've done all the work God sent me to do," or, "Why am I still here? I just take up space." One elderly woman, newly widowed, said, "Why don't I just die?" Older women often view their economic and health problems as the result of their personal failings. They are not aware that there are other old women who are struggling with the same issues (Brown, 1978; Sommers, 1984).

Many older women are unnecessarily lonely, because they reject close relationships with other women in their age-group as unsatisfying (Butler & Lewis, 1982). Often they feel that something is "not quite right" if they are not in the company of a man. This attitude can become more of a problem with age, because fewer and fewer men are available. Elderly women outnumber men three to two. For the oldest women, this inequality is even more pronounced. In 1982, there were 80 men for every 100 women in the 65 to 69 age-group. But in those aged 85 and over, there were only 42 men for every 100 women (U.S. Bureau of the Census, 1983); see Figure 4-2.

Being old and female in the United States is frequently synonymous with being poor; 72 to 75% of the elderly below the poverty line are women, and 72% of the aged who receive Supplemental Security Income (SSI) are

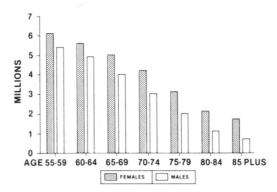

FIGURE 4-2 Population 55 years and older by age and sex, 1982 (numbers in thousands). *Source:* U.S. Bureau of the Census, Projections of the Population of United States: 1982–2050. *Current Population Reports,* Series P-25, No. 922, Oct. 1982, as it appears in U.S. Senate Special Committee on Aging in conjunction with the American Association of Retired Persons. *Aging America: Trends and Projections* (2nd ed.). Washington, D.C., 1984, p. 9.

women. Most women do not receive any type of pension, and only a small percentage (2%) receive widows' survivor benefits from their husbands' pensions (Block, 1983; Women's Studies Program and Policy Center, 1982). In part, women are excluded from survivor benefits because their husbands can choose to have pension benefits paid out entirely during their lifetime. Monthly payments are then higher during the husband's lifetime, and stop when he dies. In some pension plans, men can make this choice without informing their wives. In those cases, although income is sufficient while the husband is alive, poverty descends suddenly on the unsuspecting newly widowed woman. Widowhood can extend over many years. The average age when women become widows is 59 years, and the woman who becomes a widow at age 65 lives, on the average, another 18 years (U.S. Bureau of the Census, 1984). Even when the woman is left with what appear to be adequate resources, medical bills can quickly consume them, reducing the woman to poverty. The myth of the rich widow is just that: a myth. Elderly men are much more likely to be wealthy than are their female counterparts. In 1981, 9% of elderly men had incomes over $30,000, but only 1% of the women had comparable incomes. For that same year, the average income for a white woman 65 and over was $4,900. White men of the same age had an average income of $8,600. The picture is even bleaker for elderly women of color (U.S. Senate Special Committee on Aging, 1984).

This disturbing financial picture is further complicated by the fact that many women have been taught to leave financial management to the man even if that man was not competent financially or did not want financial responsibility. First their husbands managed their finances, then, when they became widows, they relied on their sons or some other male kin or on male lawyers or bankers. Thus most older women are ignorant and virtually helpless when they are eventually forced to handle their own money and as a result become dependent on the good intentions and good judgment of others.

Some elderly widows, lonely and with no male relative to help them with financial affairs, fall prey to male strangers who offer help. In one urban area, for example, a smooth-talking contractor succeeded in ingratiating himself with several mentally impaired elderly women and convinced them to sign over the title to their homes. This he did either by outright fraud (having them sign legal documents and not telling them what they were) or by promising to take care of them for the rest of their lives. He then placed the women in nursing homes or otherwise abandoned them. Newspaper accounts noted that in each of these cases, the victims were from a generation in which women were encouraged to rely on the male in the family to make decisions. The contractor sometimes endeared himself to his victim by developing a mother–son type relationship. With others, he took the role of the gigolo. Through the diligent efforts of authorities (and because one woman was capable of testifying), the contractor was apprehended, tried, and convicted. He was sentenced to three years in connection with the one case. Several of his victims were too mentally impaired to testify, and so the man could not be tried for defrauding them.

Most women who marry will be widowed. In 1981, more than half (51%) of women 65-years-old and over were widowed, whereas only 1 out of 8 elderly men were widowed. These facts reflect the fact that women usually marry men who are older than they are and usually outlive their husbands. Also, most men who are widowed or divorced quickly remarry, often to a woman younger than 65 years old (U.S. Bureau of the Census, 1984). Widows are much less likely to remarry, either because they choose to remain single or because the pool of available males is so small. For those 75 and over, the figures are remarkable; 7 out of every 10 men are married, whereas only 3 out of every 10 women are married (U.S. Senate Special Committee on Aging, 1984). This means that most women will be single in old age whether or not they were married at one time. It also means that they are more likely to be poor. Older women who are married or living in multigenerational housing have higher incomes than do women who live alone (U.S. Bureau of the Census, 1983). And of course, if older women become poor and disabled and are forced to live alone, they quickly become dependent on the good graces of others.

In the 1980s, more and more elderly women are living alone. In 1982, 30% of the elderly lived alone, most of them women (U.S. Senate Special

Committee on Aging, 1984). The trend toward living alone in old age is probably due in part to the false value American society places on independence, on not needing anyone to help out with daily living. This attitude results in many elderly people feeling humiliated and shamed when they finally must accept help because of their infirmities. Few elderly women live in intergenerational households, with children or with other relatives in the home. But as age increases, the number of women living with others increases, suggesting that the women are taken in by their relatives when they can no longer meet their personal needs in their own homes (U.S. Senate Special Committee on Aging, 1984). This fact becomes critical in considering elder abuse, because preliminary research indicates that most victims are women over the age of 75 with significant mental and or physical impairments which require assistance with daily living. Often, a medical emergency, such as a stroke or fractured hip, precipitates the change in living arrangements, and the elder is taken into the relative's home upon discharge from an acute hospital. Discharge planners and physicians can help elders and families plan realistically during this time by encouraging them not to make hasty and permanent decisions based solely on the crisis situation.

Greed

Human greed is the last of the societal attitudes that are implicated in elder abuse and neglect. A caregiver may wish that a dependent elder would die and "get out of the way" so that the inheritance can be passed on. Some caregivers, trusted by the impaired elders, have proceeded to expropriate their funds or property, rationalizing their behavior by saying, "I know she would want me to have it if she were in her right mind," or, "Dad always said he wanted to pay for the kids' college education," or, "I need the money now and there is a lot left over after her care is paid for. Why shouldn't I have it now? She's taken care of and besides, I'll always take care of her if she runs out of money."

These rationalizations ignore the fact that the elder's resources legally belong to her and do not revert to the heirs until the elder dies. One grandson could not wait.

A Court Investigation Unit got a call from a convalescent hospital administrator. The administrator was concerned because the grandson of a longtime resident had come in and asked for a list of nursing homes which would accept Medicaid patients. The grandson told the administrator that he had been advised by an attorney to transfer all his grandmother's assets (two parcels of real property plus a substantial amount of cash) into his name and to place his grandmother on public benefits. He quoted the attorney as saying that no one would ever check. The administrator knew that the grandson was his grand-mother's legally appointed conservator.

When the Court Investigator arrived at the convalescent hospital, she found other matters to be concerned about. The activity director told her that the grandson had confided in her too. He told her that while his mother had been alive and serving as co-conservator for his grandmother, she had taken money from the conservatorship estate "anytime she wanted." That was why, he said, his mother had often been delinquent in paying the convalescent hospital bills. Now that his mother was dead, the grandson felt justified in taking money from the estate himself. He and his wife had recently returned from Hawaii and he implied that he had used his grandmother's assets to pay for the trip.

The grandmother's clothing was in poor condition; she wore hand-me-downs donated to the nursing home. Personal items such as lotions and powders were provided to her by charitable organizations and by donations from private individuals at Christmas time. The hospital staff had shamed the grandson into buying one blue dress for his grandmother. However, the grandson regularly claimed reimbursement for clothing in his accountings to the court. The investigator wondered if that was how he had financed his trip to Hawaii.

No rental income was listed for either of the parcels of real property. The grandson occupied one of the parcels but appeared to be paying no rent to the estate. Further, he charged his grandmother's estate for maintenance and repair of the property.

Upon completion of her investigation, the court investigator wrote a polite although pointed letter to the grandson asking questions regarding the man-agement of his grandmother's estate. When he did not reply, she referred the matter to the court and the grandson was ordered to come to court and make an accounting directly to the judge in open court.

SUMMARY

Throughout this chapter on theories of causation of elder abuse and neglect, the focus has been on *probable* causes. As O'Malley et al. (1983) note, these hypotheses about the causation of elder abuse and neglect are not mutually exclusive. For instance, a stressed caregiver could have come from a home filled with violence but, in addition, she could be mentally ill or demented and also trying to cope with an elderly woman who is physically and mentally impaired. Such combinations are probably more common than one "pure" causative factor. Elder abuse and neglect are probably the result of a multiplicity of factors.

The theories described in this chapter have arisen from the preliminary research and exploration on the subject of elder abuse and neglect. Other research such as studies on domestic violence where the research and documentation are more mature have also contributed. The field of gerontology, too, has much to contribute to the understanding of elder abuse. No doubt further research will refine, confirm, or take issue with some of these theories. But for now, they provide a logical framework which can help practitioners understand the phenomenon of elder abuse and neglect.

II Elder Abuse Diagnosis and Intervention

Systematic and realistic interventions can lead to satisfactory results even with difficult cases. The purpose of Part II is to present components of the Elder Abuse Diagnosis and Intervention (EADI) Model. This model, which takes an eclectic approach in treating elder abuse and neglect, is the result of having examined various assessment and intervention strategies in different disciplines: geriatric nursing, medicine, social work, public health, psychiatry, and psychology. The EADI Model consists of two phases. The Diagnosis Phase consists of taking the referral, preparing for the assessment interview, and conducting the assessment. Specific protocols and questions are offered to assist the practitioner in identifying elder abuse and neglect in her practice.

The Intervention Phase offers crisis intervention, short-term treatment, and long-term treatment strategies that can individualize the intervention with the elder and the abuser. Termination issues for each of these strategies are also considered. Termination in the Intervention Phase depends on the chosen intervention strategy. A referral to other agencies and plans for follow-up and monitoring procedures may be made. In some cases, termination consists of the practitioner rehearsing with the client and family some future problem scenarios and solutions.

The first stages of the EADI Diagnosis Phase are described in Chapter 5. Issues that arise when the practitioner accepts a referral are presented. People refer suspected cases of elder abuse and neglect for a variety of reasons, not always out of concern for the elderly client. From the moment a referral is received, the practitioner begins to gather information and develop strategies. Suggestions are made on how to prepare for initial contact and how to obtain access in order to interview the client.

Chapter 6 describes the rest of Phase I, presenting the assessment protocol that is used to diagnose elder abuse and neglect. Signs and symptoms that may alert the practitioner to elder abuse and neglect are listed. The methods for conducting the functional assessment and the physical exam of the client are described in detail. The specific questions and strategies to be used when interviewing the alleged abuser may alleviate some of the practitioner's anxieties in this difficult period of the assessment process.

The first half of Chapter 7 discusses the factors that affect the choice of intervention method. Among them are the client's capabilities and cooperation as well as the degree of the abuser's pathology. The second half of Chapter 7 describes how the practitioner can utilize crisis intervention strategies to handle medical and financial emergencies. In crisis situations, treatment begins immediately, and the practitioner often functions as a case manager, organizing other practitioners and institutions to save the elder from further harm.

In Chapter 8, the focus of short-term treatment is on problem resolution with an eye to the future. Since many elder abuse and neglect victims will choose to remain with the abuser, it is necessary to work with them as a unit without taking sides. Environmental change, reality orientation, and education can help to prevent and eliminate abusive incidents. Common practitioner oversights are also presented through case illustrations in Chapter Eight.

Chapter 9 describes long-term treatment including individual therapy, group therapy, and family therapy to stop elder abuse and neglect. In practice, it may take several months for the practitioner to sort out alternatives and options before the appropriate mix of services is in place. Motivations of the elder and of the abuser are also factors. Long-term treatment may be more appropriate when abuse is long-standing and for elders who respond to a more gradual intrusion of change.

Chapter 10 describes legal intervention, ranging from the least restrictive to the most restrictive legal options that are available to the practitioner and the abused or exploited client. Highlighted are remedies that do not require court involvement, such as helping the client with the direct deposit of his pension check to a bank or obtaining a protective payee. Also highlighted are remedies that require court involvement, such as guardianships or conservatorships. Criminal proceedings are also described. In addition, this chapter gives practitioners suggestions on how to have impact on the judicial system and how to give court testimony.

5 Diagnostic Phase I: Preparation for Assessment

THE EADI MODEL

The Elder Abuse Diagnosis and Intervention (EADI) Model is the result of a desire to present practitioners with a consistent and coherent set of principles and methods to treat elder abuse and neglect. Since resources and the amount of time that is available for a practitioner to carry out a treatment plan vary with agencies and settings, it is sensible to take an eclectic approach. The different treatment approaches that were studied all have a goal of changing, modifying, or improving the client's situation, but the manner in which the goals are accomplished differ among the various approaches (Simon, 1970; Strickler & Bonnefil, 1974).

The EADI Model is an amalgam of different approaches and consists of two phases. Phase I, the Diagnosis Phase, utilizes the traditional psychosocial casework approach (Gambrill, 1983; Lowry, 1957; Simon, 1970); crisis intervention (Golan, 1978, 1979; Parad, 1971; Rapoport, 1962, 1970); and psychiatric diagnostic techniques (Folstein, Folstein, & McHugh, 1975; Goodwin & Guze, 1984; Kahn, Goldfarb, Pollack, & Peck, 1960; Katz et al., 1963). The nonvoluntary client, a person who does not initiate the request for help but finds himself face to face with a practitioner, may present with ambivalent feelings and with behaviors that commonly label him as "resistant." Mitchell (1973), Wasserman (1979), Murdach (1980), Butler and Lewis (1982), and Cormier and Cormier (1985) provide suggestions that will engage the client in the helping process, making the transitions from "doing to and for" to "doing with."

Phase II, the Intervention Phase of the EADI Model, is composed of three different sets of strategies: crisis intervention, short-term intervention, and long-term treatment. Ideally it is the need of the client that determines the type and length of treatment. However, various other factors intervene:

agency mandate and budget, availability of resources, and the amount of time the practitioner has to provide treatment. Treatment modalities that are utilized in this phase are rich and varied: the psychoanalytic approach as applied to a geriatric population (Bosch, 1980; Butler & Lewis, 1982); learning theory (Carkhuff & Anthony, 1979; Cormier & Cormier, 1985); learning theory as it is clinically applied for the treatment of batterers (Ganley, 1981; Roy, 1982; Sonkin & Durphy, 1982; Sonkin, Martin, & Walker, 1985; Star, 1978; Walker, 1979, 1984); pragmatic approaches that are used to diminish and prevent child abuse and neglect (Kempe & Kempe, 1978; Steele & Pollock, 1968); environmental therapy (Butler & Lewis, 1982); group therapy techniques (Burnside, 1976; Ebersole, 1975, 1976, 1978, 1981; Foster & Foster, 1983); and family therapy techniques (Herr & Weakland, 1979).

Having a variety of options allows the practitioner to be flexible and creative in her approach. None has a goal of "curing" the client and treating every problem presented to the practitioner. In many cases the focused and individualized treatment plans that are developed by the practitioner may be a combination of two or more treatment approaches.

The termination period of the Intervention Phase differs in each strategy. It is an important time during which the practitioner and others in her agency can evaluate their practice, the purpose for involvement, course of treatment, and the treatment outcomes. Ideally, termination occurs because treatment goals have been met. In reality, other considerations intrude. Termination may be at the client's request, or it may be due to the agency's policy that dictates the length of practitioner involvement. An important step in any of the treatment strategies is the development of follow-up and monitoring plans, which lets the elder know that help is available in the future as the need arises or when the elder chooses to ask for it (Golan, 1978; Parad, 1971; Rapoport, 1970). Legal issues weave in and out of all three intervention strategies and a separate chapter, Chapter 10, "Legal Intervention," is devoted to them.

This chapter describes in detail the role of the practitioner in the first half of Phase I, the Assessment Phase. In this period, an assumption is made that "forewarned is forearmed." Cautious collection of available information and the formulation of a tentative treatment plan prior to making the first contact are compatible with crisis-intervention guidelines.

THE REFERRAL

The purpose of the assessment process is to obtain information and an understanding of the client in his situation that will predict and guide the practitioner's intervention. It also marks the beginning of an individualization process that continues until termination (Simon, 1970).

The assessment process usually begins with an initial phone call to the practitioner. From the moment the practitioner receives the phone call, she must function as a first-class strategist and use all available resources, internal as well as external. That is, the practitioner must use all of her five senses and rely on intuition as well as use concrete, agency resources. In this phase, the practitioner's actions are guided by several assumptions:

1. Practitioners of different agencies need each other to treat elder abuse and neglect successfully.
2. People who report elder abuse and neglect may themselves be abusive. The practitioner cannot assume that reports are made solely out of concern for the elderly.
3. In general, people who report elder abuse and neglect expect prompt action on behalf of the victim.

Referrals may come from practitioners, relatives, friends, neighbors, or concerned citizens. Each of these referring groups presents different problems or issues, and the practitioner must take them into consideration during the initial phone call. Regardless of who makes the referral, demographic data and patient information should be obtained:

1. Client's name, address, phone number, age, gender, ethnic background.
2. Client's close relatives and friends and their phone numbers, collateral agency contacts and their phone numbers.
3. Alleged abuser's name, address, and phone number, physical description and knowledge of his behavior, relationship to client, and length of relationship.
4. Description of abuse and neglect, suspicions, and evidence obtained to date. Dates of prior contacts, action taken, and by whom are very helpful.
5. Physician and other known practitioners and their phone numbers.
6. Referrer's name and contact phone numbers, description of referrer's involvement in case to date, how long referrer has known client.

Referral by Practitioners

Practitioners who refer cases may be colleagues in the same agency, employees of another agency, or those in private practice in the community. Some may be mandated to report elder abuse and neglect; others may call for different reasons. The practitioner must clearly understand the purpose of the referral, which may be one of the following:

1. The practitioner is to assume care of the client after the referral is made; the case is transferred permanently.
2. The practitioner is asked to do a one-time-only assessment and refer the case back to the referring practitioner or agency.
3. The practitioner is asked to function as a consultant, to give advice or suggestions via phone or in the company of the referring practitioner during her investigative contacts.
4. The practitioner is asked to collaborate on a case and assist in the development of an assessment and treatment strategy that is to be mutually agreed upon by the referrer and the practitioner accepting the referral.

At first contact, the lack of clear agency role or task delineation may result in poor or missed communication, mismanagement of the case, and most important, frustration of the practitioners involved. For example, if the referrer assumes the practitioner will function as a consultant who will be asked for advice but the practitioner perceives herself to be the client's primary practitioner or case manager, the practitioner may become upset or frustrated if the referrer rejects her advice and selects a different intervention option. The practitioner must fully understand her role limitations and boundaries, especially when they are not defined by herself but by the referrer. In some cases, it may be possible or even necessary for the practitioner to declare her conditions or prerequisites for becoming involved. The practitioner may want to ask herself several questions before making a decision to accept or reject the referral:

1. *Choice:* Do I have a choice in accepting this case? Is my agency mandated to accept all referrals and act on them?
2. *Time:* Do I have the time to devote to this case? How many contacts am I able to handle? Will my involvement result in a worse outcome than if I did not become involved?
3. *Fees:* Practitioners in private practice may ask, Do I want to be paid for my services and expenses incurred? How much shall I charge? Will I see this client at no charge if no one can pay for my services?
4. *Role comfort:* Will I be comfortable as a consultant even if I disagree with the intervention option(s) selected by the other practitioner?
5. *Agency policies:* Do agency policies mandate specific types of intervention? Can I remain within the confines of agency guidelines and accommodate the referrer at the same time? Will the agency support me even if boundaries are transgressed?

In any case, a collegial relationship that has open communication and cooperation is most likely to promote a satisfactory working environment.

Referral by Relatives

As with referrals from practitioners, it is important to understand clearly the purpose of the referral when a relative calls:

1. The relative may feel that another relative is being abusive or neglectful and would like an investigation.
2. The relative has been accused of being abusive or neglectful and would like an investigation to prove his innocence.
3. The relative is a stressed primary caregiver of the elderly client and would like help to prevent an abusive or neglectful situation.

The practitioner should be aware that motivations for reporting a case vary among relatives. A relative could be upset about the contents of the elderly client's will or may be engaged in "sibling rivalry" with another relative and feel compelled to "turn in" the other relative. To clarify the nature of the referral, the practitioner may ask:

1. How did you hear about our program or agency? Relative's possible response: "I read about your program in the newspaper. People feel I'm abusive. I want you to come to our home to do an investigation and prove to them I'm innocent."
2. Why are you calling now as opposed to a month ago or a year ago? Relative's possible response: "Well, I thought my brother was going to take good care of my mother, but lately I've seen him change. He's been yelling at her more often."
3. What are your expectations of our program? Relative's possible response: "I want you to help me with my alcoholic brother. He comes over to harass me and my mother. He shoved me around last week and I am wondering if I should press charges against him. I want him to stop this behavior."

A case may be inappropriate for the agency or the type of practice in which the practitioner specializes. At this point, the practitioner may refer the caller to another agency. Unlike the referral from another practitioner, when a referral is by a relative the practitioner must make it clear to the referring relative that his referral does not exonerate him or dismiss him from being investigated and interviewed in the same manner as those he accuses of being abusive or neglectful. To convey a stance of neutrality, the practitioner may say:

"Mr. Smith, I'm glad you are concerned enough about your mother to call and make this referral. However, I want you to know that our assessment process involves interviewing everyone, including yourself and the alleged abuser. We do not presume anyone's innocence or guilt and will defer judgment until our investigation is completed."

Referral by Others

A survey of 17 states' adult protective services agencies' reporting data conducted by the Alliance/Elder Abuse Project revealed that nonmandated reporters generated the largest number of referrals (1983). These referrers may be a neighbor, an apartment manager, a friend, a concerned citizen, or an anonymous caller. These referrers often have known the client for many years and may have observed the steady mental or physical decline of the client. Sometimes these referrers have observed the abusive or neglectful relationship between the alleged abuser and the client over a period of time and feel compelled to report the situation because they can no longer remain passive observers. They may report the client's situation also because of a recent newspaper or television report on a situation similar to the one they have observed.

The anonymous caller presents a challenge. The practitioner should accept all information in an objective manner and not press for the caller's name. Without knowing who the referring person is, the practitioner is reduced to guessing the purpose of the call and how to proceed without jeopardizing the safety of the elder and the outcome of the case. Fear of reprisals could be the main motivation for remaining anonymous. The practitioner may inform the referrer about the protection offered by the state's elder abuse reporting law, if one exists. The referrer should be informed that confidentiality is practiced in the agency to the extent possible and that their state law provides for immunity from civil and/or criminal liability for reporting the abuse or neglect, and for giving court testimony for reporting. A caller may say she does not want to testify on the case, and the practitioner cannot guarantee the caller that she will never be subpoenaed. However, the practitioner can reassure the caller that cases seldom come to trial and it is highly unlikely that the caller will ever have to testify. Although confidentiality can be offered, no practitioner can guarantee a "fail safe" system, since most elder abuse and neglect cases involve communication among several agencies' practitioners. Mistakes do happen, and the primary practitioner cannot monitor everyone's actions. As the public becomes better educated about elder abuse and neglect and learns about agencies to which they can turn with trust and hope, reports will increase in volume. It is important to acknowledge the referrer's concern and courage, and to thank her for picking up the phone, dialing, and finally completing the referral, sometimes after months of deliberation.

PREPARATION FOR INITIAL CONTACT:
CASE PLANNING

Successful intervention is a result of adequate planning and anticipation of problems which the practitioner must be prepared to handle, should they arise. At this point, the following steps may be useful to follow.

Make collateral contacts promptly to assess the seriousness of the situation. The practitioner should determine whether the case that is referred requires immediate attention. Based on the nature of the presenting problem, the practitioner should decide whether the client should be seen immediately or whether contact can be deferred for a few days. Chapter 7 discusses crisis-intervention techniques in greater detail. Quick phone calls to collateral contacts or people who have recently seen the client can help the practitioner make this decision. Whenever possible, the practitioner should call the client's physician, home health nurse, or medical group to ask what the plan of action should be if the practitioner finds the client in need of immediate medical care. Sometimes it is difficult to contact medical practitioners by phone on short notice. Nevertheless, to reflect careful planning, the practitioner's notes should indicate that an attempt was made to contact them. If a medical practitioner is consulted and placed on "standby" status during this case planning phase, the practitioner will later save precious time and be able to act promptly and institute the agreed plan of action. If the medical practitioner is unavailable, it may help to leave a detailed message explaining the importance of the call. Sometimes the medical practitioner will respond promptly if she realizes the practitioner is waiting for her consultation before proceeding with the assessment.

Practitioners seem to be divided on the issue of doing collateral contacts without the client's consent. Some practitioners feel it is unethical to call a client's medical practitioner and obtain confidential medical information, while others feel it is a prudent step to take. Practitioners who are mandated by state law to investigate reports of elder abuse and neglect and mental health professionals who must assess the client for involuntary commitment usually are permitted to obtain confidential information. One way to handle this issue is to call the medical practitioner and to give, not obtain, information. For example:

> "I am aware you are (the nurse, doctor, hospital) providing care to Mrs. Smith. There has been a complaint of abuse or neglect and she has been described as being listless and unable to get out of bed. I am considering a home visit soon and want to know what you would want to do if I find her to be in need of medical care."

It is up to the medical practitioner to share information or to provide suggestions for treatment without breaking confidentiality. She may merely state that if necessary, the client should be transported to a specific hospital where the medical practitioner has hospital privileges, or she may ask to be contacted from the client's home or after the client has been seen. Sometimes a medical practitioner will readily provide information on the client's current health status and medications if she feels the situation warrants it.

Become familiar with available information. Valuable information may be obtained from other practitioners who have had previous contact with the client and/or the alleged abuser. Some agencies have statewide computers that can inform the current practitioner if the client's case is active in another unit or office. Previous reports or charts, if they are available, should be studied. One city has a formal agreement with the police department which allows their state agency to receive information regarding the alleged abuser's criminal record. People known to have been threatened by the alleged abuser should be interviewed in order to determine what the safest approach for completing the assessment is. For example:

An attorney assigned as the guardian ad litem in a difficult guardianship process called the hospital social worker involved in the same case. He asked her how she handled the friend of the alleged incompetent, an elderly female. This client was easily swayed by her friend, who was demanding and verbose. The social worker described the friend's personality and made suggestions on how to approach him and to obtain his cooperation in completing his investigation.

In another example:

A protective services practitioner who did not check on the alleged abuser's background did a home visit alone to interview a client who lived with an abusive man. She found no one at home. Later, she found out that this man had been convicted of rape and murder in the past and had a record of assaulting women. Given this information, she realized she should not have done the home visit alone and decided that on her next visit she would go with another worker or ask that the interview be held instead at her agency.

Document a tentative plan. Once the practitioner has information from collateral contacts and available reports, she can document a tentative treatment plan. The plan can serve as evidence to anyone who may criticize the practitioner's intervention. A plan that reflects planning and forethought may prove to be valuable later if the practitioner is accused of being capricious or sloppy, or acting mostly on emotions (Gambrill, 1983).

Be familiar with the protocol questions and gather forms and equipment for the interview. It may be helpful to memorize the questions to be asked in the interview or to be prepared to read them from a printed sheet. The practitioner should bring appropriate forms with her such as release of information forms for interagency communication, or consent forms to obtain services and to be photographed.

Rehearse and have ready intervention options. The practitioner should anticipate the need to introduce intervention options to develop the client's belief in interventions. It is helpful to have in mind a range of services available specific to the client's situation. A brochure containing resources the client may use can serve as a calling card and can be slipped under the door. The practitioner is at a disadvantage if she is unprepared to "sell" herself in the first few minutes of the initial interview.

Rapoport (1970), in formulating short-term treatment techniques utilizing the crisis intervention approach, states:

> The primary need of the client is to experience in the first interview a consider-
> able reduction in disabling tension and anxiety. One way in which this is
> achieved, which may be specific to brief treatment approach, is by the worker's
> sharing tentative hypotheses and structuring a picture of the operating dynamics
> in language that makes sense to the client. This enables the client to get a
> manageable cognitive grasp of his situation, and usually leads to a lowering of
> anxiety, trust in the worker's competence, and a feeling of being understood.
> (p. 288)

Develop a prompt sheet or card of your coping strategies. Many contacts in elder abuse and neglect work are adversarial in nature and can be stressful. It is at times helpful to "feed" oneself by using a prompt card that provides support and lists ways to get through a stressful interaction (Gambrill, 1983). The card can read:

"I am an effective practitioner."
"These people can use my services."
"I have dealt with angry people successfully."
"I can get backup help if I need it."
"Don't panic; count to three and try another approach."

Do not work alone. Before contacting the client or abuser, it is helpful to spend 15 minutes to review a case with a colleague or a worker from another agency or discipline. The practitioner can discuss the tentative treatment plan and ask for comments, additions, and suggestions. Invariably practitioners with different areas of expertise who are farther removed from the situation can clarify the practitioner's goals or add options missed by the practitioner for the case. Furthermore, their support will give the practitioner the confidence and emotional backing that are necessary to investigate a difficult case.

FIRST CONTACT

Having gathered whatever information is available to the practitioner, through either review of written documents or contacts with professionals and people familiar with the situation, the practitioner initiates the first contact.

In the home: drop-in visit versus visit by appointment. There are both advantages and disadvantages to either dropping in on a client or visiting him by appointment. The method of choice depends on the practitioner's perceived acuity of the client's condition, the client's ability to consent to the interview, and the perceived cooperation of the alleged abuser. Dropping in on a client is chancy. The client may not be in and time is wasted, especially if many miles are driven. However, if the case is presented as having emergency or life-threatening conditions, or if the practitioner is unable to contact the elderly client by phone and feels that sending an appointment letter will take too long, then a drop-in visit may be justified. The practitioner may feel that visiting an elderly client unannounced will provide her with a realistic picture of the client's functional and environmental conditions and prevent a cover-up of signs of abuse and neglect. However, drop-in visits are disadvantageous because they can alienate both the client and the alleged abuser and put them on the defensive if they feel the visit was meant to "catch them in the act." The practitioner is perceived as a threat, with the client and others feeling a loss of control over their own situation (Wasserman, 1979). The resentment and defensiveness that are developed from an initial drop-in visit can hinder future contacts and prevent the development of an ongoing relationship, especially when the client is ambivalent about receiving services. In most cases, an accurate portrayal of the home situation may be obtained without dropping in through the administration of the elder abuse protocol as described in Chapter 6.

Whenever possible, the practitioner should call the elderly client to arrange the visit and state the time and date of the appointment. Regardless of who made the referral—an agency worker, relative, or anonymous person—it is necessary to speak to the client directly. When the referral is from another agency's worker, the practitioner should elicit her help to call and prepare the client for the impending visit. When the referral is from a relative, it is not possible to assume that the client will be told about the visit. On the phone, the practitioner may say,

"Please put your mother on the phone; I want to introduce myself and let her know I'll be visiting her."

When the client comes on the line, say,

"Your son has asked me to come by to discuss some services for which you may qualify. I would like to come by tomorrow at 2:00 P.M.."

It is important to be positive and firm. It may be necessary to compromise on the appointment time or another detail, but a rejection can be avoided by preparing the client and others for the visit. Formally establishing contact directly with the elderly client conveys many things: the practitioner does not intend to use the referral person as her sole means of obtaining and giving information from or to the elderly client; the practitioner respects the elderly client and assumes that he wants time to prepare for the visit; if the practitioner is expected to visit and does not barge in, she will be met with less resistance when she is in the home and attempts to engage the client in a conversation.

Sometimes a client is a prisoner in his own home. The caregiver may field telephone calls by using an answering machine or may attempt to prevent the practitioner from contacting the client by saying he is sleeping or cannot come to the phone right then. Even if the client is perceived as being in need of immediate contact, the practitioner should attempt to call the client. If there is no answer, the practitioner can later justify the drop-in visit by saying that an attempt was made to contact the elderly client by phone but there was no answer. Another method to use is to call one to two hours before visiting the elderly client. Within that short period, everyone involved will be alerted to the practitioner's visit and she will not be perceived as dropping in unannounced. Last, if the client has no phone or if the practitioner wants to save time, she may want to drive to the client's home and say,

"I was in the neighborhood and in order to save time, I thought I'd stop by to see if you had time to see me. If this time is inconvenient, I would like to make an appointment with you."

"Neutral territory" setting. The practitioner may wish to consider interviewing the elderly client outside the home if she has difficulty speaking up due to lack of privacy or others' interruptions. For instance, in the case planning phase the practitioner may have found out that the client has been attending a day center for adults. Instead of a home visit, the practitioner may wish to approach the client in that setting without letting others know. Staff of the center must agree to maintain confidentiality. Prior to meeting the client at a place where others may observe the interview, the practitioner can ask that a private room be set aside for a specific time period. Staff are to keep from talking about the visit with other center participants. It is better if no explanations about the practitioner's presence are given. It is up to the client to respond to inquiries himself.

Other neutral settings may be a coffee shop or a car. The practitioner can interview the elderly client as he is transported to a medical appointment or grocery store. Ambulation and mobility capabilities should be taken into consideration. Because elder abuse and neglect clients are often frail and vulnerable, it is doubtful that the practitioner will interview them while participating in activities requiring strenuous movements or walking great distances.

Agency or clinic setting. Clients very rarely seek help for elder abuse and neglect; they often present themselves to agencies and clinics for resolution of other problems. If elder abuse and neglect are suspected, the practitioner must seize the opportunity to assess the situation. Precautions must be taken to maximize privacy and confidentiality for it is not uncommon to discover during the assessment that the person accompanying the elderly client to his interview is an alleged abuser. A terrible mistake can be made by interviewing the person accompanying the elderly client before the client is interviewed and by stereotyping him as a "normal" caregiver. An elderly client may become more reluctant to disclose important information when he quietly observes the practitioner befriending the very person from whom he is trying to seek protection.

In a medical clinic, if a physician suspects elder abuse but lacks the time to do the elder abuse and neglect assessment, she may say to the elderly client that he will be seen by another practitioner to determine what services he may require, being careful to not mention the word "abuse."

Hospital emergency room. Hospital settings are assumed to be one of the safest places or havens to protect, at least temporarily, the elderly client from the alleged abuser. Unfortunately, not all hospitals have staff trained to detect and treat elder abuse. Therefore the onus is on the practitioner to prepare the hospital staff. When taking the client to a hospital, it is best to call the emergency room ahead of time and speak to the triage nurse or social worker. A summary statement may save the client hours of waiting (see Chapter 7 for format of statement). The statement may be filed in the chart for others to read, especially if a decision is made to admit the client, and different staff treat the client on a hospital floor. Carefully prepared written work and clear verbal communication add credibility to the practitioner's presence in the emergency room. The practitioner's self-assured style may have a calming effect on staff who are uncomfortable with elder abuse cases. Furthermore, the practitioner will less likely be perceived as someone "dumping" the client in the emergency room or manipulating the staff to examine the client for problems that are not serious.

The hospital practitioner who suspects elder abuse and neglect or who is approached by an agency practitioner as described in the previous paragraph has the role of hospital-wide advocate. That practitioner should find a private setting to interview the elderly client and inform the staff about the special nature of the case. Certain equipment should be ready for the assessment: camera, consent forms, tape measure, sketch sheet, note paper, and pen. The hospital practitioner should be prepared to explain the institution's procedures and to serve as liaison since hospitals can be an intimidating setting for the client, the client's advocate, and nonhospital practitioners.

Access

Gaining access into an elderly client's home is more difficult than approaching him in an agency or hospital/medical setting. In most cases the practitioner has no authority to gain access without the property owner's consent. Legal remedies such as a court injunction are used as a last resort. States laws vary on the criteria for the protective services practitioner to obtain court permission to enter a home to complete an investigation. A practitioner can assume that she will gain access if she approaches the home visit with the goal of being perceived by the client and others in the home as someone helpful and friendly, able to provide services at no or low cost, and/or able to alleviate problems for the entire family. As mentioned above, several experts in the field of crisis theory stipulate the goal of the initial contact to be the alleviation of tension and anxiety (Golan, 1978; 1979; Parad, 1971; Rapoport, 1970).

The practitioner's car should be parked in front of the client's home in case additional help is required. An ambulance driver or a law enforcement officer who is called to the home will be able to identify the correct house easily. At the client's door, proper identification is necessary, preferably with a photo of the practitioner, especially if the visit is unexpected. The elderly client should not be expected to open his door to just anyone. If the practitioner anticipates difficulty with access, she may ask the client's neighbor, friend, church member, or apartment manager to accompany her. The client may open the door if a familiar, trusted voice is heard through the locked door.

Home health nurses and public health nurses are rarely denied access to elderly clients' homes. O'Malley et al. (1983) state that "access is gained most successfully by nursing personnel who are non-threatening, have the reputation of being helping professionals, and emphasize the effects of illness in the ability of the elderly person to function (p. 1003)." A nonmedical practitioner may have more clout if she is perceived as being part of a medical team. Some protective services workers have learned how to take pulses and blood pressures as a way of assisting their clients and gaining acceptance. If a client's condition requires skilled nursing services, it may be helpful to ask a home health nurse to make the initial contact to the home and discuss other agencies' services that the nurse feels may be helpful to the family. An effective approach used by some home health agencies is to have their nurse and social worker visit the client as a team. Sometimes pairing up with another agency practitioner works. In one case, a public health nurse, an adult protective services practitioner, and a hospital social worker did a home visit together with good results.

Conflict Situation Versus Treatment Situation

The practitioner must remember that access is dependent on her ability to convince the client that suggested options have merit (Gambrill, 1983). Not all clients welcome practitioners' offers of help. A treatment situation means that a client's cooperation exists and that the practitioner is able to proceed with the assessment and treatment plan. Conversely, a conflict situation is one in which an involuntary client has not consented to intervention, and bargaining and persuasion techniques must be used to promote client cooperation (Murdach, 1980).

Bargaining can be seen as a process of progressing through several phases:

1. Introduction.
2. Discovering the bargainable, which consists of defining bargainable objects, the range of disagreement, and possible areas of agreement.
3. Establishing areas of agreement, which is easier if objects are quantifiable and the process does not involve basic moral or ethical commitments.
4. Critical bargaining, during which proposals and counterproposals are offered; it is the compromise and concession stage.
5. Public presentation of results, when the cementing of the agreement is marked by public display (Mitchell, 1973).

Initial steps during the elder abuse and neglect assessment phase may take the following form:

1. *Introduction*. Tell the client and/or caregiver who you are in a nonthreatening manner: "I am a counselor from (agency). Here is my card. I am here because our agency received a call of concern about you."
2. *Discovering the bargainable*. Put forth some service options which the client may consider: "Your doctor has asked me to come by to see if there are any services for which you may qualify. I would like to show you a list of services available to senior citizens. It is a part of my job to make these services available to as many senior citizens in the city as qualify. One of the outcomes of today's interview may be in a plan that may include delivery of 'meals on wheels,' chorework or housekeeping services, or more monthly income. You (your son) and I could work together to discuss and develop a plan like this."

Once the client exhibits signs of willingness to participate further in a discussion, the practitioner can proceed to the other phases of the bargaining process in the ensuing assessment phase.

Continuum Of Approaches

Sometimes the practitioner will be met at the door by a caregiver who does not wish to be bothered. If the friendly, diplomatic approach does not result in access, a more authoritative stance may be utilized. The following approaches may be used to gain access, and they are listed from least confrontive to most confrontive:

Offer services. "I am here to see whether you and your mother need services. Your mother requires increased care since her stroke, and it is difficult for one person to do all the work." The caregiver should not be faulted or put on the defensive.

Offer to be an advocate for the caregiver. "I'm here to do whatever I can to help people realize you are doing your best. Many people do not realize how much work is involved in caring for a frail, elderly person. Will you please take me through a typical day so I can understand your role?"

Use ascribed authority. "Before you slam the door on me, I want you to know that as a representative of my agency, I must obtain certain information on the client. I am an official representative of the county, and we are responsible for your mother's health. If I am unable to obtain the information today, I'll have to keep returning till I do. I want to work with you. I have successfully been doing this type of work for the past five years and know how to get the job done. Cooperate with me and I will leave as soon as I complete my assignment. I may have to call for assistance from the pay phone."

Call for assistance: "Our agency has received information that abuse has taken place. I want to spell your name correctly so I can give it to the police. I want you to know that you are quoted as saying, 'Shove it,' to me (the practitioner writes as she talks). All you are demonstrating is that the concerns seem valid. I want you to know that I will be back soon with the police."

The practitioner should use her level of fear as a barometer for the danger level of the situation and at the same time not be intimidated by hostile behavior. If weapons are in sight, it may be best to leave and return with a law enforcement officer. The practitioner is in control of the situation just as she would be if the setting were her own office. The practitioner is on a mission to rule out elder abuse and neglect and to determine whether intervention is necessary. Threats should not be made by the practitioner unless they can realistically be carried out. The practitioner must remember that she has an obligation to obtain access to the client and that she has the ability to bargain with the client and/or caregiver in order to get beyond the first few minutes of the introductory phase and be permitted to proceed to the assessment phase. The following words represent rules that may produce a successful introduction phase:

1. *Tactics:* The practitioner should have bargaining and persuasion tactics well rehearsed, proper identification, and service delivery options ready for presentation.
2. *Tact:* The practitioner is to use diplomacy with perseverance, and avoid confrontations if at all possible.
3. *Talk:* The practitioner should avoid pauses in the conversation, speak in a calm manner, and not give the client or caregiver the opportunity to deny access.
4. *Time:* The client and caregiver should be allowed time to feel comfortable with the practitioner.

Lowry (1957) discusses the hazards of working within a certain amount of time and/or a limited number of interviews in the context of short-contact casework. The practitioner is warned that if time is limited overdirection in the interview may result, with too many questions being asked in an effort to obtain information quickly. Practitioner anxiety may inhibit creative and accurate assessment of the client's situation:

> Because of the sense of being pressed by time, we may yield to the impulse to move along in the interview at a pace which we ourselves set. This may result in a loss of valuable understanding that might have been achieved had the other person been allowed to move more nearly at his own pace, particularly in the early phases of the interview. It is true that there is a need for discriminating direction of the interview on our part, but this direction should stem from our perceptions and thought processes rather than our feelings of urgency. (Lowry, 1957, pp. 53–54)

The practitioner is reminded that significant material may emerge spontaneously after attention is paid to the establishment of a relationship and some of the client's feelings of ambivalence and threat are addressed. Questions should be spaced sensitively and be related to areas of the client's immediate concern. Sometimes it takes 20 to 30 minutes to put the client at ease or to let the client and/or caregiver become familiar with the practitioner. Accepting a cup of coffee may help to break the ice. The practitioner may want to disclose bits of information about herself to diminish feelings that she is a threat. In the first interview, if an understanding has been established about the reason for the home visit, that is a goal accomplished in itself. Sometimes obtaining access and alleviating fear are the main goals of the first interview, and the practitioner may want to return at another time to proceed with the elder abuse and neglect assessment.

SUMMARY

Careful assessment of a case of elder abuse and neglect and successful interventions depend on meticulous planning prior to the initial contact with the elder and the alleged abuser. At times contacting others who are already involved will save the practitioner time and ensure client and practitioner safety. The following chapter addresses the assessment process in detail.

6 Diagnostic Phase II: Assessment

Assessment of a client for elder abuse and neglect may require several contacts over a period of time, and can be a very time-consuming process. This chapter describes the use of a written protocol which will help the practitioner focus efficiently, thus conserving time and energy. A concise, easy-to-use form for the protocol is located in Appendix A. It consists of guidelines for interviewing the elderly client and caregiver individually to identify and assess the possibility of elder abuse and neglect. The assessment protocol contains four sections: (1) assessment of the client's functioning, (2) a physical examination of the client, (3) interview of the potential abuser, and (4) collateral contacts.

RATIONALE

Originally written in 1981, the protocol was designed to be used by health care professionals in many disciplines including nursing, social work, physical and occupational therapy, psychology, and medicine (Tomita, 1982; Tomita, Clark, Williams, & Rabbitt, 1981). It was developed after reviewing protocols used to assess for child abuse and neglect and other forms of domestic violence such as sexual abuse and assault, and battered women syndrome (Anderson, 1981; Johnson, 1981; Klingbeil, 1979; Klingbeil & Boyd, 1984). The protocol assumes that in order for health care professionals to detect, intervene in, and prevent cases of elderly abuse, three major barriers must be overcome (Rathbone-McCuan & Voyles, 1982). One barrier is denial by many health care professionals that abuse and neglect exist within their own client populations. For example, it may be difficult to believe that an 80-year-old woman who is seen regularly for therapy at a hospital with bruises on her upper extremities is being physically abused by her caregiver. For fear of being too intrusive, the practitioner may be reluctant to inquire about the bruises, or may not know what to do if the abuse is recognized or acknowledged by the client.

The absence of written procedures for case detection is the second barrier (Rathbone-McCuan & Voyles, 1982). Few health care professionals are aware of or have routine materials which outline reporting or intervention procedures for domestic maltreatment of the elderly. The practitioner will be more likely to inquire about an elderly patient's bruises if she has training in detecting abuse and neglect and feels comfortable with a protocol that has been made available to all staff in her agency.

The third barrier is the lack of service and support options for the abused elderly person, the abuser, and the family. A practitioner is more likely to get involved in an elder abuse case if she feels treatment options exist for all involved.

The protocol is necessary because older adults do not report elder abuse and neglect just as they do not report their complaints to medical practitioners till the conditions have reached an advanced state. Williamson et al. (1964) found that among 200 patients over age 65 who were examined for physical and psychiatric disabilities, the men had an average of 3.2 disabilities with 1.87 of these disabilities unknown to their family physician. The mean number of disabilities for women was 3.42 with 2.03 of these disabilities unknown to their families or to their physicians. Physicians practicing in a metropolitan area were less aware of patients' difficulties than were physicians who lived in small, close-knit communities and who perhaps knew their patients better because of the communities' cohesiveness and informal communication network, the study found. Any general practitioner who relies on the self-reports of illness is likely to be seriously handicapped in meeting the needs of old people. If elder abuse and neglect could be considered a disability that can be reported too late, then the need for periodic medical examinations which would include a protocol to assess and treat elderly abuse and neglect is supported. The protocol can also be adapted easily for use in the client's home by social workers and home health nurses.

METHODOLOGY/TECHNIQUE

Each case and each interview session has its own "personality" with a unique tone, feeling, process, and pace. The practitioner should anticipate that things will inevitably go wrong during the process, and that the ideal one-hour interview does not exist. At times, signs and symptoms will elude the practitioner because false assumptions have been made and attention has not been paid to important details.

The following basic tools will be required in conducting any assessment:

1. Sketch sheet or trauma graph (see Figure 6-1, p. 123).
2. Tape measure.
3. Camera, film, and flash.
4. Paper and pen.
5. Consent and release of information forms.

The sketch sheet and camera are used to document injuries and/or other evidence of elder abuse and neglect. A tape measure or other measurement tool is needed to measure injuries accurately. The practitioner will need to record verbatim both the elderly client's and the alleged abuser's statements. Discrepancies between the two may point to elder abuse and neglect. The practitioner should anticipate which consent forms the client will need to sign and have them in hand. They may include forms consenting to intervention by a practitioner representing a particular agency, allowing exchange of information between agencies involved in the client's care, or allowing photographs to be taken of the client's injuries. These forms should either be gathered together in a packet and taken along on each home visit or be kept on file in the health care or service agency.

It is important to conduct the interview in a nonjudgmental manner. Personal feelings should not be allowed to interfere with giving the best possible care. The client should not be diagnosed prematurely as being a victim of elder abuse and neglect. Nor should the caregiver be told about treatment plans until all the facts are gathered. Special attention should be paid to trauma, nutritional status, recent change in physical and mental condition, and the client's financial status and home situation. A good way to remember the essentials of interviewing techniques is to think of them as the "five P's," that is:

1. Privacy.
2. Pacing.
3. Planning.
4. Pitch.
5. Punctuality (Villamore & Bergman, 1981).

Privacy.

It is essential that the client be examined alone, without the caregiver being present. Sometimes considerable energy is required to negotiate privacy with the client, especially when the caregiver is reluctant to leave the client alone with the practitioner, citing a variety of justifications, such as:

"I have an appointment elsewhere in an hour and you are going to make me miss that appointment. We can do this faster if you interview us together."

Or, "My mother doesn't know what she's saying half the time. I'll tell you what you need to know."

The practitioner may emphasize the need for privacy by saying something like this:

In a home setting: "Our agency insists on client confidentiality. I need to speak with your mother alone. I'll talk to her first in that room. After I'm done, I would like to talk to you so you can tell me how things have been here. Are you able to take a walk outside or go somewhere while I'm interviewing her? I'll take around 45 minutes with each of you."

In a clinic or agency setting: "Thank you for bringing your mother to this clinic. I will interview her first and would like you to wait in the waiting room or if you'd like, you can go get a cup of coffee. It will take approximately 45 minutes. Then I would like to talk to you and ask you some questions about your mother's home situation."

The interview setting should be a room with four solid walls and a door, where there is the smallest chance of being interrupted or eavesdropped upon. Failure to take these precautions may result in a less successful interview. For example:

A hospital social worker conducted her elder abuse and neglect interview of a 68-year-old woman in the patient's two-bed hospital room. The patient's roommate was away, attending a physical therapy session. The interview was proceeding smoothly and the patient was beginning to disclose information, when the patient's roommate returned earlier than expected. The patient then became noticeably withdrawn and tried to avoid being overheard by speaking very softly. With only a fabric partition separating the two patients' bed spaces, the social worker belatedly realized she should have conducted the interview in a private office down the hall.

If privacy is not available in the home, the practitioner should consider interviewing the client elsewhere. For instance, the client might be interviewed in the car while being driven by the practitioner to a doctor's appointment, or the practitioner may arrange to meet the client in another setting. The practitioner needs to bear in mind that he is the one responsible for the physical setup of the interview. Being in someone's residence requires that the practitioner respect both the person and her property. At the same time, both client and caregiver tend to perceive the practitioner as someone who has expertise in interviewing people and who will provide gentle guidance and structure to help them feel secure. The practitioner may feel uncomfortable about "calling the shots" in a client's living room. But it may be necessary to ask the client to turn off the tele-

vision and to sit down to talk. After conducting several elder abuse and neglect assessments, the practitioner will become more comfortable with
these techniques and have an easier time "directing" clients and caregivers in their homes.

Pacing

It is important to pace the interview evenly, while at the same time providing support to the client and to the caregiver. In spite of time restraints,
questions should be worked into the conversation in a relaxed manner. The
client should not be rushed, even though she may respond to important
questions in a tangential manner, or with metaphors, or in such a way that
the practitioner is forced to read between the lines. While talking or listening, the practitioner should be attuned to the client's nonverbal behavior,
i.e., body posture, facial expressions (particularly those revealing emotions),
and vocal tension. Lowry (1957) states:

> As case workers we really need four ears: one with which to listen to *what* is
> being said; one to attend to what is *not* being said; one to hear *how* it is being
> said; and one to heed the feelings *unexpressed*. (p. 55)

Planning

As it was noted in Chapter 5, it is important to have a goal or behavioral
outcome for each case and each interview, and this requires memorizing
preplanned statements and responses. It may be helpful to use prompt cards
or written reminders of ways to cope in a tense or difficult situation. Before
going to a client's residence, the necessary forms should be gathered, to
avoid having to return for a signature at a later date.

Pitch

It is helpful during an interview to speak in a well modulated tone of voice
and to avoid sounding excited or surprised. A friendly tone of voice and facial
expression will help the client develop confidence and trust in the practitioner.

Punctuality

If an appointment has been made, it is important to arrive promptly. This
shows respect and can help to develop trust. Some elderly clients will wait
all day for the practitioner, worrying that they may have been forgotten.

SUSPICIOUS SIGNS AND SYMPTOMS

On first contact, it is necessary to watch for signs and/or symptoms which may indicate that the client is being abused or neglected. These may include the following.

The client is brought to a hospital emergency room by someone other than the caregiver, or the client is found alone in the home. For example, if the client is brought into the emergency room by a law enforcement officer or a neighbor after having been found wandering outside, or if the client dials an emergency number but is unable to answer the door when help arrives, it may be that the client has been abandoned or has been living in an unsafe setting for long periods of time.

Prolonged interval between injury/illness and presentation for medical care. The practitioner should ask himself why the client or the caregiver waited so long to seek treatment for the client's injuries. Suspicious injuries may include week-old bruises and gangrenous feet. The assumption cannot be made that all caregivers mean well. Failure to seek help in a timely manner may be the result of the caregiver's desire not to spend money on medical care, of ignorance, or of a need to minimize the severity of the client's problems until they no longer can be ignored.

Suspicious history. If the client is new to the medical clinic or agency, the practitioner should wonder whether the caregiver or the client is doctor or agency "hopping" in order to hide previous injuries. The practitioner's suspicions should be raised if the description of how the injury occurred is inconsistent with the physical findings, if the client has a history of similar episodes, or if the client has too many "explained" injuries or offers explanations for injuries which vary from time to time.

Medication noncompliance. A check of the client's pharmacy profile or medication bottles may indicate that medications are not being taken or administered by the caregiver as prescribed.

INTERVIEWING THE CLIENT

Functional Assessment

The guidelines for conducting a functional assessment are part of the protocol that is located in Appendix A. The purpose of the functional assessment is to find out with whom the client interacts frequently, and on whom she depends for social, physical, and/or financial support. This may be accomplished by obtaining a detailed account of the client's typical day and by making an assessment of level of independence. In this section are compiled specific questions which should be asked in the order listed. The people mentioned by the client during this assessment will form the pool of people who must be considered as possible abusers. It is important to begin with more general, nonthreatening questions and to leave more emotionally laden questions until later. This method of assessment requires writing the client's responses down verbatim to the extent that note taking is possible. Some practitioners may be reluctant to write during the interview, fearing that it will inhibit the client. If it would disrupt the interview process, the practitioner may decide not to take notes at the time. Upon leaving the interview site, he can then drive a few blocks away, stop, and write down everything he can remember, especially quotes. Later, he may be able to check with the victim and/or the abuser for confirmation of certain facts. These notes may be required for later use in a legal proceeding and will help the practitioner recall actual statements made by the client during the contact. The practitioner can explain the necessity of note taking to the client by stressing the need to remember important information and to avoid repeating questions. Tape recorders can be used if the client is comfortable with the technique and has been assured of confidentiality.

Collect pertinent data. The interview begins with the practitioner asking easy questions which will help to put the client at ease. It may be helpful to ask about services the client has already obtained and to collect information to determine whether the client qualifies for a service. Sample questions include:

"What is your correct address?"
"How long have you lived in your apartment?"
"Do you live alone?"
"Do you have a bus pass?"
"Do you receive meals on wheels?"
"What is your current income?"

Some clients may feel that questions about their income and savings are insulting, but it is necessary to obtain financial data to determine the client's eligibility for programs such as chore services and transportation. It is also important in ruling out financial abuse.

Ask the client to describe a typical day. Finding out how the client spends a typical day allows the practitioner to determine the degree of her dependence on others and to find out who the client's most frequent and significant contacts are. Sample questions include:

"I would like you to tell me what a typical day is like for you. For example, what do you do from morning to night on any given day?"
"What time do you get up in the morning?"

"Do you need help getting out of bed?"
"Are you able to walk to the bathroom by yourself?"
"Who helps you?"

While the client responds, the practitioner should take down what she says verbatim. The notes may look like this:

Client states she wakes up by self around 7 A.M. daily; lies in bed and waits for spouse to help her out of bed. Some mornings he is late in helping her. States, "I just lie in bed and wait till he comes." As she is sight impaired and needs assistance with walking to the bathroom, she sometimes wets the bed.

Breakfast is eaten at 8 A.M. and consists of . . .

It is important to go through the entire day, from the time the client awakens until bedtime, and to ask who helps or is supposed to help the client, who the client relies on, and how often these helpers are in contact with the client. The client invariably will mention significant others in her life, i.e., her spouse, children, friends, household help, or neighbors. At this point in the interview, the practitioner should obtain their names and phone numbers if possible. Usually, an abuser is known to the client. Thus anyone mentioned as a helper or contact may be an abuser.

Assess the client's ability to perform the activities of daily living. Several excellent checklists such as the Index of ADL by Katz et al. (1963) in Appendix D are available for assessing the client's ability to deal with daily living activities. Basic living skills which require assessment are the client's ability to groom herself, to dress, to walk, to bathe, to perform toileting activities, and to feed herself. While taking down the client's answers, the practitioner should be thinking about what kind of help the client would require in order to remain independent.

Ask the client about her expectations about care. Sometimes there is a discrepancy between what the caregiver and the client expect of each other. Abuse can, at times, be the result of these unrealistic expectations, so it is important that the practitioner compare the client's statements with those given by the caregiver.

Gradually, the practitioner may begin to explore the subject of abuse more specifically.

Have the client report any recent crises in family life. At this point, the client may be willing to tell the practitioner about major problems in the home, or reveal that she has concerns about a certain family member.

Ask about alcohol problems, drug use, illnesses, behavior problems among household or family members. Some questions the practitioner may ask here include:

"Is there anyone you know who has problems with alcohol, drugs, or with
controlling his or her temper?"
"Is there anyone who has been having a particularly bad time lately?"

*The practitioner should next begin to ask the client about abusive in-
cidents. This part should include questions about whether she has ever been
shoved, shaken, or hit, tied to a bed or chair, or left locked in a room for
long periods.* The practitioner should also ask whether the client has been
yelled at or threatened. If the response is yes to any of these questions, the
practitioner should ask when it happened and where the client was hurt. Ask
her to point to those parts of the body which were injured and to demonstrate how she was struck (i.e., open hand or closed fist, how often). Ask how
long the client was restrained and when it happened. The practitioner
should narrow the focus of the interview to the specific incident or incidents
mentioned by the client and obtain more detail, e.g., what seem to be the
precipitating factors for the abuse and how often the abuser repeats these
incidents.

At this point in the assessment, clients usually respond to direct questions
with a "yes" or "no," as long as they perceive the practitioner to be trustwor-
thy. Very few clients refuse to answer specific questions about elder abuse
and neglect if they are asked in the right way. These questions must be
asked, even if the client is perceived as confused or has been labeled
"demented." Despite some memory loss, clients still may recall recent
abusive incidents. Others may recall only incidents which occurred in the
remote past and may say they have not been abused recently. Some clients
may admit readily to being victims of elder abuse and neglect, but they may
refuse to name the abuser. It is possible, however, to determine who the
abuser is likely to be from the pool of names obtained during the "typical
day" assessment, and from clues the client gives inadvertently. For example,
the client may say, "I don't want to tell; she might get mad at me." The
practitioner will want to be alert for abuse by a female, possibly someone the
client has named earlier in the interview.

It is helpful to prepare the client for these delicate questions by putting
her at ease and by allowing time for the practitioner and the client to get to
know each other. This is why the "typical day" assessment should ordinarily
be conducted first. Some clients will deny the abuse or neglect, but this
should not deter the practitioner from asking specific questions. The practitioner is never able to determine abuse and neglect without giving the
client an opportunity to speak on the matter.

Questions regarding financial abuse should be asked in the same manner
as those related to physical abuse. The determination of financial abuse may
be made by asking the following questions:

"Have you signed any forms or documents lately that you didn't quite understand?"

"Has anyone asked you to sign anything without explaining what you are signing?"

"Is anyone taking your checks?"

"Has anyone accompanied you to your bank and had you withdraw money for her use?"

"Who owns this house? Is it in your name?"

"Do you suspect anyone is tampering with your savings or your other assets?"

In addition, the client should be asked whether she is getting enough to eat and drink, and whether her medications are being given on time. The practitioner should also ask whether the client has been yelled at or threatened. In order to determine how she copes with the abuse, the client should be asked how she responds in abusive situations. The client's responses to these questions may range from, "Oh I just expect him to have his way all the time so I don't fight back," to, "I hit her back and told her no one pushes me around like that."

Because some clients may be victims of multiple types of abuse, the practitioner must be sure to ask questions regarding all possible forms of abuse.

Determine the client's current mental status. The purpose of conducting a mental status exam at some point during the interview is to add credibility to the client's report of elder abuse and neglect and to counter attempts by others to dismiss the client's allegations with statements such as, "Oh she made up the story," or, "She's senile. She doesn't know what she's saying." Evaluation tools such as the Mini Mental State Exam (Folstein et al., 1975), Dementia Scale (Kahn et al., 1960), and Symptoms of Depression (Goodwin & Guze, 1984) are easy to administer and to score (see Appendices B, C, and E). If the client's scores are high, her statements will have more credibility. If the client does poorly, on the other hand, it may indicate that she is incapable of caring for herself, or to give consent for intervention. The practitioner's case plan may later need to include finding someone to assist the client.

Assessing Injuries

Practitioners who are not in the health care field are sometimes uncomfortable about examining for injuries. They may feel they lack training, or they may have been schooled to assess the client verbally only. Nevertheless, it is possible to review the client physically while at the same time protecting the client's modesty. While still in the client's home, the practitioner should tell the client that he would like to take a quick look at the client's scalp, arms, and legs to make sure they are all right. For example, the practitioner might say:

> "Mrs. Smith, I would like you to roll up your sleeves for me so I can take a peek at your arms."
> "Will you please let me look at your neck and feel your scalp?"
> "Do you hurt anywhere in particular? Show me."
> "Would you mind rolling up your pants so I can look at your legs?"

If the client does not mind complying with the request for this examination, the practitioner should proceed and ask to be allowed to look at her back and chest. The practitioner should say:

> "I'd like to look down your collar for a second, look at your back."
> "Will you please unbutton your front so I can look at your chest?"

In a medical setting, it is necessary to examine the patient after she is undressed and gowned. Symptoms of abuse and neglect may be overlooked unless the entire body is examined carefully. All findings should be recorded on a sketch sheet or trauma graph (see Figure 6.1).

Document:

1. The size of the injury.
2. The color of the bruise or injury.
3. Its shape.
4. The injury's location.

On an inpatient hospital floor, part of the assessment of abuse and neglect requires that documentation be made in detail in the patient's chart. Findings should be described explicitly and the patient's statements recorded in quotes. Suspicion should be aroused if the patient's version of how she was injured is different from the caregiver's. The patient's trunk and extremities should be sketched, and bruises, lacerations, or other injuries drawn according to size, color, shape, and location to call attention to the seriousness of the problem. The sketches should be signed and dated by the practitioner. Such eye-catching sketches in the chart are very important for future reference and intervention as well as for staff education. Interdisciplinary collaboration can be especially helpful during this assessment. For example, the caregiver may state that the patient's bruises are from repeated falls. If the physical therapist, after several sessions, finds that the patient ambulates independently with no assistance, does not fall, and has a normal gait, then it is necessary to consider elder abuse and neglect as a possibility. In another

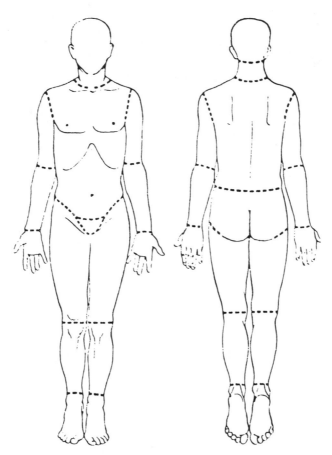

FIGURE 6-1 Sketch sheet to document physical injuries.

example, a patient with organic brain syndrome may be admitted to the hospital with bruises of unknown etiology. If the caregiver feels the patient bruises easily, the nursing and physical therapy staff can observe how easily the patient actually bruises. If the patient develops no new bruises from routine handling such as being turned or transferred from walker and/or from being restrained with wrist or waist restraints and belts, and if bruises presented upon admission fade away during the patient's hospital stay, then the patient should be viewed as a possible victim of abuse and neglect.

If an injury is from an accident, the way the injury occurred should be determined. When the client says she fell, it is not enough just to note that the client fell. The client should also be asked, "What were you doing when you fell?" "Was anyone with you at that time?" "Show me how you got this bruise." The client's responses should then be recorded.

The client should be assessed for injuries to the head, scalp, or face. Bruises and hematoma that are distributed bilaterally, on both sides of the body, or that are symmetrical should be noted on a sketch sheet. A hematoma is a mass of blood confined to an organ or an enclosed area, such as the spleen, a muscle, the chest, or the head. A hematoma that is located in an arm or a leg causes increased girth or swelling of that extremity. The practitioner may see an accompanying bruise or discoloration in the adjoining skin area. The bruises may be shaped like the object that was used to inflict the injury. Some hematomas are not diagnosed by visual exam. For example, a subdural hematoma which creates pressure on the brain is detected by computerized axial tomogram (CAT scan). A "spongy" scalp, or

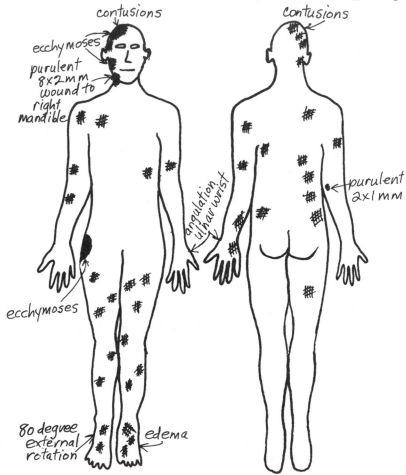

FIGURE 6-2 Case example A.

one that is very soft to the touch, may be the result of hair pulling. If round bruises are found on both upper arms or near both shoulders, the client may have been held by the shoulders and shaken. The sketches shown in Figures 6-2, 6-3, 6-4, and 6-5 represent documentation of clients' injuries. Each sketch should contain the client's name, the date of the exam, and the signature of the examiner. Later, they can be used as evidence in a court hearing, such as a guardianship proceeding or when a protective order is needed.

Suspicious bruise sites include the upper arm or thigh, and the inner arm or thigh. Bruises which are clustered, as if from repeated striking, or which are shaped like thumb/finger prints are also suspicious. If new and old bruises are present at the same time as if from repeated injury, or if injuries are present which are at different stages of resolution, elder abuse and neglect must be considered. The following chart will help to determine the age of bruises:

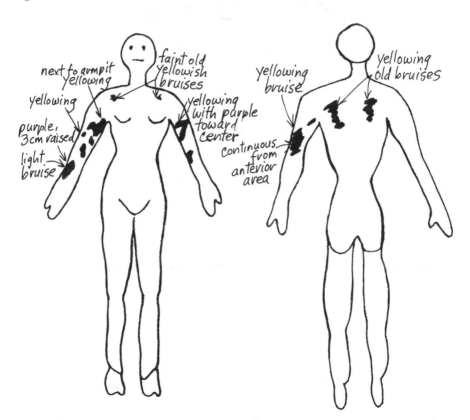

FIGURE 6-3 Case example B.

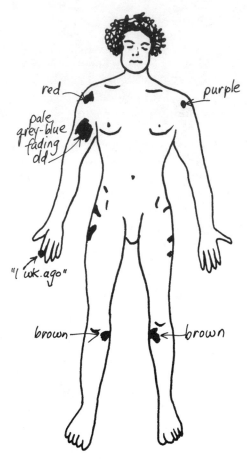

FIGURE 6-4 Case example C, front view.

Dating of Bruises

0–2	days	swollen, tender
0–5	days	red-blue
5–7	days	green
7–10	days	yellow
10–14	days	brown
2–4	weeks	clear

If bruises are noticed after the client has changed health care practitioners or after she has had a prolonged absence from a health care agency, the practitioner should consider and take steps to rule out elder abuse and neglect.

Besides bruises, other symptoms should also be noted. Marks around the wrists, ankles, and under the armpit may indicate that restraints have been

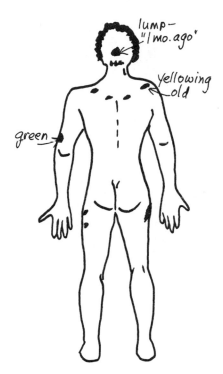

FIGURE 6-5 Case example C, rear view.

used. If the client has joint contractures, that is, her knees or hips are stiff from lack of use or movement, it may indicate neglect. Contractures and poor muscle tone may also be a sign that the client has been tied down or confined to a bed or chair for long periods of time.

A neurological exam may be conducted if changes in the client's mental status are evident from a previous examination.

In a medical setting, diagnostic procedures, as indicated by the client's history, may include the following:

1. Radiological ("X-rays") screening for fractures.
2. Metabolic screening for nutritional, electrolyte, or endocrine abnormalities.
3. Toxicology screening for over- or undermedication.
4. Hematology screening for a coagulation defect when abnormal bleeding or bruising is documented.
5. Computerized axial tomogram (CAT scan) for major changes in neurological status or head trauma that could result in subdural hematoma.

6. Gynecological procedures to rule out venereal disease from sexual assault.

Sexual abuse/sexual assault is underreported and underdetected partially because of societal attitudes that stereotype the elderly as being sexually inactive and unlikely to be victims of sexual assault. Practitioners must pay close attention to the client's statements and questions, which may provide hints that sexual abuse or assault has occurred. For example, an 80-year-old client might ask a practitioner if she could become pregnant. She may actually be asking indirectly for help. Such questions should not be laughed off or dismissed as absurd.

Taking Photographs

While sketches are useful, photos taken during the exam are preferable. Photos of injuries should be taken during the physical exam, assuming the client has given consent to be photographed by signing a release form. If the client is unable to give consent because of illness or inability to comprehend the request, pictures may still be taken. It may be necessary to find a substitute who can later give permission to use the photos. Some state laws permit protective service workers to take photographs. Some law enforcement personnel will also take photographs when called to the scene. They usually must be notified to bring a camera with them in advance.

Cameras with film that develops instantly are practical because retakes are possible if the photos are under- or overexposed. However, instant development film can distort color, depending on the camera's angle or lighting. Therefore, it is advised that a color guide be placed next to the subject for future reference. Placing a coin next to injuries will give the viewer an idea of the size of the injury. Close-up photos of the injury are not enough. It is advisable to take a full-length photo of the elderly client which includes her face and the injury, in case anyone attempts to challenge the photo's veracity.

"You Won't Tell, Will You?"

After finishing the interview with the client and beginning to interview the caregiver, special attention must be paid to the concerns of the client. Regret, fear, and anxiety may surface after the client has admitted to being a victim of elder abuse and neglect. These feelings may show up in fearful questions such as, "You won't tell, will you?" "Now what are you going to do?" The client may fear reprisals if the caregiver finds out what the client has disclosed. The client may also have ambivalent feelings toward the abuser. She may be upset about being abused but may sacrifice her needs in order to keep the abuser from getting into trouble or being arrested and jailed. The client may also be frightened if she thinks the practitioner is considering removing her from her own home, regardless of the reason. Sadly, in more than one instance, an elder abuse and neglect victim has been removed from the home for safety reasons, only to have the abuser move into or take charge of the now vacant house.

After completing the interview with the client, the practitioner should be straightforward and reassuring. He should give the client an example of what will be said to the caregiver. The practitioner may say:

> "We need to collect more data or information about your situation. I am going to talk to your son to see what his concerns for you are. I will not tell him what we discussed, even if he asks me what we talked about. For example, I will not say to your son, 'Your mother just told me you've been hitting her (taking her money, etc.). I am going to have you arrested.' Instead, I will say to your son, 'I'm trying to determine what services your mother may require and would like your perception of how she has been doing.' I will not say anything that will get you in trouble, OK? I will attempt to work with both of you to help you improve your situation."

INTERVIEWING THE CAREGIVER

The practitioner interviewing a family member or caregiver who is suspected of being abusive or neglectful may feel anxious. Interviewing a caregiver or family member who has little knowledge can be anxiety-provoking and/or uncomfortable for him. This section of the evaluation is probably the most difficult to complete because the practitioner is faced with someone who is, or may potentially be, dangerous to the client *and* the practitioner. It is difficult to predict the caregiver's response to specific questions, because abusers come in all sizes, shapes, and colors. For instance, known abusers at one agency have included a bleached-blonde, pleasant-looking daughter who worked as a nursing home aide; a tall, thin, articulate son who expressed a desire to take good care of his father; and a dapper, white-haired elderly male who appeared for his interview in a double-breasted suit. It is very important to interview the caregiver immediately after the client is interviewed. The caregiver will not have a chance to collude with the client or ask the client what was discussed earlier. A primary method of uncovering elder abuse and neglect is to find inconsistencies in stories or reports given separately by the client and the caregiver. When these inconsistencies are uncovered, it is then necessary to proceed with a longer investigation, including prompt collateral contacts.

It is advisable to stick to the format of the protocol—it can provide a "security blanket" for the practitioner during a very emotion-laden interview. It is best to maintain a friendly disposition and to speak in a well-modulated tone of voice, so as not to excite anyone. The practitioner should matter-of-factly record the caregiver's responses verbatim. If it is not possible to document every statement verbatim, the practitioner may write key words that may trigger his memory later as he reviews his notes. Some clients may look nervous about the practitioner's note taking and have difficulty focusing on the questions asked. Rather than quit taking notes, the practitioner may acknowledge the client's apparent concerns by stating, "It is difficult for me to remember everything that you said. I need to record what you say so I don't make mistakes. You can read my notes before I leave if you would like to."

The caregiver may resist being interviewed by the practitioner. If the protocol is introduced as a standard part of the exam, however, and is read by the interviewer, the caregiver may be less defensive and less likely to feel singled out or unjustly accused of wrongdoing.

The interview with the caregiver may include the following questions and statements:

> "Thank you for waiting while I interviewed your mother. Now it's your turn. I need your help—I am doing an (psychosocial) assessment of your mother's current functioning and situation, in order to determine what services are appropriate at this time. I would like to spend some time with you and have you tell me your perception of how things are here."
>
> "Tell me what you want me to know about your mother."
>
> "What is her medical condition? What medicine does she take?"
>
> "What kind of care does she require?"
>
> "How involved are you with your mother's everyday activities and care?"
>
> "What do you expect her to do for herself?"
>
> "What does she expect you to do for her? Do you do those things? Are you able to do them? Have you had any difficulties? What kind?"
>
> "Please describe how you spend a typical day."
>
> "How do you cope with having to care for your mother all the time?"
>
> "Do you have supports or respite care? Who and what?"
>
> "Are there other siblings who help?"
>
> "What responsibilities do you have outside the home? Do you work?"
>
> "What are your hours? What do you do?"
>
> "Would you mind telling me what your income is?" (If this question seems touchy to the caregiver, the practitioner might say, "I just wondered if your family can afford the pills she needs to take.")

The practitioner should assess the caregiver's degree of dependence on the elderly client's income/pensions/assets through the following questions:

"Is your mother's Social Security check directly deposited in the bank?"

"Who owns this house? Do you pay rent? Whose name is on the deed?"

"If you help your mother pay her bills, how do you do it? Is your name on her account?"

"Do you have power of attorney? Does it have a durable clause? When did you get it?"

Questions will seem less provocative if the caregiver perceives the questions to be client-centered, and perceives the practitioner as someone who wants to make a detailed assessment of the client's situation rather than focusing on the caregiver's behavior or actions. All or most of the above questions serve that purpose. If the caregiver seems suspicious or slightly defensive, repeat the fact that she is being helpful by providing this information and that services for which the client may be eligible may benefit the caregiver as well. The practitioner needs to use assertiveness, as well as the bargaining and persuasion tactics which are helpful when working with involuntary clients. These tactics were described earlier in Chapter 5 and may be helpful to keep the caregiver talking while the practitioner assesses the client's condition and physical surroundings.

When the client presents with a serious physical or mental condition, even more delicate questions must be asked; it is best to save these questions for the end of the interview, when most of the necessary information has been gathered and a defensive response from the caregiver can be risked. Abuse and neglect must not be assumed. The burden of denial must be placed on the caregiver. The following appropriate questions can be asked to determine the caregiver's responsibility in causing the elder's condition:

"You know those bruises on your mother's arms (head, nose, etc.), how do you suppose she got them?" (Document response verbatim. If possible, follow up with a request that the caregiver demonstrate how the injury may have happened.)

"Your mother is suffering from malnourishment and/or dehydration." Or, "Your mother seems rather undernourished and thin. How do you think she got this way?"

"Is there any reason you waited this long to seek medical care for your mother?"

"Caring for someone as impaired as your mother is a difficult task. Have you ever felt so frustrated with her that you pushed her a little harder than you expected? How about hitting or slapping her? What were the circumstances?" (Document response verbatim.)

"Have you ever had to tie your mother to a bed or chair or lock her in a room when you go out at night?"

"Have there been times when you've yelled at her or threatened her verbally?"

At one hospital, many abusive caregivers interviewed denied or minimized their responsibility for the elderly client's injuries or precarious situation. When interviewing the caregiver, the practitioner's primary goal is to gather information and to document the information accurately. It is not to argue, dispute, or challenge the responses of the caregiver. In the intervention phase, after all information is gathered, the practitioner may decide to be confrontive, but the goal in this phase is to gather information.

When the Abuser Denies Abuse

The questions listed above provide the caregiver with an opportunity to admit frustration, stress, loss of control, or any "wrongdoing." This admission may be sincere ("I just lost it; I couldn't take one more night of her whining, and I'm sorry"), or it may be insincere, that is, the admission or apology is made only to get the practitioner "off my back." At this point, the practitioner must make a judgment about whether he is faced with a sincere, stressed caregiver who needs assistance, or with a pathological caregiver who feels she has been "caught in the act" and so must cooperate with the practitioner. The caregiver's affect while discussing the abusive situation may help the practitioner assess the caregiver's sincerity. Furthermore, verification of the caregiver's specific response may be obtained by interviewing others who know both the client and the caregiver such as neighbors, friends, relatives, and personnel of agencies involved in providing care to the client.

COLLATERAL CONTACTS

Collateral contacts must be made promptly, before the caregiver attempts to collude with others. The number of contacts made by the practitioner may range from two to 20 people who have knowledge of both the client's and the abuser's behavior, and who are good sources of information. Concerned people who possess important information are usually reluctant to become involved if they anticipate a court appearance or having to face the caregiver at a later date. The practitioner may need to appeal to them as "good Samaritans" in order to aid the client and to ensure confidentiality. When possible, collateral contacts may be made even before interviewing the client and the caregiver. The caregiver and client may be asked, "Who else should I talk to?" "Who can tell me more about your mother's condition?" "What are your neighbors' names? I may interview them to see what they know about your mother."

SUMMARIZING

Summarizing may be done separately with the client and the caregiver. After completing the interviews with the client, caregiver, and/or collateral contacts, the practitioner should give the client a summary of what has occurred. The practitioner might say, "Based on what you're telling me, you would like some help with household chores. It must be difficult to have to rely on your son to do everything for you." Findings are stated in a factual manner: "Based on what you've revealed, your son mistreats you. You are frightened of your son and yet you love him. As frightened as you are of him, you are also saying you feel safe when he is around and are glad when he comes to your home, talks to you, opens your mail, and fixes your meals." Next, the client is informed that only with her permission will intervention or treatment options be explored. In the initial interview and throughout the treatment process, besides reducing tension and anxiety, a major goal is to provide the client with a feeling of hope for improvement and relief. A feeling of hopelessness can serve as a barrier to motivation and change. Hope or optimism is directly related to the practitioner's degree of therapeutic enthusiasm. The practitioner must play an active role in conveying to the client that change is possible, that the client can obtain some improvement in his situation (Golan 1979; Rapoport 1970).

When summarizing with the caregiver, the practitioner should thank the caregiver for her cooperation and contribution. The practitioner should *not* disclose his plans or strategy for intervention. Very often the (abuser) caregiver begins to develop her own strategy when she realizes that the practitioner is concerned about the client's current situation. The urge to confront the abuser should be fought. Instead, the practitioner may inform the caregiver that he will proceed at a cautious pace and with the client's permission, determine the client's individualized treatment plan. The practitioner may feel he is being deceptive, but should remember that the client's safety is at stake, and that the status quo should not be disrupted until better conditions can replace or improve it.

DIAGNOSIS

After reviewing the client's history, physical exam, the caregiver's history, and information from collateral contacts, the client may be given a tentative diagnosis. This may be one of the following:

1. No evidence for elder abuse and neglect.
2. Suspicion of neglect.
3. Suspicion of abuse.
4. Positive for abuse, neglect, or gross neglect.

SUMMARY

Elder abuse and neglect are typically hidden phenomena. Phase I of the EADI Model provides a protocol to systematically determine whether elder abuse and neglect exist. Occasionally a situation will be characterized by the need for immediate action on the part of the practitioner and the assessment phase must be collapsed and combined with treatment on first contact. The following chapter describes immediate actions the practitioner can take in crisis situations.

7

Intervention Phase: Considerations and Crisis Treatment

Due to the variety of situations that are presented to the practitioner regarding elder abuse and neglect, Phase II of the Elder Abuse Diagnosis and Intervention Model provides several approaches for intervention: crisis intervention, short-term treatment, and long-term treatment. This chapter describes factors that influence the practitioner's choice of intervention and then describes crisis intervention. The practitioner is provided with options that may be initiated immediately and do not require prior legal action. Interventions that do require prior legal action are described in Chapter 10.

FACTORS INFLUENCING INTERVENTIONS

Client's Capabilities

After the practitioner has interviewed the client and the alleged abuser, his next task is to determine whether the client has the capability to consent to treatment and to decide what should be the course of treatment. Specific assessment tools will enable the practitioner to determine the client's general level of physical and mental capacities. If the client is not oriented to time, place, and/or person or has a low score on a mental status exam and does poorly in her assessment of activities of daily living and advanced living skills, then finding a surrogate decision maker should be considered. The practitioner should bear in mind that these assessments may require several contacts in order to be completed. Practitioners from different disciplines are sometimes consulted, and these assessments can be carried out simultaneously with other intervention options. In hospital geriatric evaluation units, an elderly client's work-up to determine her capabilities includes:

1. "Dementia" work-up to rule out reversible illness:
   a. Laboratory tests.
   b. Chest X-ray.
   c. Urinalysis.
   d. Computerized axial tomogram (CAT scan).
   e. Electroencephalogram (EEG).
   f. Skull X-ray.
2. Administration of a mental status exam to determine mental capabilities (see Appendix C).
3. Assessment of basic and advanced living skills to determine functional capabilities (see Appendix D).
4. Neuropsychological tests, when indicated.
5. Administration of a questionnaire to rule out depression (see Appendix E).

Neuropsychological testing performed by a clinical psychologist is indicated if the client's mental status exam shows capabilities in some areas but not in others and there is no clear explanation for these differences. Psychological tests can more clearly pinpoint the client's "pocket of deficiencies." For example:

A sociable and conversant client hospitalized with a broken hip was alert and oriented on admission and initially perceived as capable of caring for herself. Later, she was perceived to be uncooperative by staff in performing grooming, dressing, and ambulation activities. Psychological testing showed the client was losing some ability to digest and retain new information and that she was not capable of remembering everything that the physical therapist told her in previous sessions. The treatment plan was subsequently modified to add written cues to the verbal cues to help the client progress in her recovery.

It is necessary to perform an assessment for depression because some people may look and act "senile" or "demented," but may in fact be suffering from a depression that may be reversible with medications. Factors to consider when assessing for depression are listed in Appendix E.

The practitioner may feel uncomfortable about using the aforementioned tools, thinking that he needs to be a specialist in order to use them. However, case managers, social workers, and nurses are known to have utilized these tools with no problems during home visits for a preliminary assessment. Being familiar with these tools will enable the practitioner to refer the client for a further work-up to the appropriate agency. Time and again, the client has been too quickly labeled "competent" or "incompetent" without adequate information that justifies the use of these labels. The practitioner's assessment of the client's capabilities has to be done carefully in order to establish an appropriate treatment plan and to hold up in a legal proceeding. With adequate information, an assessment team can recommend with confidence someone other than the abusive caregiver to be the limited or full guardian of the elderly client when it is necessary. In some instances the abusive caregiver has obtained her own legal counsel and contested the guardianship that was initiated on behalf of the client by the practitioner or others. Assuming the guardianship will be challenged, the practitioner must be prepared to defend the reasons for declaring the client incapable and assume that he must make a court appearance. In these cases, information must be gathered in depth, and all contacts, observations, and statements must be documented carefully and accurately.

After all specified assessments are completed, the client will fall into one of the following main categories:

Capable and consenting. The client scores high in the dementia and functional assessments, manifests the ability to integrate information, and consents to treatment.

Capable and nonconsenting. The client scores high in dementia and functional assessments, understands her circumstances, but does not consent to treatment or services for a variety of reasons.

Incapable and consenting. The client scores low in the assessments yet requests assistance or services.

Incapable and nonconsenting. The client does poorly in the assessments, is incapable of giving consent for treatment or services, refuses services, and requires surrogate representation.

Emergency client. The client is in danger of irreparable harm to self or property, which may be due to an acute medical condition, unsafe environmental conditions, or sudden and rapid loss of finances or property.

Client Cooperation

It is easy and often pleasurable to work with a capable, consenting client because she is motivated toward change and often expresses gratitude for the practitioner's time and concern. On the other hand, it is frustrating to work with the capable, nonconsenting client. She is aware she is a victim of abuse or neglect but chooses to remain in the abusive situation. The client's willingness to consent to treatment and her degree of involvement can depend on several factors such as her motivation to change her behavior or environment, her capacity to engage in a treatment relationship, and opportunities and resources available to effect change. Before becoming angry at the client or feeling that she is foolish to remain in the victim role, the practitioner should examine factors influencing the client's choice to remain in the abusive situation. The client may choose to remain in an abusive situation due to fear, hope, love, low self-esteem, financial dependence, emotional dependence, isolation, duty, lack of proper help from outsiders, and the abuse not being severe enough to make the client want to leave (Elliott, 1983; Star, 1978).

Ambivalence is a concept that is acknowledged by practitioners but is not dealt with adequately. It is an inherent part of the beginning phase of treatment. Any practitioner working with abused elders has been told more than once, "No, I don't want your services," and has felt frustrated. It may be liberating to the client to hear the practitioner address the ambivalence saying, "Perhaps you are having some thoughts as to whether or not you want a stranger like me to help you." Attending to ambivalent feelings early in the treatment period will decrease the chance of conscious or unconscious sabotage by the client (Wasserman, 1979).

Gambrill (1983) cautions the practitioner to refrain from labeling the client as "resistant." When the client fails to comply with the practitioner's expectations and does not talk about issues which the practitioner feels are important, the client may not be "resistant," but instead may be struggling with discomfort, possibly due to a previous negative relationship with a practitioner or because she has never related with a practitioner under similar circumstances. The client may also be struggling with having to take responsibility for her own actions. All new situations can threaten the elder, and the worker can show the client that he is aware of these feelings by saying, "Perhaps you are wondering what I'm doing here." "You must be wondering if I'm going to ask you to leave your home." Or, "Getting to know a new person takes time" (Wasserman, 1979). Cormier and Cormier (1985) define resistance as "any client *or* therapist behavior that interferes with or reduces the likelihood of a successful therapeutic process and outcome." They state that most if not all clients display resistive behavior at some time during therapy. This includes not only involuntary clients but also the voluntary and self-referred. Resistance may occur when the elder lacks necessary skills or knowledge or has pessimistic expectations or anxious or negative thoughts. Discussing her situation with a practitioner may require change on the part of the client, but she may not yet feel prepared to change. Sometimes the client may seem uncooperative because she may want to avoid painful topics and may have ambivalent feelings toward change and toward the abuser.

Practitioner variables also affect resistance. Sometimes practitioners label clients as resistant to explain their treatment failures. As a result, Cormier and Cormier (1985) suggest that the practitioner avoid personalizing client resistance and be accepting of himself. The practitioner can also help by encouraging client participation in the therapy by acknowledging his own anxiety and discomfort about his competence. Rather than viewing the client as uncooperative, the practitioner should view this period as an opportunity to examine how his own behavior and attitudes could be influencing the client's participation.

Butler and Lewis (1982) describe why some elders resist mental health treatment. These reasons may be applied to any "helping" situation. Elders may be resistant because they desire independence, taking pride in their perceived self-reliance. They also hold on to what they have because they fear change and the unknown. They do not seek treatment because they fear certain diagnoses. They may have symptoms of a condition of which a deceased friend or spouse died and may not realize that the state of the art has advanced and the condition can be treated. Low self-esteem, already mentioned earlier, may be due to having absorbed society's negative attitudes toward aging. Other factors contributing to low client participation may be anxiety, low motivation, lack of information or misinformation, interfering beliefs and attitudes, distractions, interfering life circumstances, poor rapport, lack of participation in choosing the treatment procedures, and lack of social supports for participation. Physical and mental impairments also contribute to low participation (Gambrill, 1983).

Pathology of the Abuser

Some abusers as well as elders may seem resistant but are on guard because they fear being misunderstood and labeled forever as mean and awful. They also fear that they will not have the opportunity to tell their story. Others are obstructionistic, and intervention often depends on the abuser's willingness and ability to stop the abusive behavior. The guilt-ridden, overburdened caregiver who recognizes that her abusive behavior is unacceptable may be more receptive to intervention than the severely disturbed caregiver who denies any wrongdoing or feels her behavior is justified. Sometimes the abuser will take responsibility for the abuse only after legal intervention such as a protection order is initiated. The less cooperation the abuser offers, the more drastic the intervention is likely to be against her.

It is imperative that the practitioner determine early in the assessment and intervention phases the severity of the abuser's pathology and whether the client is in a life-threatening situation. This is especially important if the client chooses to remain with the pathological abuser. Joint sessions in which feelings such as anger, resentments, and jealousy are aroused may lead to an abusive episode after the interview when no witnesses are present (Star, 1978). With this in mind, it is suggested that the practitioner not provoke the abuser but instead carefully plan the intervention steps and not take any drastic action in opposition to the abuser unless the client *clearly* supports the intervention choice.

Very often court-mandated treatment for a spouse or child abuser is necessary due to her characteristics of denial, minimization, externalization, and impulsivity (Ganley, 1981). The abuser will not voluntarily seek help for the above reasons. Because the study of elder abuse and neglect is in its nascent stages, special programs have not yet been developed for courts to mandate abusers of the elderly to seek treatment. It is not yet known whether abusers of the elderly can be treated together with batterers of women and children in existing programs.

Severity of Situation

The severity of the situation dictates the type of intervention and how quickly intervention should occur. For example, if someone is removing large sums of money from a client's bank account in a short period of time, immediate intervention is necessary. If, however, the client has the ability to defend herself in a neglectful or abusive situation and is not in immediate danger, the practitioner will probably have time to do a full assessment of the situation, do collateral contacts, and carefully develop a treatment plan.

Quality of Practitioner–Client Relationship

The development of a positive, therapeutic relationship between the client and the practitioner will maximize the chance of mutual cooperation and a positive treatment outcome. Villamore and Bergman (1981) note that "an ongoing semitherapeutic relationship may have greater long-term benefits than any specific service." Traditional intensive psychotherapy, described in Chapter 9, is not necessarily the sole or the most effective treatment modality for elderly clients, who may be reluctant to go to mental health clinics or private practitioners.

Stone (1979) notes that on the average, one-third to one-half of clients in a medical setting do not follow treatments prescribed for them even when instructions are clear. It is the quality of the interaction between the practitioner and the client that influences the degree of client compliance. The practitioner may have angry feelings and may be tempted to terminate the relationship if the client seems uncooperative and consumes precious amounts of time. The practitioner might justify terminating the relationship by citing a heavy caseload, but it should be remembered that the ambivalent client can benefit from regular contacts and eventually may choose to accept the practitioner's suggestions and offers of help. For example, a hospital emergency room may offer intervention options to a woman diagnosed as a victim of battering. If she chooses to return to the battering situation, she is informed that battering usually escalates to more serious forms and that she is free to return for help in the future. She may return three or more times before she requests active intervention such as a referral to a battered women's shelter.

Having described influential factors in the intervention phase, the use of crisis intervention in elder abuse and neglect will now be discussed.

CRISIS INTERVENTION

Crisis Theory

A crisis is "an upset in a steady state." This definition was developed by Caplan in 1960 (Rapoport, 1962). Crisis theory is a combination of different behavior science theories and practices. The study of crisis theory originated with Lindemann and Caplan and has been expanded by Rapoport (1962, 1970), Parad (1971), and Golan (1978, 1979). It has also been applied to therapy with groups and families in crisis (Langsley & Kaplan, 1968; Parad, Selby, & Quinlan, 1976; Umana, Gross, & McConville, 1980). Its application to social casework has been made in the last 20 years, and practitioners who work with elder abuse and neglect can utilize this approach, especially when time constraints prevail.

There is a difference between a problem and a crisis. With a problem, an elder does not require new methods of coping; her current coping mechanisms are adequate to overturn the situation. In a crisis, the client must readapt to the situation and learn new methods to decrease her feelings of anxiety and helplessness. The practitioner treating elder abuse and neglect, therefore, should be armed with specific sets of practice techniques that the client will wish to use, given her discomfort.

Crisis theory provides guidelines and techniques for intervention and has been used extensively in medical settings, mental health centers, and crisis clinics. Golan (1978) summarizes the basic tenets of crisis theory which can be applied to elder abuse and neglect:

1. Crisis situations may occur episodically. They may be initiated by a hazardous event, may be finite, and may be the result of external or internal stressors. Crises may be composed of a single occurrence or a series of successive mishaps which may build up to a cumulative effect.

2. A crisis is a disturbance in the homeostatic balance and puts a client in a vulnerable state. To regain her equilibrium, the client first uses her customary repertoire of problem-solving mechanisms, with an accompanying rise in tension. If the client is not successful in regaining her equilibrium, then utilization of new, emergency methods to cope is observed.

3. If the problem continues and cannot be resolved, avoided, or rede-fined, tension mounts, resulting in disequilibrium and disorganization. This period is called the state of active crisis.
4. A client may perceive the initial and subsequent stressful events as either a threat, a loss, or a challenge. A threat may result in feelings of anxiety. Loss may result in feelings of deprivation, depression, or a mourning state. The client who feels challenged by a crisis may experi-ence a moderate increase in anxiety, but also hope and expectation.
5. A crisis is not to be equated with illness. It is not an illness nor a pathological experience. Instead, it reflects a realistic struggle in the individual's life situation. It may reactivate earlier or unresolved or partially resolved conflicts so that the client's response to the current crisis may be inappropriate or exaggerated. Given this, there is an opportunity for the client to resolve her present difficulties and also to rework a previous struggle and to break the linkage between past events and the current situation.
6. Each particular type of crisis follows a series of predictable stages which can be mapped out and plotted. It is possible to anticipate emotional reactions and behavioral responses at each stage. If a client fixates at a particular phase or omits a phase, it may provide clues to where the client is "stuck," and what lies behind her inability to do her crisis work and master the situation.
7. The active state of disequilibrium is time limited, commonly lasting from four to six weeks. Parad (1971) reports that a specific number of interviews are part of a crisis-oriented treatment contact. Interviews range from 1 to 12 with the average number of contacts being 6. These interviews may take place daily within one week, or be spaced out over a month.
8. During the resolution of the crisis, the individual tends to be amenable to help. It is during this period that the client is more open to outside influence and change. If intervention occurs during this period, a minimal amount of effort can produce a maximal effect.
9. The last period in a crisis is the reintegration phase, when the client may emerge with newly learned adaptive styles. If help is not available during a crisis, sometimes inadequate or maladaptive patterns may be adopted by the client, which can result in her weakened ability to function adequately in the future.

Parad (1971) considers the practitioner to be a participant, observer, and change agent during a crisis situation. It is a period when immediate therapeutic contact and precisely articulated diagnostic formulation occur. It does not lend itself to a period of systematic history taking. Rapoport (1962, 1970) and Parad (1971) emphasize the need for an unencumbered method for intake. There should be no wait list to obtain help, and there is no separation between study, diagnosis, and treatment aspects of the case.

Capitalizing on the client's readiness to trust during this period of confusion, helplessness, and/or anxiety, the practitioner must work fast and be actively involved. The practitioner in a crisis will be able to operate quickly based on past clinical experience, knowledge of personality organization, and ability to appraise the significance of the client's behavior on the basis of overt communication and marginal clues (Golan, 1978). The emphasis of crisis intervention is on cognitive restructuring and accomplishing tasks in order to achieve a positive resolution of a specific crisis (Rapoport, 1970). However, even cognitively impaired people can benefit from this model because the emphasis is on restoring comfort and safety. For example:

> A 95-year-old man was referred by a neighbor to an outreach agency for older adults after he was observed to be a captive in his own apartment. Two young men, described as large and threatening, had moved into the man's apartment and claimed to be his caregivers. When the worker did his initial visit, he found an extremely frightened man who slept on the living room sofa. The younger men had taken over his bedroom, and the apartment was extremely dirty and cluttered. The worker immediately assessed the man as in need of a medical exam and as cognitively impaired in certain areas. While he was aware of the goings-on in his apartment, he could not provide information about his income and was obviously intimidated by his "caregivers." In a brief moment when the worker and elder client were alone, the worker whispered, "Do you want me to get you out of here?" The frightened man nodded yes emphatically. Focusing on the client's need for a medical checkup and not antagonizing the younger men, the worker left to work on a planned admission to a local hospital. After he obtained the cooperation of the client's physician and nurse, the worker returned to the apartment the next day, accompanied by several law enforcement officers as a safety measure, and transported the client to the hospital. Within a short period, the client was relocated to a safer apartment, was assigned a limited guardian for his estate, and began enjoying a tension-free life.

This example shows that the treatment structure in crisis situations does not rely on the development of a quality relationship between practitioner and client. Instead, treatment relies on the client's readiness to accept help due to discomfort and anxiety in order to regain a sense of autonomy or to reestablish her equilibrium (Strickler & Bonnefil, 1974).

Professional intervention in crisis situations can be broken down into three steps: (1) formulation, (2) implementation, and (3) termination (Golan, 1978). Formulation includes establishing contact with the client, finding out what is going on, determining whether or not a crisis exists, and setting up a working contract for future activity. Implementation includes identifying and carrying out tasks, as well as organizing and working over data in order to bring about behavior change. The last phase, the termination phase, involves arriving at a decision to terminate, reviewing progress made in the treatment situation, and planning for future activities.

FORMULATION AND IMPLEMENTATION

At the time of the initial contact with a possible case of elder abuse, the practitioner's first task is to determine whether a crisis exists, how urgent the client's plight is, and whether immediate action is needed. In many instances, referrals will be presented to the practitioner as if they are emergencies. But upon closer examination, the practitioner discovers that the situation is ongoing and not even at a crisis point, although the referrer perceived it as a crisis.

An emergency is defined as a situation in which either the client or her property is in danger of irreparable harm and immediate action is required (Villamore & Bergman, 1981). Treatment begins on first contact because there is not enough time for a formal and separate study period. There are two common types of emergency situations the practitioner may face:

1. Medical/physical emergencies in which the client requires prompt medical attention.
2. Financial emergencies resulting from sudden withdrawal of funds from the client's bank account or other financial misconduct.

In these hazardous events, the client may feel a threat to her life, security, and assets. Fear, anxiety, helplessness, and confusion may accompany the stressful situation. The client is more likely to be open to practitioner intervention at this time.

Medical/Physical Crises

Immediate intervention or action by the practitioner may be required in any of the following situations:

1. The client is alone and is unable to get up to let the practitioner in.
2. The client is unresponsive and, when finally aroused, is confused and disoriented.
3. The client shows a "failure to thrive" and is found
   a. Lying in urine and feces.
   b. Unable to obtain nourishment and fluids.
   c. Dressed inappropriately for weather conditions.

    d. With untreated sores or injuries.

    e. Unaware of or unable to explain a, b, c, or d.

If upon arriving at the client's residence the practitioner can see through the window that the client is unable to open the door, he should search for a neighbor or apartment manager and attempt to obtain an extra key or assistance in entering the residence. It may be necessary to call a law enforcement officer, who can suggest ways to gain entry, or call for additional assistance, if it is needed. Forced entries are justified only when the situation is perceived as an emergency. Chapter 10 describes in greater detail the involvement of law enforcement personnel in these situations.

When the practitioner reaches the client, the next step should be to make sure she is oriented in regard to person, place, and time. This can be done by asking:

1. What is your name? (person)
2. Where are you? (place)
3. What year is this? (time)

If the client is unable to answer any or all of these questions, further medical evaluation may be required. Disorientation can be the result of lack of food or due to an acute medical condition such as a stroke or over-medication. It does not necessarily indicate the presence of a psychiatric disorder.

Untreated sores, wounds, or other medical conditions may go undetected unless the practitioner is alert for telltale signs. A client lying under blankets or wearing heavy clothing and socks may have hidden injuries. The practitioner can ask the client gently to uncover herself or ask the client's permission to look under the covers. A quick look takes only a few seconds and does not require that the client fully disrobe. If the client and practitioner are of opposite sexes, awkwardness may be eased if the practitioner is comfortable with the situation, maintains eye contact, and proceeds slowly, explaining at each step what is being done. A strange or foul odor may be a clue that the client requires medical attention. One adult protective services worker reported missing the seriousness of a client's situation because she concentrated on the verbal interaction and did not use her senses of sight and smell:

> "I went to see a man who was lying in bed with a blanket up to his neck. He smiled throughout the interview and assured me he was fine. I left after he refused all of the services I offered. Later our office received another call about him. When I interviewed him the second time, I removed his blanket and found a huge pressure sore on his back."

Although the written protocol in Chapter 6 probably will not be able to be completed at this time, attempts should be made to gather as much information as possible. If the caregiver is present, an interview should be conducted to determine her knowledge and awareness of the situation, and the practitioner should try to obtain an explanation of how the condition(s) evolved. The client and/or caregiver may be asked:

1. When was the last time you (your mother) went to the bathroom?
2. You are (your mother is) soiled. Are you aware of this? Can you (she) clean yourself (herself)?
3. What did you (your mother) eat for breakfast this morning? What did you (she) drink and how much?

The practitioner should document *verbatim* their responses to the questions asked. Discrepancies, inconsistencies, and "holes" in their explanations may be helpful in detecting abuse and neglect. For example:

An 84-year-old woman was brought to the emergency room unresponsive and malnourished with bruises on her face, arms, and right thigh. Upon questioning, her caregiver stated that earlier in the day he dragged the client to the dining room table and sat her up. He stated that she then ate meatloaf, mashed potatoes, and peas by herself. The staff had difficulty believing the client was recently able to do anything for herself, much less sit up at a table and hold a utensil to feed herself. The staff began to suspect abuse.

Having determined the client's current status, the practitioner moves quickly from the formulation phase to the implementation phase. He determines the availability of internal, intrafamilial, and community resources that can be mobilized quickly to restore a degree of equilibrium (Rapoport, 1970). When appropriate, the practitioner should let the client know that a "checkup" at a hospital or clinic will be necessary. In Chapter 5, emphasis was made on the importance of calling the client's physician before the home visit to develop a plan of action should the client need immediate medical care. A plan which includes key people being on standby will help the practitioner to obtain assistance quickly and efficiently. If the client is unable to give consent, and a caregiver is present, she must be informed that the client may require treatment outside of the home. The practitioner may say:

"Your mother isn't well and we need to help her. I am going to call her doctor (or the nearest emergency room consulting nurse, etc.) to discuss her condition. She may need to be seen by a doctor today and I will probably need to call for an ambulance."

In suspected abuse cases, neither family members nor the alleged abuser should be relied on to transport the client to the treatment site. An ambulance or cabulance may need to be called. Because the client will be billed for private transportation services, consent should be obtained. Transportation by a law enforcement officer is not billed but may not always be available. It will help out the ambulance company if it can be informed ahead of time of the client's approximate height and weight, and whether a stretcher or wheelchair will be required. If the client is overweight or immobile and in a second floor bedroom or a basement room, two or three people may be required to transport the client up or down the stairs.

The practitioner should accompany the client to the treatment site and exchange information with the treatment staff. It is best to speak directly to the medical practitioner when conveying a suspicion of abuse and neglect and the need for the medical practitioner to document findings in detail. Not all emergency room personnel or other medical professionals have been trained in assessing and detecting elder abuse and neglect. To expedite case management, the practitioner should prepare a referral note on a sheet of paper large enough to keep it from being lost or misplaced. The referral note should contain the following information:

1. The practitioner's name, title, agency, and phone number.
2. The client's physician or treatment agencies and their phone numbers.
3. The names and phone numbers of the client's significant others.
4. The names and phone numbers of the client's neighbors.
5. Information gathered so far on circumstances surrounding the injury or illness.
6. The practitioner's concerns, suspicions, and warnings regarding physical abuse, neglect, or financial exploitation of the client.

Valuable time and information can be lost when the agency practitioner provides verbal information to the admitting clerk, assuming it will be forwarded to the examining practitioner. Taking a few minutes to write the referral note and/or requesting to speak to the examining practitioner will promote a careful assessment.

If the client is admitted to a hospital, the agency and medical practitioners must maintain contact with each other and develop a discharge plan together.

Financial Crises

Certain financial situations can be as serious as medical crises. Some elderly clients have suffered financial and/or material abuse which has taken their entire life's savings, pension checks, real estate property, or valuables, causing them irreparable harm. Others have had to spend large amounts of money to recover their assets through the legal system. For a practitioner to intervene successfully in financial abuse, he must assume that the client's report of financial loss is correct and that abuse has occurred. Some emotional signs of a crisis in a client may be anxiety, tension, shame, hostility, depression, and guilt. Cognitive confusion may also be observed (Rapoport, 1970). Practitioners should take prompt action and must have a thorough knowledge of the options available in financial emergencies. When the practitioner is disbelieving of the client's report, the delay may allow the financial abuser to further dissipate the client's assets and to escape accountability for her actions.

Financial abuse can take many forms. Acquaintances, friends, or relatives may add their names to the client's checking and/or savings account, claiming that this will make it easier to pay the client's bills and to assist the client in the event of illness or accident. When there are unexplained withdrawals from the client's account, prompt action is necessary. Consider the following example:

> A 75-year-old woman was hospitalized after suffering a stroke and was visited by an 80-year-old sister who lived in another state. She brought with her a joint account signature card from the client's bank and asked the client to sign it. The sister's name was added to the account. The sister immediately withdrew $7,000 and returned to her home state. The abuse was discovered accidentally when a close friend of the client happened to meet the hospital social worker one evening and asked if the staff were aware of the sister's actions.

Sometimes a caregiver or friend may forge a client's signature to withdraw money, alter a signed check, or ask a client to sign a blank check. In these instances, the practitioner has several options open to him:

Call the bank to place an alert on the account. The practitioner may wish to find out the name and branch of the client's bank. He can call and ask to speak to the bank manager. The practitioner should identify himself and his agency, and explain the purpose of the phone call. Banks vary in how much information they will give a practitioner. Some banks will indicate only whether there are sufficient funds to cover a check for a certain amount, while others will answer yes or no to general questions that are asked by a practitioner. For instance, the practitioner might inquire whether the client's account balance is in four figures and if the amount is a high or low number. Most bank managers appreciate calls of concern, and while they are unable to provide detailed information by phone without the client's written consent, they will take information and alert tellers and other bank branch offices to watch for unusual activity in the client's account.

Transport the client to the bank to discuss the incident with the manager. When possible, the practitioner should consider taking the client to the bank where the bank manager can speak directly with the client. A client in a nursing home or a hospital may be allowed to go out of the institution on a pass granted by her physician. The practitioner should call to prepare the bank manager for the visit. It will be necessary to go to the client's home or institution early enough to prepare the client emotionally and physically for the visit. If the practitioner's agency forbids the use of personal vehicles, other transportation options include senior escort services and public or volunteer transportation. Some practitioners who choose to transport clients in their vehicles have arranged with their insurance agent to increase their coverage at a nominal fee. A folding wheelchair may be necessary if the client is unable to walk long distances or to stand for long periods of time. In order to be free to aid the client, the practitioner should consider using a taxi or having someone else do the driving. At the bank, the practitioner should explain the purpose of the visit and allow the client to express his concern.

Help the client close her current account and open a new account that is inaccessible to others. In the aforementioned case:

> The hospital social worker, once alerted, asked the client if she let her sister put her name on her checking account. The client nodded yes. The worker then asked her if she was aware that $7,000 was withdrawn from her account. The client became visibly upset and said "no." She indicated she wanted her sister to stop withdrawing any more money. The worker took the client to the bank. The bank manager knew her well and had visited the client at her home in the past to complete other transactions. The manager recommended that the woman close the current joint account and transfer her money to a new account to which her sister would not have access. Phone calls to the client's sister made prior to the bank visit indicated that the sister left the state with the client's checkbook and had been writing checks on the account. Everyone involved later agreed that immediate transportation of the client to the bank probably prevented additional thousands of dollars from being withdrawn from the account.

Bring bank personnel to the client's home. If a client is unable to go to the bank because of illness or impairment, or if the practitioner feels a bank visit may be too exhausting or upsetting for the client, the practitioner may ask a bank representative to visit the client in the home or institution. During the visit, it is important to ensure privacy and to make sure the conversation is not overheard by others in the home. The bank representative can then ask the client whether he was aware of the unusual activity on the account, and in cases of forgery, ask the client whether she wishes to pursue legal action. Banks may be particularly concerned about forgery because in some instances lawsuits have been filed against banks when signatures were not checked and forged checks were cashed.

Obtain a consent form or letter from the client to inquire about her account. If a bank representative is unable to visit the client, an alternate plan is to request information on the client's behalf through a release of information form or a letter requesting that the bank provide the practitioner with specific information. It is helpful to know the client's account number and bank branch. The letter might read:

October 15, 198——
Dear Bank Manager of _____ Bank:
   I am unable to go to the bank myself so I am asking Mr. John Smith, Case Manager for the Division on Aging, to obtain for me my current bank balance. I am concerned that someone is taking money from my account. My phone number is 555-4469. Please call me if you require more information.

                                        Sincerely yours,

                                        _____
                                        (signed) Jean Jones
                                        Account # 000-00-0000

   The practitioner should be prepared to present proper identification along with the letter. Copies of the letter should be made for the client and the practitioner.
   Generally speaking, bank representatives are helpful to clients and their advocates when presented with adequate information and documentation.

TERMINATION

In crisis intervention, there is no separation of diagnosis and treatment activities. Treatment begins in the first session. Termination in crisis intervention is also combined with these other two activities; it is not a separate and distinct phase. During termination, the practitioner reviews the progress made during the course of his contact with the client. He can discuss future strategies such as who and when to call for help. Hopefully by this time, the client has developed an awareness of the realistic aspects of this stressful situation and can move to a level of mastery over a short period of time.
   An important goal in termination is the development of a method for monitoring the client. The client should be left with the knowledge that she may return for services. It is helpful to routinely build in a method for following up with a client. This could be done in person within a few months, or by a telephone call. In addition to restoring the elder's emotional equilib-

rium, a major goal of crisis intervention is the development of foresight. Before closing the case, the practitioner may utilize role rehearsal and anticipatory guidance to prepare the client for similar future incidents. For example, the practitioner may want to write names and phone numbers of agencies and people the client should call if she is not getting her medications regularly and is feeling ill, or if she is threatened again to sign over her Social Security check to her grandson. At the time of termination, the client hopefully has developed new ties with persons and resources in the community (Golan, 1979).

SUMMARY

This Intervention Phase of the EADI Model can be considered a process during which the client and the abuser may reveal a variety of conflicting feelings. The client's capabilities and willingness to cooperate will affect the intervention outcome, as will the abuser's pathology and the severity of the situation.

In cases of elder abuse, medical and financial crises can arise at any time, and practitioners need to be alert to the possibilities in each and every situation. Prompt action can mean the difference between life and death, or between financial comfort and poverty. The next chapter describes short-term interventions that the practitioner can utilize when no emergency situation exists.

8 Intervention Phase: Short-Term Treatment

Some elder abuse situations such as those described in the previous chapter are best treated by crisis intervention strategies. Still others benefit from long-term treatment methods. This chapter focuses on short-term treatment as it applies to elder abuse and neglect.

In short-term treatment, the concept of "cure" is abandoned. It is essential that goals be limited and that the practitioner genuinely accept this limitation. This may be difficult for the practitioner, especially when clients present with a multitude of problems and situations which will not be handled within a short period of time.

Short-term treatment involves immediate problem solving and the restoration and enhancement of client functioning. In this method, goals are concrete and specific, marked by the use of referrals to other agencies. These goals are determined by what the practitioner considers to be the "useful next step" (Rapoport, 1970). The practitioner is not necessarily the ongoing worker, but refers the client for case management. The practitioner makes a plan that does not necessarily include herself. For example, a practitioner may come into contact with the client only during the diagnostic workup phase. She may be the practitioner responsible for obtaining a diagnostic assessment to rule out elder abuse and neglect. This can be done by doing the assessment herself or by requesting a geriatric evaluation in the home or at a clinic, working with other professionals. Sometimes a short hospital stay or repeated home visits are necessary to assess the client and to develop a case plan. The client with medical problems such as malnourishment, dehydration, or pressure sores may be admitted to a hospital from home. The hospital staff should be alerted to rule out elder abuse during the client's inpatient admission. The practitioner who does not have time to follow a client for a long period, for example, beyond three months, may conduct the diagnostic assessment and then refer the client to another agency for long-term follow-up or for monitoring.

Less emphasis on relationship development is placed in short-term treatment than in long-term treatment. The short-term treatment practitioner stays involved until long-term care and monitoring plans are developed. Emphasis in brief treatment is on the development of foresight through educational techniques and anticipatory guidance. Brief treatment often is not by purpose or plan, but is labeled retrospectively.

In terms of time, short-term treatment may involve up to a dozen interviews spaced out over three to six months. Diagnosis and treatment are often combined, which means that the treatment goals and strategies may change from time to time as new facts emerge. Short-term treatment is a *different* method of intervention rather than less treatment. It is attractive to many practitioners, for it is one way that they are able to see as many clients as possible within time and fiscal constraints. In many communities, this treatment method is used by practitioners in protective service agencies. Short-term treatment is not for psychiatric clients who are in a chronic state of crisis and who often have continually erupting crises and require services over an indefinite period of time. These clients require indefinite case management, structure, and ongoing care and may need to be referred to agencies such as community mental health centers where they can be cared for adequately.

The major limitation of short-term treatment is the lack of time to develop a positive therapeutic relationship that often is required before change can occur. Rapoport (1970) suggests that focus should be on the client's motivation to seek relief from discomfort, which short-term treatment can accomplish, rather than on the client's motivation to make permanent behavior changes.

COUNSELING ISSUES IN SHORT-TERM TREATMENT

While elder abuse and neglect detection and assessment tools are now being developed in greater quantity than five years ago, specific counseling techniques for elder abuse victims and abusers are only now being developed. A few helpful counseling guidelines now exist (Rathbone-McCuan, Travis, & Voyles, 1983; Villamore & Bergman, 1981). Methods used to work with child abuse and domestic violence victims and abusers are being reviewed and their applicability to treating elder abuse and neglect are being explored. The following treatment suggestions are the result of a review of literature on counseling, child abuse, and domestic violence in combination with direct field experiences. These are general guidelines and in no way represent proven methods for treating all aspects of elder abuse and neglect. They are subject to modification as more knowledge is gained from new research and practitioner experiences. A wide range of interventions are presented because the types of clients and abusers are so diverse.

Client Advocacy and Abuser Accountability

Professionals currently are divided on whether it is possible to fulfill the role of advocate for both abuser and victim with impartiality. Many professionals can be "pro-victim," but have difficulty being perceived as "pro-abuser." They feel that the abuser is not deserving of their attention, and he should be left alone or punished. The practitioner often has angry feelings that distance her emotionally from the abuser and lead her to view the victim as the sole client. This stance in part can be influenced by the practitioner's schooling, which emphasized individual therapy, by the agency's philosophy and mission, and by the lack of practitioner role models to treat both victim and abuser.

The intervention most frequently chosen by practitioners when dealing with a pathological caregiver is physical separation of the abuser and the elder, especially when other interventions have failed or when the elder's life is endangered. Often this means the elder will be placed in a nursing home, usually a painful step because most elders want to remain at home, even if they are being abused and even if they are physically and/or mentally impaired. Most elders, and indeed most of the general population, view nursing homes as houses of decay and death and as the only alternative to living at home.

The effect of separating the abuser and the victim remains an unsettled issue for both child abuse and spouse abuse. For cases of elder abuse, the reality of the situation should guide the practitioner: cases that require permanent separation of the client and abuser comprise a small percentage. Most or many of the cases involving elder abuse and neglect involve the victim choosing to remain in the abusive situation, which results in provision of services to an intact but stressed family.

Counseling techniques addressing the needs of both victim and abuser should be learned. Factors influencing the practitioner's ability to maintain concern for the caregiver as a person include the practitioner's knowledge of formal and informal resources and ability to refer as well as the support received from her agency (Rathbone-McCuan et al., 1983). Many agencies do not have adequate staff to treat both client and caregiver and therefore may emphasize contacts with clients alone.

Ganley (1981) supports the ability of a practitioner to treat both the client and the abusive or neglectful caregiver. Rather than being a supportive counselor to both in the traditional sense, the practitioner becomes an advocate for the client and is a monitor of the abuser's behavior, making him accountable for his actions. The goal of joint counseling is to stop the battering and is based on social learning theory, which holds that behaviors are learned from one's family of origin, culture, and prior experiences. These behaviors can be unlearned and replaced with acceptable alternatives.

COUNSELING THE ELDERLY CLIENT

Counseling Methods

Choice of Style

The practitioner has a choice in selecting her counseling style. Szaz and Hollander (1956) discuss three models of the physician–client relationship that may be applied to elder abuse and neglect work. The first is activity–passivity, the second is guidance–cooperation, and the third is mutual participation. Short-term treatment often requires that the practitioner be active and directive, while communicating concern and authenticity (Rapoport, 1970). The practitioner will choose to be active when the client is in an emergency situation or is incapacitated. Szaz and Hollander caution the practitioner not to utilize this model unless absolutely necessary, and to examine whether the active role is chosen to support feelings of authority and superiority. To this point, Stone (1979) suggests that if the patient is incapacitated and immediate action is not crucial, a guardian must be found to consent to treatment.

The guidance–cooperation model dominates present medical care delivery and may be the one most frequently chosen by the practitioner treating the elder abuse and neglect client. The client is suffering from pain, anxiety, and fear and wants help and is willing to cooperate with the practitioner, who can present options and facts and gently guide the client toward the treatment plan of choice. Szaz and Hollander (1956) again serve as the practitioner's conscience, asking her to examine whether her motives are due to needs for mastery and superiority over the client.

The third model of mutual participation or the contractual model is one in which the client has control in decision-making. Here the practitioner and the client have equal power, are interdependent, and will relate in a mutually satisfying manner. The model is not appropriate for children or those who are cognitively impaired, very poorly educated, or profoundly immature. While it may be difficult to accept the fact that the client may choose to disagree with the treatment plan, some comfort may be had in knowing that options have been presented and that the practitioner did her best to educate the client about his situation. Szaz and Hollander (1956) put forth reminders that to be an effective practitioner, the therapeutic relationship is a process, one in which the client may progress from being a passive client to becoming a cooperative client and ultimately to being a partner in the management of his care. The practitioner must have the ability to recognize these changes and be able to make corresponding changes rather than labeling the client as "difficult" or "uncooperative." The potential for a positive intervention outcome may be maximized by being aware of the following counseling issues.

Resistance

Cormier and Cormier (1985) discuss many specific techniques that the practitioner can utilize when working with the resistant or involuntary client. For example, they suggest that when clients lack necessary skills or knowledge, resistance may occur. In those instances, the provision of informative details and skills training may be helpful. When elders have pessimistic expectations within the treatment relationship, instead of countering with statements of optimism, their pessimism should be acknowledged. For example, instead of saying, "You don't sound hopeful that I'll be able to improve this situation but I will do my best to work this out successfully," the practitioner may instead say, "Perhaps it is best that we start out uncertain and doubtful that things will improve right away. We may not make any headway with your son for a while."

When clients have negative or anxious thoughts, Cormier and Cormier (1985) suggest providing support and exploring the elder's fantasies, expectations, and fears in detail. The elder may have inaccurate beliefs such as, "If people find out I'm being beaten by my son, they'll wonder what I did to deserve this." Also, to combat the elder's fear of failure, the practitioner may want to give him tasks that are easily handled before suggesting a larger task that may be overwhelming and discouraging to the elder. Last, the practitioner is advised to place little emphasis on her role in any changes the client has made and to focus on the client's contributions instead. "Take a low profile, speak softly, and carry a tiny stick" (Cormier & Cormier, 1985).

Courtesy

Being courteous also helps to improve the elder's willingness to work with the practitioner. For example, the client should be alerted to the practitioner's impending absences and other disappointments. The client may take a while to trust the practitioner and begin to count on the regular contacts. To avoid the client's feelings of rejection and lowered self-esteem, the practitioner should inform the client at the beginning of the relationship whether the contact will be short-term or time-limited, and whether she is a student practitioner and will be on vacation between quarters or is a practitioner who anticipates absences from her agency work.

Trust

It may be necessary to build a relationship of trust with an elder abuse victim before confronting him with the reality of the abuse. The practitioner should carefully consider how the confrontation should be done or if it should be done. It may be possible to resolve the situation without a flat-out confrontation. Many older adults are uncomfortable with direct confrontations but may be willing to work with the practitioner to eliminate the abuse. This may also be true of the caregiver. If the client is treated against his will or has had promises broken, he may experience ambivalence and an inability to trust the next practitioner. If the current practitioner experiences difficulty establishing a relationship with the client, it may be helpful to explore the client's past experiences with other practitioners. The client may reveal that he fears being victimized by the practitioner again, fears being misunderstood, having his rights stripped from him, or being let down as in the past. Unfulfilled promises may be more harmful than no promises. Acknowledging that the counseling relationship is a process during which the client slowly learns to trust the practitioner, it is necessary that each client be assigned to one practitioner on whom he can rely and with whose style he can become familiar. The main practitioner can serve as the case manager, directing the comings and goings of other practitioners and orchestrating collaborative activities among agencies.

Privacy

The practitioner should counsel the client in privacy. In the assessment phase, emphasis was placed on maintaining privacy to promote disclosure of painful and sensitive information. Having entered the intervention phase, the practitioner must continue to interview the client in private settings. Later on, as treatment progresses and the client believes the practitioner sincerely wants to help the abuser too, joint sessions will be possible. Family treatment is further described in Chapter 9.

Acceptance

The practitioner should allow for the client's need to talk and desire to be in charge of his own situation. The client may take months or even two to three years to finally end the abusive relationship. During that period he may need a friendly visitor to simply talk about his doubts, anxieties, frustrations, and ambivalence. He may ask for active intervention later, when he feels it is the "right" time, and that "right" time may not jibe with the practitioner's time frame.

The expression and management of the client's feelings can lead to tension discharge, a goal in itself in short-term treatment. Without judgment, the practitioner can validate the clients' conflicting feelings. For example, she can say, "I believe you when you say you love your son," or, "You don't like having your son threaten you but you don't want him to be arrested either." Later, the elder may say, "Well, even love may not be worth all of these beatings" (Elliot, 1983). If the practitioner attempts to interpret rather then merely paraphrase the client's statements, she should be cautioned to make these interpretations in a tentative, nonthreatening manner, and not in a way that is beyond the elder's grasp (Golan, 1978).

Intervention Options

The intervention options that are available for the elder abuse and neglect client are diverse. The practitioner can provide reality testing, assist with restructuring the elder's environment, utilize the educational and prevention models to develop client foresight, provide concrete assistance and services, as well as intervene indirectly. These options are detailed in this section.

Reality Testing

The practitioner can be a direct influence on the elder by providing information and advice which will combat excessive fantasies, magical thinking, regressive behavior, and other maladaptive coping patterns such as somatization and withdrawal from reality (Golan, 1978). An elder may attempt to dismiss the practitioner's offers of help, claiming he is capable of handling his own affairs. He may in fact be pseudo-independent and require assistance. For example, if the client claims that he can do his own monthly budget, the practitioner can ask him to sit down and do a budget with her. Or if the elder says he is capable of doing his own grocery shopping, the practitioner can ask the client what he has been eating and to show her what foods the elder has available in his refrigerator and cupboards. The client should be allowed to arrive at his own conclusion that perhaps a little bit of help may be useful.

Some elder abuse and neglect clients may maladaptively generalize their feelings after being victimized, and as a result may require reality testing. For instance, an elder whose trusted friend expropriated $8,000 from his savings account began to verbalize a general mistrust of everyone. He began to jeopardize his social supports as he kept meaningful people at a distance, saying people were interested only in his money, and that no one should be trusted anymore. In her multiple contacts with him, the practitioner repeatedly reminded him, "That's how your friend was; not everyone is like him." She also helped him restore his faith in others by accompanying him to the bank and introducing him to the bank manager, who agreed to monitor the transactions of the elder's account. In many instances, rather than rely on client self-determination, it is appropriate to advocate a particular course of action or to give an opinion about a maladaptive resolution to the elder's problem (Golan, 1979; Rapoport, 1970). The client who believes that the relative's abusive or neglectful behavior will cease through faith and hope will need to be reminded that wishing away a problem will not work and that perhaps he should consider other specific options.

Some elders blame themselves for creating the abusive or neglectful situation. Statements such as, "If I weren't such a burden he wouldn't be so angry," or, "Everyone would be better off if I were dead," can alert the practitioner to remind the client that he is not responsible for the abuser's behavior. For example, the practitioner may react with, "Spilling a glass of water does not justify a slap. In any circumstances, it is wrong to be hurt like that." The elder must be encouraged to express his feelings to others to prevent self-blame. Eventually he may come to the conclusion on his own that there was nothing he could have done to prevent the abusive episode (Golan, 1978).

Development of Foresight

A major goal in short-term treatment is to prepare the elder for the possibility of future incidents of abuse and neglect. This "rehearsal for reality" (Rapoport, 1970) includes anticipatory guidance and role rehearsal. As the client integrates new behavior, he must also anticipate the related reactions of others who may not appreciate his newfound strength.

The practitioner can assist the client with anticipating scenarios that can result in more abuse and neglect by focusing on the previous incident. The elder is asked to recall the conflict situation or problems that led to the call for help, focusing on precipitating stressors. Then the practitioner and elder can discuss new behaviors and plans which can be activated if a similar incident occurs. In one protective services agency, a potential client is asked to develop a future plan of escape from the batterer as a condition for receiving agency services. This requirement shows the client that the practitioner takes the abuse seriously and so must he. It also helps the client to think beyond his current helpless feelings and to think about what solutions are possible. This anticipatory process can serve to restore the elder's emotional equilibrium.

Educational Therapy

Teaching the client about new methods for dealing with abuse and neglect is extremely effective in short-term treatment. The practitioner can model appropriate behavior which the elder may adopt. She can also provide extensive information regarding the client's social and legal rights, and intercede with medical and legal authorities to explain complex procedures. Modeling and teaching are effective during the "teachable moment" when the client is vulnerable and open to new information (Rapoport, 1970).

The client can benefit from empowerment training that will help him acquire or strengthen a positive, powerful self-image. The client's training may include taking assertiveness training classes to learn to say no to unreasonable demands, and to stand his ground in times of adversity. For example:

> In one state with a large rural population, it was common for alcoholic sons to threaten their mothers with physical violence if they did not hand over their Social Security checks. The mothers, accustomed to sharing whatever they had, readily handed the checks over and then had no funds to purchase food for themselves. Community workers taught the mothers assertiveness, after which they felt less intimidated by their sons. They were then able to refuse to give the adult sons the checks which they themselves needed for the basic necessities of life.

Training also may include taking self-defense classes to overcome fear. Participants are taught to fend off an attacker and recognize situations in which they are vulnerable (Kenoyer & Bateman, 1982). These classes are offered in many senior centers or government-subsidized apartment houses for the elderly. Also offered in these settings are classes sponsored by local law enforcement agencies on how to secure one's residence. The client can also be taught not to take the same route from his residence to the grocery store or bank while he is carrying cash and other valuables. Perpetrators may observe his patterns and then assault him. Handbags should be worn inside the client's coat. In the home, cash and other valuables should be kept out of sight of visitors and family members. When possible, the elderly client should be educated about direct bank deposits of his Social Security or railroad retirement checks.

The client may also be instructed on techniques of self-care to reduce dependency on the caregiver. For example, the practitioner may introduce aids that make the client less dependent such as a reacher or dressing stick, commode chair, simplified clothing, and special eating utensils. Devices such as medication boxes enable the elder to take medications correctly and may also keep him from being a burden on the caregiver.

The practitioner should also educate the elder that battering is usually recurrent and escalates, and that action may be necessary to protect himself. While the client may resist any interventions, the practitioner can take an educational approach and inform the client about what is known so far about the cycle of violence. The practitioner should inform the client that battering can escalate in severity and frequency if no changes are made, and that it is understandable why he may choose not to leave the abusive relationship, especially in the calm, loving respite phase when the batterer is remorseful, attentive, and loving, and swears that he will never be abusive again (Walker, 1979). The client may experience the abuser's recurrent episodes of violent behavior followed by the respite phase before he realizes he is supporting a chronic condition by remaining in it. Educating the client and then being available when the client makes the final decision to seek active intervention may be all that the practitioner can do for the moment.

Environmental Therapy

In short-term treatment, one of the practitioner's roles is to determine the client's capacity to understand and utilize community resources. The offering and delivery of concrete services are proofs of the practitioner's sincerity to assist the client. The practitioner may counteract past disappointments and help build a trusting relationship by delivering services when she says she will. If possible, the practitioner should act first on problems that are perceived by the elder and/or caregiver. The general rule of thumb is to provide services while maintaining the client in the least restrictive environment. The Continuum of Care scale (Figure 8-1) lists environmental options by degrees of restriction, beginning with the least restrictive environment at the bottom.

Services such as meals on wheels, chore services, and home nursing care may enable the client to remain in his own familiar surroundings. For example, rather than relocating a failing client who is unable to prepare meals or pay his own bills, the practitioner can refer him to a home-delivered meal program and the local service agency that dispatches volunteers to assist with paying bills on a monthly basis. Promises of services should not be made without knowledge of the client's income and assets since qualifying for these services is based on income. The pertinent data obtained earlier in the assessment phase will now be useful. Only after all possible in-home services fail to maintain the client's freedom and safety in his own home should consideration be made to place him elsewhere.

Unfortunately, in some cases a client may require a move from his familiar environment. The main reason for such a move is the client's need for 24-hour care that cannot be provided in the home by himself or others. The client's emotional and physical safety is seriously jeopardized by remaining

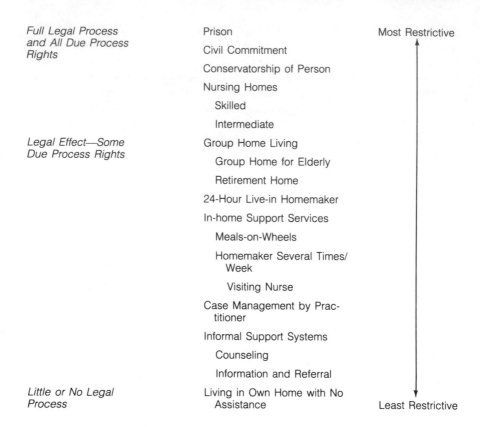

*Full Legal Process
and All Due Process
Rights*

Prison

Civil Commitment

Conservatorship of Person

Nursing Homes

   Skilled

   Intermediate

*Legal Effect—Some
Due Process Rights*

Group Home Living

   Group Home for Elderly

   Retirement Home

24-Hour Live-in Homemaker

In-home Support Services

   Meals-on-Wheels

   Homemaker Several Times/
   Week

   Visiting Nurse

Case Management by Prac-
titioner

Informal Support Systems

   Counseling

   Information and Referral

*Little or No Legal
Process*

Living in Own Home with No
   Assistance

Most Restrictive

Least Restrictive

FIGURE 8-1 Continuum of care. (Modified from Consortium for Elder Abuse Prevention, *Protocols,* Mount Zion Hospital and Medical Center, San Francisco, 1983.)

in the home. The chapter on legal intervention will discuss measures to keep the abuser away from the home, but sometimes even legal interventions will not rectify the situation and the client must relocate. Relocation, especially to a more confining environment that results in the loss of privacy and familiar things, should be a plan of last resort. Some housing alternatives, depending on the client's activities of daily living abilities, are share-a-home, adult family home, boarding home, retirement home, and nursing home. The elderly client may be afraid to admit to being a victim of abuse and neglect because he envisions being sent to a nursing home against his will. The abuser may have intimidated him by saying, "If you tell them I hit you and took your money, they'll send you to a nursing home where you'll rot and die." Remembering this, the practitioner must examine all housing alternatives listed on the Continuum of Care Scale. If a nursing home is deemed the most appropriate choice, the nursing home staff should be made aware of the client's victimization, because it is not uncommon for the abuser to go to the nursing home to remove the client because he needs the client's monthly pension check. If not watched, he may threaten the client with harm, force him to sign checks and property over to him, and hasten his death by suffocating him, or turning off his oxygen supply. The decision flow chart (Figure 8-2) by O'Malley et al. (1983) may help the practitioner determine what type of services can be offered.

Preventive Counseling

The practitioner can encourage the client to make reasonable requests before confrontations. This will help to reduce the client's anger and guilt (Schmidt, 1980). A client may feel that he is a burden to the caregiver and

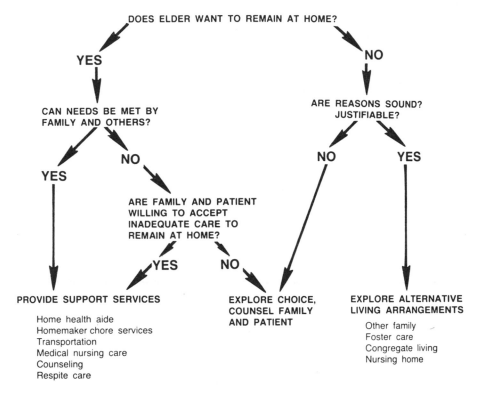

FIGURE 8-2 Decision flow chart for abuse or neglect of elderly person dependent on others for care. (Reprinted, by permission of the authors and the publisher, from O'Malley et al., Identifying and preventing family mediated abuse and neglect of elderly persons. *Annals of Internal Medicine,* 1983, *98*(6), 998–1005. Copyright 1983, American College of Physicians.)

not deserving of asking for any changes in his situation. For example, the client may want the caregiver to drive him to a local restaurant where his friends meet regularly for coffee but may not have the nerve to speak up. The practitioner can rehearse with the client how to bring up the matter and be present when he makes the request.

Activity With Collaterals

Interpersonal and institutional resources can assist the client in developing a pattern of seeking and using help. Natural and created groups can provide comfort, support, and need satisfaction from these relationships. Some elders benefit from a change of residence, or their environment can be made safer when friends, neighbors, and practitioners from different agencies and within the same agency develop a mutual plan of action that is carried out by all.

The client can feel more secure when he knows his community will provide aid when necessary. Increased monitoring from outside of the home can come from daily telephone reassurance checks such as "dial-a-care," from being part of a neighborhood block watch program that is sponsored by a law enforcement agency, or by filling out a postal alert card, whereby the mail carrier will contact a local agency if the client fails to pick up his mail for a specified number of days. "Neighbor helping neighbor" programs or "gatekeeper" programs are a cost-effective way of assisting the elderly client. In some cities, utility meter readers, home fuel deliverers, and other groups have been trained to look for signs of foul play or neglect and to report their findings to a designated agency.

With the elder's permission the practitioner can also call or visit people who come in contact with the elder and ask them what they think they can do to assist the elder. Some neighbors may choose to not get involved at all. Others may offer to "drop by," wash and set the elder's hair, and call the practitioner when there is a cause of concern. If the client belongs to a social group, its members may take turns transporting him to group activities. Many times neighbors who live alone exchange house keys and may be willing to check on each other's well-being. Professionals in the community may help as well, as when an outpatient clinic social worker collaborates with the elder's protective services worker to arrange medical intervention when it is needed. Furthermore, the practitioner may help the client enroll in an adult day-care center that provides a hot-meal program and transportation services to and from the center. The staff of the center can be alerted to monitor for signs and symptoms of abuse and neglect and to talk to the client about his concerns. Or they may alert the referring practitioner to follow up on concerns of their own, choosing not to take a chance of alienating the client by confronting him with the abuse.

Satisfactory resolution of financial exploitation incidents have necessitated collaborative activities by practitioners and financial institution personnel. In general, financial institutions are aware of exploitation attempts on the vulnerable elderly and attempt to monitor their regular customers' banking activities. Training has been conducted in some banks to make tellers aware of all possible fraud schemes. The practitioner covering a certain geographical area may want to drop in at local financial institutions and introduce herself to the branch managers. Later, when a specific problem arises with a mutual client, the bank staff may respond quickly. Having met the practitioner, the bank staff will know where to turn and call for assistance.

Bank personnel welcome calls from workers who suspect that an elder's account is being exploited. The bank staff will look at signatures closely and may choose to withhold funds. They may put an alert on the account. The alert may appear on the computer screen at the time a transaction is attempted, and/or the alert may be circulated by written communication between branches. Unfortunately, only the elder's "home" bank has the immediate alert; it is not possible to do a statewide alert all at once. If a client's funds are being withdrawn by a joint tenant of the account, the client or the client's substitute must close the account as soon as possible to avoid further depletion of funds. Once a signature is on an account, it is not removable. A new account will be opened in the client's name so that he will have access to his funds. If someone attempts to withdraw funds by forging a client's signature or changing the amount on a check, the client is notified by the bank as soon as possible. The client then fills out a fraud form, "Affidavit of Forgery," if the amount involved is $350.00 or more. It is up to the client to fill out the form. If the client chooses not to fill it out, the bank will not pursue the matter further.

Indirect Intervention

Short-term indirect interventions sometimes consist of documentation, reporting, and referral to another profession or agency for follow up. Documentation and treatment of elder abuse are done indirectly and directly and may take place in the home, the emergency room, and outpatient clinic, or a hospital inpatient floor. The in-home physical or occupational therapist, upon noticing suspicious signs of abuse, may refer the client to an agency nurse or social worker to study the problem, and they may work together to document symptoms of abuse and develop an interdisciplinary treatment plan. On the inpatient service, indirect interventions are also used where the abuse is documented and the assessment protocol is administered, but often no further action can be taken, primarily because the victim resists any changes in the situation. The client's refusal of help can be frustrating to the staff. However, a small amount of comfort can be obtained in the realization that abuse and neglect are clearly documented in the chart and that other staff who treat the client on the next admission or visit to the emergency room will be alerted to the problem and offer services again.

The practitioner should become familiar with her state's elder abuse mandatory reporting laws. In most states, practitioners including nurses, psychologists, social workers, pharmacists, and physicians are required to report suspicious cases of elder abuse and neglect. The agency mandated to accept all reports and to investigate them is usually the state's social and health services agency staffed by protective service workers. Once a report is made, the protective services worker will conduct an investigation and offer appropriate services to the client and/or caregiver. If the referring practitioner chooses to remain involved with the client and to work with the protective services worker, that should be known at the time the report is made. Protective service workers often appreciate the support and resources provided by other agency practitioners.

Having described treatment of the elder, the next section describes short-term treatment of the abuser.

TREATMENT OF THE ABUSIVE CAREGIVER

Several types of approaches are used with the abuser: a therapeutic plan, an educational plan, resource linkage, and monitoring for crisis.

Therapeutic Plan

This approach involves repeated home or office visits to evaluate the caregiver's functional capabilities, clarify role expectations, reduce conflict, and assist families in communication and decision making. This section provides specific counseling techniques that can be used with the caregiver.

Management of Practitioner's Feelings

The practitioner's first difficulty is in the management of her feelings toward the abusive caregiver. Angry feelings are easily aroused when the practitioner remembers the abusive incident and has feelings of revenge and of wanting to make the abuser "pay" for his actions. As child abuse experts remind all involved that "a hurt parent is a hurt child"; an analogy that can be made here is, "a hurt caregiver is a hurt elder" and treatment must be offered to the caregiver as well (Steele & Pollock, 1968). The abusive caregiver who is overwhelmed with the tasks involved in taking care of an elder may enter the counseling relationship feeling that he will be attacked and as a result be defensive. He may be yearning for love and affection and want to be acknowledged as someone who tried his best under the circumstances. The practitioner is advised to ask the caregiver questions carefully and share similar situations in order to universalize the caregiver's situation. The caregiver's ability to identify with the practitioner is a good sign that he feels understood (Steele & Pollock, 1968). Attention must be paid to the caregiver as a person. The time spent with him must not be used to ask about the elderly client. The focus during short-term treatment is on the caregiver and his issues, not the elderly client. It is wise to develop a relationship with him and to cultivate a genuine liking for him. Simple things can help create a relationship between a caregiver and a practitioner. For example, the practitioner may tell the caregiver that she likes a picture on the caregiver's wall or something he is wearing. Talking about those items will help to develop the relationship on a genuine basis and the caregiver will feel more accepted. Sometimes even talking about the weather will put both practitioner and caregiver at ease. In turn, the abuser will probably be more cooperative with a suggested treatment plan. The practitioner must pay attention to positive traits of the abuser, and not just his shortcomings. Focusing solely on negative traits can keep the practitioner from remaining focused on the main goal of treatment—to stop the abuse and neglect.

Social isolation and having no one to talk to may contribute to decreased self-esteem and increased frustration. The practitioner's task is to help the abusive caregiver develop skills to engage in social activities. The task begins with the practitioner providing regular contacts, visiting the caregiver regularly or requesting that a volunteer visit him regularly for the purpose of support and having a friendly visitor to share the day. Periodic phone calls to inquire about the caregiver's progress may help. Once the caregiver feels accepted and comfortable with the practitioner as a friendly visitor, he may feel comfortable enough to consider increasing his contacts to include others in the community.

Acknowledgment of the Relationship's History

The practitioner can acknowledge to the caregiver that she is aware that his situation has been a difficult one for many years, that the elder has a history of being difficult to please, or that the elder has at times been unduly nasty toward the caregiver. While this acknowledgment does not condone the abusive or neglectful behavior, it will help the caregiver feel that he is being treated fairly and that the practitioner is not "taking sides." The practitioner may discover that the abusive caregiver has been victimized at some point in his past, either as a child abuse victim, as a victim of economic recession by being laid off from a job, or as a victim of a mugging. Exploring how he feels or has felt as a victim may help him to understand his victim's feelings and to develop empathy. The abuser and victim may share similar feelings such as fear, hopelessness, self-blame, and anger. A caregiver who must tolerate an elderly client's abuse may have ambivalent feelings yet still perform caregiver tasks out of love, duty, or a strong sense of responsibility. The practitioner can promote a more positive relationship by acknowledging the caregiver's ambivalence and accepting his negativity and pointing out that in spite of the negative feelings and past hurts, he is doing his best. For example, the practitioner may say, "Sometimes your father treats you like a slave and doesn't express gratitude, but you still visit him every day and try to help out. I can see why you sometimes feel like abandoning him." She can also suggest that the task be distributed among other family members and agency personnel.

Provision of Reality Testing and Structure

Sometimes the caregiver's past difficulties with the elderly client began when the caregiver was a child and the elderly client was then the powerful authority in control. With the tables turned, with the elder declining in function and in need of support and assistance, the caregiver may still be living in the past and have unrealistic expectations that the elderly client is still capable of managing his own affairs and telling the caregiver what he wants in the way of help. The role of the practitioner is to emphasize that "now" is not "then," that the client has aged (Schmidt, 1980). This attempt to improve reality testing may have to be repeated in ensuing counseling sessions. A useful tool is to show the caregiver results of the client's mental status and functional assessments that indicate mental and/or physical impairments.

If there is a possibility of abuse and neglect, it is best for the practitioner to be frank and honest, raising her concern to the caregiver, and in a manner that says help is available to correct the situation. A caregiver may acknowledge being abusive or neglectful, but may not take responsibility for his behavior and instead blame the victim or external factors, i.e., "I was so drunk I didn't realize what I was doing"; or, "Those pills changed me into a different person; I'm usually not that way"; or, "She called me a nasty name so I had to teach her a lesson." The practitioner can refuse to support the externalization of blame, pointing out that while alcohol and drugs may have disinhibitive and cognitive effects on some people and contribute to inappropriate behavior, other people are not abusive when under the influence of alcohol or drugs. Still others continue to be abusive when they are sober or free of drugs. Battering may coexist with alcohol and drug use, but the two do not share a cause-and-effect relationship.

Collaborative data from others may be used to combat minimization and denial of abuse and/or neglect. The abusive caregiver must be aware that while he may not perceive himself as abusive or neglectful, others do.

Collateral contacts, especially with persons who have known both the elderly client and the caregiver, are valuable for obtaining information that can be presented to the caregiver. One caregiver may continue to deny his abusive or neglectful behavior in spite of the information, but another may realize that he has been "caught" and cannot get away with the abusive or neglectful behavior any longer (Ganley, 1981).

Emphasizing self-control is another method the practitioner may use to assist the caregiver with changing his behavior. It is possible to encourage the abusive caregiver to spend his energies on learning to control his own behavior rather than focusing on the victim's behavior and trying to control him. It is necessary to remind the caregiver that his abusive behavior is not caused by the victim; rather his behavior is a result of learned and observed experiences and it is possible for him to change. The abusive caregiver must also be reminded that while external stressors such as unemployment and racism cannot always be controlled, his response to these stressors can be controlled, and acceptable methods of expressing them can be learned. When the abusive caregiver stops blaming others for his problems, he gives up feeling that only others' actions can make him happy as well. He can learn that as he takes responsibility for his behaviors, he can learn to be in control of them. His happiness or unhappiness will be a result of what he does or does not do for himself (Ganley, 1981). An attempt to stop the caregiver's abusive behavior can be made by focusing on clear expectations for behaving, usually with a time frame attached to them. For example, the practitioner can provide structure to the relationship by presenting verbal and/or written instructions to the caregiver in the following manner:

1. Effective immediately, you will make a conscious effort to stop assaultive behavior.
2. By February 25, you will return the items that you removed from your mother's home. You understand that failure to do so will result in a formal report to the authorities.
3. By March 1, you will identify someone to call and to talk to when you are feeling frustrated.
4. By May 1, you will use alternate behaviors to striking out. Alternative behaviors are: (a) count to 20 before responding to other person, (b) walk around the block once, (c) write a sentence beginning with "I feel _____ (frustrated, angry, upset) because _____ or _____."

Problem Resolution

Anticipatory counseling may be utilized to prevent family confrontations. The practitioner can sit down with the caregiver and discuss items to be negotiated (i.e., leaving the elderly client in the care of a companion so the caregiver can have a free day) long before the situation arises. Discussion of touchy issues when both the elder and caregiver have the time and energy to discuss them will help to avoid verbal and emotional confrontations that may further alienate each other. Sometimes the caregiver may assume that the elderly client is incapable of engaging in decision-making activities regarding his care, especially if the elderly client suffers some degree of cognitive impairment. The practitioner can help to relieve the caregiver's guilt and frustration by holding joint family conferences and treating the elderly client as if he is cognizant of the counseling activities and capable of participating in problem solving, i.e., deciding how often the caregiver should have "days off" and deciding at what point the client will require 24-hour care in a facility. While the impaired client may not comprehend everything that is discussed, he may have moments of lucidity and make a few contributions (Schmidt, 1980). Most likely he will have more of a commitment to a solution if he is included in the problem-solving process.

Educational Plan

An educational approach to problem resolution is often the least threatening counseling technique. Whenever possible, the practitioner can inform the caregiver of assistance for which he may qualify. He may qualify for services such as respite care, volunteer visitor programs, and cash grants for caring for the elder. A caregiver may be reluctant to accept outside help, thinking that he must do everything by himself. Several sessions may be required to convince him that it is acceptable to have help.

A practitioner has heard an ill-informed caregiver make such statements as, "Oh, he can walk if he wants; he's just faking it to get attention. To teach him a lesson I just ignore his cries for help." To diminish unrealistic expectations of the elder, the practitioner can take an educational approach to teach the caregiver what he can and cannot expect from the elderly client. The caregiver can also be told of groups he can join to learn about subjects such as the psychological aspects of aging, chronic illnesses, sensory deprivation and communication, and utilization of community resources. The caregiver can also be helped with literature written in lay terms which describes ways of taking care of a dementia patient in the home, home safety lists, and the do's and don'ts of drug use (Hooyman & Lustbader, 1985).

As the caregiver conducts himself in an appropriate manner and fulfills his role as caregiver and family member, praise and support must be given whenever possible. The practitioner can give suggestions and guidelines on what are appropriate caregiver tasks, such as laying out clothes for the elderly client who is unable to get to his closet and select clothing to be worn, or preparing a main meal on a daily basis.

While it is still not known how spouse battering is similar to elder abuse, it can be assumed that the elderly client can be in increased danger if he chooses to remain in an abusive setting in which the abusive caregiver does not make an effort to change his behavior. The caregiver must be taught that what is known so far shows that physical abuse can escalate in severity and frequency, and that there are three phases of battering: (1) tension-building phase, in which the victim attempts to cope with minor battering incidents; (2) explosion or acute battering phase, in which there is a lack of predictability and control; and (3) the calm, loving respite phase, in which the abuser is remorseful and obtains absolution by being kind and generous (Walker, 1979). There is no guarantee that the abuse will stop after the third phase unless the caregiver attempts to change his behavior. Sometimes the only emotion that an abusive person has felt acceptable to express is anger. He reacts with anger no matter what happens and no matter how else he may be feeling. Where other people may react with embarrassment if the elderly client yells at them in public, or be worried if the elderly client is two hours late coming home from an outing with others, a caregiver may express his embarrassment and anxiety by yelling at the elderly person. He may never have learned to express the whole range of emotions such as hurt, disappointment, joy, shame, and worry. The practitioner can be helpful by interpreting some of these angry outbursts (Ganley, 1981; Sonkin & Durphy, 1982). For example, she may say, "If my mother had been that late coming home, I would have been worried sick"; or, "I always get embarrassed if someone yells at me in public, especially when I'm trying to be helpful and I feel that I don't deserve such rudeness."

Resource Linkage

Resource linkage may occur as part of the educational plan, but also can be implemented as a separate component. Locating respite care for the caregiver or day care for the elder in order to give family members a rest, obtaining cash grants for the caregiver when possible, and identifying appropriate community resources are ways to relieve the burdens of caregiving on family members.

Monitoring for Crisis

The practitioner should discuss with the caregiver resources that are available when the caregiver feels abusive and needs support. Crisis clinics exist in almost every city and are available 24-hours a day. Some are connected with inpatient psychiatric units of general hospitals. The practitioner's agency may have a 24-hour hot line, or the practitioner may give the caregiver phone numbers of people available for crises. These numbers and the plan of action for crises should be rehearsed early in the counseling process.

The abusive caregiver may be very threatened by the prospect of being on his own should the elderly client choose to ask him to leave his residence. He may not receive free room and board any longer. The client may choose to vacate the residence and leave the caregiver with the responsibilities of paying his own rent and supporting himself. The caregiver may not have the capacity to fend for himself and may contemplate suicide. Taking a nonthreatening, educational approach, the practitioner can discuss this with the caregiver and agree on intervention strategies if a crisis occurs (Ganley, 1981).

To summarize, working with the caregiver may in the long run be an effective use of the practitioner's time. In reality the majority of elder abuse and neglect victims will most likely choose to continue living with the abuser. Extremely pathological caregivers who are unwilling or unable to change their behavior probably constitute a small percentage of caregivers. It is possible for the practitioner to work with the abusive caregiver if the focus of the counseling is on stopping the abusive behavior. The practitioner's main task is to hold the abusive caregiver accountable for his behavior. She can teach the caregiver that his abusive behaviors are not caused by the client, and that inappropriate behaviors are learned, can be unlearned, and can be replaced by more acceptable behaviors. By providing support and acceptance and at the same time defining clear behavioral expectations, the caregiver may become more comfortable in fulfilling appropriate roles. The abuse or neglect may then cease.

TERMINATION

In short-term treatment, termination is often initiated and discussed in the first interview. The client, either the elder or the abuser, may negotiate with the practitioner the numbers of contacts and formulate criteria for ending treatment. Termination may occur when clients *begin* to find solutions to their problems (Rapoport, 1970). The practitioner may have difficulty "letting go" and be tempted to maintain contact for a period beyond the predetermined time. She may justify the prolonged treatment period by saying the client is still "shaky." The focus of short-term treatment is not to promote dependency but to maximize the client's functioning and growth potential. For all people, not only those who are identified as clients, there are periods of adaptive and maladaptive functioning. Clients may be ambivalent toward help or not want immediate assistance. They may take a while to decide to focus on solutions. For example, a client may change his mind about pressing charges against a caregiver who has just stolen several thousand dollars. If the practitioner can anticipate that ambivalence will be a common occurrence, she may be more realistic about treatment outcomes and not blame herself if the client rejects what seems to be a sensible treatment plan.

In some cases, the practitioner should allow herself time away from clients. She feels as if she is banging her head against the wall when a certain client taxes her patience, repeatedly changes his mind about receiving help, or shows no progress in mastering his environment after multiple home visits. The practitioner may want a breather and should feel free to say to the client, "It's time for me to take a break from this situation. I feel that for the moment I've done all I can to assist you. I'm going to attend to some other matters for a few weeks and return to see you next month. Let's make an appointment to meet in one month and I will call you in two weeks to say hello." While the practitioner may be tempted to terminate the relationship permanently, distancing herself from the situation may refresh her and enable her to examine the difficult situation with greater objectivity; new solutions or ideas may emerge from this break.

The practitioner should not have a sense of guilt and failure if the elder and/or the abuser refuses help or seem to make no progress within several treatment sessions. With an "open door policy," the elder or the abuser may return for help. Rapoport (1970) states:

> . . . we expect that a problem solved should stay solved for all times. Reapplication for service should be viewed positively. Experience has shown that clients who return after a brief period of help need even briefer help the second time. They may use a second period of help to consolidate previous gains. In other instances, the need for help the second time may be unrelated entirely to the first situation, and should be dealt with in accordance with current need. (p. 303)

COMMON OVERSIGHTS

Even an experienced practitioner occasionally misjudges a situation. She should not castigate herself for these lapses. The following situations illustrate typical errors and omissions and they may help the practitioner to be alert to similar situations in her practice.

1. A practitioner was called by the management of a facility to investigate a case of possible neglect. One of their patients was being cared for by private duty nurses who refused to let the staff of the facility examine the patient. When they were finally able to examine the patient by forcing the issue, they found that the elderly woman was covered with 13 pressure sores. Some of the sores were extremely wide and deep, exposing bone. Others were covered with black material. Facility staff

took photographs of the pressure sores and showed them to the investigator. The practitioner did not go and look at the pressure sores herself, which she later realized was an error of omission. If she had been called to testify on the situation, she would not have qualified as an eyewitness to the client's condition. She also felt that had she personally assessed the client, she would have gained more energy to work on the case and advocate more rigorously for the elderly woman.

2. In another instance a practitioner mistakenly interviewed the caregiver before the client. The client became suspicious of the practitioner's motivations, feeling that since the practitioner had interviewed the caregiver first, he would take sides with the caregiver and not believe her explanation of the home situation. When the client was interviewed after the caregiver, she asked the practitioner why he interviewed the caregiver first. The patient had been trying to alert the staff that she was being abused by the caregiver.

3. One practitioner made the mistake of not watching a caregiver actually leave the premises as asked. The practitioner had asked the caregiver to wait her turn to be interviewed and to walk around the block. He assumed that she went out of the house; however, as he began interviewing the client, the caregiver returned and was able to eavesdrop on the entire interview.

4. In another instance a practitioner interviewed a caregiver first and believed the caregiver's explanations for the condition of the elder without verifying the information from third-party contacts. She closed the case and provided no assistance to the elder who was, after all, her client.

5. A practitioner looked for a family member in a tavern in order to interview him. The practitioner rationalized that in order to keep other family members from overhearing the interview with this particular individual, he would interview him in the tavern he frequented. When he was able to catch up with the family member, that person felt insulted that the practitioner would find him in a tavern. He said that the practitioner must consider him a heavy drinker who had nothing better to do than to sit in a tavern all day long. As a result he refused to cooperate with the practitioner, calling him a "meddlesome social worker." Looking back, the practitioner felt that he should have accorded the family member the courtesy of being sent an official letter requesting an appointment. If he had not responded to the letter, the practitioner would have been more justified in looking for him in his usual hangout.

6. In one instance a practitioner allowed a caregiver to set up an interview with the elderly client without her knowledge. As a result, the client expressed surprise that the interview was scheduled and refused to cooperate with the practitioner.

7. A practitioner was hasty in removing a client from her home and assumed that he would be able to obtain short-term housing for her, either in the community or at a hospital. He was unsuccessful in placing his client immediately and realized that he should not have removed the client from her home without adequately planning and obtaining confirmation that housing was available.

8. In another situation the practitioner failed to interview the alleged abuser due to time constraints and because the proof seemed fairly substantial that he had perpetrated an act of enormous financial abuse upon the client. One year later he called the practitioner and threatened a lawsuit saying, "There must be some way I can get at you; you never talked to me and I never had a chance to tell my side of the story; I want to sue you. How can I go about it?" The practitioner realized that he should have interviewed the abuser and that if he had, he most likely would not have been subjected to the threats.

The practitioner should not permit herself to become immobilized by errors of omission and commission. Acting in good faith, using commonly known techniques, and following agency policy will usually suffice. When errors are made it is best to note them, to realize what corrective measures are necessary, and to correct the situation to the extent possible.

SUMMARY

Short-term treatment may last from three to six months. Elders and abusers may progress from denying the abuse or neglect and refusing help, to feeling ambivalent toward each other and/or toward the practitioner, to finally accepting services in the form of a concrete service or by receiving counseling to explore alternate methods for handling abusive situations. Some clients and abusers may never directly admit that abuse and neglect have taken place. Several interventions may be chosen from the diverse list of options that have been described in order to individualize a client's treatment. While it is not possible to always expect that the client or abuser will exhibit permanent behavior changes within this short period of time, some positive outcomes can be expected. Mainly through educational counseling and reality orientation, the abused elder can develop foresight and learn what he can do to protect himself and to develop a sense of autonomy. With the abuser, the practitioner can make him more accountable for his behaviors. In a few sessions, she can provide support, reality testing, and structure as well as teach the abuser more appropriate ways of expressing himself. When time permits, collaborative intervention methods can also be developed by the practitioner. The next chapter describes long-term treatment methods.

9   Intervention Phase: Long-Term Treatment

This chapter will focus on the long-term treatment of abused and neglected elders, their abusers, and their families. While many cases will be resolved during an immediate crisis or with short-term treatment, other cases will have to be followed for two years or longer. It may be that agencies identifying themselves primarily as delivering protective services will engage in more crisis and short-term treatment while nonprofit agencies which have fewer time and budget constraints will be better able to offer long-term services.

Long-term treatment is characterized by several variables. The relationship between client and practitioner is more involved and may be marked by transference and countertransference between the two parties. Transference refers to the unique, highly emotional attitude the elder develops toward the practitioner which represents a repetition of the elder's fantasy wishes concerning people from the past—now, however, projected onto the practitioner (Arlow, 1979). Thus an elder may relate to the practitioner as if he is a child to be advised or a magical figure who can cure everything that is wrong. Countertransference refers to the feelings that are engendered in the practitioner in relation to the elder. These feelings are related to the practitioner's unresolved childhood fantasies and may interfere with his relationship to the elder (Arlow, 1979).

Intrapsychic issues such as long-standing family conflicts may be handled in long-term treatment, although in-depth probing and confrontation should be done only by those who are trained specifically to do so. In long-term treatment, unlike crisis and short-term treatment, the emphasis is on perceptions and feelings which emerge over a period of time. When individuals and families have a long-standing history of abusive behavior, long-term treatment will tend to be more effective than crisis intervention or short-term treatment. The slower pace may be more appropriate for some families. Also, it may take a longer period of time to find the proper mix of services. Finally, some abusive situations simply do not resolve unless long-term treatment is employed.

Various treatment modalities will be presented in this chapter. Individual counseling for both victim and abuser will be discussed, and group work for both will be explored. A four-phase approach to counseling will be suggested which can be used for victims, abusers, and families. Issues of termination and follow-up, phases sometimes forgotten by practitioners, will be highlighted following the family treatment section and will apply to elders and abusers as well as families.

In order to reduce the incidence of elder abuse and neglect, the practitioner must focus on overall program planning as well as individual cases. For that reason, long-term environmental therapy issues are included at the end of the chapter.

COUNSELING OLDER ADULTS

Traditionally, long-term counseling or psychotherapy has not been available to older people. The elderly have not been viewed as proper "candidates" for treatment for a variety of reasons despite the fact that the later stages of life involve more losses, crises, and real-life changes than any other period of life: loss of spouse and friends, bodily changes, chronic illnesses, coming to terms with the way one has lived one's life, and the fact of impending death. All types of depression as well as other mental disorders rise markedly with old age (Burnside, 1976; Butler & Lewis, 1982).

Butler and Lewis (1982) believe that professionals in the field of mental health suffer from ageism and negative countertransference when it comes to old people and this is why there is so little long-term treatment of the aged. Ageism prevents therapists from seeing old people as unique human beings separate from their chronological age and protects therapists from having to deal with their own aging and eventual death. Negative countertransference takes place when "mental health personnel find themselves perceiving and reacting to older persons in ways that are inappropriate and reminiscent of previous patterns of relating to parents, siblings, and other key childhood figures" (Butler & Lewis, 1982, p. 176). Thus practitioners working with the elderly have to deal with leftover feelings from the past as well as all the negative attitudes toward older adults that are prevalent in our society and enmeshed in institutions and individual psyches.

Therapists and indeed all practitioners have negative attitudes toward the aged by virtue of having been raised in this society. In addition to the aged stimulating feelings about one's own old age and death, working with them can arouse conflicts about one's relationship with parental figures. A therapist (or any other practitioner) may feel he has nothing useful to offer an older person because he believes that older people are incapable of learning or examining their behavior, or because he thinks that all old people suffer from untreatable organic brain disease or "senility." Additionally, a practitioner may fear that the older person will die during the treatment process (Butler & Lewis, 1982).

Very little definitive research has been done with respect to the benefits of psychotherapy or counseling in the elderly. However, in the absence of compelling scientific evidence proving otherwise, clinicians have concluded from their own experiences that it is possible to do significant work with older people both individually and in groups (Butler & Lewis, 1982; Foster & Foster, 1983; Goldfarb & Sheps, 1978; Herr & Weakland, 1979).

Because of the paucity of mental health practitioners interested in working with the elderly, practitioners will need to consult their peers on a regular basis and in fact may wish to establish regular peer supervision meetings. One practitioner who did this found it most helpful; the group was able to alert her when she failed to observe that a physically impaired spouse was in fact becoming the target of increased abuse by his wife. The practitioner then realized that she had become inured to the situation and had begun to tolerate the physical abuse to the point of not even recognizing when it had escalated. She confronted the situation and, because it was becoming dangerous for the physically and mentally impaired man to remain in the home with his wife (who despite counseling did not appear to be able to control her actions), helped the wife place her husband in a reputable nursing home.

Individual Counseling

Themes

Common themes in individual counseling sessions include expressions of guilt and atonement, expressions of grief and the need for restitution, issues of identity and autonomy, need for assertion, and desire for a new start and second chance (Butler & Lewis, 1982). All of these themes are pertinent to working with abused and neglected elders. There are also themes that are specific to abusive situations. Stopping the abuse is the major theme, but other issues are also important such as reducing the amount of isolation and dependency the elder feels, assisting the elder to work through self-blame as well as blaming others, helping the elder learn to set limits on the abuser if the two are to continue to live together, and if the abuser is an adult child, helping the elder learn to see the child as an adult with rights and responsibilities.

Practitioners in the human services field frequently underestimate and undervalue their contributions to the mental health of older people. One should never assume that something helpful is not being accomplished by listening to an abused or neglected elder. It is impossible to calculate the enormous relief an elder experiences upon being able to openly discuss the abuse and neglect to which she has been subjected (London, 1985). By simply listening, a practitioner performs an invaluable service.

Phases of Counseling

Counseling is an active process through which a person in distress, by interacting with an interested counselor, becomes aware of the source of her distress and learns to take steps to resolve it. Carkhuff and Anthony (1979) outline four steps in the counseling process. While the model is based on learning theory, it can be adapted to other psychological theories and applied to working with elders, abusers, and families.

Phase one, the Involving Phase refers to the time during which the practitioner and client(s) first meet and determine the arrangements under which the counseling will proceed. The second phase is the Exploration Phase during which time the client(s) and practitioner explore the problem, describe it, and detail attempted solutions that have failed. The third phase is the Understanding Phase. During that phase, both practitioner and client(s) come to comprehend the role the client(s) play(s) in perpetuating the problem. In the fourth phase, termed the Action Phase, the practitioner and client(s) focus on various courses of action, test them out, and evaluate them.

Issues of termination and follow-up are also important and will be dealt with in the section following the family treatment section. Phases will vary in length with each elder because of the uniqueness of each person, but basically, each counseling relationship with abused or neglected elders has these phases.

Involving Phase During this phase the elder and the practitioner are getting to know each other and are negotiating the circumstances under which counseling sessions can best proceed. Burnside (1976) believes that a contract should be arranged between the elder and the practitioner. The contract should be printed in large letters on white paper and a copy made for each person; it can then be reviewed periodically, even at each meeting if the elder has trouble grasping the details due to anxiety or memory problems. Burnside cautions that meeting times be carefully selected so that they fit the elder's daily schedule. Flexible scheduling may help. When an abused elder told her practitioner at the first session that she could not possibly come in for weekly sessions, the practitioner reminded her that she had important issues to talk over and suggested that she consult her schedule when she got home and consider coming in every two weeks. The elder left the session, returned home and called the practitioner within one hour to tell him that she would be able to come in every two weeks. Practitioners should remember that abused elders will quite likely have high anxiety during the first few meetings due to breaking the taboo of not talking about the abuse and neglect. In those cases, the elder may wish to work on other issues first such as grief, loneliness, or family conflicts, or the need for concrete services. For example:

> One practitioner was immediately aware that there was financial abuse as well as physical and psychological neglect in a situation but chose to build up a relationship carefully over a period of two months with the elderly woman by giving concrete services such as providing transportation to a doctor, bringing in a homemaker, listening to her, and in general, "doing a lot of hand-holding." When the practitioner sensed that the "time was right" and that she had the trust of the elderly woman, she gently confronted her by saying to her, "You know, something's not right here. You don't know where your money is going or how much you should have, your son-in-law and grandchildren won't take you to the doctor or get your medication for you, and you are very lonely and get left alone all the time. You've also told me that they grab you and yell at you and have threatened to kick you out of the house by saying, "I have the power to put you on the streets." At that point, the elder was able to admit that there were problems and could proceed to explore them.

The practitioner can periodically "test the waters" to see whether the elder is ready to confront the abuse. In some instances the abuse and neglect will be stopped without directly confronting it; the elder gains enough self-esteem and ego-strength through the counseling sessions to confront her situation and resolve it.

In the involving phase, the practitioner must take many factors into account. Sensory loss may be present in the form of vision and hearing impairments as well as decreased taste sensation. The senses of touch and smell seem to decline the least (Herr, 1976). Therefore, the practitioner needs to consider how noisy the physical environment is, how comfortable both persons are, and how the chairs are arranged.

The frequent presence of chronic illnesses in the aged means that energy levels and attention span must be considered; sessions may have to be shortened at times or initially contracted to be for 30 minutes with the option of continuing to a full 50 minutes if the elder feels energetic on that particular day.

Simple acts of human warmth like hugging, holding hands, supplying longed-for candy, or even a hamburger can enhance the counseling relationship by helping the elder experience trust and caring. However, a caveat must be added here. There are those who would interpret touch as sexual invitation. There are others who abhor being touched and who cannot tolerate being indulged. This is particularly true with elders who have paranoiac thinking. With those clients, the practitioner must be careful not to get too emotionally or physically close because it is frightening to the elder. A firm, warm detached manner serves those clients better and so does scrupulous honesty (Butler & Lewis, 1982).

Exploration Phase In this phase, the counselor helps the elder expand on the concerns that have been stated in the involving phase. If the abuse and neglect have been openly stated as issues, it may be helpful to ask the elder to describe the abusive incident(s) in detail. If the elder can remember what triggered the abuse incident, it may be possible to devise ways of avoiding abuse in the future. It is important to keep in mind that the elder may not be able to fully answer questions relating to the abusive incident(s), because of denial or anxiety or memory problems which may result in the incident(s) being fogged over. It is also important to remember that victims of abuse tend to minimize the severity and history of abuse (Sonkin et al., 1985). A specific technique for eliciting the abuse incident is to ask the elder to imagine what happened, to reconstruct the incident to the best of her ability, and then to describe it, but this time with an ending that she prefers. This will give the practitioner some clues as to the elder's functioning as well as the fantasies she may be entertaining. Possibly, the desired outcome can be made a reality during the action phase of the counseling sessions. In that sense, the cycle of violence can be broken.

An advantage of doing counseling with older people is that they have a history of having had to face difficulties, even survival issues, and there is the distinct possibility that they have evolved coping strategies of which they are not consciously aware. The counselor can draw on this healthy part of the elder's psyche by asking about past crises and how she lived through them. Basch (1980) emphasizes that counselors must learn to build on strengths and not continually search for pathology.

Understanding Phase The third stage of helping the elder stop abuse occurs when the counselor assists the elder in understanding the situation and grasping what her role is as well as figuring out what the elder would like to have happen to make her life better. In the following case example, one counselor helped an abused elder understand her situation more clearly.

A 78-year-old widow and her 49-year-old daughter in a rural area began living together after the death of the daughter's husband who had been physically abusive to her. Shortly after his death, she had a psychotic break, and following a hospitalization, went home to live with her mother; she literally had no place else to go. The two women lived together peaceably until a mass murderer in a nearby community began striking randomly. The daughter became extremely fearful and taped the windows and doors shut. When her mother tried to get out, she repeatedly struck her and threw furniture at her. The mother feared for her life and called the police when the daughter was in the other room. The police came but did not exercise their powers to involuntarily hospitalize the daughter. The daughter retaped the door the police had used to enter, and when the mother tried to get outside again, she physically abused her. Again the mother called the police and again no action was taken to address the abuse. The day after the second incident, the mother called her private physician, seeking treatment for her injuries.

After the physician referred the matter to a family service agency, the counselor assigned to the case contacted the mother, and having ascertained that the daughter had somehow reestablished treatment with a psychiatrist, invited the mother to come in "to talk things over." This the mother did, although she initially expressed ambivalence and at one point during the first session tried to terminate the counseling before it had begun. She consented to continue only after the counselor made adjustments in the counseling schedule and reminded her that things were indeed very troubled between her daughter and herself right now and that it would help to talk it over with someone outside the family. Thus, a crisis situation evolved into a long-term treatment situation.

After establishing some groundwork and setting a contract with the mother, the counselor proceeded to learn more about the situation by asking questions of the mother. The story that emerged was of a family composed of mother, father, and daughter. The daughter was "treated like a little princess" and always indulged. The family was somewhat isolated and tended to focus on the daughter. Unlike most children, the daughter never went through a period of rebellion. She continued to be the "good" daughter and behave as she was told.

During the understanding phase of the counseling sessions, the counselor focused on several issues and interpreted them to the mother. Because the mother was alternating between blaming her daughter and blaming herself for the incidents, the counselor pointed out and sought to undermine the blaming by helping the mother focus on getting the abuse stopped and developing a more mature relationship between mother and daughter. He dealt with self-blame by reminding the mother that rebellion is a normal part of growing up and that her daughter had somehow not gone through this phase, something that was hardly the mother's fault. The counselor put the blame outside of both mother and daughter, enabling the mother to move on to other matters such as learning to relate to her daughter in an adult way instead of treating her as a teenager and telling her how to dress and act. He also empowered the mother by reminding her that the house belonged to her and that she had the right to make the house rules. He then proceeded to help the mother make the rules and rehearse how to communicate them to the daughter. The abuse stopped. The daughter remained in therapy and the two professionals conferred with the consent of their respective patients. There is the possibility that joint therapy with mother and daughter will take place in the future and, in essence, give both women a second chance.

Some elderly accept abuse because they feel they deserve it, either because they have absorbed the negative stereotypes about aging or because they abused the adult child who now abuses them. One elder said, "I know how my son feels and why he hits me. I felt the same way when he was a child. You know, frustrated. I used to hit him. Probably more than I needed to. He used to make me so mad. I know he loves me though." The counselor asked the mother to explore how she felt about hitting her child when she was a young mother and asked her to describe the scenario. He then helped her to identify the particular frustrations and conflicts that she was feeling as a young mother and helped her explore why it was that she resorted to hitting her child "more than I needed to." He helped her accept her feelings of guilt by acknowledging that perhaps she was more aggressive than she needed to be but that the past could not be changed. The next step was to help her forgive herself and move on to confronting the situation in which she now found herself. The counselor universalized the situation by stating categorically that it is wrong to hit old people and that not all old people are hit by those they love. He pointed out that her other children and grand-children loved her and they did not hit her. Therefore, hitting need not be a part of love. He also reminded the mother that all adults are responsible for their behavior unless they are declared incompetent and told her that her son was capable of learning not to hit her. He asked the mother to con-sider how long she must atone for her past actions by being abused in the present.

Action Phase During this phase, the elder and the counselor focus on various courses of action, test them out, and evaluate them. The action might include an act of assertion with the abuser, seeking treatment for a long-standing medical problem, asking for services from various agencies, finding another living arrangement, or initiating legal processes such as locating a suitable person to serve as conservator or filing a restraining order that would effectively get the abuser out of the house.

The period of introducing services or trying on new behaviors should be viewed by the elder and the counselor as a trial period, a time when options are still open and changes can be made. Snafus should be taken in good cheer and appropriate adjustments made to accommodate the "wrong" de-cisions. Even when services delivery is going smoothly, it is rare that all problems will be solved immediately, and there may even be flare-ups of the abuse from time to time, especially psychological abuse, which seems to persist even if physical, financial, and violation of rights abuse are stopped.

Group Therapy

Group work is common with older adults. In all likelihood, elder abuse and neglect exist in this population, but it is not addressed directly. It is unlikely that a group could be formed expressly for the purpose of focusing on elder abuse and neglect mainly due to the powerful forces of denial, shame, fear of exposure, and guilt. There are also problems of mobility and transportation, especially among the old-old, the most likely victims of abuse and neglect.

It is important to focus on the various groups to which elders belong because domestic abuse and neglect could become an issue at any time and group leaders need to know how it can arise, which type of group will precipitate it, and what can be done about it. Any member of any group could be an abused or neglected elder or could have been abused in earlier years as a child or a spouse. There is also the possibility that a group member has a history of abusing other family members or is currently abusive or neglectful.

The groups in which elders participate can be categorized loosely as those which are formed in institutional settings such as nursing homes and those that take place in community settings such as doctors' offices and mental health clinics (Burnside, 1976; Butler & Lewis, 1982; Ebersole, 1976; Foster & Foster, 1983). The population of the two groups is different; those who are institutionalized tend to be a decade older than those living in the community, and while both groups have members with mild dementia, the community group has, as would be expected, less severe dementia. The institutionalized elders are usually widowed, while elders living in the community frequently live with a spouse (Berger & Berger, 1973; Ebersole, 1976; Foster & Foster, 1983).

Institutional Groups

Several different types of groups have been developed, mainly by nurses, to assist institutionalized elders, many of whom have become regressed and isolated (Butler & Lewis, 1982; Ebersole, 1976). The groups include reality orientation, sensory retraining groups, resocialization or remotivation groups, reminiscence groups, and music groups.

The aim of reality orientation groups is to help the cognitively impaired person make the most of her intellectual assets by bringing her into contact with reality and helping her stay in touch with it. The techniques deal directly with the classic symptoms of disorientation, confusion, and memory deficits through intensive mental and memory stimulation (Burnside, 1970; Ebersole, 1976; Ireland, 1972; Taulbee & Folsom, 1966). Blackboards, large clocks, newspapers, calendars, and visual aids are used, and basic information is given repetitiously in an effort to help the elder become aware of time, place, and person.

Sensory retraining groups were devised for severely regressed elders who have deficits in motor and cognitive abilities and difficulty distinguishing sensory stimuli. The elder has multiple sensory losses which result in withdrawal from normal interpersonal communication. The training is geared toward engaging the older adult by using a variety of stimuli, such as music, various foods, and objects (Foster & Foster, 1983). Some of the earliest and most lasting impressions involve the tactile and olfactory senses. It is surprising what the smell and feel of home-baked bread can stimulate in a group of elderly people (Burnside, 1971).

In remotivation groups there is a structured group program with those who can function on a verbal cognitive level. Group discussion centers on activities in everyday life and on such subjects as current events, plant care, grooming, and dining in public. The aim is to resocialize the person and arouse her interests in the environment around her by helping her learn or relearn a wide variety of informational knowledge.

Reminiscence groups are helpful because there is evidence that thinking about the past occurs throughout the life span and that it accelerates with age. Many elders are reluctant to reminisce due to various fears including the fear of being thought crazy, concern that it is a sign of dementia, or worry that thinking about the past will activate painful memories which will be difficult to handle. Some irrationally fear that by reminiscing they will become lost in the past and be unable to function in the present. Other elders question the value of reminiscing or are reluctant to indulge in it because there are no peers with whom to discuss the past. However, several researchers and clinicians have called attention to the psychological gains that can be made by using reminiscence in both group and individual work (Butler, 1963; Butler & Lewis, 1973, 1982; Ebersole, 1975, 1976, 1978; Ebersole & Hess, 1981; Fry, 1983; Huber & Miller, 1984; Ostrovski, 1977). One researcher (Romaniuk, 1983) found that reminiscence can be used as an assessment tool with organically impaired people who are suspicious or resistant to being interviewed.

Hennessey (1976) believes that music therapy can be an important adjunct to remotivation group therapy. It can also be used in reminiscence therapy. The music should be chosen carefully, and elders should be solicited as to their desires. Music can recreate the past and evoke emotion. It can also be used to evoke current feelings and thoughts.

Fry (1983) noted that reminiscence training or therapy offers certain advantages over other methods of increasing psychological well-being. It is a cognitive activity that originates from the client's memory, which means that no special setting conditions, client characteristics, or methodological tools are needed. The client's personality is immaterial except that it is more effective if the client is verbal and cooperative. Fry also noted that this type of mental activity may not be appropriate for those with psychotic ideation.

Community Groups

Community groups generally focus on higher functioning elders. However, many of the most common themes are the same as with those elders who are institutionalized: losses (family/friends), finances, dependency, aging, reminiscing, and hope versus despair. Community aged also express frequent concern about loneliness, losses of health and functioning, family intactness, quality of available services, power versus weakness, and passivity versus activity (Butler & Lewis, 1982; Foster & Foster, 1983). There are also life crises for the elderly just as for younger people; retirement, widowhood, impending death, chronic illness, change in living arrangements. It is at those points in life that group therapy may be especially useful (Butler & Lewis, 1982).

Traditional psychotherapeutic group therapy with the aged is similar to group therapy with other age-groups in that psychotherapeutic principles apply, i.e., use of confrontation and importance of expressing negative feelings (Butler & Lewis, 1982). They are especially helpful in treating depression.

Life Review Therapy In 1963, Butler proposed that reminiscence has particular meaning for the aged. He theorized that the aged use their reminiscences to engage in what he termed "life review." Life review appears to be a normal-health mental activity, an arena of rich historical material that many elders are ready and eager to explore. It might be the task of the group leader to unblock those who have faltered in their life review process for fear of their memories, for lack of validation of the importance of the memories, or simply because a listener and sorter is needed for some. In group therapy, members can bring to mind troubling parts of their own histories and enlist group support in achieving resolution. And, it is here, of course, that the potential for eliciting domestic abuse and neglect issues arises.

Group Therapy and Elder Abuse

Issues of domestic violence including elder abuse and neglect can arise in any one of the groups. They may emerge in direct statements, but more likely the references will be indirect via such statements as, "I was harder on my daughter than I needed to be," or, "My son doesn't treat me right." Although these seem like minor cues, it is important to realize that abusers and victims tend to deny and minimize abuse incidents (Sonkin et al., 1985). Therefore, these statements are cues to be explored either within the group context or individually.

The issue of domestic abuse and neglect may emerge if the leader(s) bring it up first, perhaps as part of mentioning several things that can be difficult in life. It could also emerge when current events are being discussed; there are frequently news stories about domestic violence in the newspaper or on television. Leaders may decide to do education around the subject by way of helping elders spot, prevent, and combat abuse and neglect. In those instances, permission can be given for elders to speak to the leader privately or within the group. Deprivational behaviors may be a tip-off that an elder has been abused and/or neglected. Those behaviors include clinging to the leader, expressions of desperation and panic, hypervigilance, and gobbling down refreshments that are offered as part of group meetings. The many indicators of abuse also apply to the group situation (see Chapter 3). Many clinicians have had the experience of reaching out to touch an elder, particularly an impaired elder, and had the person recoil and cower as if the practitioner was going to hit her.

In some instances, elders may take a leader aside and wish to speak privately about domestic violence problems. Conversely, there may be times when a leader will take the initiative and speak to an elder outside of the group, especially if the elder seems particularly upset about issues around domestic violence or has talked openly about abuse or actually comes to group with bruises that are inadequately explained (see Chapter 6 for assessment techniques). When approaching an elder about possible personal abuse, practitioners should be prepared for initial denial, even if it is obvious that abuse is taking place. However, if a door is left open in the form of an accepting statement, the elder may return for help. Such a statement could be, "Well I'm glad to hear that everything is all right in your life. But I want you to know that often older people are abused, just like children and wives are sometimes abused. And it doesn't mean that you have a bad family or that you have to leave your family or that anyone has to go to jail. So if that ever happens to you, I want you to know that you can come to me and I'll help you."

TREATING THE ABUSER

Themes

Some of the themes in working with abusers are the same as when working with elders: combating isolation, dealing with guilt and self-blame or other-blame, confronting dependency issues (although from a different perspective), denial and minimization of abuse and neglect, and learning to set limits. Other themes will be unique to the abuser: becoming financially independent of the elder, dealing with substance abuse, handling feelings that are both current and historical toward the elder, confronting the physical and/or mental failing of the elder and eventual death, separation and loss. Still other themes will be lack of privacy or time for recreation, health problems, fatigue, role stress, personalized feelings of failure, shame at feeling resentful or angry, personal goals that have been delayed or denied because of the pressures of caregiving, lack of rewards for being a caregiver, and absence of help from other family members or society in general.

Individual Counseling

Earlier in this chapter a model consisting of four phases for counseling elders was introduced. Although many of the themes will be different, this model can also be implemented when doing individual counseling with abusers.

Involving Phase

In the involving phase, the emphasis is on meeting the abuser and setting up a regular system for contact. In the following case example, the practitioner perceived that the alleged abuser was badly in need of treatment, and she left the first interview session with a counseling commitment from the alleged abuser.

> One practitioner made a home visit on a referral and found a male abuser who initially was resistant to seeing her. By the end of the visit, he had agreed to come to her office for regular counseling appointments. The man was a caregiver for his grandmother and financially dependent on her. The grandmother was sure that her grandson was getting a better deal than she was, even though he did all the housework and physically cared for her. He was an alcohol abuser who had recently joined Alcoholics Anonymous. The practitioner told the man that he was obviously doing a job for which he was getting little recognition and that he looked very stressed to her—which he did. She told him that she was concerned about him and offered him the time and place to talk over his problems. After some initial reluctance, he gratefully accepted her offer.

In this instance, the practitioner was firm in her approach and convinced the abuser that she had something to offer. She "hooked" him by appealing to his needs for recognition and his need to talk about the caregiving and the problems it was causing for him. Other abusers will behave differently, either by being very candid about the abuse or by denying or minimizing it in some way. A sympathetic approach will frequently be successful in helping an abuser decide to enter into a treatment relationship with a practitioner. It may be helpful to approach all abusers as stressed caregivers in the initial stages of abuser treatment.

Exploration Phase

In the exploration phase, the focus is on enabling the abuser to tell his "side of the story." Often, through ventilation, the intensity and emotionality of the situation are diffused. This is not to say that some caregivers do not have personality disorders. They do, and the key to understanding the difference lies in asking questions that relate to the past (Cutler, 1985).

Another value in hearing the abuser out is that, frequently, no real productive work can be done to resolve the abusive situation until the abuser has been fully heard and understood. The abuser may sabotage work done with the elder unless he feels the practitioner is paying serious attention to him too.

Feelings that are particularly important to explore and express are anger and ambivalence because it is just these feelings that the abusive caregiver may be repressing and ignoring. Also, expression of these feelings will serve to ameliorate guilt in the present and the future. There may be shame about these feelings. In a counseling context, the shame can be addressed.

Some caregivers are surprised when they do not feel affectionate toward the elder or when their affection is insufficient to provide emotional gratification. Guilt results even though the caregiving may be perfectly adequate. Jarrett (1985) suggests that caregivers be helped to realize that it is only recently that there has been a cultural imperative to feel affectionate about the person for whom one is caring. Previous generations have cared for their frail elders on the basis of felt obligation based on kinship systems. Those systems have been seen as exhibiting positive concern about the well-being of all relatives. When there is a need for help, one does what one can. Being a "good" daughter or son does not rely on feeling affection; it relies more on feeling and showing concern for the welfare of the parent/kin and giving what can be given to the limits of one's ability (Jarrett, 1985).

Practitioners who have an aversion to dealing with abusers can use the exploration phase to try to understand the frame of reference the abuser has and to see whether there is anything with which they can identify. However, some abusers will be unlikable no matter what the practitioner does. It is then that the importance of pride in a job well done comes to the fore. Liking a client and identifying with him may provide motivation for the practitioner to do good work, but it is not always necessary.

Understanding Phase

The third stage of counseling occurs when the counselor helps the abuser gain an understanding of the abuse and his role in it. It is during this phase that accountability issues arise. Many abusers project blame on the victim or on external circumstances. The counselor can help the abuser realize that he has a role in the abuse for which he is responsible, no matter how many provocations he feels he may be receiving from the victim or the outside world. Some abusers will continue to deny that they have a role but will change their behavior nonetheless. The following case example illustrates how a practitioner worked with alleged abusers who never admitted to the abuse.

An 82-year-old woman lived with her son and daughter-in-law, who were financially dependent on her. They were also dependent on her for housing. There was evidence that all three were abusers of alcohol and that a priest-friend of the mother's who visited frequently was also an alcoholic. Over a period of two years while a practitioner had been working with her, the elderly woman sustained three major fractures: two hip fractures and a broken arm. The practitioner suspected abuse but had no proof. Following the third frac-ture, the woman complained to hospital staff that her daughter-in-law had pushed her. The daughter-in-law and son maintained that the woman fell. The hospital social worker consulted a second practitioner, who was known to have handled several elder abuse cases. This practitioner visited the elderly woman and listened carefully as she described how awful her daughter-in-law was and decided that she should go and see this "terrible person." She made an appointment with the younger woman and her husband, and upon meeting them was startled to see a dejected man and a haggard, drawn woman who walked with her head down. The woman looked "beaten down," and the practitioner's heart went out to her. She determined by listening that the daughter-in-law was a stressed caregiver; she was doing all the housework, taking physical care of her mother-in-law, and even walking her mother-in-law's dog. She said that no one appreciated what she was doing and she felt that her mother-in-law was very demanding. The son expressed feelings of helplessness and hopelessness about his current life situation.

The practitioner "felt in my gut" that the alleged abusers were in need of treatment. She consulted with the family's first practitioner, who agreed. She then contacted her supervisor, who also agreed. Her own agency could not provide expert consultation for her, so she privately contracted with a clinical social worker who was experienced in couple's therapy and alcohol abuse.

Thereafter, the family's first practitioner and she met with the entire family and proposed that the son and daughter-in-law come for weekly visits to talk over their problems. The couple became very excited and kept all their couple therapy appointments. Individual therapy was initiated for all three as well, and family visits were interspersed with the couple and individual therapy.

Individual therapy for the son revolved around his feelings about himself and what he wanted out of life. An only child, he felt diffusely guilty about his mother and was conflicted as to his responsibilities. He felt inept both as a father and as a son. He also felt that he was in competition with the priest-friend for his mother's affections.

The daughter-in-law was encouraged to ventilate her rage and anger about all the work she was doing without any rewards. She was helped to learn that there were other ways she could deal with her anger and that she was functioning in a situation which most people would find difficult and draining. It was also emphasized that she was not a bad person for "complaining." She was helped to ease off on the amount of work she was doing and to let a newly hired housekeeper pick up the slack. She was also helped to examine the situation from her mother-in-law's perspective, which enabled her to become less defensive when the elderly woman made demands on her.

At the end of each meeting, the practitioner asked the individual, "What did you get out of this meeting?" The emphasis was on empowering the individuals and helping them to realize that they could be in control of their lives.

The son and daughter-in-law were also helped to become financially independent of the older woman. The son was eligible for disability benefits as well as housing. The couple made application for both as a result of the counseling. The treatment goal of stopping the abuse was reached, although the abuse was never confronted openly and neither was the alcoholism. Eventually, all three parties made the decision to stop living together. Nevertheless, the son and daughter-in-law decided to take the caregiver class that was offered by the agency in order to learn more about aging and the needs of the mother.

The foregoing case aptly illustrates the importance of working with abusers as well with victims. In many senses, abusers are frequently victims themselves. The case also demonstrates how the understanding phase of counseling can flow into the action phase.

Action Phase

This is the phase when practitioner and counselor alike begin to focus on remedies to the problems which by now have been clearly identified. Most likely, the first focus should be on what the abusive caregiver feels is the most problematic issue. There are many strategies that can be used in the active phase of long-term counseling. In addition to the concrete educational strategies detailed in the short-term treatment section (Chapter 8), the following suggestions will serve to guide the practitioner in long-term treatment.

Personal Goals The practitioner can draw on the personal dreams and hopes of the abusive caregiver and help him realize them, to whatever extent possible. For example, one caregiver felt purposeful and more relaxed when he was able to return to art classes after the practitioner helped him arrange for a neighbor to be with his demented wife while he was gone.

Getting Help Most abusive caregivers need help, and the practitioner is in a position to see that they get it. Caregivers may not confide their problems to other family members because they rightly sense indifference (Cutler, 1985; Headley, 1977). Some caregivers may not ask for the help of other family members because they have gained the elder's confidence and so are able to use the elder's money for their own uses. Also, a new will may have been made and the caregiver is loathe to expose the elder to other family members for fear that the elder will come under their influence and make out a new will.

For some, the use of in-home respite has met with success. In one model research project, elder abuse aides went into the homes of abusers and their victims on a regular schedule and provided companionship and support of various types (Wolf & Pillemer, 1984).

Positive Benefits of Caregiving Many caregivers derive positive benefits from being caregivers, but they do not value those benefits if they are not reinforced. Practitioners can elicit this information and thereby reinforce the positive factors. Some caregivers feel pride in fulfilling an obligation or in recognizing that they have the ability to cope with difficult situations (Sommers, 1985).

Caregiver Health Frequently, because caregivers themselves are older adults or under a great deal of stress, they develop health problems. Some of those problems are physical such as hypertension, ulcers, and other stress-related conditions. Other caregivers are badly in need of treatment for schizophrenia or substance abuse. In the action phase, the practitioner can arrange for treatment as appropriate.

Placement In the abusive family, the time may come when the caregiver cannot control himself and the physical and psychological abuse to the impaired elder is escalating. As one practitioner put it, "It's a judgment call. When the elder is frankly in danger and all other alternatives and options have failed, the abuser must be confronted with the reality of the need for placement." It may be necessary to call in reinforcements at this time such as an adult protective service worker or other family members or family doctors. Abusive caregivers are reluctant to place not only because they deny the abuse or think, "It's not that bad," but because they also may believe that they are still capable of doing the caregiving. Reluctance to place is frequently related to financial reasons.

Financial Independence Wolf et al. (1984) found a high correlation between physical elder abuse and financial dependence of the abuser on the victim. Therefore, one goal of long-term counseling would be to help the abuser become financially independent and, probably, establish a separate household. Employment counseling may be needed. Some abusers will be resistant to this and offer various rationalizations. Nevertheless, it is a worthy goal. Even if complete financial independence is not possible, the abuser may be able to establish a separate household so that he can have his own life, perhaps supported by a monthly check from the elder. In those cases of financial abuse where the abuser continues to appropriate the elder's income and bank accounts, legal action of some type may be necessary to ensure that the elder's money is used for her.

Accountability Throughout the long-term treatment of the abuser, the counselor must have the means of monitoring the care of the elder if the two are still living together. Practitioners should be open regarding the monitoring activities, and abusers should clearly know that abuse incidents will be treated with the utmost seriousness. In cases where the elder is alert and able to communicate, the practitioner can ask the victim directly whether the abuse is continuing, decreasing, or changing in some tangible way. In cases where the elder is unable to express her concerns, external monitoring through homemakers and other practitioners may be needed.

Groups Treatment With Abusers

To date, there are no known groups for elder abusers. However, there are groups for men who batter women and there are groups for caregivers of elders. It is likely that if and when there are groups specifically for elder abusers, principles from each type of group will be integrated into program design. For that reason, the two types of groups are briefly described here. There is also the possibility that court-mandated treatment of elder abusers would be helpful in some instances, e.g., to get psychiatric treatment for a schizophrenic adult child or to ensure that an abuser continues to participate in a substance-abuse program. Most states have laws that relate to forms of physical and psychological violence, as well as damage to property. Judges use these laws to enforce court-mandated treatment for woman batterers, and they may well choose to apply them to elder abusers, particularly if there is a demand that they do so.

Group Treatment For Woman Batterers

In the past six years, specific treatment programs geared to helping men who are physically violent in their relationships with women have evolved around the country (Roberts, 1984; Sonkin et al., 1985). The programs are pioneering and represent the first attempts to directly address the feelings and attitudes that lead men to batter women. Groups for abusers with anger management problems can be useful to (1) help the abuser learn ways to express anger constructively, (2) learn new ways of communicating a wide range of feelings, and (3) help the abuser be accountable to his peers, often his most severe critics. Practitioners who decide to form groups for elder abusers may develop similar projects in similar fashion.

With woman battering, length of time in counseling is a factor because the longer a man is exposed to counseling, the more likely he is to learn new ways of behaving. Sonkin et al. (1985) believe a minimum of one year is needed and, in many cases, more than a year. Court-mandated treatment may be the only way to enforce long-term treatment because it can allow for the time that is necessary to make lasting changes.

Caregiver Groups

The evolution of groups to help caregivers of frail elders is a recent development and one that shows great promise (Clark & Rakowski, 1983; Crossman et al., 1981; Hayes, 1984a, 1984b; Schmidt & Keyes, 1985). Themes in caregiving groups include feelings of entrapment and isolation, change in familiar roles that accompany caregiving, a sense of disruption in life, difficulty in distinguishing between *caring* and *curing*, and a desire to resolve past feelings of guilt and inadequacy with regard to the relationship with the elder (Hayes, 1984a).

Issues of elder abuse and neglect may emerge in caregiver groups. Hayes (1984b) studied three support groups formed for the purpose of assisting caregivers. In those groups, the caregivers reported that sometimes physical, emotional, financial, or medical abuse occurred when the caregiver was frustrated in his attempts to develop a loving relationship with the impaired elder. Caregivers also reported that they emotionally mistreated an elder out of frustration, and that for some, it was linked with the feeling that they were not prepared to deal with the stress involved in assisting an impaired elder. Instances of abuse often occurred when unresolved childhood issues accompanied the stress of caregiving. Hayes noted that families often delay institutionalizing an elder against medical advice and that this can sometimes be termed medical abuse because the elder is not receiving proper care and supervision.

In one caregiver group, the caregiver/abuser/wife met with a support group for several months and talked about pushing her impaired elderly husband around from time to time. The group was understanding of the stress that led her to do that without giving sanction for it. Eventually, after the physical abuse escalated, the man was placed in a nursing home at the social worker's insistence. It was not until several months after the husband died that the woman was able to acknowledge fully why she could not constructively confront her actions. She told the social worker (who had helped her with the funeral arrangements) that, "If I had been able to admit that he was disabled, then I couldn't have stood it because I would have had to face his eventual death and I knew I couldn't stand that." She defended herself from this knowledge by continuing to think of her husband as normal and by physically abusing him as a way of trying to get him to fulfill his former roles.

The next section deals with family treatment.

FAMILY TREATMENT

Introduction

In some situations, the only way to proceed to resolve an abusive situation will be to engage the entire family in solving the problems which created the situation in the first place. Family treatment may be on an emergency basis, a short-term basis, or a long-term basis. Much depends on the skill of the practitioner/counselor and how fast the family can mobilize to solve the problem. Family treatment is included in this chapter because it is sometimes a parallel activity to long-term treatment of the victim and the abuser.

Whether to treat the elder abuse and neglect victim and abuser separately or as a family depends on several factors: the pathology of the abuser, the wishes of the client, and the severity of the situation. Success often depends on the attitude of the practitioner and the degree of comfort he feels in the presence of the family, which will include the abuser. There are times when it may not be appropriate to treat the family as a whole. It may not be the treatment of choice if there are ongoing threats to the elder by family members. Revelations that occur in the family treatment meeting may be cause for abuse to the elder after the meeting is over particularly if "family secrets" have been told.

Working with the Family

The process of working with a family begins when the practitioner first becomes involved and proceeds through several phases: exploring the problem, understanding the family system and solutions that have been tried as well as determining the goals of the family, and taking action to correct the difficulties (Carkhuff & Anthony, 1979; Herr & Weakland, 1979). Phases of termination and follow-up are important and will follow this section. Each family will proceed differently through the phases, although there are commonalities that will be observed by the practitioner.

Involving Phase

At the outset, it is important to realize that the presenting complaint of an individual may in fact be a cry for help from the family system. The elder who complains of abuse and neglect may be signaling to practitioners that here is a family in trouble. The practitioner can simply ask to meet with all family members to talk over the problems that seem to be coming up. With elder abuse and neglect cases, the focus might be a recent hospitalization or a call for help from the elder or another family member on a seemingly unrelated problem. Sometimes, families are reluctant to involve an elder in the treatment because they feel she can't participate meaningfully. They may feel that she is confused, or "too fierce to be faced, too impotent to be counted, or too vulnerable to be told" (Schmidt, 1980, p. 267). Practitioners can remind families that elder's confusion may fluctuate depending on the time of day and that even elders who are not totally oriented are aware of their own feelings and may be sensitive to the way they are treated (Schmidt, 1980). Involving elders reduces the chances of their being treated like objects.

Exploration Phase

In this phase, each member of the family has the opportunity to talk about his or her perspective of the "problem." The more explicit each person can be, the better the chances for solution because specific interventions can flow from specific problems. Problems that are named and categorized are frequently easier to solve (Herr & Weakland, 1979).

A useful part of the exploring phase is to ask family members what they have tried to do to solve the problem (Herr & Weakland, 1979). By learning the details of what has been tried, the counselor can get a good idea as to how the family copes and how they go about solving problems. Families can also be asked to identify strategies or actions they have taken that seemed to have a positive impact on the "problem."

Understanding Phase

In this phase, each family member can be asked to explore and accept responsibility for his or her role in the difficulties the family is experiencing. The practitioner must also take steps to understand the family, such as determining the extent of the family system, questioning where the counselor fits in the system, and trying to figure out the family rules. The counselor may become part of the family system and be seen by different members of the family in different ways. For instance, the elder may see him as the son she wanted her abusive daughter to be, the daughter may see the counselor as competition for her mother's affections, and the son-in-law may see the counselor as a younger brother. It is important for the counselor to recognize these issues so that he does not begin to act them out unconsciously.

Family rules are attitudes and values that are usually unconscious and dictate how family members should act with each other (Herr & Weakland, 1979). Examples of family rules are the following: "No one but Mother can express anger in this family." "Only Dad can make decisions regarding Mom's health." "We don't tell our business to outsiders." "It is all right to hit each other in our family."

There may be an identified patient in the family, someone other family members feel "needs help." Frequently, it is the elder who is the identified patient, but in fact, all family members are experiencing distress and are in need of assistance.

Another important question to be answered is "How is power exercised in the family?" Often some apparently powerless people are in fact in total control of the family even though they may feel helpless (London, 1983). It is particularly important that the counselor resist "rescuing" the elder who illegitimately plays the powerless victim and claims to be persecuted.

Still another issue for the practitioner to consider is whether this family is enmeshed or disengaged. Enmeshed families have very close connections, and it is difficult for family members to see each other as separate. Separation itself is seen as a threat. This is why some families have difficulty understanding that an elder member is ill or impaired. Enmeshed families have trouble distinguishing tasks that must be done when a crisis hits, and they frequently become confused and paralyzed. Disengaged families are distinguished by the relative absence of strong connections. Family ties may be weak or nonexistent. These families have trouble coming together to solve a crisis (London, 1983).

Action Phase

In the action phase, the family mobilizes to realize the goals that they may have voiced earlier, and the counselor uses the information he has gleaned about the family in earlier phases to suggest interventions that fit the family system. In the following case example, the treatment was firm, confrontational, and short-term.

An elderly man who lived in the same apartment house as his daughter fell and broke his hip. He was hospitalized, and when he was discharged, his daughter took him in to live with her. She started collecting his benefit checks by becoming his subpayee. She also moved her son into the father's apartment.

In time, the father recovered and began to resume his former life. He started seeing his woman friend again and told his daughter that he wanted to move back into his own apartment and that he wanted to handle his own money again. The daughter refused. The father complained to the manager of the building, who in turn contacted legal services for the elderly. An attorney came out to see the father and informed him of his legal rights. The father, who was cognitively clear and able to take care of himself, surmised that the reason his daughter did not want to restore power to him was because she did not approve of his woman friend and was afraid that he would give his money to the friend instead of to the family.

After the attorney's visit, the father again demanded that control of his funds be returned to him and that he be permitted to live in his apartment. Again, the daughter refused. The father telephoned the attorney, who again came out, but this time held a meeting with the entire family. She heard the daughter out carefully. By doing so, she determined that the daughter had no substantial basis for continuing to force her father to live with her and for collecting his benefit checks. She informed the daughter and the grandson of the elder's rights and told them that they were in violation of local rent control laws. She also told them that the elder had a right to return to his apartment and resume control of his finances and his social life and that if he was not permitted to do so, she would take legal measures to see that his rights were honored. Within a week, the daughter relented and the father was restored to his former position.

In the foregoing case example, the resolution was rapid and clear cut. Practitioner time was limited. Although there were several phone calls, there was only one visit to the father and one family session.

TERMINATION ISSUES IN
LONG-TERM TREATMENT

How the counseling relationship is terminated greatly influences the long-term outcome of the treatment (Herr & Weakland, 1979). Termination of a case of elder abuse and neglect when the abuse and/or neglect has been stopped is frequently problematic for counselors, both because they are concerned about the continuing safety of the elder, who is often frail, and because a relationship has been formed with both the elder, the abuser, and possibly other family members. There may even be a strong tendency on the part of the counselor to hang onto a case that has been successfully resolved simply because so many other cases are difficult and do not have clear-cut endings or successful resolutions.

Wolf and Pillemer (1984) note that theoretically once the treatment goals are met, the case should be closed. Practitioners may find it difficult to let go. In some situations, clients, whether they be elders, abusers, or families, may be more than ready to move on, but the practitioner becomes anxious and wonders, "Is she really ready? Will she be all right?" There are three reasons why practitioners find it difficult to let go (Herr & Weakland, 1979). First, there is an emotional attachment if the work has been done well;

termination means the end of that special attachment. Another stumbling block for the practitioner is that termination means that he is admitting that he has helped as much as he is capable of doing. And third, termination means that the practitioner is no longer indispensable in the client's life. It may be appropriate for the practitioner to check in either by telephone or via the services which are going into the home. Terminating the case may result in backsliding because the client's dependence on the relationship was what made cooperation with delivery of services possible. The client does not want to lose the relationship the practitioner has so carefully built up because, in many instances, it is the only one she has and she feels understood. Thoughtful practitioners realize this only too well and will help their clients form other relationships before initiating termination.

Elements of Termination

Terminating can be an art and, in order for it to be successful, should include three elements (Herr & Weakland, 1979). The client or family should be given the opportunity to take responsibility for their own solutions so that they can have a sense of accomplishment. This can empower them even though they may be reluctant to accept credit for what they have done to make their lives better. The counselor can point out all the things that they have done to make the counseling work successful, e.g., keep appointments, follow suggestions, and entertain new ideas. The next element in terminating is to anticipate what could go wrong in the future, even though the client may not wish to hear it. Frequently, the client or family has become accustomed to the abuse and neglect and feels "naked" when it stops. They may sabotage their progress consciously and unconsciously and bring on abuse again if possible future problems are not discussed. Herr and Weakland (1979) suggest that it can be almost fun and certainly creative for the counselor and the client or family to think of ways that they can undermine the progress that has been made.

The last element of termination involves being restrained about the future and letting the client or family know that they are not expected to live "happily ever after" with no real-life problems. Without this element of termination, they may feel that they are expected to live in the euphoric state they now feel after solving some of the problems. They may define themselves as failures if they have any future difficulties or if the abuse or neglect recurs.

Finally, the counselor may wish to leave the door open by telling the client or family that they may return or call if a problem recurs or even if they do not have problems. It can be helpful to tell a client that she can call to report successes or tell the counselor how well she is doing. The latter will reinforce the progress of the client, validate the counselor, and provide a positive experience for both. It can also alert the counselor to problems that may be developing in the client's life.

Follow-up Phase

Realistically speaking, some abused and neglected elders cannot remain in their homes without the continuing involvement of a practitioner. There may be a dearth of supportive services, particularly in rural areas, and the practitioner may be the only possible person to provide continuity and supervision for such things as getting the elder to the doctor and making sure that the chore worker comes in on a regular basis and knows what has to be done. Additionally, the practitioner may be the only confidant a pressured caregiver has. The follow-up phase may not be as intensive as the counseling phase, and the practitioner may not see the client or caregiver as frequently or may use the telephone to make contact and "check in." In some communities specific agencies are delegated to do follow-up and monitoring.

Standby

Some clients may not be able to utilize counseling sessions throughout all the phases and may need to move more slowly, contacting the practitioner sporadically to do specific parts of the phases. This may be particularly true for clients who are quite capable and alert but are having difficulty taking action. One legal service provider reported that she was contacted several times over a period of two years before one man had the courage to go ahead with a restraining order which would get his abusive son out of the house. This long-term relationship was difficult for the practitioner. The case had come to her as an emergency situation when the elderly man was badly beaten by his son, who was also taking his Social Security checks. The practitioner had been eager to move on the case and the man wanted "something to be done about the way my son treats me," but he could not accept the intervention of a restraining order for a period of two years. He was capable of understanding his situation and therefore no involuntary court action (guardianship or conservatorship) was appropriate. It was agonizing for the practitioner to have the man call periodically to check out all his options once again, to seek still more detailed information about the restraining order, and to test the practitioner to see whether she would still help him. The practitioner later said, "They didn't teach me that in law school." In retrospect, she had been on standby for two years. However, in doing so, she had supported the man's right to self-determination, a basic principle of applied gerontology (Quinn, 1985).

ENVIRONMENTAL THERAPY:
DEVELOPING PROGRAMS AND NETWORKS

Treatment of individual clients by a few practitioners specializing in elder abuse and neglect will not satisfy a community's need for greater participation by staff of all agencies involved with the elderly. The development of an elder abuse and neglect program can be divided into three phases, the agency assessment phase, the initiation phase, and the community networking phase.

Phase One: The Agency Assessment Phase

Before embarking on a successful agency assessment program, several assumptions must first be made:

1. Elder abuse and neglect exist in the agency's client population.
2. One person alone cannot detect and treat elder abuse and neglect.
3. Education and training of all staff in an agency treating the elderly is necessary.

Before a successful program can be launched, one or more practitioners in the agency must be aware that some of the clients currently being served are or will be victims of abuse and neglect and that these cases need to be detected and treatment must be provided.

In this phase, a commitment must be made by a department or unit (i.e., nursing, physical therapy, medicine, social work, psychiatry) to study the problem and to designate one practitioner as the agency's "elder abuse practitioner."

Given departmental sanction, the designated practitioner should feel free to begin an assessment of the staff's current knowledge of elder abuse and neglect. The practitioner may choose to develop his own questionnaire or assessment form. Results of the questionnaire that is administered may reveal that the staff in general is not familiar with the term "elder abuse" and has not detected many cases of elder abuse and neglect. Their findings may support the need for an agency-wide training program on the use of a uniform protocol.

Phase Two: The Initiation Phase

This phase consists of relationship development and the provision of direct services. The practitioner must initiate contacts with directors of other units in the agency in order to inform them that an elder abuse program is needed in the agency and that an elder abuse program is about to be initiated. If unit managers and staff of departments perceive the practitioner as being helpful or "taking a load off their backs" instead of being someone who creates more work for them, they will collaborate with the practitioner to treat the elder abuse victim.

The practitioner must request speaking or training time at meetings that are held regularly in the agency. For example, in a teaching hospital, medical grand rounds, social work grand rounds, nursing inservice education meetings, journal club meetings, emergency room orientation sessions, and student seminars are some of the gatherings at which the elder abuse program staff can present information on elder abuse and neglect and offer services. Care should be taken to develop strong relationships with agency managers or hospital medical chiefs and to show them how their employees may benefit from training. They may then ask their supervisees to cooperate with the practitioner by treating or referring cases. Unit managers may invite the practitioner to lecture on elder abuse once a month, for example, when a hospital emergency room's new rotation of medicine and surgery residents attend an orientation session. Even if only 20 minutes of the two-hour orientation session is allowed to lecture on elder abuse, these presentations may result in earlier, more frequent detection and documentation, which are necessary for successful intervention.

In medical settings, every patient who is suspected of being abused should be referred automatically to the practitioner by the attending physician for follow-up services. The elder abuse program staff can interview the patient on the inpatient floor if she has been admitted or call or send a letter to the patient in order to inquire about her general health and offer general follow-up services. Elder abuse need not be mentioned if the patient is contacted at home. General, nonthreatening inquiries can be made instead, giving the client an opportunity to accept or reject help.

Phase Three: The Community Networking Phase

This third phase consists of developing working relationships with practitioners from other agencies. The diagram in Figure 9-1 shows how many specialty agencies must work together to provide appropriate protective services to the client and/or the caregiver.

Special attention must be paid to finding key contacts in various agencies to assist the client. Nonprofit or volunteer payee/guardianship programs, protective services agencies, the city attorney or county prosecutor's offices, and legal services agencies are some of the legal entities that may agree to assist the practitioner. As these agencies provide additional services, their staff will learn about the practitioner and eventually begin to make referrals and request inservice education on elder abuse and neglect. Several com-

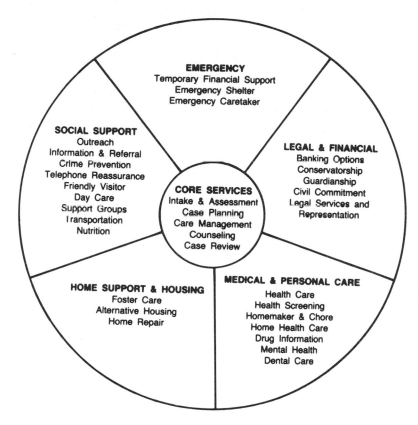

FIGURE 9-1 Range of services needed by protective client. (Reprinted, by permission, from *Improving protective services for older Americans, a national guide series.* University of Southern Maine, 1982.)

munities have developed elder abuse network teams that consist of representatives from legal, mental health, home health, hospital, senior information and assistance, case management, protective services, and law enforcement agencies. Meeting once or twice a month, these teams discuss cases that require multi-agency intervention. These teams also discuss cases that have been terminated in order to review lessons that were learned and to formulate improved intervention techniques for treating similar cases in the future. Meeting regularly creates an appreciation of each agency's capabilities as well as limitations, and decreases the chance of territoriality struggles and misunderstandings. Some agencies develop written agreements that list the manner in which one agency will assist the other. This simplifies the practitioner's efforts to obtain assistance and information on a given case. For example, protective services agencies have developed agreements with law enforcement agencies which stipulate that a law enforcement officer will respond in a timely manner to a practitioner's request for assistance at a client's home. The protective services agency reciprocates by agreeing to respond as soon as possible to a law enforcement officer's request for assistance in a difficult case that requires social services.

Last, development of a data-collection system is necessary whenever an elder abuse and neglect program is started in order to promote uniform reporting, to centralize services, to avoid duplication of services, to retrieve information quickly, to follow cases throughout the agency system for a designated period of time, to follow cases referred to other agencies, and to have data available for research activities.

SUMMARY

The interventions described in this chapter consist of individual, abuser, family, community, and agency responsiveness. The intervention phase can be considered a process during which the client and abuser may reveal a variety of conflicting feelings. They may progress from denying the abuse or neglect and refusing help, to feeling ambivalent toward each other and/or toward the practitioner, to finally accepting services in the form of a concrete service or by receiving counseling to explore alternate methods for handling abusive situations. Some clients and abusers may never directly admit that abuse and neglect have taken place. Several interventions may be chosen from the diverse list of options that have been described in order to individualize a client's treatment. When time permits, community education and training of colleagues are intervention methods that can also be utilized by the practitioner.

10 Legal Intervention

The practitioner involved in elder abuse and neglect cases will undoubtedly be involved with the legal system. This chapter discusses legal options to be utilized by the practitioner. The advantages and disadvantages of these legal interventions are outlined. Actual legal tools are located in Appendices F, G, and H. In addition, suggestions are given on how the practitioner can conduct himself in a court room, give court testimony, document findings, prepare for legal involvement, and be involved with the criminal justice system. Last, the strengths and limitations of mandatory reporting laws on elder abuse and neglect are discussed.

ACTING IN THE LEGAL MODE

Traditionally a service practitioner has had little to do with legal issues insofar as his client is concerned. In fact, he may have fear and trepidation of being involved in legal issues, as if they were beyond his ability to learn or to comprehend, or as if something terrible could happen to him. Furthermore, the prospect of being sued is always held over the practitioner's head, and while it is true that a suit could be brought, for anyone can try to sue anyone for anything, the likelihood of the practitioner being sued for work in the course of his prescribed duties is extremely remote. Yet the practitioner is often told that he must limit his activities because "you might be sued." This is not to say that the practitioner should act without discretion. Many people fear attorneys, and older people may see attorneys as having a great deal of power. If a practitioner feels comfortable with attorneys and legal issues, his clients will feel more at ease. The practitioner should be aware that he is potentially liable for acts of omission as well as commission. He may expose himself to liability if he fails to report acts of abuse and neglect, fails to report crimes, fails to treat the client according to agency guidelines, or fails to utilize the least restrictive alternative when treating the client. With regard to acts of commission, the practitioner is liable if he breaches confidentiality or fails to respect the client's right to due process. The latter may occur when the practitioner subjects the client to relocation or medical treatment against her will. In an emergency situation, the practitioner should consider calling either a law enforcement officer or a member of the fire department to transport the client instead of transporting the client in the practitioner's car. This would protect the practitioner from liability should an accident occur in his vehicle or if the client dies en route to a treatment facility.

Elder abuse clients need legal protection, and the practitioner needs to know what is available. He needs to be working in a "legal mode" at all times, because with elder abuse clients, there is always the possibility that the practitioner's report will be needed by a judge to validate the need for a conservatorship or guardianship, to keep an abusive relative from being appointed the conservator or guardian, or to provide the basis for requesting that a judge issue a protective order. The practitioner cannot do the work and forget about going to court, not if he wants to protect his clients and be involved in the "real" world. The practitioner should assume that he will be going to court with each elder abuse case, and it is likely that the abuser will have her own attorney, who may try to disprove what the practitioner has to say. There are ways of protecting, of documenting, of giving testimony, and of proceeding in a calm and rational manner. There are certain things that judges and attorneys look for. The practitioner might be surprised to learn that he is viewed as an expert, as the person who will have solid, workable recommendations, and who is knowledgeable about community resources, assessment, and client functioning—the knowledge and skills the practitioner already possesses. It may even be possible to develop a team approach to an elder abuse situation when working with an attorney and a judge. One judge has suggested that the practitioner attend court hearings, and learn to understand court proceedings in his community. This would enable the practitioner to observe the manner in which the various parties conduct themselves and to become familiar with legal terminology. Another judge has agreed to preside over mock court hearings to help a practitioner rehearse his testimony and to help him be as comfortable as possible in the actual proceedings.

In some ways, the practitioner may not have much choice about being involved in legal proceedings. Beginning in the late 1960s, many states, motivated by changes in the philosophy of treating elderly people in state hospitals and by the expectation that there would be funds forthcoming from the federal government to treat that population in the community, began discharging large numbers of frail and vulnerable elderly into unprepared communities. The increased numbers of needy older people were added to those frail elders already present in the community. One response to this increased numbers of at-risk elders has been the upsurge in adult protective services units, which will be discussed in the next chapter.

The practitioner can assist the client in obtaining legal counsel and may look to several subgroups in the legal profession for assistance. A private attorney who specializes in probate law may be most helpful when a guardianship or conservatorship is needed and in cases of complex financial exploitation. Government funded legal services agencies, especially those with senior citizen units, may be helpful in actually representing an elderly client and can suggest legal options in cases involving fraud, financial exploitation, abuse, and other domestic violence acts. Public defenders may sometimes become involved with victims of elder abuse and neglect. Some courts will pay a private attorney to represent a client who is unable to afford her own legal counsel.

LEGAL DEVICES

Least Restrictive Options

The philosophy of using the least restrictive option is a concept that is known to both the practitioner and the lawyer. It is generally accepted by those working in the field of protective services and by those in legal services that the client in need of assistance should not be intruded upon any more than is necessary in order to keep body and soul safely together. The client should be provided with the assistance which allows for maximum personal liberty and independent control of her life. It is a basic mental health principle that the more the client feels in control of her life, the more mentally healthy she will feel.

This concept applies to both the personal and the environmental care of the client as well as the handling of her material resources such as bank accounts, real estate, stocks, bonds, and jewelry. When considering which type of intervention to use, the least restrictive option should be the first choice. Ideally, the more restricting the option is, the more due process there is and the more opportunities the client has to object and state her preferences. Due process may not exist or it may be "on the books," but in fact, the elderly client may have no *real* way of protesting or having her views heard. Unless she is informed of her rights, she will not know what they are. For example, in California, there have been provisions for years which permit the client to object to the possibility of having a conservatorship placed over her. However, if she cannot read the citation (due to poor vision or illiteracy) that is delivered to her to give notice that proceedings are forthcoming, if she does not know her rights, such as the right to protest and to have an attorney, she does not effectively have due process rights even if they are written in the law. It was not until a revision in the law provided for a representative of the court to interview each of the proposed conservatees and to tell them about their legal rights that "due process" had any teeth in it.

In going over the various legal options that are listed in Figure 10-1, the practitioner will be able to see how each one of them can be abused: good, honest dealings are always dependent on the person who is handling the affairs of another, no matter how many legal protections are built in. Anyone in a position of trust is also in a position to be abusive. On the other hand, a legal device may be a means of preventing further abuse by placing more responsible and capable individuals in charge of the situation and moving out the abusers.

Legally speaking, the Continuum of Legal Options scale begins with the client being unable to write the checks due to a physical impairment, but

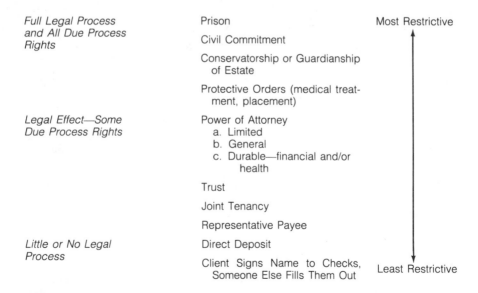

FIGURE 10-1 Continuum of legal options. (Modified from Consortium for Elder Abuse Prevention, *Protocols,* Mount Zion Hospital and Medical Center, San Francisco, 1983.)

being able to sign them if someone else fills them out. In some cases a client can take care of her financial affairs if someone helps her every month by going over the bills. However, the client is at risk for exploitation if she is unaware of the check's amount or is incapable of understanding why a check is being written.

Direct Deposit

Proceeding up the scale of options, direct deposit of the client's checks is the second least restrictive legal device. The client who receives Social Security benefits, Supplemental Security Income (SSI), civil service, railroad retirement checks, or Veterans Administration (VA) payments may have her checks mailed directly to her bank, credit union, or savings and loan account. The advantages to direct deposit are that the check cannot be stolen, misplaced, or destroyed. In order to arrange for a direct deposit, the client may go to the bank to obtain necessary forms to request the direct deposit of her check. She may ask that the practitioner accompany her. Once the forms are filled out, the bank will send the completed form to the source of the client's monthly check and in approximately 60 days the client's check will be deposited directly. A disadvantage of direct deposit is that the check may not arrive on the same day each month. The client may not know that a check is late being deposited and may write checks when she has insufficient funds to cover them.

Joint Tenancy

Joint tenancy means that two people share equal title to an asset, a bank account, or a piece of property. When an asset is in joint tenancy it is not part of a will; on the death of the individual it immediately becomes part of the survivor's property whether or not it was her property originally. Joint tenancy can be used with bank accounts and real property. Most married couples hold all their assets in joint tenancy. The abuser who is intent on defrauding the elderly client will ask that the client add the abuser's name to the deed on real property by telling her, "I will help you stay out of a nursing home if you will put my name on your property or deed." The perpetrator may mislead the elder by simply putting a document under the elderly client's nose and demanding that she sign it without telling her what it is for. Banks allow anyone to add a name on an elderly client's account, especially if the bank knows that the elderly client has no transportation or is not ambulatory. More than one bank account has been cleaned out in this manner. Banks are now becoming more concerned about exploitation of the elderly.

Representative Payee

If a client is unable to manage her benefits properly, due to a mental or physical disability or a drug or alcohol problem, she may require a representative payee. A representative payee is a person designated by the Social Security Administration or other federal agency to receive the check of the client for the purposes of paying the client's bills. A relative, a friend, or an agency may ask to become the representative payee. If a suitable person cannot be found within the client's social circle, the Social Security Administration or other agency may help. Anyone may make a referral to the Social Security Administration to recommend that a client be assigned to a representative payee. In order to obtain a representative payee for the client, the practitioner may call the local Social Security Administration office and information will be taken by phone. A field representative will then do an investigation and may request that the prospective payee go to the local office of the Social Security Administration to fill out forms. Sometimes the procedure can be done by mail. In any case, another form is sent to the client's medical practitioner, which asks for the practitioner's opinion regarding the client's ability or inability to handle her finances. The form is then returned to the Social Security Administration. This process takes approximately 90 days. Caution should be taken in selecting the payee, for some have been known to abscond with the client's money.

The representative payee must make an accounting to the Social Security Administration upon request, usually annually. In practice, accounting is difficult to enforce and a payee may abuse her privileges by keeping the client's money. A concerned person or the client may request removal of the payee either because the client feels that the payee is no longer needed or because the payee fails to fulfill her duties. Sometimes a form filled out by the client's physician will suffice as evidence that a client has improved in her mental or physical condition and no longer requires a payee.

Power of Attorney

A common legal device is a power of attorney. A power of attorney is a written agreement authorizing one or more persons to act for or represent the individual signing the document. The person granting the power of attorney must be competent at the time of signing the document or otherwise the power of attorney is invalid. The power of attorney represents a voluntary action on the part of the person requesting it. It means giving up some control, sometimes upon recognizing that physical functioning is becoming impaired. The power of attorney can be granted on a permanent basis or on a temporary basis and the person who serves can be a financial advisor, a relative, or a friend. The individual signing the power

of attorney is designated as the "principal" and the person to whom authority is given is termed the "attorney-in-fact" or "agent." In spite of the name,
no lawyer is involved unless a lawyer prepares the document or serves as
the attorney-in-fact. This power of attorney is revokable at any time by
the principal. If a practitioner finds that the power of attorney is being
abused, it is his responsibility to let the elder know that the power of attorney is revokable and to assist the client in the process of revoking the
instrument.

Powers of attorney may be limited and specific, or general. In addition,
most states may permit a power of attorney to be durable and continue after
the principal becomes incapable or incompetent. The limited or specific
power of attorney is just what it says, for a specific act. For example, a
limited power of attorney may be granted to cash a check or to draw on a
bank account or to sell real property. This will allow a person who needs
assistance in the paying of her bills by writing and signing checks to grant
another person access to his bank account without giving her as many rights
as would a joint tenancy. Some financial institutions have their own power of
attorney documents. An attorney-in-fact may use the funds only for the
benefit of the principal. Creditors of the attorney-in-fact may not have access
to the account as would the creditors of a joint tenant. A general power of
attorney usually gives the right to the attorney-in-fact to handle all financial
affairs. This type is often used when a person needing help has physical
limitations. If the power to engage in real estate transactions is one of the
powers given, then the power of attorney must be recorded with the county
recorder. When a power of attorney does not have a durable clause, both the
limited and general powers of attorney become invalid when the principal
becomes incompetent or incapable. In practice, however, many families
continue to use the power of attorney long after the principal begins man-
ifesting incompetent behavior.

Durable powers of attorney take two forms: one for health care and one for
estate matters (see Appendix F). Generally, a durable power of attorney for
finances or estate matters and a durable power of attorney for the principal's
health care are two separate documents and the attorney-in-fact handling the
estate matters need not be the same person handling health matters. A
durable power of attorney means that the principal, while presumably
competent, designates an attorney-in-fact to make medical decisions and/or
manage her property in case of future incompetency. Either power of
attorney may take effect at the time it is signed or may have a "springing"
clause and take effect only when the principal is declared incompetent as
specified by the principal. For example, a principal may designate that a
durable power of attorney take effect when two physicians agree that she can
no longer handle her affairs. Support for this type of power of attorney is
increasing across the country among both attorneys and state legislators. The

underlying assumption of a durable power of attorney is that self-determination ahead of time is preferable to a guardianship or a conservatorship which may be imposed involuntarily at a later time, is public, may be expensive and complicated, and might be imposed for only one act of mismanagement on the part of an elderly client.

While a power of attorney may be entirely appropriate in many cases, it has some implicit limitations. Chief among them is that there is no supervision of the attorney-in-fact. Most states provide that the court can make an investigation if there are charges of impropriety, but the community at large may not know that and an overburdened court may not have designated staff to do the investigations. In one state, there are court personnel specifically assigned to do investigations. Another problem is that no attorney-in-fact is bonded. If there is dishonesty or wasting of funds, there is no means of recovering the lost assets. Nevertheless a power of attorney can be a useful tool, especially when long known and trusted people are available to serve and there are others who are in contact with the elderly client on a regular basis and could spot abuse. It is likely that more powers of attorney will be used in the near future, especially the durable power of attorney.

In general, the more specific terms of the power of attorney, the less likely it will be abused. The practitioner may suggest that the client limit the conditions of the power of attorney and that the conditions for revocation and continuation be spelled out. Power of attorney forms are available in most stationery stores. However, extreme caution must be taken in filling out a general power of attorney form that will give the attorney-in-fact more privileges than desired by the principal. Powers of attorney do not need to be recorded with the county recorder's office, but it is a good idea to record powers of attorney involving financial matters. Any power of attorney may be revoked immediately if the principal so desires. A revocation has been done even if the capacity of the principal is in question or after the principal is found incapable. This may be done when the client does not recall granting the power of attorney in the first place, and there appears to be abuse. If the client is unconscious or incapacitated and is unable to revoke the power of attorney and the power of attorney is being abused, an interested person or practitioner may have to resort to finding a way by which the power of attorney can be revoked. This can be done by having a guardian or conservator appointed. When revocation of a power of attorney is being initiated, the principal or her substitute should call the attorney-in-fact immediately and state that a revocation is forthcoming. This telephone call should be documented in writing. The phone call gives the attorney-in-fact due notice to cease immediately using the power of attorney and is followed by a letter sent by certified mail. If the attorney-in-fact uses the power of attorney after the verbal notification, the courts may hold her liable. A revocation may be simply written as in the following example:

John Smith
1234 Cherry Lane
Des Moines, CA 02222
June 8, 19——

Mrs. Mary Jones
P.O. Box 12345
222 Box Street
Los Angeles, CA 91111

Dear Mrs. Jones:

I, John Smith, rescind the general power of attorney that was granted to Mary Jones on December 24, 19——.

I request that all copies of records of my accounts, bank books, checkbooks, and my identification cards be turned over to me by July 9, 19——.

Thank you for your prompt attention to my request.

Sincerely,

John Smith

A durable power of attorney for health care can be revoked verbally at any time as long as the principal has capacity. The burden is on the principal or her substitute to notify all parties who may be relying on the power of attorney about the revocation as soon as possible before further costly transactions are made. It is advisable to record the revocation with the county recorder even if the power of attorney was not recorded when it took effect.

Protective Orders

A protective order must not be confused with a protection order, the latter being a tool under the laws of domestic violence. The protection order will be covered in the criminal remedies section of this chapter. Protective orders fall between conservatorships and powers of attorney in terms of restriction. Like a conservatorship, the courts become involved, but unlike a conservatorship where the powers of the conservator are widespread, an order is specific, for one particular situation. For instance, a protective order may enable a client to be medically treated or moved from a dangerous residence. A judge must be presented with convincing evidence before she will sign an order. Some states have time-limited guardianships that operate on the same principle as protective orders. Often the protective legal order that affects the client is done "for her own good." Often it is an involuntary measure; the client does not want the protective order. Most states provide for no formal avenue for the client to voice her opinion or objections about the legal order, and there is wide disagreement as to who should be subjected to these protective procedures. Often the lawyer and the practitioner involved with a mutual client may seem to be at odds. The social worker may say that a client needs help and the lawyer may say that the client's most important right is the right to be left alone, the right to personal freedom. Disagreements are real and valid for both disciplines. The truth lies in the middle and could be discovered by each knowing more about the other's discipline so that the practitioner will not think that all lawyers are heartless and want to prevent frail elderly people from getting help and so that the attorney will not think that practitioners want all their clients to be under guardianships over their objections and without any civil rights protections.

Trusts

Trusts are often used by persons with significant financial assets or for persons with small estates for purposes of financial management and probate avoidance. A trust requires a trustee, generally someone other than the person creating the trust, to serve as trustee. The trustee can be any person qualified to serve or any entity qualified to serve, such as the trust department of a bank. With this type of arrangement, financial management is assured, but the client's personal and medical needs will not be supervised. A trust officer will not go to the client's home on a regular basis to supervise the care he is receiving.

Conservatorships and Guardianships

Conservatorships are called guardianships in many states. Some states have both conservatorships and guardianships; the first is for the purposes of handling a client's estate and the second is for the purposes of handling a client's personal affairs and/or estate. Appendix G contains a letter to newly appointed conservators. In some states there are only conservatorships when referring to adults in need of assistance and other states have both. For purposes of simplicity, in this text the terms "guardianships" and "conservatorships" will be used interchangeably.

Conservatorships or guardianships have not always enjoyed good press or public relations. In truth, it has been the alternative of first choice in too many situations that might have yielded to a less restrictive legal option if only there had been someone available to serve and if the client had been capable of giving consent. There are several reasons why conservatorships have been used as the "solution" to the unmet needs of a dependent adult. One common reason for resorting to conservatorships is the lack of awareness of other legal options available for handling the finances and personal affairs of an individual. Another reason may be convenience, that is, time may be pressing and the nursing home wants a "responsible party" to sign a client in and to make sure that the bills get paid. In one city some nursing home operators for a time tried to insist that everyone who was admitted to their facilities should be under conservatorship. Another reason for turning to a conservatorship may be necessity. A very sick and confused person in an acute care ward of a hospital who is unable to handle her affairs may require a conservatorship. There is no way of knowing whether her physical health and mental status will return to baseline functioning. After a conservatorship is established, the patient may improve considerably and she may no longer require a conservatorship, at which point the conservatorship may be terminated.

Time-pressing matters may also create the need for a guardianship. Perhaps the finances are being dissipated by a person who is in the manic phase of a manic-depressive illness and there is concern about protecting the bank accounts so that money will not be lost entirely. Last, most people know that a guardianship is under court supervision and guardians are bonded. This can be very reassuring. However, the quality and quantity of court supervision may vary from county to county. Just as practitioners are learning to discard nursing home placement as the only way to take care of physically and mentally frail elderly, so the practitioner must learn to think of using legal devices other than guardianship.

Why have conservatorships been viewed so negatively by some professionals involved with the elderly? There are many good reasons, and some states have moved to revise their laws incorporating the objections of civil libertarians, whose main focus is the preservation of due process protections. A main objection is that in many states, a medical or psychiatric diagnosis alone can make an adult eligible for a conservatorship, no matter how well the individual is functioning and taking care of her personal and financial needs. Thus, if a person carries the label schizophrenic, she could be subject to a conservatorship. Similarly the term "old age" is still incorporated in many state laws as a sole reason for needing a conservatorship. Some have called that ageist. Functional ability should be the criterion for a conservatorship, that is, the ability to manage financial resources and to provide for personal needs, such as food, clothing, shelter, and medical care. Another objection has to do with the global concept of "incompetency." In most states, incompetency means that the conservatee or ward can do nothing for herself. The conservator or guardian is in total control. It has been argued that conservatorships should be tailored to assist the individual only in the area(s) where there are difficulties. There should be flexibility and the elder should be allowed control over those areas where she is capable of making decisions. Another cited difficulty is that court proceedings for appointing a conservator are sometimes too informal, that they are done without due process protections for the proposed conservatee or ward, or that all the requirements for notice to a proposed conservatee or ward are not strictly followed. For instance, a proposed conservatee may never be informed of an impending conservatorship or be discouraged from attending the proceedings when she is capable of doing so. Thus, unless she has hired an attorney to represent her, which is highly unlikely, there may be no opportunity for the proposed conservatee to put forth her position. Another objection is the expense involved in setting up the conservatorship. There are fees and costs which can range from $700.00 to $2,000.00, depending on the problems involved in the case.

Courts are prejudiced in favor of granting guardianships, not denying them. Families and relatives, the usual heirs to an elder's estate, are viewed more favorably by the law as proposed guardians than are friends and strangers, even though there may be obvious conflicts of interest. For example, the guardian may not want to spend money for the ward's care and support because she is preserving the estate so that she will inherit as much as possible. On the other hand, there may be no one else available to serve as the guardian, and it may be the wish of the proposed ward that this particular individual serve. When a spouse or relative is unable to serve, the court has the ability to appoint others to serve as guardians. Some states have public guardians and/or nonprofit corporations that fulfill certain criteria to serve as guardians. Professional people and agencies are increasingly serving as guardians and now are able to earn a living at being professional guardians. The court sometimes holds a professional guardian to a higher standard than a family member who may not have the opportunity to know resources and agencies.

Reforms of Conservatorship and Guardianship Laws Those who are concerned with the way the laws read regarding conservatorships and guardianships propose several reforms, many of which are embodied in the recent revisions of some states. For example, in California, the concept of conservatorship was created to eliminate what was felt to be the stigma of guardianships where a person legally was labeled an "incompetent" or an "insane person." Now an individual under a conservatorship is simply termed "conservatee." A guardianship now applies only to children. There are no findings of incompetency and the law looks strictly to functional abilities, not diagnoses, to determine the need for a conservatorship. The term "old age" does not appear in the text of the law. A conservatee retains certain rights unless the court makes specific determinations. These are the right to vote, the right to handle any earnings, the right to have an allowance, the right to marry, and the right to make medical decisions. Although the law may not be as flexible as some would like, there is an obvious attempt on the part of the legislature to allow judges to tailor the conservatorship to the conservatee.

With changes in the conservatorship law came the role of the court investigator. In California, each of the 58 counties has a court investigator, with the larger counties having more than one investigator. The investigator is responsible to the judge he serves and must make reports on proposed conservatees and supervise existing conservatorships on a regular basis. The investigator generally sees a proposed conservatee prior to the appointment of a conservator, one year thereafter, and then every two years. The investigator also responds to complaints from conservatees or others, including practitioners in the community. The investigator follows up on problem situations such as elder abuse and neglect, makes recommendations to the judges, and informs conservatees and proposed conservatees of their legal rights. For instance, those who are subjected to a conservatorship have the right to attend the hearing, protest the establishment of a conservatorship, ask for someone other than the proposed conservator to be her conservator, and have legal representation. If the court investigator thinks an attorney is needed to protect the rights of the proposed conservatee, the investigator can make that recommendation to the judge, who then will appoint an attorney.

On review of the conservatorship, the investigator determines whether the conservatorship is still needed, and if not, assists the conservatee in obtaining a termination of the conservatorship. Previous to the existence of investigators, conservatees usually were unaware that termination was a possibility. The court investigator represents the judicial system's best attempt to humanize situations that are difficult for all concerned. Appendix G contains more information on conservatorships in California.

Utilizing Guardianships or Conservatorships Conservatorships or guardianships are not always imposed involuntarily. In fact, most are uncontested. An individual can nominate anyone she chooses to serve as a guardian prior to the need for a guardianship. She may state, in writing, that should she become incapable of handling her own affairs she would like a specific individual appointed as her guardian. Thus, some self-determination is possible. Some states have conservatorships which pertain to involuntary mental health commitment and are distinctly different from traditional probate conservatorships.

When should a practitioner consider a conservatorship for a client? First the practitioner must make sure that the code requirements are met by the individual whom the practitioner wishes to conserve. Generally speaking, now that other legal devices are available, a conservatorship should be used only when another device will not do the job adequately, i.e., more protection is needed, or the elder has become too impaired to sign a power of attorney, or third parties such as banks, brokerage houses, and title companies will not recognize a power of attorney but will honor conservatorships. A conservatorship may be a way of permanently blocking an abuser from access to an elder's financial assets. It can also be valuable when there are a number of adult children and only one or two want to be involved with the parent. The fact that the court records are public and can be examined by the other children at any time may serve to avert family feuds. Conservatorships are also advised where there are substantial assets so that the person managing those assets is bonded. Many older persons want conservatorships because they know there is court review. Prospective conservators may welcome a conservatorship for the same reason. Some states have written instructions to conservators outlining their responsibilities (see Appendix G). A conservatorship is appropriate for someone who needs help and objects to help but clearly lacks the capacity to carry on for herself. In fact, although civil libertarians see conservatorships as always involuntarily placed over unwilling subjects, most older people do not object to a conservatorship. Many welcome it and feel relieved that they do not have to be responsible for their affairs or that, at last, help is available. Some elderly people know that they are losing capacity to handle their affairs.

Depending on her capabilities, a person under a guardianship may lose civil rights such as (1) the right to manage property, or personal and financial affairs, (2) the right to contract, (3) the right to vote, (4) the right to drive, (5) the right to choose a residence, and (6) the right to refuse or consent to medical treatment. Removal of such rights is a very serious act, and the practitioner should recommend to the court the removal of as few rights as possible.

For expediency, some states have forms available for medical practitioners to fill out which indicate the client's functional ability. Other states ask that physicians comment only on whether or not the client is physically able to be present in court since the criterion for conservatorship is the client's functional ability and not her medical diagnosis. For states in which medical letters are currently required, it is important that the medical practitioner write a letter which includes a functional assessment of the client.

In some states a special guardianship or a limited guardianship is available for a specific situation. For example, if a proposed ward is in need of emergency surgery and is not able to consent to surgery and no next of kin can be found, a limited guardianship may be initiated by an agency or hospital attorney. A limited guardianship automatically terminates after the specified intervention is completed or on the predetermined date.

The shortcomings of a conservatorship must be mentioned. For states in which the ward or conservatee is still labeled "incompetent," the psychological ramifications of being stigmatized with such a label may be considerable. The public and open nature of the proceedings can also be a disadvantage. The proposed ward may feel humiliated and on the "hot seat." Conservatorships in states with no court investigators as described in this section generally are not fully monitored by the court system. Although a termination of a conservatorship is possible, it is very difficult to effect, especially when the ward or conservatee is unaware that she is being abused or neglected (*Guide*, 1981). If a conservator is found to be abusive of her privileges, anyone may ask to modify or terminate the conservatorship. Terminating a conservatorship requires returning to court for a hearing, and this process must be coordinated. It is difficult for the conservatee to effect the termination by herself. It can be costly to hire an attorney to terminate the conservatorship except in states where there are public defender agencies willing to do the task.

Having discussed guardianships or conservatorships, the remaining items on the scale are civil commitment and prison. These are the most restrictive devices and they carry the most due process rights protections. These options are placed on the scale so that the practitioner can see the progression of deprivation of rights and have some idea of the meaning of due process protections.

CRIMINAL REMEDIES

While the least restrictive legal devices just described involve the civil section of superior court, criminal remedies involve the criminal section of the court. This means that the criminal justice system, including law enforcement agencies, prosecutor's offices, courts, jails, and prisons, are involved. In a criminal case, the victim is a witness, not necessarily the moving party in the case. It is the prosecutor's office or the government, not the victim, that decides whether or not a case will be brought to trial.

Working with the Police

A case involving the criminal justice system begins with a call to a law enforcement agency to request assistance. The standard emergency telephone number can be used to make a report. The practitioner can begin by identifying himself and giving the purpose of the call. A uniformed officer will be dispatched to take a report from the victim. It is preferable to speak to supervisors who are sergeants. They will probably have more experience in matters related to elder abuse and neglect. When possible, the practitioner should request that the client be interviewed by an officer in street clothes instead of a uniform. The uniform may intimidate the victim and prevent her from disclosing important information. After making the phone call, the practitioner should remain with the client at the scene of the incident to provide information to the officer and to be a source of support.

When the practitioner has difficulty gaining access to a client and fears for the client's safety, he can call the standard phone number and ask an officer to "check on the well-being" of his client. A law enforcement officer will visit the client's residence but may not use force to enter on the first visit unless he feels that the client is in immediate danger. It may take additional reports of concern for the officer to make a forced entry.

The practitioner may ask that the responding officer bring a camera if there are physical injuries sustained by the elder and/or if the residence is in a state of extreme neglect. The practitioner should ask the officer to make a report on each incident to which he responds so that a paper trail is established and there will be documentation which may be used at a later date. The practitioner may say to the officer, "I am establishing a chain of evidence and I need you to make a report." The practitioner should always obtain the police report number for future reference.

In some states, the law enforcement officer may not arrest anyone on the scene unless there is repeated or ongoing violence. In states where domestic violence laws stipulate automatic arrest of perpetrators, officers have no choice but to arrest them. Some states have penal code sections that hold caregivers responsible for the abuse they have willfully inflicted (see Appendix H). In cases where explicit threats are made involving weapons, an officer may confiscate the weapon for "safekeeping."

After evidence is gathered, the law enforcement officer's report is turned over to the prosecutor's office. The prosecutor, a lawyer for the government in a criminal case, determines whether or not there is sufficient evidence to press charges for which a case is brought to court. It is up to the prosecutor to decide whether or not he will file charges against a wrongdoer. Very few cases of elder abuse and neglect reach the criminal justice court system, partly because of the elderly victim's reluctance or inability to ask that charges be pressed, especially if the charges are against a relative or someone she has known for a long period. Prosecutors are reluctant to bring cases of elder abuse and neglect to trial when the elderly victim is unable to be a credible witness, especially when the victim is incapable of recalling details of the crime, due to an intermittent memory loss.

A person who is abusive may be charged with criminal trespass, false imprisonment, malicious mischief, reckless endangerment, or one of several types of assault. For theft and fraud, an abuser may be charged with one of several degrees of theft or burglary, extortion, forgery, or possession of stolen property. It is very difficult to make a charge of neglect; however, a person held against her will may have the perpetrator charged with false imprisonment. The wrongdoer may also be charged with malicious mischief or reckless endangerment (*Advocate's Guide*, 1983).

Theft charges are very difficult to prove unless a paper trail is developed to prove that the crime did take place. Proof of intent to deprive the client of funds or property is very difficult, especially if the victim is unable to counter claims by the wrongdoer that the property was a gift or promised to her.

Role of the Practitioner

The practitioner can play an important role in helping the elderly victim decide whether she would like the prosecutor to press charges against the wrongdoer. In some instances it may be helpful for the victim to have charges pressed in order to help the wrongdoer obtain court-mandated counseling. When pressed charges result in a conviction, the wrongdoer may also be mandated to make restitution to the victim for medical care and property loss or destruction. The wrongdoer may also be ordered to have no more contact with the victim, thus providing a safer situation for her. The wrongdoer may be deterred from committing further abusive acts if she knows that she may be arrested and charged.

Pressing charges can be difficult for the victim. The benefits to the victim and to society at large must be weighed against the strain of pressing charges. The victim may be pressured to drop charges by the abuser or others or be made to feel guilty for being a cooperative witness. She may feel that it is wrong to imprison a member of her immediate family. Having to recount the fraud or abusive incident may be too traumatic for the victim, and she may refuse to participate in the criminal proceedings. The practitioner should accompany the victim when she is interviewed by the prosecutor, who must decide whether adequate evidence is available and whether the victim will be a cooperative witness. Prosecutors specializing in domestic violence cases advise the practitioner to counsel his client carefully before deciding to proceed with the prosecution process, which can be lengthy. The victim must remember that once she agrees to have charges pressed, she is no longer in "control" of the case. Only the prosecutor can dismiss charges prior to the trial. If the victim changes her mind before the trial, the charges will not be dropped automatically (*Advocate's Guide*, 1983).

While one victim may refuse to be involved in criminal proceedings, another victim may want justice to prevail, and it is important for the practitioner to support a victim who wants to pursue every avenue of prosecution. The victim must withstand multiple delays in the criminal proceedings, be willing to be interviewed by both the prosecutor and the attorney for the defense, be consistent in telling her story, and not be afraid that the abuser, who sometimes may be out of jail on bail, will torment her. Some communities have victim/witness advocacy groups that can provide supportive counseling to victims who are trying to decide whether or not to press charges or who have pressed charges and need maximum support until the case goes to trial. Staff members of these groups can help the victim to decompress afterwards.

Currently, prosecutors are being criticized by the media for not working hard enough to bring cases involving elder abuse and neglect to trial. The U.S. Attorney General's Task Force on Family Violence (Attorney General, 1984) made specific recommendations for prosecutors: that prosecutors work with victim/witness advocacy providers, prosecute whenever possible, and develop special units to process family violence cases. Medical and service professionals must work closely with prosecutors and others in the criminal justice system so that abusers will be charged. Impeccable documentation and medical assessments are necessary in order for the prosecutor to do his job.

Protection Order

A protection order directly addresses an abusive situation. Approximately 43 states make protection orders available through domestic violence laws. Originally designed to address the problem of spouse abuse, these laws can be used to apply to the older adult who is being abused. They make it possible for a judge to order an abuser to move and stay out of the house and order the abuser not to contact the abused in any way. A judge can also order the offender to pay the fees for the victim's attorney and order the offender to obtain counseling. These orders are enforced by the police if the abuser violates the order. A violation is deemed a crime and the abuser can be arrested. An abuser can also be ordered to make restitution to the abused, to "make whole" or return her to the status she enjoyed prior to the abuse.

A protection order is not to be confused with a protective order, which was discussed earlier. The benefit of a protection order is that it can be granted whether or not another legal action is pending. It is also different from a restraining order and a no-contact order. In some states a restraining order can be obtained only when the victim is involved in another legal action such as a divorce, guardianship, or child custody proceeding. A no-contact order is used in criminal proceedings. After criminal charges are filed, a no-contact order can be issued to an alleged offender as a method to keep him from making contact with the alleged victim pending the outcome of the trial.

A protection order can be issued in situations of domestic violence which include not only actual physical harm or injury but also threats or actions which cause a victim to fear immediate physical harm. The victim can obtain immediate help by filing a request with the court for a protection order. In many cases a temporary protection order is issued immediately, pending an investigation and a hearing which occurs usually within 14 days. The practitioner should advise the victim that once she files the protection order, she should not invite the abuser back into her home. This has been known to happen; the abused victim files a request for a protection order, is granted the protection order, and then has a change of heart. Such a scenerio makes it difficult for a police officer and prosecutor to do their share of law enforcement.

DOCUMENTING FOR COURT

A booklet by Collins and La France (1982) on protective services and the law outlines what documentation is necessary for successful court intervention: case notes, statutory chart recording, compilation of exhibits, and casework recording. Additionally, many courts give credence to documented quotations gathered during the practitioner's assessment.

From the beginning of his involvement the practitioner should record all dates, contacts, home visits, and telephone calls. Firsthand knowledge of a client's behavior is weighed more than behavior that is reported by others. Hearsay evidence sometimes is admissible into the court. Statutory chart recording consists of recording observations factually and applying them to statute and policy definitions of situations such as emergency, abuse, incompetency, and imminent danger. The booklet recommends that the practitioner develop a chart that lists the definitions in one column and show in an adjoining column the practitioner's gathered facts and dates related to the specific situation. In addition, witnesses, their addresses, and phone numbers should be listed. Such a chart would be read easily by the court and provide clear data to help the court make necessary decisions.

The practitioner should compile his exhibits and have available a list of all collateral contacts who have reports or firsthand knowledge. Certified copies of documents, copies of contracts and agreements associated with the case, law enforcement reports, medical and professional reports all should be gathered in logical form. Photographs, when available, should be added to this portfolio. When, where, and by whom the photos were taken should be recorded. Last, the practitioner may wish to prepare a casework recording for the court's consideration. This is a typed summary reflecting the practitioner's notes, charts, exhibits, and opinions. It is essential that the worker separate facts from his subjective or professional opinions. Recommendations and treatment plans should also be written in separate categories. Included in this recording are the practitioner's initial assessment and treatment plan and subsequent modifications. The practitioner should always remember that the actual case notes may be subpoenaed by the attorneys or by the court. Other methods for documenting evidence during the assessment phase have been covered in Chapter 6.

PROVIDING COURT TESTIMONY

The thought of having to testify in court can be anxiety producing for the practitioner. It can also be an exhilarating experience and one that can bring a great deal of focus to the practitioner's work. There are some principles to giving testimony. They should be reviewed repeatedly prior to having to give testimony or whenever encountering the legal system.

Before giving any testimony or relating a case to a legal professional, the practitioner should rehearse his facts from the documents which he has carefully executed all along while working on the case. Whenever possible the practitioner should be prepared to present information obtained during the assessment phase. He should assume that there will be another attorney representing the abuser and that he will be cross-examined. He must try to anticipate questions that might be asked and have answers ready. He should be aware of "holes" in his testimony and be prepared to have answers. It is quite likely that the attorney for the other side will find the "holes" and will try to use them to discredit the practitioner. The practitioner should talk to others who have given testimony in the past to obtain their advice. If possible, the practitioner should sit in the courtroom of the judge before whom testimony will be taken to become comfortable with the judge's style. When testifying, the practitioner should be as precise as possible about dates and events. His answers should be brief and precise, stated clearly without mumbling. He should be honest but if a mistake is made he should admit it. If the practitioner has "axes to grind" he should leave them outside the courtroom. The practitioner must at all times be objective and factual, not opinionated. The practitioner may be tempted to exaggerate when he feels that he will not be believed. He should stick to the facts and give an opinion only when asked. If the practitioner does not understand an attorney's question or wants to buy a little time to think through his answer, he may ask to have the question repeated. If he does not know the answer to the question, he should say so. He should take his time and not let anyone rush him. He will want to give the best testimony possible. The practitioner's role is to answer questions and not ramble. Ostensibly the courtroom process is one of searching for the truth of the situation. It can be assumed that the judge is trying to focus on what will be in the best interest of the client. In some states the judge must favor relatives, and so if testimony is being given that undercuts the practitioner's side of the matter, he should be prepared to be especially knowledgeable and factual. The practitioner should not be surprised if his report is challenged. It is considered as one more piece of evidence. Strength lies in the fact that the practitioner is presumed to have nothing to gain in the legal matter and that he has only the interest of his client at heart. It must be remembered that the court must consider all evidence, not just the report of the practitioner. The judge may give the benefit of the doubt to family and long-term friends, but if the practitioner's evidence is to the contrary, the judge must weigh it carefully.

The practitioner's dress should be conservative in style and color. Most judges are conservative, but even the ones who are liberal minded lend more credibility to people who are conservatively dressed. The practitioner's posture should be good and he should not interrupt the judge or the attorney. The practitioner should try to act natural and speak in a clear tone of voice. Although nervous, he should try to appear confident. He is a professional with credentials and would not be on the witness stand if he did not have something important to relate to the court on behalf of his client. He should have in mind clear-cut recommendations that he feels would remedy the situation the client is in. The judge and attorneys will look at the practitioner as an expert in his field who is prepared to give intervention options.

The cross-examination period is the most difficult part of giving testimony. The legal system is adversarial and the opposing attorney's job is to try to shake the practitioner in his testimony. The practitioner may be accused of making up the story he is reporting, or of having a personal interest in bringing the case to court, or of acting on emotions and not on facts. A practitioner who is not used to being attacked for "doing good" should not take accusations personally, because it is the defense attorney's job to defend his client even if that client is abusive (Havemeyer, 1980). Prosecutors will frequently advise the practitioner not to bring to court information that has not been subpoenaed but rather to bring prepared materials such as the typed summary and chart recording in the previously mentioned portfolio. If the defense attorney observes that the practitioner is carrying information that may benefit his clients, he will ask to have access to it and be granted this request. The practitioner may bring to court the portfolio that he has prepared, but for practical purposes in giving verbal testimony, it is best for the practitioner to write notes on a small piece of paper or card to refresh his memory, keeping in mind that either attorney has a right to see the card. The practitioner should attempt to memorize the facts and dates and be able to recount chronologically the activities leading up to the court proceeding.

HAVING IMPACT ON THE LEGAL SYSTEM

As the practitioner becomes more aware of the law in protective services, he will want to become more familiar with it. He will also want more access to the courts in order to gain the best results for his client.

The practitioner must realize that the court is an independent body, not in existence to support only the practitioner's stance. He may feel angry toward the court if his "side" does not prevail. The court must consider all facts and all evidence before making a final decision. Given this lengthy system of checks and balances, it is incumbent upon the practitioner to be as prepared as possible.

The practitioner can write to judges or attorneys if he feels he has information that will be helpful in a particular case or if he wants to establish an ongoing relationship. The practitioner can do this by writing a letter introducing himself. The letter should be brief, respectful, and professionally typed. The practitioner may well have special information about his case that no one else has. For example, he can be reasonably certain that neither the attorney nor the judge has ever been in the home of the abuser or the victim. He may be the only one who can give the facts of the situation and prevent an abusive caregiver from becoming a guardian or conservator. The practitioner may have important information about the mental status of the client. However, the legal standard for incompetency or incapacity to determine guardianships may be different from the practitioner's standards. Each profession seems to have its own standards for this subject, and a judge's standard must be the same as those legislated by his state. If the practitioner understands the standards under which attorneys and judges must function, he will be less frustrated.

Instead of waiting for a court hearing to take place, the practitioner may want to request a meeting with the judge to discuss mutual concerns. For example, he may approach the judge by saying, "I often have information on cases that come before you. I would like to discuss with you how I might best make this information available to you on a regular basis so that you will have all of the facts in front of you at the time of the hearings you conduct." Not all judges will respond but some will, and the practitioner must remember that judges cannot be stereotyped. They may be liberal, progressive, naive, isolationist, sophisticated, unexpectedly compassionate, or unfamiliar with medical conditions affecting the elderly or with resources that can be of assistance. A judge may come from a different economic class than the client and may never have been exposed to the kinds of problems faced by the protective services practitioner. Nevertheless, many people, including judges, know that elderly people are being abused and neglected.

At times the practitioner may ask for a meeting in a judge's chambers. Time in chambers is an informal problem-solving practice that enables all parties to get away temporarily from the legal procedure, which is a sparring, adversarial process, and to get to the point. It also saves certain people from being exposed publicly regarding embarrassing information. At the hearing the practitioner may request the client's attorney to ask the court if it would entertain a chamber session. This can be done at the beginning of the court process. What goes on in chambers is not recorded. It is a discussion process. Decisions made in open court go on record.

It is advised that when the practitioner goes to court he remain during the entire course of the hearing to make sure that everything he wants to have expressed or presented in court is accomplished. At times attorneys, who have many different pieces of information to present, may lose a piece or two and may benefit from prompting by the practitioner.

When having contact with the legal system, the practitioner should not present himself as impassioned for any particular cause or issue because it turns people off. If the practitioner shows a lot of emotion, his credibility will be questioned. If he has strong feelings about a case, he is advised to discuss them and ventilate with a co-worker or supervisor, but not in court. When the practitioner is speaking to legal professionals, it is best to understate a case and use facts to convince, not feelings. When first making contact with the court, the practitioner must realize that he will have to prove himself to the court over a period of time, sometimes for months or one to two years. He should not "buddy up" to court personnel. They serve the general public and must not give the appearance of being biased toward certain practitioners. Court workers are very aware that some people will try to curry their favor and they will be on guard. The practitioner needs to be sincere and consistent in working with court personnel. They will help when possible.

Another way for the practitioner to have impact on the legal system is to learn about the laws that affect his client population. The practitioner can begin by going to the law library and asking for information on guardianship, conservatorship, and power of attorney laws in his state. Groups may be formed to study and understand the laws. If the practitioner has located a sympathetic attorney, he may invite her to attend the study group. The attorney chosen should be one who is both knowledgeable about the laws in question and sympathetic to the practitioner's position or at least willing to learn about it. An attorney who specializes in issues regarding the elderly is most knowledgeable in this instance. The practitioner should not look to the attorney as the sole authority on legal matters but rather as one who can give him information and perhaps one side of the issue as the practitioner travels on the road to becoming an expert on protective services laws. The practitioner may also want to find out who is available for public speaking and guest lectures and who will come to the practitioner's agency to teach staff about geriatric law. There is probably at least one legislator in the practitioner's state who is sympathetic to older people and their problems. The practitioner can attempt to find out who they are and make acquaintance with them and their staff. He can learn about impending legislation and give input so that the laws are realistic and can support his practice. Some practitioners are now being asked for input on proposed legislation and are able to effect appropriate changes in protective services laws.

The practitioner may want to find out when hearings are held on con-servatorships or guardianships in his county. Since most of these hearings are public, anyone has a right to attend them. The practitioner may call the superior court and attend these hearings to acquaint himself with the judicial mind. If anyone should ask the practitioner why he is present, he should speak honestly. The practitioner may say that he has many clients who come under guardianships and that he wants to educate himself so that he can be more knowledgeable about the field. Courts tend to respect the learner, the practitioner who methodically and rationally tries to learn more about the functioning of the court with an altruistic goal in mind. Court personnel on the whole like to think that they are helping people; they are aware that going to court can be a momentous experience for most people, and they will make it easier if they can. Some judges are very supportive of the practition-er's desire to learn more about the court system. These judges have offered to perform mock court, to give the practitioner a tour of the court system, and run them through a typical hearing. Agencies may want to consider these judges' offers and make court tours and rehearsals a standard part of their staff training program.

The practitioner has a right to approach judges and legislators. They are public officials, appointed or elected. They must be responsive to their constituencies. Most are aware that there are increasing numbers of older people who vote and that their livelihood depends in part on them. Addi-tionally, older people have good press now, and there is a national conscious-ness of many of the problems that are part of old age. There is also a climate for the practitioner to become involved. He has a better chance of finding a sympathetic ear now than 10 years ago. The field of geriatric law is moving rapidly, and the practitioner is in a very good position to influence it.

MANDATORY REPORTING LAWS

Most states have passed mandatory reporting laws on elder abuse and neglect within the last five years. Debates regarding the pros and cons of mandatory reporting seem outdated at this time. However, it may be worthwhile to discuss in general the strengths and limitations of these laws. First, state laws vary in their definitions of elder abuse and neglect, stan-dards for reporting, penalties for failure to report, and types of immunity provided to the reporter. Currently, statistical systems in some states lump together self-neglect and neglect cases, and abuse categories include one-time-only muggings, abuse by caregiver, abuse by nonrelatives, and abuse by strangers. It is difficult to study these subgroups when they are lumped into general categories. Furthermore, if a client is a victim of multiple forms of abuse and neglect, she is counted as a client more than once. Clearly these statistical systems can be improved, and in the next 10 to 15 years the nation will see more uniform definitions and improved methods of gathering data. A standardized data-gathering system may be in the offing should Congress pass a federal law mandating nationwide reporting and information gathering on cases of elder abuse and neglect.

Increasing press reports of elderly people who are killed by relatives or locked in rooms for months by their paid caregivers may provoke legislative bodies to pass laws protecting the elderly. It must be emphasized that the passage of elder abuse mandatory reporting laws is just the beginning of a long process. The practitioner looking at the development of the child abuse and neglect and domestic violence movements can see that those groups have taken 15 to 25 years to progress from coining terms such as child abuse and neglect and battered women, to making them household words. Progress has been gradual and has included passing laws that encourage the reporting of child abuse and neglect, the development of agencies to treat these populations, and finally the refinement and modification of the laws through legislation. Training is now taking place among law enforcement agencies and the legal system to make their staff more sensitive to the plight of these victims. Awareness training and related activities were unheard of 15 to 20 years ago. As a further sign of progress, agencies are now networking so that the victim can give her report to fewer people and be subjected to less trauma. The domestic violence laws, such as the protection order which mandates an abuser to stay away from the victim for periods of up to a year, seem to make concrete the enormous problems faced by the victim. Fortunately, the elder abuse client is able to take advantage of laws that were designed originally to help spouse abuse victims.

An ideal mandatory reporting law on elder abuse and neglect contains three main parts: reporting, investigation, and service delivery. Some laws are only for reporting elder abuse and neglect, leaving the community agencies to develop their own criteria for investigation and service delivery. Most laws provide immunity for anyone who reports elder abuse and neglect and give permission to a mandated agency to perform the investigation. These laws have heightened many professionals' awareness of the problem and propelled them to provide training to staff and other groups in the community. The laws have also increased the numbers of reports of elder abuse and neglect.

A serious problem facing protective service agencies when a mandatory reporting law is passed is the lack of adequate staffing to take the reports, investigate them, and offer services to the client and the caregiver. The practitioner may wonder whether it is worthwhile to report the case, knowing the mandated agency is poorly staffed. However, each practitioner has an obligation to make these reports and continue to provide services to these cases so that the mandated agency can take its statistics, often astounding in numbers, to the legislature to appeal for budget amendments. It is hoped that once legislators become aware of the problem and are presented with convincing statistics, they will allocate additional enforcement monies.

Proponents of mandatory reporting laws believe that interventions in crisis situations will occur sooner since no court order or a preponderance of evidence is necessary to initiate an investigation. Most mandatory reporting laws permit an investigation should there be a mere suspicion of elder abuse and neglect. Another benefit of the mandatory reporting law is that it assists unconsenting and endangered adults who may be labeled victims of self-neglect. These adults may be too weak or frightened to ask actively for help and may be brought to an agency's attention by a neighbor or concerned citizen who is aware of the mandatory reporting law. While agencies are criticized for potentially abusing mandatory reporting laws and "yanking" people out of their own homes, these critics should be aware that protective services and other agencies and professionals have their own standards for intervention and are not lax or unethical. Protective services practitioners respect due process, have standards of evidence required by the courts, and are not without their own agencies' checks and balances. Critics who accuse practitioners of unnecessarily committing clients to mental health in-stitutions are reminded that a psychiatric involuntary commitment pro-cedure remains outside the boundaries of what is covered under the manda-tory reporting law on elder abuse and neglect. It is a separate procedure with separate criteria for involuntary commitment, and should remain so.

While there are many advantages that support the passage of mandatory reporting laws, its limitations must also be mentioned. First, critics have asked, What good is a law when there are no money and services available to enforce the law? To this criticism, a point must be made that protective services are the responsibility of the entire community, that it cannot be tackled by one agency that is short on funds. In this time of budget problems (there seems to be no time when an agency is free of budget problems), all agencies must band together to provide a community-wide response system. This statement does not detract from admitting that states as well as the federal government must increase, not decrease, funds and support activi-ties involving intervention and treatment of elder abuse and neglect. Man-datory reporting laws are frequently criticized as being too intrusive, be-cause an elderly person has a right to privacy regardless of her condition and situation as long as others are not being harmed. According to this view, a victim of self-neglect has a right to remain in her own situation and refuse help regardless of her mental status and her ability to consent to services. Critics also state that many cases of self-neglect or neglect are already known to agencies and authorities and no intervention has taken place. The passage of a law does not guarantee increased services. Mandatory reporting laws are also criticized for jeopardizing the relationship of a client and a professional. Some physicians say that a client will not return for much-needed services if she learns that her physician must report her abusive situation, sometimes against her wishes. Another criticism of mandatory reporting and the investigation of elder abuse and neglect cases is that the involvement of an agency professional with improper solutions may be worse than the problem itself. The practitioner is, therefore, cautioned to proceed judiciously and to ask himself if his intervention is harmful or will worsen the client's current situation.

Mandatory reporting laws may reinforce ageism in this society, because people may feel that if older people require special legislation for protection then they truly must be weak and vulnerable, incapable of caring for themselves, not strong enough to hold their own in society. Fiscally speaking, critics have said that only a small percentage of the elderly are being abused and, therefore, why should governments spend millions of dollars on a small population when greater numbers of elderly have basic needs that are more important—food, clothing, medical benefits, and energy assistance. These critics argue that money should be channeled into these basic need areas rather than spent on a small subgroup of the elderly.

Mandatory reporting laws are feared by certain people who feel that these laws will sanction medical procedures against the client's will, such as keeping her alive or providing medical care which she clearly does not want but against which she is too weak or too impaired to express an objection. For example, a terminally ill client may want to be left alone to die in her own home, but a protective services worker may facilitate the transportation of this client to a hospital where she will be fed by tubes and be kept alive. Her condition may slowly improve. These critics may be silenced by pointing out that most practitioners know when a client is capable of giving consent and understands the consequences of refusing services. The practitioner will not intervene or interfere in that client's way of living or dying.

The laws are also criticized as restricting an adult's physical movements. It is feared that a practitioner will remove a client from her own home or the client may feel she is being incarcerated in a hospital against her will and make statements such as, "Why did you put me in this jail? I didn't do anything wrong." Here again the client's right to refuse treatment and the right to self-determination should be respected, and the community should be provided with some education on the goals and purposes of the mandated agency and its limitations in order to dispel these fears.

Most states are passing mandatory reporting laws and this trend will continue. The stated strengths and criticisms of the laws point to the need for further refinement. The legal and helping professions must work together to refine these laws.

SUMMARY

The practitioner who makes it a point to understand all legal options available to his client will be able to serve his client in an expeditious and efficient
manner. He should expect to be involved in court proceedings and, therefore, become familiar with his community's civil and criminal justice systems
and their personnel. He can work on issues involving elder abuse and
neglect in several ways: as a clinician helping his client understand legal
procedures; as a proponent of change in laws affecting his client, including
mandatory reporting laws; and as an advocate of practitioner–attorney team-
work whenever it is possible.

Practice Issues

The first two parts of this book describe the complexities of elder abuse and neglect work. The practitioner must be prepared to utilize a variety of diagnostic and intervention techniques, depending on the situation and condition of the elder and the abuser. Having to consider so many variables in any given situation, the practitioner faces many challenges. This part discusses some of those difficult practice issues.

Chapter 11 describes the problems faced by practitioners who provide protective services. Dilemmas, conflicting principles, and trying experiences make an already difficult job more difficult. The responsibilities of others who come in contact with protective services practitioners are also specified.

Working with abused and neglected elderly can drain the practitioner of precious energy. The adversarial nature of the job sometimes makes it difficult for the practitioner to relax and enjoy the work day. Chapter 12 describes the types of feelings the practitioner may experience and the actions that can be taken to combat practitioner burnout.

11 Protective Services and Elder Abuse

This chapter describes protective services in the generic sense, their history and philosophy, and the problems and issues facing the practitioner who works with frail elderly and attempts to detect and treat cases of elder abuse and neglect. The purpose of this chapter is to assist all practitioners in understanding difficulties facing workers who provide protective services and to appreciate the complexities of providing protective services to victims of elder abuse and neglect. This chapter also describes differences in job conditions between the practitioner who provides protective services in the normal course of her work and the public agency adult protective services (APS) practitioner who is mandated by a state law to accept and investigate reports of elder abuse and neglect. Intervention models that might be used by the practitioner are also offered in this chapter. While it is recognized that protective services are now provided to adults who are 18 years old or older and can include the developmentally disabled, the mentally retarded, and the psychiatrically impaired client, they will not be covered in this chapter, which will focus only on the elderly client.

DEFINITIONS

What is a protective services program? What makes it different from a social services program? What are its special features? A protective services program combines a multitude of services and draws on nearly every resource available to elders in any given community. It is not to be confused with "in-home care," "long-term care," or "legal services" exclusively. Instead, a protective services program is a unique mixture of legal, medical, and social services that permit the broadest array of interventions. These services are frequently provided by several agencies which may collaborate. For example, a public health nurse, an APS worker, and a lawyer might work together to develop appropriate interventions for their mutual client. The mandated agency practitioner may act as the coordinator of the interventions of several agencies and be the main contact person with the client. Protective services involve intervention by an outsider into the personal affairs of the adults who are seen as needing protection of some type. There are several definitions of protective services. One definition focuses on the adult's situation and the concept of endangerment. Protective services are for

> Adults who are in danger of losing their life, liberty, health, or property, through the actions of others or through their inability to care for themselves and who would receive little or no help except through the services of an external intervenor. (Collins and La France, 1982, p. 2)

Protective services include a mixture of services, and their clients are also a unique mixture of people. They fall into several main categories: voluntary or involuntary, neglected or self-neglectful, abusive or abused, compliant or noncompliant with their medical care, and consenting or not consenting to intervention. Clients who typically fall under the auspices of protective services also fit the profile of the elder abuse victim. The client is usually female and over 75 years of age. Those who are assisting her with activities of daily living such as bathing, grocery shopping, and meal preparation are becoming exhausted. The client has several physical ailments and sometimes is suffering from mental confusion. Sometimes her behavior is bizzare and outrageous and does not conform to community standards. While some protective services clients welcome intervention by a practitioner, others will accept it only reluctantly or reject it outright (Collins and LaFrance, 1982). These clients are referred often by practitioners from other agencies such as utility companies, meals on wheels, senior center programs, and law enforcement. Concerned citizens are becoming more aware of the needs of frail elders and the agencies that serve them. Reports of endangered elders are made increasingly by friends, neighbors, apartment managers, and relatives.

ORIGINS

The notion of protective services grew out of governmental concern for adults who had difficulty managing their own affairs. The passage of the Social Security Act in 1935 marked the beginning of protective services when state departments of public welfare and several private service agencies began providing assistance to the aged, blind, and disabled. In the

1950s and 1960s, protective services were offered to people who were unable to manage their own resources or to protect themselves from harm. Elder abuse and neglect were not introduced as a special problem with its own set of principles for assessment and intervention until the late 1960s and early 1970s, when the U.S. Department of Social and Rehabilitation Services funded demonstration grants to initiate the National Protective Services Project. As part of that project, protective services clients were identified and intervention techniques were developed. Several important questions were raised such as, Did the receipt of protective services hasten the client's death or impede his freedom? Was societal disorganization, not the client's "deviance," responsible for the numbers and types of elderly in need of protective services? Attempts to answer these questions have helped guide policymakers of protective services and continue to be debated as the practice of protective services evolves (Blenkner, Bloom, & Nielson, 1971; Bloom & Nielson, 1971).

In 1975, Title 20 of the Social Security Act mandated and funded protective services for all adults 18 years old or older with no regard to income. Additionally, emphasis was placed on clients who were found in situations indicating abuse, neglect, or exploitation. With this federal mandate, most states created adult protective services (APS) units in their social service agencies, while other states contracted with public and private agencies to provide protective services with Title 20 funds.

Policies and standards concerning the delivery of protective services have changed throughout the last 50 years, reflecting each state's perceptions of their problems. The focus of APS has expanded and evolved from treating the impaired, low-income elderly, to treating all adults over 18 years of age without regard to income, and more recently to treating elder abuse and neglect victims as a special population. APS units have become better known since the passage of mandatory reporting laws by 37 states. They have become synonymous with the reporting and investigation of elder abuse and neglect.

PHILOSOPHY

At the 1982 conference, "Improving Protective Services for Older Adults," which was attended by social work and legal professionals at the University of Southern Maine, a theory of adult protection was formulated with the hope of stimulating discussions and creating greater clarity with regard to the functioning of protective services. These four principles, combined with a set of guidelines developed by Havemeyer (1982a, 1982c), serve to guide the protective services practitioner.

When interests compete, the practitioner is charged with serving the adult client. The worker is not charged with serving the community's concern about the client's safety, the landlord's concern about crime or morality, or the concern of the client's family about their own health or finances. The client has the right to be annoying, eccentric, and even foolish. For example, he may eat out of garbage cans, wear three shirts at once, be observed talking to himself, own 12 cats, have candy and soda pop for breakfast, lunch, and dinner, and not be in need of any protective services intervention.

A stressed caregiver or apartment manager may make a referral out of concern for the client. As much as the referrer may want to be helpful, it is the client's circumstances and wishes for help that are the primary determinants for intervention. The practitioner cannot always intervene just because the community says, "Do something." The practitioner's role is to be an advocate for the client, and to maintain and uphold the client's rights. The client also has the right to divest himself of his wealth, to give away his savings while he is alive. Wills may be contested by relatives after the client's death, but these relatives may not dictate how the client is to spend his money while he is still alive.

When interests compete, the adult client is in charge of decision making until he delegates responsibility voluntarily to another or the court grants responsibility to another. The client retains all constitutional rights unless he is declared incapacitated or incapable of giving consent or of handling his own affairs by a court of law. Services may not be imposed on those who are competent and who refuse to accept them. Deprivation of personal liberty must be carried out in accordance with due process law. The client has a right to marry whomever he chooses unless he has been declared by a court of law to be incapable of contracting a valid marriage. An agency may receive a complaint that an 80-year-old man is about to marry a 21-year-old woman who will probably inherit his $100,000 savings after his death. The woman is perceived by the referring caller to be exploitive, marrying the older person for his money. In such a case, the practitioner may not do anything if the 80-year-old man is capable of deciding what he wants for himself.

On the other hand, depriving people of their rights can sometimes be protective. Due to the immoral and unethical nature of some situations, the practitioner may be required to intervene, especially if funds are diverted and the client is subjected to undue influence. At times, a protective legal device may be necessary. For example:

One man who had inherited wealth had married four times because he was incapable of resisting the women's desires for marriage although he did not want to be married. He was relieved when the court took away his right to remarry for the fifth time.

When interests compete, freedom is more important than safety. The client has a right to be left alone, no matter how unsanitary and primitive his residence may be, and he has a right to refuse treatment. Recently, there have been several widely publicized cases involving elderly who have refused medical treatment and for whom guardianship proceedings were initiated. Professionals were divided as to whether the clients were incapable of giving consent for medical care. These cases serve as reminders that practitioners do not necessarily agree on what is best for the client, that a client has the right to refuse treatment even if to do so would result in imminent death, and that it is sometimes very difficult for a practitioner to support the client's decision, especially when the client chooses not to alleviate his painful medical condition and subsequently dies. Every attempt should be made to gain the cooperation of the client before any action is taken. Involuntary intervention will not be initiated unless the client is incapable of caring for himself and/or he is in an emergency situation which is threatening to himself or others. Only with proper evaluations and in the absence of all other reasonable alternatives will the practitioner obtain legal authority to remove the client's rights.

In the ideal case, protection of adults seeks to achieve, simultaneously and in order of importance, freedom, safety, least disruption of life style, and least restrictive care alternative. Services should be provided for the shortest period of time and to the simplest extent necessary. The practitioner should involve those familiar to the client, including relatives, friends, and agencies to the extent that they are willing and able to provide help. If no one else is available to assist or advocate for the client, the practitioner is obligated to assist the client. The intervention that is chosen will be balanced against the possible impact that it will have on the client's self-esteem, will to live, and feeling of control over his own life.

PROBLEMS AND DILEMMAS

As the practitioner proceeds judiciously in situations where interests compete, she also has the added problem of being faced with principles that sometimes conflict with each other, as well as with separate sets of values of the legal and social work professions. The two principles that often oppose each other and guide the practitioner are the principle of *parens patriae* (Latin: parents of the country) and the principle of the right to privacy. The notion of *parens patriae* originated centuries ago when kings in England had the royal perogative to delegate authority to certain members or groups to take care of the kingdom's less fortunate citizens just as a parent would care for a minor child. These citizens were often labeled "mentally infirm" and required extra care. It could be said that those who were delegated to care for these citizens or to determine what was to happen to them were the earliest forms of protective services workers. This principle of *parens patriae* crossed the waters to America and influenced the development of guardianship law and practice. States also developed the notion of police powers, whereby certain laws, regulations, and ordinances were developed to protect citizens from being harmed. Institutions were developed to care for the mentally ill. Although the *parens patriae* laws protected the majority of the citizens, these laws often came in conflict with a citizen's constitutional rights, chiefly his right to be left alone and the right to privacy. Anyone working with the frail elderly can be caught between pressure from the community to do something about a certain citizen and from lawyers who feel that the citizen's individual rights must be preserved at all costs.

A lawyer tends to interpret the world in terms of black and white through the use of clearly defined laws and constitutional rights. On the other hand, the social services practitioner is comfortable with dealing with the client's subjective behavior, the "gray areas" of a person's life that also have emotional overtones. The focus of social work intervention is on the client's condition, physical and environmental, whereas legal intervention is focused on the rights of the client and whether the client's actions are legal or illegal. A lawyer will defend her client from judicial intrusion into his life or affairs, whereas a social worker is more likely to seek judicial sanction for changing the client's situation or behavior. The legal profession uses an adversarial process to represent all sides equally, whereas the social work profession encourages collaboration, networking, and cooperation to achieve successful intervention.

These differences between the professions sometimes contribute to misunderstandings, miscommunications, and tension even though both professionals are seeking the best interests of their client (Havemeyer, 1982b). Sometimes well-meaning practitioners will bring services to a frail elder that make a difficult situation worse. The difficult question to be answered by the protective services practitioner as she sets out to see a client is, "When are services provided better than no services at all?" The principle of "do no harm" or, to put it in a more positive term, the principle of beneficence and determining the most therapeutic environment should guide the protective services worker in her efforts.

While there is a consensus among states to define an adult as 18 years old or older, every state seems to define protective services and their agency goals and objectives differently. Some protective services agencies consider the elderly to be their target population, while others do not; some states take a crisis-oriented approach by assisting mainly adults in emergency situations, while others focus mainly on clients of self-neglect or attempt to prevent clients from being harmed or harming others. Some protective services agencies consider their main purpose to be the prevention or alleviation of abuse, neglect, or exploitation; others consider their purpose to be the provision of services, using environmental supports to reach the client and to compensate for the older person's deficiencies. In spite of the specific goals and objectives which are developed, the ultimate intervention plan that is chosen for a specific client is affected by the client's situation and variables such as

1. The adult's functioning.
2. The circumstances or situation in relationship to the adult's behavior.
3. Action by a third party detrimental to the adult.
4. The problem that brings the adult to the agency's attention (Burr, 1982).

These different variables make it impossible for the practitioner to treat her clients successfully unless she is aware of the intervention options available in her community and the guiding principles of protective services.

An important distinction must be made between the right to refuse the investigation and the right to refuse services: when an agency is mandated to investigate a report of elder abuse or neglect, the client and those involved in the client's life must cooperate with the investigation. The practitioner has the right to insist on entering the client's residence, and in some states as a last resort she may obtain a court injunction to gain access. Once the assessment is completed, however, the client has the right to refuse all services and be left alone. Victims of elder abuse and neglect have rights that sometime impede the practitioner's attempt to deliver services. The practitioner must remember that unless the client is declared incompetent by a court of law, the client has the right to decide what services he will accept or reject.

Another dilemma facing the protective services practitioner is the problem of disagreeing with what the elder thinks. Beside struggling with the conflicting principles of *parens patriae* and the right to privacy, the practitioner is in the dual position of being an advocate for the elder's wishes and at the same time being the bearer of bad news. For example, the practitioner may find herself in the position of having to confront a client with his inability to handle his finances and his need for a conservatorship. Or a worker may solicit the trust of her client after offering medical services and promising a better situation. The treatment plan may unexpectedly include a hospitalization and a temporary nursing home placement, which in the client's eyes are forms of punishment. He may feel betrayed by the practitioner. Another dilemma facing a practitioner results from inadequate staffing in her agency. Since the passage of mandatory reporting laws, staff are now faced with climbing numbers in their caseload while staff positions are being reduced. In some states, cases have doubled or more than doubled after the passage of mandatory reporting laws. Heavy caseloads and inadequate staffing put the practitioner in the nearly untenable position of wanting to provide follow-up services for clients but having to maintain a short-term, crisis-oriented approach, and terminate cases as soon as possible.

UNIQUE ASPECTS OF APS

While all practitioners involved in protective service cases share similar problems, critical differences separate the state or county APS worker from an agency worker who is not mandated to receive and investigate reports of elder abuse and neglect. The APS worker is unable to "pick and choose" her cases: state mandatory reporting laws force the APS worker to accept all reports. This situation was recently referred to as the "Statue of Liberty" concept, whereby clients with whom other agency practitioners do not want to work or are unable to handle are referred to APS as a last resort. The public's lack of understanding about the role and limitations of APS creates unrealistic expectations that the APS practitioner can solve anything and everything. As a result, the APS practitioner's caseload often is filled with the most troubled people in society. The APS worker cannot be expected to work with every frail elder, for there are too many to handle.

Second, the APS worker may feel powerless as legislative mandates, not her statements and suggestions, affect her practice. She may feel that "higher ups" or those far removed from the realities of her work conditions dictate her job activities and are unaware of the complexities she faces. The passage of elder abuse and neglect reporting laws have resulted in more "spotlighting" of APS practitioners and more pressure to do well. It is no longer adequate to protect a client by placing him in a boarding or nursing home: the client must also be protected from abuse or neglect in those placement settings.

Multiple Dilemmas

With a burgeoning caseload, the APS supervisor is often unable to assign all referred cases for immediate assessment as the law requires. Many of these unassigned cases are perceived by the referring person as in need of immediate attention, and frustration mounts as weeks go by with no action. As mentioned in Chapter 7, crisis theory promotes early intervention during the state of active crisis, when clients are most vulnerable and amenable to change. The APS worker knows that the opportunity to constructively effect a change in the situation is being missed but is unable to investigate all new referrals at once.

To further complicate matters, the APS worker who is mandated to accept and investigate reports has received little training. Her actions are also sometimes hampered by the unwillingness of others to cooperate or an agency's inability to release information about a client in a crisis without the explicit consent of the client. Furthermore, during the investigation period, the practitioner must struggle with the issue of confidentiality, and attempt to collect information from others while taking precautions not to divulge information about the client and the referrer.

Criticism of APS

Given the dilemmas and problems facing the APS practitioner, it is no wonder that she is often a target of criticism as she attempts to fulfill her responsibilities. One criticism is that the relationship between the practitioner and client is impersonal. Owing to high caseloads, the practitioner is unable to develop the one-to-one, in-depth, quality relationship that is required to understand fully the wishes and behavior patterns of her client. A second criticism is that there are no checks and balances in APS. Some critics have suggested that the APS practitioner has more "power" than law enforcement officers, who have to cite the Miranda warnings before proceeding to question a client. For instance, practitioners providing protective services can coerce a client into allowing the worker into his home and have the client removed from the home for emergency medical care against the client's will. In these cases, the client may be too weak or unable to protest because of physical and/or mental impairments. The protective services worker has been criticized for prematurely changing her client's residence, and/or institutionalizing the client, which some observers feel hastens death and makes mortality rates higher for protective services clients than for those receiving no protective services at all (Mitchell, 1979).

The protective services practitioner sometimes is viewed by the legal profession as being "trigger happy" by petitioning for guardianship for her client, with the sole purpose of "shoving him into the nursing home." A good nursing home is often a haven and the most appropriate choice of treatment, especially for a malnourished and dehydrated client who has been grossly neglected in his own residence. Some critics feel that not enough has been done to maintain the frail and vulnerable elderly client in his own home before the initiation of a nursing home placement. This criticism does not take into account the frequency with which severely impaired elderly lack insight into their dire circumstances. The following quote captures this dilemma, which is faced by anyone working with the frail elderly:

It appears to be part of the nature of people with mentational disorders to resist social assistance, partly because of the justifiable fear that such aid will result in their being removed from their homes and placed in institutions forever, until death. Given the existing social system, however, institutionalization often seems to be the treatment of choice. (Bloom & Nielson, 1971)

The act of transferring a frail elder from one setting to another has come under scrutiny. The results of the protective services demonstration project at the Benjamin Rose Institute included a discussion on whether or not intervention by protective services could result in a premature institutionalization, resulting in what may be called "transfer trauma" and premature death (Blenkner et al., 1971). This is a very controversial question and several recently published studies point out that the issue remains unresolved. It is impossible to point a finger at protective services and say that premature death results from intervention (Borup, 1984).

Another complaint about protective services is that reports are made because the caregiver is burdened by caring for the client and that protective services intervention mainly helps to relieve the stress of the caregiver but in doing so restricts the client's freedom and may result in his loss of control and privacy. Some clinicians feel that when protective services relieve stress of the caregiver, it is a positive outcome. Another concern is that very little follow-up results after a report of elder abuse is made. People who report sometimes feel that while they have made every effort to seek help for a frail and vulnerable elderly client, "the protective services worker did nothing." This is due in part to the protective services agency's inability to report the results of its investigative efforts to every referring person. The public may not witness the practitioner referring the case to another agency for additional services or being confronted with a competent elder who absolutely refuses any intervention. In an ideal situation, some practitioners have found that making a quick call to the referrer to provide general information without breaching confidentiality, or a brief form letter, can help referrers realize that the APS worker "did something."

SOCIETAL RESPONSIBILITY

What is society's responsibility in treating the elder abuse and neglect victim? What are the responsibilities of others who come in contact with practitioners providing protective services? If society lacks the proper resources for housing its frail and vulnerable elderly or for providing adequate in-home services which would maintain a client in the community, and as a result the client is found wandering in the streets and sleeping in the park, is this client truly deviant or a victim of elder abuse and neglect, or is he also a victim of inadequate community resources? Is the unfortunate elder prematurely labeled due to inadequate social policies? It is impossible for a protective services practitioner to be the sole provider of services for every elderly person who is victimized or who seems eccentric or "abnormal" or "deviant."

It is not enough for society as a whole to turn to agencies that work with frail elders and say, You do it. The protection of endangered elderly is the responsibility of the entire community, not just one agency. Professionals from all disciplines must agree to provide backup services such as medical and legal assistance to those who work with frail elders. Protective services consist of medical, legal, and social services. One practitioner cannot provide all of these services to a client unless the rest of the community agrees to work with her. Formal agreements must be made between agencies to treat conjointly the frail and vulnerable elderly, and efforts must be made to avoid territoriality battles. Most elder abuse and neglect cases involve anywhere from two to 10 different agencies to achieve resolution, and it is unrealistic for any agency to expect one practitioner or one agency to handle a difficult elder abuse and neglect situation alone. Maximum services must be provided from all parts of society, preferably with client consent, and if not with client consent, in a sensitive and diplomatic manner which takes into account due process rights. The offering of services must be done cautiously without depriving the client of his freedom prematurely or unnecessarily. The loss of that freedom may not be worth any intervention at all. All practitioners must ask themselves, "Is our dosage too strong, our intervention too overwhelming, our takeover too final?" (Blenkner et al., 1971).

SUMMARY

Increased public awareness of the existence of agencies providing services to frail elders, in part due to the passage of mandatory reporting laws, has placed a tremendous amount of pressure on all who work with frail elders but particularly on those whose agencies mandated by state law to investigate and treat elder abuse and neglect. The practitioner has the difficult but at times gratifying and powerful role of being the regulator, the case manager, and the "balance wheel" among several disciplines. She is also in the position of being the supporter of a client's strengths and rights, an interviewer, a decision maker, and a provider of concrete services. The next chapter describes sources of possible practitioner fatigue and discouragement and how to prevent or combat them.

12 Practitioner Reactions: Burnout and Beyond

The truth was that Evelyn felt herself to be not very good with old people; she could hear in her own voice the horrid inept middle-class interfering tones she so disliked in others, the patronising kindness. No wonder the old woman had not responded. . . . What Evelyn did not tell Kate was that she was actually frightened of the old and the frail. Ever since childhood, while talking to the very old, she had been frightened by visions of herself attacking them, hitting them, assaulting them, knocking off their glasses. Evelyn, the mildest of women. These visions would appear, unsummoned, while she sipped cups of strong tea in client's bed-sitters, even while she entertained her own rambling great-aunt in larger rooms to cups of weaker tea in thinner, more fragile china. Of course, Evelyn knew that she would never assault an old person, and that these horrid apparitions must be images of her own fear of age and death, might even be some kind of safety valve. But they frightened her, nevertheless. Being a sensible woman, she looked on the positive side: she was quite good with delinquent adolescents (her own excepted) partly because she seemed to have some insight into the impulse that makes the young and the violent turn upon the weak and the defenceless, and therefore did not regard this impulse with uncomprehending disgust. She was good, also, with parents who battered their babies, a less unusual talent. But she still, in her heart, grieved over her lack of easy contact with the frail, was ashamed of the relief with which she had abandoned Mrs. Fergo to her fate. How long could she go on doing her job if these feelings grew more powerful? Had she, after all, mistaken her vocation, and was her vocation, after all, a waste of time, a job that could and should be undertaken better by bus inspectors and shop assistants?

—Drabble, *The Middle Ground*

This quotation was taken from a work of fiction and describes the feelings and reactions of an English social worker. Not all practitioners will have reactions that are this strong, but the issues of elder abuse and neglect inevitably elicit a variety of disturbing emotions. These feelings and reactions can be helpful and provide motivation and energy to inspire the practitioner to resolve a case. But they can also get in the way and drain her to the point of disturbing her personal life. This is particularly true when working with elder abuse and neglect cases because the cases can be upsetting and the feelings can be strong. Some of these feelings that arise will be discussed in this chapter and ways of coping with them will be suggested.

REACTIONS

Denial

Sometimes the facts of a case are so horrendous that the practitioner cannot believe the abuse is happening and denies it. It can be difficult to grasp the fact that an adult child would intentionally harm a parent or that a caregiver would neglect a helpless elder. The practitioner may end up saying to herself, "This can't be happening. Maybe if I look deeper into the case, it will turn out not to be abuse or neglect." The practitioner may not trust her own instincts or assessment abilities and may ask another practitioner to validate what she has uncovered. When the practitioner denies, she is in danger of colluding with the caregiver who says, "It is unavoidable that I must tie my mother up when I go to work. Otherwise, she will wander and get lost. What do you expect me to do? There's no one to take care of her and I can't afford to hire a housekeeper." Or the practitioner may summarily agree with family members who maintain that the elder is bruised because of a fall. Denial is one of the most primitive defense mechanisms available to human beings and serves to protect them when they are not fortified enough to face a shocking situation. The fact that elder abuse and neglect have been hidden for so long is partially due to denial.

Shock and Disbelief

Shock and disbelief are related to denial. Denial means that the practitioner does not see the abuse or neglect whereas shock and disbelief occur when the practitioner admits the facts of the case into conscious awareness. A practitioner who has grown up in a sheltered environment that is heavily laden with the religious injunction of honoring parents will find it very shocking to encounter situations where family members or hired caregivers are indifferent to the sufferings of an elder or inflict injuries on a dependent elder and then blame the elder for the abuse and neglect. One judge could not bring himself to believe that an adult male actually broke his mother's arm and, as a result of his disbelief, did not remove the man as his mother's conservator. Other practitioners become immobilized by their feelings of shock and find it difficult if not impossible to "work the case."

Some cases are truly revolting. Cases where there is sexual abuse of the elderly seem to elicit strong feelings of revulsion in most practitioners, especially when it is committed by a family member. Other situations that elicit revulsion are those where the elder is unkempt and filthy, and where there are gross physical injuries due to the abuse and neglect such as multiple, far-advanced pressure sores. A home environment can also be revolting:

> One woman, who was self-neglectful and had critical medical problems for which she refused to receive treatment, kept over 30 cats in her house and never let them outside to eliminate. There was cat manure all over everything. She had even let the cats excrete on the top of her television set until the screen was totally obliterated. She then purchased a second television set and placed it on top of the first. Practitioners involved in the case had difficulty coping with the stench. They took photographs of the house in order to convince a judge to sign an order that would enable the woman to receive badly needed medical treatment.

Envy

Practitioners may feel envious in certain instances. In one case, a woman new to the United States went to work for a home health agency and was sent to the home of a wealthy woman. She gave excellent care to the woman, who was literally alone in the world. Eventually the woman made out a will that left her considerable estate (over $500,000) to the housekeeper. After a thorough investigation, it was determined that there was no financial abuse in this case. But the practitioner went away wondering why she was working so hard for $20,000 a year when someone with little education and few skills was going to inherit a half million dollars with what seemed like very little effort.

Anger

The practitioner may find herself feeling very angry in certain cases and may feel that she wants to rescue the victim of abuse. This may be particularly true if the practitioner has been abused herself or has witnessed violence in her childhood home. She may want to rescue the elderly victim by charging into the home and removing him, thinking that this will solve everything and that she will be rewarded for being the savior of the elderly person. The danger of hasty interventions is that the rights of the elderly person to self-determination may be violated. His wishes and desires to remain with the abuser may be ignored. Moving too quickly in response to anger can alienate both the victim and the abuser, and they may not cooperate with the practitioner after the initial contact.

Projection of Biases

The practitioner may also feel that she wants to avenge the elder abuse victim and may say, "Lock the abuser up for life and throw away the key." A practitioner who is prejudiced against either men or women may project her biases onto the abuser or onto the victim. This stereotyping of the individuals involved prevents her from seeing the reality of the situation or from planning for effective interventions. One practitioner said of a female abuser, "You would think she would know better, having raised five children." In another instance a physician said, "What can you expect of men? They're all aggressive."

Depression

At times, the practitioner may feel depressed and overwhelmed by cases of elder abuse and neglect. There may be a sense of helplessness and hopelessness when the practitioner has not developed strategies for investigating and for effectively intervening in these cases. There may also be a feeling of not being supported by the agency that lacks adequate staff and resources. There may also be a feeling of being victimized by working in an agency whose funding has been reduced, and as a result, the practitioner has been told that she must carry a double caseload. The practitioner may be so overwhelmed that she feels like throwing up her hands and walking out. When this happens it is difficult for the practitioner to feel empowered or that anything she does is going to make a difference in her clients' lives. This feeling of powerlessness and victimization can transfer to clients.

The practitioner may also feel helpless and hopeless if the elder abuse client refuses to make any changes in his life, such as asking the abuser to leave the client's residence. Cynicism can set in, which in turn erodes the practitioner's ability to intervene effectively with the next case. The practitioner may say to herself, "Well, why get involved in this case? She's just going to say what the last three abuse victims have said, which is, she wants to continue living with her abuser. Why bother?"

Preoccupation with Cases

Cases can take over both the waking and sleeping hours of a practitioner's life. One nurse found herself thinking obsessively about an upsetting case and even dreamed about it. The case involved a 39-year-old doctor who had promised a 96-year-old wealthy, terminally ill patient that he would marry her. The doctor had known the woman for approximately four months. The nurse was outraged that a physician would behave in such a manner, and she worried that the elderly woman would not receive good medical care. The practitioner may mentally take her work home and not pay attention to family members, who in turn may complain that she does not care about them or suggest that she quit her job or work less diligently. A difficult case may be so upsetting to a practitioner that it disturbs eating and sleeping patterns. When an elder dies as a result of abuse or neglect, the practitioner may review every detail of the case and wonder whether she could have intervened more quickly or in a way that would have prevented the death. She may say, "Why didn't I trust my own instincts?" or, "Why didn't I follow up myself instead of relying on someone else to do it?"

Avoidance

Because cases of elder abuse and neglect can be so complex and at times overwhelming, the practitioner may find herself trying to avoid working on the cases or closing the cases prematurely. She may postpone a home visit or find reasons for not keeping an appointment. She may rationalize by saying, "I'll do the easy cases first today and then later in the day I'll do the more complex cases when I have the time." But somehow the time for complex cases never comes. The practitioner may look for cases to close and may say, "Well, the crisis is over and I have to get on to other cases." She may be trying to close a case prematurely by narrowly interpreting her agency's policies with regard to the length of time a case may remain open.

Impatience

Elder abuse and neglect cases are complex and take months to resolve. The practitioner who is accustomed to situations that resolve more quickly may find herself feeling impatient with the case and try to force the abuser or the victim to act more quickly. There may be impatience with other members of the team and the practitioner may blame them for impeding progress without recognizing the limitations that other professionals have. The practitioner may feel that other professionals are not as dedicated or committed as she is to resolving an elder abuse and neglect case.

Fear

Occasionally the practitioner may feel fearful either for the victim's safety or perhaps for her own. Some abusers have been charged with assault and have actually served time in prison. In the evenings and during the weekends, the practitioner may find herself worrying about the victim's safety. The practitioner may fear being attacked physically or verbally by either the abuser or the victim. There have been cases where practitioners have been threatened verbally by abusers or victims who have in essence said, "Stop meddling in my affairs," or, "I'm going to find out where you live and I'm going to harm you or your family." There are some instances in which a practitioner has had a gun pointed at her or been physically threatened. Practitioners in the helping professions are unaccustomed to having hostility directed at them. On the contrary, they are used to being thanked for their intervention. It can be very unsettling to discover that an abuser or even a victim thinks the practitioner is an enemy. This happens occasionally with an elder abuse and neglect case.

Anxiety

Sometimes a practitioner does things that are outside of agency policy; although she knows that she is pursuing the right course of action for a given client she nevertheless realizes that the agency will not defend her if she should be charged with wrongdoing. As a result she may feel very uneasy or feel as if she is out on a limb all by herself.

Overidentification

The practitioner may find herself overidentifying with either the abuser or the victim, and perhaps taking sides. It may be difficult for her not to take sides when she sees that a victim is obviously abused. However, it is important to compensate automatically when the practitioner senses that she is taking sides. Otherwise the case will not be resolved effectively.

BURNOUT

Signs of Burnout

Most people who enter the "helping professions" are deeply motivated to be of assistance to others. But over the years of active practice, the flame of commitment can flicker and dim. According to Maslach (1982), a pioneer in the study of the phenomenon of burnout, there are three major signs: (1) emotional exhaustion, (2) depersonalization, and (3) reduced personal ac- complishment. Emotional exhaustion happens when a practitioner feels drained and used up by the demands imposed by other people. There is a feeling of not having enough energy to face another day. She may feel that emotional resources are depleted and that there is no way to replenish them. She may feel that she has nothing to give her client. She may also feel that she wants to help but is simply unable to do so. She may have "compassion fatigue," which means that she has experienced her clients' pain and distress for so long that she cannot "feel" for anyone. She may find herself cutting back on involvement with others, especially those who may need her help. She may become a petty bureaucrat who "goes strictly by the book" and who pigeonholes people, responding to them only as categories and not as individuals. She may apply a formula to each and every case. A practitioner who is emotionally exhausted tries to protect herself, but her armor becomes so thick that no feelings can get through and she is viewed as being cold and indifferent to others' needs and insensitive to the feelings of others.

The second sign of burnout is depersonalization. This occurs when the practitioner sees people, especially clients, through rust-colored glasses and develops a poor opinion of them. She expects the worst of them and in fact actively dislikes people in general. She may become contemptuous of her clients and no longer care what happens to them. She may denigrate people and refuse to be civil or courteous to them. She is soured by the press of people clammering for her help.

The third sign of burnout according to Maslach is a feeling of reduced personal accomplishment. The negative feelings the practitioner has about others get turned back on herself and she feels guilty about how she has treated others. She realizes that she is turning into the very type of person she does not want to be—cold and uncaring. The practitioner may have a deep sense of inadequacy and feel that she is not the kind and sensitive person she once thought she was. Positive feelings of self-worth and self-esteem decline and depression may set in. The practitioner may say to herself, "I guess I'm just not cut out for this work." Steuer (1984) notes that practitioners working with distressed families are exposed to a great deal of grief, pain, and helplessness. Their training has taught them to empathize. But Steuer questions how much one practitioner can experience before she too becomes depressed and exhausted. Steuer suggests that the practitioner may have to get some emotional distance from cases by participating in research projects or being part of a team that treats patients and families. Steuer notes that isolation may be as much of a problem for the professional as it is for families who are suffering from stress and also suggests that a variety in the practitioner's caseload and in daily activities can be important.

Many factors contribute to burnout according to Maslach. Some of these factors are the emotional intensity that a helper must have with the people she is trying to help, the negative focusing on problems in the client's life to the exclusion of positive aspects, and the lack of supportive feedback. A practitioner frequently does not know whether or not she is making a difference in her client's life. Poor peer contact in the work setting can also contribute to burnout.

In her research studies on burnout, Maslach found that there are internal factors which play a part in burnout and that certain people are more at risk than others. It may be that by virtue of their upbringing women are more prone to suffer from emotional exhaustion and men from depersonalization and feelings of callousness. Burnout seems to be largely a white experience, although a slightly higher rate among Asian-American helpers was noted in Maslach's studies. Dramatic differences between whites and blacks were noted, suggesting that blacks do not burn out as much.

Other correlates of burnout are age, marital status, and educational level. Burnout is greatest when workers are young; it is likely to occur within the first five years of employment. Older workers are the "survivors," the ones who did not leave. People who are single seem to suffer the most burnout, while those who are married suffer the least. Divorced workers fall somewhere in between single and married people but are closer to single people in terms of emotional exhaustion. Workers with children seem to suffer less burnout. Usually, they are older, more stable, and psychologically mature people; and their involvement with their spouse and children gives them experience in dealing with conflict. Families can also be a source of emotional replenishment, and people who are married have a different view of their job than do single people; they do not depend on their jobs for their social life and have less need to obtain personal gratification from clients or colleagues. It may be that the more education a practitioner has, the less burnout she will suffer. According to Maslach those with less postgraduate training will have more burnout and those who have an undergraduate degree alone may be more vulnerable to burnout.

BEYOND BURNOUT

There are several ways to combat personal burnout. The first step involves learning to listen to one's own internal dialogue, which may be negative and destructive, and then substituting dialogue that is positive and supportive. A second area involves creating a positive work environment. The third area involves learning to "take time out," and the fourth, developing and supporting a private life that is nurturing and replenishing.

Self-Talk

Butler (1981) calls attention to the importance of how people talk to themselves in determining the direction and quality of their lives. These self-messages are frequently destructive and affect feelings, behavior, interpersonal relationships, one's sense of self-esteem, and levels of stress. The messages may be harsh, critical, and judgmental; often people talk to themselves in terms they would never dream of using with others. Other messages may urge the person to "Be Perfect," "Hurry Up," "Be Strong," "Please Others," or "Try Hard." Some self-messages prohibit an individual from taking action or expressing herself by telling her that whatever she is planning will result in a catastrophe or make her look silly or stupid in the eyes of others. She may impose negative labels on herself such as compulsive, castrating, ungrateful, or domineering. Or she may decide that she will take action only under a particular set of circumstances—which never materialize. When these negative messages dominate, life becomes routine; pleasurable activities fall by the wayside; relationships stagnate; and work becomes a bore or worse, an onerous burden.

The way out of destructive internal dialogue involves learning to listen to the self-talk, deciding whether or not it is helpful, and replacing the negative self-talk with supportive, nurturing messages. Positive messages are often permissive and build a strong foundation of self-support. Such messages may sound like this: "It's okay to be human; it's okay to make mistakes," or, "It's okay to support myself and allow myself to succeed," or, "It's okay to say no to activities that do not reflect my intrinsic feelings at the moment." Butler notes that many of the ways we talk to ourselves reflect messages we received in childhood. They may have been helpful in earlier years but need to be discarded in adulthood. The process of changing the messages may involve talking directly to the little child still within, supporting her, and giving her recognition for her accomplishments. For instance, one of the authors told herself that she should hurry up and do more work in the field of elder abuse and neglect because the need is so great. She found herself feeling harried and dissatisfied with the work she was already doing. When she realized what she was telling herself, she replaced the "Hurry Up" message with the realization that it took 25 years for spouse abuse and child abuse to come into the conciousness of America and for coping strategies and clinical expertise to be developed. The professional must remind herself that she is a pioneer in the field of elder abuse and neglect and that there are no pat methods or "cookbooks" to teach her how to perform every act of intervention. As she treats cases, she is developing techniques that will be used in the future by others. She should avoid comparing herself to her colleagues, wondering whether her statistics, her casework techniques, or her thoroughness make her a more effective worker. The "Be Perfect" message can handicap the practitioner who finds that she can do one case extremely well and intensively but may not be able to put out as much intense energy for each and every case. It is important for the practitioner to catch this destructive self-talk and acknowledge that it is happening. She can then build in positive responses such as, "No one can do it all by themselves," or, "This is a difficult case," and, "I am a good worker and I do care about people." The practitioner can use these phrases to give herself support and to remind herself that she does good work.

Creating a Positive Work Environment

In many agencies the focus is always on the negative aspects of the clients' lives and an atmosphere of gloom may permeate the agency and inhibit positive working relationships or problem solving. The practitioner can create a positive work environment in several ways. One way is to develop close working relationships with colleagues. This can be done by consulting colleagues in a problem-solving way with regard to cases that are difficult or perplexing. By consulting colleagues the practitioner will gain more energy and ideas, which will help her to continue working in a given case. The practitioner who shares ideas and takes the time to discuss case problems with others can combat negative feelings such as envy, jealously, and accusing others of laziness. Learning how others handle their difficult cases will help the practitioner realize that they too have a difficult time handling these cases and that they did not intervene successfully "by magic." It may be helpful for the practitioner to identify colleagues within the agency who are helpful and who have positive energy to share. This person may be a secretary, an administrator, or a co-worker. The practitioner should avoid colleagues who have primarily a negative focus on their work or on life in general. They will not be helpful, and in fact they may make the practitioner feel depressed and ineffective, as if nothing she does can help her client or help her to feel better about her work. Mentor relationships, in which an experienced worker volunteers to teach a less experienced worker about a complex job or skill, can be extremely helpful. Mentor relationships can extend over a period of time and can help a practitioner develop into a mature worker. Another way a practitioner can grow and mature in her work is to create opportunities for positive feedback. For example, one supervisor makes it a point always to tell her supervisees when anybody says anything positive about them. In another example, one agency encourages its clients to fill out evaluation forms which tell the agency about its effectiveness as well as where it needs to improve or change procedures. Still another way to encourage positive feedback is for the practitioner to tell individual clients or other practitioners to give feedback. She can ask whether a certain intervention worked or not, thereby creating a problem-solving situation.

Practitioners can help each other in other ways. They can make joint home visits and agree with each other before going to the home visit which person will be "the good guy" and which person will be "the bad guy." This can help in an interview so that the alleged abuser has a "good guy" with whom he can identify and accept services. Colleagues can help each other also when trouble in a difficult interview is anticipated. Co-workers can agree to interrupt the interview if the alleged abuser has a known history of assault. The interviewing practitioner can also ask co-workers to sit in on an interview as an observer for safety purposes.

The practitioner can plan each day so that it is more focused and more comfortable. For instance, it may be helpful to evaluate the exact workload at the beginning of each day in order to set priorities at that time and to make sure that the goals are realistic for each day that is being considered. The practitioner should be very specific with herself so that when she reviews her activities at the end of the day, she will have a sense of accomplishment and will be able to acknowledge to herself that she did a good job.

The practitioner can also vary her routine during the day. She may schedule the most difficult clients just before lunch or just before a break. She can also vary her interview schedule or get out of the office during different times of the day. By varying her work routine, the practitioner will experience a greater sense of control over her life and will combat feelings of helplessness.

Another way to combat burnout is to take things less personally and to realize that a client is not acting out just to make the practitioner uncomfortable. If a practitioner can avoid emotional overinvolvement and not take home people's problems, she will not feel so overwhelmed. A practitioner does not have to *feel* a client's pain and stress in order to help that client effectively. Sometimes giving talks about the job and the issues that are encountered in the work situation helps to diversify the workload, but the number of these talks should be limited so that the practitioner will not feel exploited.

Time Out

Working with elder abuse and neglect cases can be very intense, and it is critical that the practitioner take time to rest and refresh herself. This can be done by taking work breaks and using them to relax and focus on something other than cases. Some people meet friends for lunch, read fiction, or exercise. Breaks should not be used to catch up on work. If they are properly taken, they help the practitioner to focus more effectively on cases and to decrease errors of judgment. The practitioner can take many breaks during the day, even while dealing with clients, and can use a break to defuse an emotional situation. A client can be obnoxious, intimidating, and unlikable. One worker put an irate caller on hold for a few minutes while she calmed down and gathered her wits. Another practitioner left an intense interview situation, saying she was going to get a file. She took that time to consult briefly with a co-worker.

Sometimes it is important to get completely away from a work situation. There are times in a working career when a two-week vacation is inadequate. One practitioner took a three-month leave without pay in order to have time for herself. At the beginning of the leave she could not imagine returning to her work with frail elders ever again because she felt "used up." By the end of the third month she still did not feel ready to return to work so she made arrangements to have another month's leave. By the end of the fourth month she was missing her clients and was eager to return to work. It took her over a year to recover financially from the leave, but the sense of recommitment to her clients and her higher energy level made it worthwhile.

Developing a Supportive Private Life

Another way to cope with burnout is to become involved in educational activities such as teaching, writing, and consulting, or taking classes to develop professional skills which may help the practitioner obtain distance from her workload. The practitioner may find engrossing hobbies that are very rewarding and get her mind off her work. Diet and exercise are very critical. The practitioner who makes sure to maintain her own good health by having regular medical checkups and by maintaining a diet that is healthful and constructive will have more energy and enthusiasm for her work. Exercise should be a part of every practitioner's regime; it refreshes the mind and discharges muscle tension. Some find meditation very helpful in relieving the mind from thinking about cases all the time. Another way to gain distance is to have friends who are outside of the field of the helping professions. Sometimes when practitioners are gathered at parties they can only talk about their cases. This focusing on cases gives the practitioner no rest to cure the emotional exhaustion that she may be feeling from working with difficult cases. It is important to have friends outside of the helping professions because they bring an entirely different perspective to the world of the practitioner. The practitioner should also be very careful to nurture the relationships that she has in her home environment for, it is these relationships that provide the balance which permits her to work with elder abuse and neglect cases.

Sometimes it can be difficult to make the transition between working and being at home. Some clinicians have said that the time period between 5:30 p.m. and 7:00 p.m. every work day is one of the most difficult time periods they face as they try to move from their work scene to their home setting. Some practitioners take that period as time out for themselves and go into a den and read a paper, or get into a hot tub, or take a walk before going home or right after getting home. It is also helpful not to talk about work immediately after getting home even if it has been a difficult and emotionally exhausting day. It is better to decompress as much as possible, to have dinner with family or close friends first and then to talk about a case or incident. This way friends and family will not feel used for the practitioner's ventilation. Also the practitioner will not feel that she is totally immersed in the case for every single moment. In addition, Maslach has reported that a good marriage or an intimate relationship is paramount in fighting burnout.

SUMMARY

Burnout is an occupational hazard when working with elder abuse and neglect cases. Its effects are destructive and rob a practitioner of creativity, spontaneity, joy, and a feeling of having done a job well. Coping with burnout is a responsibility of each practitioner and cannot be delegated to co-workers, to the agency, or to the community. The practitioner who tackles burnout head-on will feel more in control of her life and her work.

13 Epilogue: Future Directions

Having presented much of what is now known about elder abuse and neglect, issues that merit study and attention in order to advance the field of elder abuse and neglect are discussed, and in some areas, specific recommendations are made.

RESEARCH

The cause or causes of elder abuse and neglect must be examined through further research, and the profile of the elder victim and the abuser must be more closely identified. The theory of the stressed caregiver as a reason or explanation for elder abuse and neglect has received a great deal of attention, but this is most likely not the only cause. Focusing on this hypothesis alone may prevent the practitioner and researcher from developing other hypotheses and may in fact serve to excuse the stressed caregiver for the abuse and neglect. Anyone who is abusive is responsible for her actions no matter why she did the abusing. The context of elder abuse and neglect situations needs to be studied. Does abuse occur more frequently when the elder's needs for care escalate and caregivers lose their sense of time and space? If the abuser and victim began to live together in recent years, how did it come about, and who supports whom? How does alcohol intake and drug abuse relate to abuse and neglect? Are abuse incidents preceded by conflicts which erupt into arguments? Are others present in the home when it happens? What is the quality of the relationships? What has been the history of dependent relationships in this family, of child-rearing practices? Are abuse and neglect more likely to occur when the elder and caregiver are of opposite sex but become more involved because of the elder's needs for intimate care? What are the immediate precipitants to an incident (Galbraith & Zdorkowski, 1984; Pillemer & Finklehor, 1985; Wolf et al., 1984)?

Wolf et al. (1984) observe that most elder abuse victims are women and most abusers are men. They suggest that feminist theory be integrated into research design so that the abuse and neglect can be examined as a social problem that may be caused and/or supported by the patriarchal system. Certainly, this is the focus of some theoreticians who deal with woman battering (Martin, 1976; Walker, 1984).

Pillemer and Finklehor (1985) observe that most studies have been done by interviewing practitioners and urge future investigators to focus on talking to the victims themselves and to those who are alleged to be the abusers. They also call attention to the importance of control groups and the need for general population surveys. Additionally, the consequences of abuse and neglect need to be studied. Is learned helplessness really a sequela to elder abuse and neglect? Are elders hospitalized frequently as a result of abuse and/or neglect? How often does nursing home placement result?

Other areas calling for more research attention are types of abuse, including specific physical syndromes. Hopefully, attention will also be given to strategies for intervention, and the guidelines detailed in this text will be examined closely.

TRAINING ISSUES

All professional schools should incorporate issues of elder abuse and neglect into their curricula. This includes all health care professionals as well as legal professionals and those who are being trained in gerontology. Continuing education should be made available to all these professionals on a regular basis, and they should be aware of typical cases of elder abuse and neglect that they may come across. Certain professions may see one kind of abuse more often than others. Annual conferences should include training sessions on elder abuse and neglect. Conferences focusing on domestic violence, gerontology, and protective services issues should routinely offer sessions on issues of elder abuse and neglect. It is probably best that those who do the training have caseloads that include elder abuse and neglect, so that their clinical methods are fresh and they are able to speak directly from experience. Seasoned practitioners should also consider training other professionals in their communities because this will help to develop cohesiveness among the various agencies that deal with elders and lend credibility to the issue of elder abuse and neglect.

RESOURCES

There has traditionally been a lack of resources for temporary shelters for victims of elder abuse and neglect. Some existing facilities such as convalescent hospitals and retirement homes could provide this resource. Undoubtedly victims of elder abuse and neglect require different levels of care, and it may be that retirement homes could take in the elder who is continent, alert, and oriented, whereas the elder who is incontinent, impaired, and wanders might be cared for in a convalescent hospital. Observers have called attention to the need for a 24-hour hot line whereby people concerned about elder abuse and neglect or victims themselves could call and report the abuse or neglect. Before 24-hour hot lines are installed, support services should be available on a 24-hour basis to back up these calls. Then callers need not be told to wait until the next morning when staff can come on duty to take care of their problems. Another issue having to do with resources is that adult protective services agencies customarily have low staffing. These agencies are looked upon as the official agencies to whom most mandatory reporting of elder abuse and neglect must be directed. They are increasingly unable to meet the needs of all frail elders in the community. This is particularly true since the passage of mandatory reporting laws in the last few years. The size of caseloads has increased dramatically, but the amount of money allotted for staffing, training, and education has diminished.

THE LEGAL SYSTEM

Many laws are on the books with regard to assault and battery, financial exploitation, and harassment of individuals in general. These laws should be enforced when they apply to elders as well as to other age-groups. Some observers have suggested that special laws be passed with regard to abuse and neglect of elders and others have felt that the current laws are sufficient. Direct recommendations with regard to the legal system follow:

1. There should be an expansion of the court investigation system in all states. Courts should have direct and impartial knowledge of the situations in which a frail elder finds herself when she is the subject of a conservatorship.
2. Banks should be given immunity from civil suits if they report financial abuse to the police or the court. Banks, judges, and attorneys are in the best position to observe financial abuse.
3. Written police reports should have a special category for indicating when the case involves elder abuse and neglect. This would facilitate data collection and the study of elder abuse and neglect cases.

4. Prosecutors should take elder abuse and neglect cases just as seriously as they do any other case, and they should press charges just as they do with other cases.

MANDATORY REPORTING LAWS

Currently, mandatory reporting laws are uneven across the states in definitions and penalties for not reporting. Furthermore, they tend to concentrate on physical abuse and neglect alone. This ignores the very substantial amount of financial abuse that exists. Hopefully, a national council or coalition on elder abuse and neglect will develop and will take upon itself the task of bringing uniformity to the various mandatory reporting laws. At present, a number of professions are mandated to report, but bank personnel, judges, and attorneys, those who are most familiar with financial abuse, are not mandated to report and probably should be.

PRACTICE ISSUES

The practitioner is likely to find himself working with the entire family system when working with elder abuse and neglect. Some agencies and practitioners feel they can only be pro-victim and may want to leave the treatment of batterers to other specialty agencies and practitioners. However, most victims will probably choose to continue living with their abusers, especially if they are family members. The practitioner may as well resign himself to treating the family as a system and learn family and joint counseling techniques.

A specialty practice may develop for those who are working with elder abuse and neglect. These specialists should receive training in gerontology as well as legal issues and medical conditions that traditionally affect the elderly. Additionally, they should receive specialized training in the signs and symptoms of abuse and neglect and be trained in investigation and intervention techniques. Elder abuse and neglect clinicians should develop closer working relationships with domestic violence clinicians. There should be a cross-fertilization of investigation and intervention techniques between the two areas so that those working with elder abuse and neglect will not have to reinvent the wheel. They should also be sharing common dilemmas, which will enable them to band together to lobby for effective legislation and budgets to meet the needs of domestic-violence victims. In some parts of the country, attempts are being made to form family violence coalitions that are composed of agencies that treat the various types of domestic violence: child abuse and neglect, sexual assault, spouse abuse, and elder abuse and neglect. These groups call attention to the learned nature of family violence, the common history of maltreatment of family members who are weak or dependent, and the strong likelihood that the numbers of reports of those who are victimized in domestic violence will increase.

In dealing with abusers who are elderly, specific techniques may have to be developed by therapists who are already working with batterers. They may not be aware of the prevalence of elder abuse and neglect. Although geriatric mental health is a new and growing specialty, too few therapists are interested in it.

The last practice issue concerns recommendations to judges and to those officials who deal with judges, such as probation officers. The judge who often determines the treatment of the batterer and grants protection orders for victims is usually a generalist, and he is seldom well trained in domestic-violence issues. He often welcomes specific recommendations from the practitioner, especially if those recommendations are backed up by a clear-cut rationale that shows how the practitioner arrived at his conclusion. A judge also tends to be impressed by the person who actually appears in front of him. Therefore the practitioner concerned about the treatment of the batterer and victim should go to court to give his report. This kind of follow-through by the practitioner will ensure better treatment for the batterer and for the victim.

The contents of this book only begin to teach the practitioner how to assess and treat elder abuse and neglect. The field of elder abuse and neglect is in its infancy, and a great deal of work remains to be done in the areas of research, training, development of legal response, resource development, and clinical practice.

Appendixes

APPENDIX A
Elder Abuse and Neglect: Written Protocol for Identification and Assessment*

"Tools" Needed

1. Sketch sheet or trauma graph
2. Tape measure
3. Camera, film, flash
4. Paper and pen
5. Consent and release of information forms

General Interview Techniques (Villamore & Bergman, 1981)

1. Privacy
2. Pacing
3. Planning
4. Pitch
5. Punctuality

ASSESSMENT

History

Methodology Technique

1. Examine client alone without caregiver.
2. Explain to caregiver he/she will be interviewed separately after client is interviewed; this is part of routine exam.
3. Do not rush during interview. Provide support to client and caregiver. Work questions into conversation in relaxed manner.
4. Do not be judgmental or allow personal feelings to interfere with providing optimal care. Do not *prematurely* diagnose client as a victim of elder abuse or neglect; do not tell caregiver what treatment plans are until all facts are gathered.
5. Pay special attention to trauma, burns, nutrition, recent change in condition, and financial status.
6. Do collateral contacts as soon as possible with others, i.e., visiting nurse, neighbors, friends, to obtain additional information.

*Source: S. Tomita. Detection and treatment of elderly abuse and neglect: A protocol for health care professionals. *PT & OT in Geriatrics,* 1982, 2(2):37–51.

Presentation

Signs and Symptoms Suspicious for Abuse/Neglect

1. Client brought in to hospital Emergency Room by someone other than caregiver.
2. Prolonged interval between trauma/illness and presentation for medical care (i.e., gross decubiti).
3. Suspicious history: client is new to system with history of "shopping" or "doctor hopping." Description of how injury occurred is alien to the physical findings, either better or worse; client has injuries not mentioned in history; has history of previous similar episodes; too many "explained" injuries or inconsistent explanations over time.
4. Medication bottles or the client's pharmacy profile indicates medications are not being taken or given as prescribed.

Functional Assessment Evaluation

1. Administer Mini-Mental State Exam or Dementia Scale to determine current mental status. (Kahn-Goldfarb Dementia Scale: 1 point each if patient knows age, day, month, year, month of birth, year of birth, street address, city, President of the United States, last past President of United States) (Poor = 0–2, Fair = 3–7, Good = 8–10).
2. Collect pertinent data: i.e., length of time at residence, medical insurance source, income source(s).
3. Assess client's ability to perform activities of daily living—i.e., ability to do self-care, ambulation status, ability to do meal preparation, pay bills, shop; mode of transportation, etc.
4. Ask client to describe a typical day to determine degree of independence or dependence on others, most frequent and significant contacts, who and how often seen.
5. Ask client role expectations of self and caregiver.
6. Have client report recent crisis in family life.
7. Ask if there is alcohol use, drug use, mental illness, or behavior dyscontrol among household or family members.
8. Ask directly if patient has experienced:
   a. Being shoved, shaken, or hit (record verbatim; when, where on body, examine body).
   b. Being left alone, tied to chair or bed, or left locked in room (record verbatim; when and duration).
   c. Having money or property taken or signed over to someone else. Determine current assets, financial status (specify).
   d. Withholding of food or medication or medical care, being oversedated with medication or alcohol.
   e. Being threatened or experiences fear of caregiver.
9. Assess how client responds in situations listed above.
10. Ask client how he/she copes with stress and upsetting incidents.

11. Assess degree of patient's dependence on caregiver alone for financial, physical, and/or emotional support.

Physical Exam

1. In medical setting, a standard comprehensive examination should be completed on a gowned undressed patient (no exceptions). In home, attempt review of body while protecting client's modesty.
2. If injury is due to an accident, document circumstances (i.e., client was pushed, client has balance problem, patient was drowsy from medications and fell).
3. Examine closely for effects of undermedication, overmedication, assess nutrition, hygiene, and personal care for evidence of abuse/neglect (i.e., dehydration or malnourishment without illness-related cause).
4. Assess for
   a. Burns, unusual location or type.
   b. Physical or thermal injury on head, scalp, or face.
   c. Bruises and hematomas:
      (1) Bilaterally on soft parts of body, not over bony prominences (knees and elbows). *Inner* arm/thigh bruises are *very* suspicious.
      (2) Clustered as from repeated striking.
      (3) Shape similar to an object or thumb/finger prints.
      (4) Presence of old and new bruises at the same time as from repeated injury, injuries in different stages of resolution.

Dating of Bruises

0–2 days	swollen, tender
0–5 days	red-blue
5–7 days	green
7–10 days	yellow
10–14 days	brown
2–4 weeks	clear

      (5) Presence of bruises after changing health care provider or after prolonged absence from health care agency.
   d. Mental status and neurological exam changes from previous level.
   e. Fractures, falls, or evidence of physical restraint. Contractures may indicate confinement for long periods.
   f. Ambulation status: poor ambulation may be suggestive of sexual assault or other "hidden" injuries.
5. Observe and Document
   a. Size, color, shape, and location of injury. Use sketch sheet and/or take photographs.
   b. No new lesions during patient's hospitalization.
   c. Family/caregiver(s) do not visit or show concern.
   d. Client's affect and nonverbal behavior: abnormal/suspicious behavior of client—extremely fearful or agitated, overly quiet and passive, or expressing fear of caregiver.

    e. Your intuition that all is not well between patient and caregiver.

    f. Client–caregiver interaction: if the caregiver yells at client and client yells back, determine if they "need" to yell at each other and/or if this is a long-term pattern with which both are comfortable. On the contrary, if the verbal threats or yelling incidents are "new" behaviors and the contents of the yelling indicate escalation toward more abusive acts or severe verbal abuse, the practitioner should be concerned.

6. In medical setting, diagnostic procedures as indicated by history or exam may include:

    a. Radiological screening for fractures or evidence of physical restraint.

    b. Metabolic screening for nutritional, electrolyte, or endocrine abnormality.

    c. Toxicology screening or drug levels for over- or undermedication.

    d. Hematology screening for coagulation defect when abnormal bleeding or bruising is documented.

    e. CAT scan for major change in neurological status or head trauma that could result in subdural hematoma.

    f. Gynecological procedures to rule out VD from sexual assault.

Interview with Caregiver

"Thank you for waiting while I interviewed your mother. Now it's your turn. I need your help—I am doing an (psychosocial) assessment of your mother's current functioning and situation in order to determine what services are appropriate at this time. I would like to spend some time with you and have you tell me your perception of how things are here."

1. "Tell me what you want me to know about your mother."
2. "What is her medical condition? What medicine does she take?"
3. "What kind of care does she require?"
4. "How involved are you with your mother's everyday activities and care?"
5. "What do you expect her to do for herself?"
6. "What does she expect you to do for her?
    a. And do you do those things?
    b. Are you able to do them?
    c. Have you had any difficulties? What kind?"
7. "Please describe how you spend a typical day."
8. "How do you cope with having to care for your mother all the time?"
9. "Do you have supports or respite care? Who and what? Are there other siblings who help?"
10. "What responsibilities do you have outside the home? Do you work? What are your hours? What do you do?"
11. "Would you mind telling me what your income is?" (If this question seems touchy to the caregiver, say, "I just wondered if your family can afford the pills she needs to take." At the same time you are assessing the caregiver's degree of dependence on the elderly client's income/pensions/assets.)
12. "Is your mother's Social Security check directly deposited in the bank?"
13. "Who owns this house? Do you pay rent? Whose name is on the deed?"

14. "If you help your mother pay her bills, how do you do it? Is your name on her account? Do you have power of attorney? Does it have a durable clause? When did you get it?"

Save more delicate questions for last:

1. "You know those bruises on your mother's arms (head, nose, etc.). How do you suppose she got them?" (Document response verbatim. If possible, follow up with request that caregiver demonstrate how injury may have happened.)
2. "Your mother is suffering from malnourishment and/or dehydration," or, "Your mother seems rather undernourished and thin; how do you think she got this way?"
3. "Is there any reason you waited this long to seek medical care for your mother?"
4. "Caring for someone as impaired as your mother is, is a difficult task. Have you ever felt so frustrated with her that you pushed her a little harder than you expected? How about hitting or slapping her? What were the circumstances?" (Record verbatim.)
5. "Have you ever had to tie your mother to a bed or chair, or lock her in a room when you go out at night?"
6. "Have there been times when you've yelled at her or threatened her verbally?"

Signs of high-risk situation:

1. Alcohol use, drug abuse, and/or mental illness in caregiver's residence.
2. Caregiver is alienated, socially isolated, has poor self-image.
3. Caregiver is young, immature, and behavior indicates own dependency needs have not been met.
4. Caregiver is forced by circumstances to care for patient who is unwanted.
5. Caregiver is unemployed, without sufficient funds, dependent on client for housing and money.
6. Caregiver's and/or client's poor health or chronic illness may exacerbate poor relationship.
7. Caregiver exhibits abnormal behavior, e.g., overly hostile or frustrated, secretive, shows little concern, demonstrates poor self-control, "blames" client, exhibits exaggerated defensiveness and denial, lacks physical contact, lacks facial or eye contact with client, shows overconcern regarding correcting client's bad behavior, visits patient with alcohol on breath.

Collateral Contacts

1. Do collateral contacts promptly before caregiver attempts to collude with patient.
2. Number of contacts may range from 2 to 17.

Diagnosis

Integrate patient history, physical exam, caregiver history, and collateral contact information.

1. No evidence for elder abuse/neglect
2. Suspicion of neglect
3. Suspicion of abuse
4. Positive for abuse/neglect, gross neglect

Types of Clients (Villamore & Bergman, 1981)

1. Competent, consenting
2. Competent, nonconsenting
3. Incompetent
4. Emergency

INTERVENTION OPTIONS

Agency/Professional Intervention

Indirect Intervention

1. Documentation—review of chart may later point to abuse.
2. Reporting—most states have Adult Protective Services Units. Approximately 40 states have some form of reporting law, some are mandatory reporting laws, some are voluntary reporting laws.
3. Referral out—refer the case to another agency for follow-up.

Direct Intervention to Client

1. Diagnostic Plan
   a. Geriatric evaluation team home visit or in-clinic assessment
   b. Short hospital stay or repeated contact for further assessment and case planning.
   c. Administer written protocol and refer case for execution of treatment plan
2. Therapeutic Plan
   a. *Repeated* home visits or appointments in office to gain trust, to persuade and bargain with elderly client, to help elder with decision making, ventilation, problem solving (takes up to *two years*).
   b. Legal intervention—use least restrictive option to the extent possible (see scale of legal interventions), i.e., apply for guardianship or protective payee status; press charges and/or prosecute.
   c. Financial crisis intervention:
      (1) Call the bank to place an alert on the account.
      (2) Transport the client to the bank to discuss the incident with the bank manager.

(3) Bring bank personnel to the client's home.

(4) Report the incident(s) to the Social Security office.

(5) Attempt to void the client's signature on forms signed without the client's knowledge or recall, on forms signed under duress, or when the client most likely was legally incompetent.

3. Education Plan/Empowerment Training to acquire/strengthen positive, powerful self-image.

   a. Assertiveness training.

   b. How to fend off an attacker.

   c. How to care better for self to reduce dependency on caregiver.

   d. Advise elder not to have observable pattern of behavior (i.e., change walking route regularly when going to and from store, bank, etc.).

4. Environmental change—use the least restrictive environmental option to the extent possible (see range of interventions).

   a. Block watch.

   b. Move to safer place, i.e., elderly housing, another friend, relative, adult foster home, boarding home.

   c. Home improvements.

   d. Increased contacts outside of home, i.e., day-care center.

5. Advocacy/Resource Linkage

   a. Assist elder with obtaining meals-on-wheels, chorework service.

   b. Link elder to natural helpers and "gatekeepers."

   c. Telephone checks, i.e., Dial-A-Care.

Direct Intervention to Caregiver

1. Therapeutic Plan

   a. Repeated home or office visits for family counseling to clarify role expectations and reduce conflict.

   b. Respite care for elder to give caregiver a rest.

   c. Obtain cash grants for caregiver when possible.

2. Educational Plan

   a. Group programs—community-wide information meetings and small informal discussion of groups. Provide information on aging resources and aging process, mutual problem solving and support. Help improve ability to cope with elder and to recognize own needs and limitations.

   b. Individual contacts, articles to explain "normal" dependency of aging, "senility," Alzheimer's disease, etc.

3. Resource linkage

   a. Strengthen resources and social supports available to caregivers, i.e., chorework, home health aide.

Staff Training

1. Teach your colleagues how to detect abuse/neglect, what intervention options are, what is being done elsewhere.

2. Offer team approach to caring of high-risk patients/clients; offer to do follow-up, share information.

Community Intervention

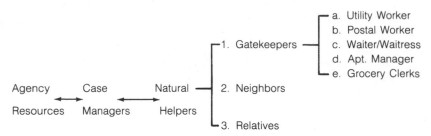

1. Train "gatekeepers" to watch for symptoms of elderly's inability to care for self, for abuse and neglect, and to report to case manager when an elder has not been seen for a long time.
2. Maintain regular contacts in your geographical area with the natural helpers and institution staff, i.e., bank personnel.
3. Always engage the natural helper's or elderly's own social systems in carrying out the treatment plan. If possible, do not "rescue."

Follow-up Process

1. In general, make appointments for initial home and in-agency visits.
2. Consider dropping in on client for second visit to put all involved "on warning" but also to display earnestness.

Limitations/When to Terminate

1. The client dies.
2. The client is competent and chooses not to accept the practitioner's help.
3. The client is no longer in danger.

APPENDIX B
DEMENTIA SCALE*

1. What is the name of this place?
2. Where is it located (address)?
3. What is today's date?
4. What is the month now?
5. What is the year?
6. How old are you?
7. When were you born (month)?
8. When were you born (year)?
9. Who is the president of the United States?
10. Who was the president before him?

   Poor = 0–2
   Fair = 3–7
   Good = 8–10

*Reprinted, by permission of the author and the publisher, from R. L. Kahn et al., Brief objective measures for the determination of mental status in the aged. *American Journal of Psychiatry,* 1960, *117*(4):326–328. Copyright © 1960, The American Psychiatric Association.

APPENDIX C
MINI-MENTAL STATUS EXAM*

ORIENTATION

Ask each of the following, and score 1 for each correct answer.

1. What is the day of the week __, month __, date __, year __, season __ ( )/5
2. Where are we: state __, county __, town __, residence number __, street name __ (or hospital and floor) ( )/5

REGISTRATION

Name 3 unrelated objects slowly and clearly (i.e., horse, watch, phone).
Ask the client to repeat them. Tell client to remember objects because he/she will be asked to name them in a few minutes. Score first try. Repeat objects till all are learned, up to 6 trials. ( )/3

ATTENTION AND CALCULATION

Ask the client to perform serial 7 subtraction from 100 or serial 3 subtraction from 20. Stop after 5 numbers and score 1 for each number (93, 86, 79, 72, 65) or (17, 14, 11, 8, 5). ( )/5

RECALL

Ask the client to recall the names of the 3 unrelated objects which you asked him/her to repeat above and score 1 for each correct name. ( )/3

LANGUAGE

1. Naming—point to 2 objects and ask client to name them. Score 1 for each correct name (e.g., tie and pencil). ( )/2

*Reprinted, by permission of the authors and the publisher, from M. F. Folstein, S. E. Folstein, & P. R. McHugh, Mini-Mental State. *Journal of Psychiatric Research*, 1975, *12*(3):189–198. Copyright © 1975, Pergamon Press, Ltd.

2. Repetition—ask the client to repeat "No ifs, ands, or buts." Allow
   only 1 trial. Score 0 or 1.   (   )/1
3. Three-stage command—ask the client to "Take a paper in your right
   hand, fold it in half and put it on the floor." Score 1 for each part
   correctly executed.   (   )/3
4. Reading—print on a blank card "close your eyes," ask the client to
   read the sentence and do what it says. Score 1 if eyes are closed.   (   )/1
5. Writing—ask the client to write a sentence; do not dictate. It must
   contain a subject and verb, and make sense. Correct grammar and
   punctuation are not necessary. Score 0 or 1.   (   )/1
6. Copying—ask the client to copy this figure
   exactly. All 10 angles and intersection
   must be present to score 1.   (   )/1

Total (   )/30 possible points

(Refer to source for scoring guidelines)

APPENDIX D
ADL EVALUATION FORM*

Instructions: For each area of functioning listed below, check description that applies.

BATHING

[ ] Independent — Receives no assistance (gets in and out of tub by self if tub is usual means of bathing).

[ ] Independent — Receives assistance in bathing only one part of body (such as back or leg).

[ ] Dependent — Receives assistance in bathing more than one part of body (or not bathed).

DRESSING

[ ] Independent — Gets clothes and gets completely dressed without assistance.

[ ] Independent — Gets clothes and gets dressed without assistance except for tying shoes.

[ ] Dependent — Receives assistance in getting clothes and getting dressed or stays partly or completely undressed.

TOILETING

[ ] Independent — Goes to toilet, cleans self, and arranges clothes without assistance (may use object for support such as cane, walker, or wheelchair and may manage night bedpan or commode, emptying same in morning).

[ ] Dependent — Receives assistance in going to toilet or in cleansing self or in arranging clothes after elimination or in use of night bedpan or commode.

[ ] Dependent — Does not go to room termed "toilet" for the elimination process.

*Reprinted, by permission of the authors and the publisher, from S. Katz et al., Studies of illness in the aged—The index of ADL: A standardized measure of biological and psychosocial function. *Journal of the American Medical Association, 185*(12):914–919. Copyright © 1963, American Medical Association.

TRANSFER

[ ] Independent — Moves in and out of bed as well as in and out of chair without
                  assistance (may be using object for support such as cane or
                  walker).
[ ] Dependent — Moves in or out of bed or chair with assistance.
[ ] Dependent — Doesn't get out of bed.

CONTINENCE

[ ] Independent — Controls urination and bowel movement completely by self.
[ ] Independent — Has occasional "accidents".
[ ] Dependent   Supervision helps keep urine or bowel control; catheter is used
                 or is incontinent.

FEEDING

[ ] Independent — Feeds self without assistance.
[ ] Dependent — Feeds self except for getting assistance in cutting meat or
                  buttering bread.
[ ] Dependent — Receives assistance in feeding or is fed partly or completely by
                  using tubes or intravenous fluids.

APPENDIX E
SYMPTOMS OF DEPRESSION*

1. Dysphoria—dissatisfaction, restlessness, malaise.
2. Sleep disturbance.
3. Poor concentration, slowed thoughts.
4. Appetite or weight change.
5. Loss of interest in usual activities.
6. Psychomotor agitation or retardation.
7. Suicide ideation, recurrent thoughts of death.
8. Worthlessness, self-reproach, excessive guilt.
9. Loss of energy.
10. Symptoms are present at least for two weeks with no other major psychiatric or organic disorder present and are not due to bereavement.

*Source: D. W. Goodwin and S. B. Guze. Psychiatric Diagnosis (3rd ed.), New York and Oxford: Oxford Press, Inc., 1984.

APPENDIX F-1
DURABLE POWER OF ATTORNEY

This is an important legal document. It creates a durable power of attorney. Before executing this document, you should know these important facts:

1. This document may provide the person you designate as your attorney in fact with broad powers to dispose of, sell, convey, and encumber your real and personal property.
2. These powers will exist for an indefinite period of time unless you limit their duration in this document. These powers continue to exist notwithstanding your subsequent disability or incapacity.
3. You have the right to revoke or terminate this durable power of attorney at any time.

ARTICLE I. DECLARATIONS

1.1 Effective date of this Power: _____

1.2 Name and Address of the Principal: _____

_____

The first person pronoun, "I", and its variations, "ME," "MINE," and "MYSELF" refer to the Principal.
THIS DURABLE POWER OF ATTORNEY SHALL NOT BE AFFECTED BY SUBSE-QUENT INCAPACITY OF THE PRINCIPAL.

1.3 Name and Address of the Attorney in Fact: SUPPORT SERVICES FOR ELDERS, INC., 50 Oak Street, San Francisco, CA 94102.
The second person pronoun, "YOU," and its variations, "YOUR," and "YOURSELF" refer to the ATTORNEY IN FACT.
When you, as my Attorney in Fact, sign on my behalf under the powers I give you in this document, you shall use the following form as authorized in California Civil Code Section 1095:

"_____ ", by SUPPORT SERVICES FOR ELDERS, INC., his/her
    My name   Attorney in Fact.

1.4 My cancellation of any part of this document: IF, BEFORE I SIGN THIS DOCUMENT, I cross out or write through any part of this document, and I put my initials opposite the cancelled part, then I eliminate that part from the powers I give you in this document.

Reprinted by permission of Support Services for Elders, Inc., San Francisco, undated.

ARTICLE II. POWERS GIVEN TO THE ATTORNEY IN FACT

2.1 I, as Principal, appoint you as my Attorney in Fact, with full power of substitution, revocation, and delegation. I give you the powers in this document to use for my benefit and on my behalf. You shall use these powers in a fiduciary capacity.

2.2 As to any assets (a) standing in my name, or (b) held for my benefit, or (c) acquired for my benefit, and subject to Paragraph 1.4, I give you these powers:

1. As to any commercial, checking, savings, savings & loan, money market, Treasury bills, mutual fund accounts, safe deposit boxes, in my name or opened for my benefit—to open, withdraw, deposit into, close, and to negotiate, endorse, or transfer any instrument affecting those accounts.

2. As to any promissory note receivable, secured or unsecured, or any accounts receivable—to collect on, compromise, endorse, borrow against, hypothecate, release and reconvey that note and any related deed of trust.

3. As to any shares of stock, bonds, or any documents or instruments defined as securities under California law—to open accounts with stock brokers (on cash or on margin), buy, sell, endorse, transfer, hypothecate, and borrow against.

4. As to any real property—to collect rents, disburse funds, keep in repair, hire professional property managers, lease to tenants, negotiate and renegotiate leases, borrow against, renew any loan, sign any documents required for any transaction in this Paragraph 4, and to sell, subject to confirmation of court, any of the real property.

5. To hire and pay from my funds for counsel and services of professional advisors, including SSE, Inc., according to the then current fee schedule, without limitations—physicians, dentists, accountants, attorneys, and investment counselors.

6. As to my income taxes and other taxes—to sign my name, hire preparers and advisors, and pay for their services from my funds, and to do whatever is necessary to protect my assets from assessments as though I did those acts myself.

7. To apply for government and insurance benefits, to prosecute and to defend legal actions, to arrange for transportation and travel, and to partition community property to create separate property for me.

8. To sign and deliver a valid disclaimer under the Internal Revenue Code and the California Probate Code, when, in your judgment, my own and my heirs' best interests would be served; to that end, to hire and to pay for legal and financial counsel to make that decision as to whether to file that disclaimer.

9. To manage tangible personal property, including but not limited to, moving, storing, selling, donating, or otherwise disposing of said property.

ARTICLE III. MISCELLANEOUS

3.1 *Severability.* If any provision of this document is not valid, all other provisions shall remain valid.

3.2 *Your freedom from liability when you show good faith.* You are not liable to me or any of my successors when, in good faith, you act or do not act under this document; but this freedom from liability is not effective in the event of your willful misconduct or gross negligence.

3.3 Where required, the singular includes the plural and plural includes the singular.

3.4 *California governing law.* California law governs this durable power of attorney in all respects.

3.5 *Reliance on photocopies.* Any person dealing with my Attorney shall have the right to rely on a photocopy of this Durable Power of Attorney declared by my attorney as being genuine, as if it were the signed, original Durable Power of Attorney.

3.6 *Signing.* I, the Principal, sign this Durable Power of Attorney on date set opposite my signature.

SIGNATURE _____ Date _____

....
)
State of California   ) ss:
City and County of San Francisco   )

On this __ day of __ in the year __, before me, the undersigned, a Notary Public, State of California, duly commissioned and sworn, personally appeared _____, known to me (or proved to me on the basis of satisfactory evidence) to be the person whose name is subscribed to the within instrument and acknowledged to me that s/he executed the same.

IN WITNESS WHEREOF I have hereunto set my hand and affixed my official seal in the County of San Francisco the day and year in this certificate first above written.

_____

Notary Public, State of California

My commission expires _____

....

Any of the following are authorized to act for SUPPORT SERVICES FOR ELDERS, INC. on behalf of _____.

_____

_____ (seal)

_____

_____

(Signed) _____

APPENDIX F-2
DURABLE POWER OF ATTORNEY
(SPRINGING)

This is an important legal document. It creates a durable power of attorney. Before executing this document, you should know these important facts:

1. This document may provide the person you designate as your attorney in fact with broad powers to dispose of, sell, convey, and encumber your real and personal property.
2. These powers will exist for an indefinite period of time unless you limit their duration in this document. These powers continue to exist notwithstanding your subsequent disability or incapacity.
3. You have the right to revoke or terminate this durable power of attorney at any time.

ARTICLE I. DECLARATIONS

1.1 Effective date of this Power: _____

1.2 Name and Address of the Principal: _____

_____

The first person pronoun, "I", and its variations, "ME," "MINE," and "MYSELF" refer to the Principal.
THIS DURABLE POWER OF ATTORNEY SHALL BECOME EFFECTIVE UPON THE INCAPACITY OF THE PRINCIPAL.

1.3 Name and Address of the Attorney in Fact: SUPPORT SERVICES FOR ELDERS, INC., 50 Oak Street, San Francisco, CA 94102.
The second person pronoun, "YOU," and its variations, "YOUR," and "YOURSELF" refer to the ATTORNEY IN FACT.
When you, as my Attorney in Fact, sign on my behalf under the powers I give you in this document, you shall use the following form as authorized in California Civil Code Section 1095:

"_____ ", by SUPPORT SERVICES FOR ELDERS, INC., his/her
      My name   Attorney in Fact.

1.4 My cancellation of any part of this document: IF, BEFORE I SIGN THIS DOCUMENT, I cross out or write through any part of this document, and I put my initials opposite the cancelled part, then I eliminate that part from the powers I give you in this document.

Reprinted by permission of Support Services for Elders, Inc., San Francisco, undated.

284

ARTICLE II. POWERS GIVEN TO THE ATTORNEY IN FACT

2.1 I, as Principal, appoint you as my Attorney in Fact, with full power of substitution, revocation, and delegation. I give you the powers in this document to use for my benefit and on my behalf. You shall use these powers in a fiduciary capacity.

2.2 As to any assets (a) standing in my name, or (b) held for my benefit, or (c) acquired for my benefit, and subject to Paragraph 1.4, I give you these powers:

1. As to any commercial, checking, savings, savings & loan, money market, Treasury bills, mutual fund accounts, safe deposit boxes, in my name or opened for my benefit—to open, withdraw, deposit into, close, and to negotiate, endorse, or transfer any instrument affecting those accounts.

2. As to any promissory note receivable, secured or unsecured, or any accounts receivable—to collect on, compromise, endorse, borrow against, hypothecate, release, and reconvey that note and any related deed of trust.

3. As to any shares of stock, bonds, or any documents or instruments defined as securities under California law—to open accounts with stock brokers (on cash or on margin), buy, sell, endorse, transfer, hypothecate, and borrow against.

4. As to any real property—to collect rents, disburse funds, keep in repair, hire professional property managers, lease to tenants, negotiate and renegotiate leases, borrow against, renew any loan, sign any documents required for any transaction in this Paragraph 4, and to sell, subject to confirmation of court, any of the real property.

5. To hire and pay from my funds for counsel and services of professional advisors, including SSE, Inc., according to the then current fee schedule, without limitations—physicians, dentists, accountants, attorneys, and investment counselors.

6. As to my income taxes and other taxes—to sign my name, hire preparers and advisors, and pay for their services from my funds, and to do whatever is necessary to protect my assets from assessments as though I did those acts myself.

7. To apply for government and insurance benefits, to prosecute and to defend legal actions, to arrange for transportation and travel, and to partition community property to create separate property for me.

8. To sign and deliver a valid disclaimer under the Internal Revenue Code and the California Probate Code, when, in your judgment, my own and my heirs' best interests would be served; to that end, to hire and to pay for legal and financial counsel to make that decision as to whether to file that disclaimer.

9. To manage tangible personal property, including but not limited to, moving, storing, selling, donating, or otherwise disposing of said property.

ARTICLE III. MISCELLANEOUS

3.1 *Severability.* If any provision of this document is not valid, all other provisions shall remain valid.

3.2 *Your Freedom from Liability When You Show Good Faith.* You are not liable to me or any of my successors when, in good faith, you act or do not act under this document; but this freedom from liability is not effective in the event of your willful misconduct or gross negligence.

3.3 Where required, the singular includes the plural and plural includes the singular.

3.4 *California Governing Law.* California law governs this durable power of attorney in all respects.

3.5 *Reliance on Photocopies.* Any person dealing with my Attorney shall have the right to rely on a photocopy of this Durable Power of Attorney declared by my attorney as being genuine, as if it were the signed, original Durable Power of Attorney.

3.6 *Signing.* I, the Principal, sign this Durable Power of Attorney on date set opposite my signature.

SIGNATURE _____ Date _____

....

State of California   )
) ss:
City and County of San Francisco   )

On this __ day of __ in the year __, before me, the undersigned, a Notary Public, State of California, duly commissioned and sworn, personally appeared _____, known to me (or proved to me on the basis of satisfactory evidence) to be the person whose name is subscribed to the within instrument and acknowledged to me that s/he executed the same.

IN WITNESS WHEREOF I have hereunto set my hand and affixed my official seal in the County of San Francisco the day and year in this certificate first above written.

_____

Notary Public, State of California

My commission expires _____

....

Any of the following are authorized to act for SUPPORT SERVICES FOR ELDERS, INC. on behalf of _____.

_____

_____ (seal)

_____

_____

(Signed) _____

APPENDIX F-3
DURABLE POWER OF ATTORNEY
FOR HEALTH CARE©

This is a Durable Power of Attorney for Health Care form. By filling in this form, you can select someone to make health care decisions for you if for some reason you become unable to make those decisions for yourself. A properly completed form provides the best legal protection available to help ensure that your wishes will be respected.

READ THIS FORM CAREFULLY BEFORE FILLING IT OUT. EACH PARAGRAPH IN THE FORM CONTAINS INSTRUCTIONS. IT IS IMPORTANT THAT YOU FOLLOW THESE INSTRUCTIONS SO THAT YOUR WISHES MAY BE CARRIED OUT.

The following checklist is provided to help you fill out this form correctly. You may use this checklist to double check sections you may be unsure of as you fill in the form. You may also use this checklist to help make sure you have completed the form properly. If you have properly completed this form, you should be able to answer **yes** to each question in the checklist.

_____ 1. I am a California resident who is at least 18 years old, of sound mind and acting of my own free will.

_____ 2. The individuals I have selected as my agent and alternate agents to make health care decisions for me are at least 18 years old and are *not:*

   • my *treating* health care provider.

   • an employee of my *treating* health care provider, unless the employee is related to me by blood, marriage or adoption.

   • an operator of a community care facility (Community care facilities are sometimes called board and care homes. If you are unsure whether a person you are thinking of selecting operates a community care facility, you should ask that person.)

   • an employee of a community care facility, unless the employee is related to me by blood, marriage or adoption.

_____ 3. I have talked with the individuals I have selected as my agent and alternate agents and these individuals have agreed to participate. (You may select someone who is not a California resident to act as your agent or alternate agent, but you should consider whether someone who lives out of state will be available to make decisions for you if and when that may become necessary.)

_____ 4. I have read the instructions and completed paragraphs 4, 5, 6, and 7 to reflect my desires.

_____ 5. I have *signed* and *dated* the form.

_____ 6. I have either:

   _____ had the form notarized; *or*

   _____ had the form properly witnessed:

      _____ 1. I have obtained the signatures of two witnesses who personally know me.

      _____ 2. Neither witness is:

         • my agent or alternate agent designated in this form.

         • a health care provider, or the employee of a health care provider.

         • a person who operates or is employed by a community care facility.

      _____ 3. At least one witness is not related to me by blood, marriage, or adoption, and is not named in my will or so far as I know entitled to any part of my estate when I die.

_____ 7. I HAVE GIVEN A COPY OF THE COMPLETED FORM TO THOSE PEOPLE INCLUDING MY AGENT, ALTERNATE AGENTS, FAMILY MEMBERS AND DOCTOR, WHO MAY NEED THIS FORM IN CASE AN EMERGENCY REQUIRES A DECISION CONCERNING MY HEALTH CARE.

Developed by the Committee on Evolving Trends in Society Affecting Life, California Medical Association, 1984. © California Medical Association, 44 Gough St., San Francisco, CA 94103. At the time this book went to press, legislation was pending that would require minor changes in the wording of this form. Copies of the Durable Power of Attorney for Health Care form that conform to current legal requirements are available at cost from the California Medical Association.

SPECIAL REQUIREMENTS

_____ 8. **Patients in Skilled Nursing Facilities.**
If I am a patient in a skilled nursing facility, I have obtained the signature of a patient advocate or ombudsman. (If you are not sure whether you are in a skilled nursing facility, you should ask the people taking care of you.)

_____ 9. **Conservatees under the Lanterman-Petris-Short Act.**
If I am a conservatee under the Lanterman-Petris-Short Act and want to select my conservator as my agent or alternate agent to make health care decisions, I have obtained a lawyer's certification.

IF AFTER READING THIS MATERIAL YOU STILL HAVE UNANSWERED QUESTIONS, YOU SHOULD TALK TO YOUR DOCTOR OR A LAWYER.

WARNING TO PERSON EXECUTING THIS DOCUMENT

This is an important legal document. It creates a Durable Power of Attorney for Health Care. Before executing this document, you should know these important facts:

This document gives the person you designate as your attorney in fact the power to make health care decisions for you, subject to any limitations or statement of your desires that you include in this document. The power to make health care decisions for you may include consent, refusal of consent, or withdrawal of consent to any care, treatment, service, or procedure to maintain, diagnose, or treat a physical or mental condition. You may state in this document any types of treatment or placements that you do not desire.

The person you designate in this document has a duty to act consistent with your desires as stated in this document or otherwise made known or, if your desires are unknown, to act in your best interests.

Except as you otherwise specify in this document, the power of the person you designate to make health care decisions for you may include the power to consent to your doctor not giving treatment or stopping treatment which would keep you alive.

Unless you specify a shorter period in this document, this power will exist for seven years from the date you execute this document and, if you are unable to make health care decisions for yourself at the time when this seven-year period ends, this power will continue to exist until the time when you become able to make health care decisions for yourself.

Notwithstanding this document, you have the right to make medical and other health care decisions for yourself so long as you can give informed consent with respect to the particular decision. In addition, no treatment may be given to you over your objection, and health care necessary to keep you alive may not be stopped if you object.

You have the right to revoke the appointment of the person designated in this document by notifying that person of the revocation orally or in writing.

You have the right to revoke the authority granted to the person designated in this document to make health care decisions for you by notifying the treating physician, hospital, or other health care provider orally or in writing.

The person designated in this document to make health care decisions for you has the right to examine your medical records and to consent to their disclosure unless you limit this right in this document.

If there is anything in this document that you do not understand, you should ask a lawyer to explain it to you.

1. CREATION OF DURABLE POWER OF ATTORNEY FOR HEALTH CARE

By this document I intend to create a durable power of attorney by appointing the person designated below to make health care decisions for me as allowed by Sections 2410 to 2443, inclusive, of the California Civil Code. This power of attorney shall not be affected by my subsequent incapacity.

2. DESIGNATION OF HEALTH CARE AGENT

*(Insert the name and address of the person you wish to designate as your agent to make health care decisions for you. None of the following may be designated as your agent: (1) your treating health care provider, (2) a **nonrelative** employee of your treating health care provider, (3) an operator of a community care facility, or (4) a **nonrelative** employee of an operator of a community care facility.)*

I, _____

(insert your name)

do hereby designate and appoint: Name: _____

Address: _____

Telephone Number: _____ as my attorney-in-fact (agent) to make health care decisions for me as authorized in this document.

3. GENERAL STATEMENT OF AUTHORITY GRANTED

If I become incapable of giving informed consent for health care decisions, I hereby grant to my agent full power and authority to make health care decisions for me including the right to consent, refuse consent, or withdraw consent to any care, treatment, service, or procedure to maintain, diagnose or treat a physical or mental condition, and to receive and to consent to the release of medical information, subject to the statement of desires, special provisions and limitations set out in paragraph 4.

4. STATEMENT OF DESIRES, SPECIAL PROVISIONS, AND LIMITATIONS

(Your agent must make health care decisions that are consistent with your known desires. You can, but are not required to, state your desires in the space provided below. You should consider whether you want to include a statement of your desires concerning decisions to withhold or remove life-sustaining treatment. For your convenience, some general statements concerning the withholding and removal of life-sustaining treatment are set out below. If you agree with one of these statements, you may INITIAL that statement. READ ALL OF THESE STATEMENTS CAREFULLY BEFORE YOU SELECT ONE TO INITIAL. You can also write your own statement concerning life-sustaining treatment and/or other matters relating to your health care. BY LAW, YOUR AGENT IS NOT PERMITTED TO CONSENT ON YOUR BEHALF TO ANY OF THE FOLLOWING: COMMITMENT TO OR PLACEMENT IN A MENTAL HEALTH TREATMENT FACILITY, CONVULSIVE TREATMENT, PSYCHOSURGERY, STERILIZATION OR ABORTION. In every other respect, your agent may make health care decisions for you to the same extent you could make them for yourself if you were capable of doing so. If you want to limit in any other way the authority given your agent by this document, you should state the limits in the space below. If you do not initial one of the printed statements or write your own statement, your agent will have the broad powers to make health care decisions on your behalf which are set forth in Paragraph 3, except to the extent that there are limits provided by law.)

I do **not** want my life to be prolonged, and I do **not** want life-sustaining treatment to be provided or continued if the burdens of the treatment outweigh the expected benefits. I want my agent to consider the relief of suffering and the quality as well as the extent of the possible extension of my life in making decisions concerning life-sustaining treatment.

I want my life to be prolonged and I want life-sustaining treatment to be provided **unless I am in a coma** which my doctors reasonably believe to be irreversible. Once my doctors have reasonably concluded I am in an irreversible coma, I do **not** want life-sustaining treatment to be provided or continued.

I want my life to be prolonged to the greatest extent possible without regard to my condition, the chances I have for recovery or the cost of the procedures.

If this statement reflects your desires, initial here _____ .

If this statement reflects your desires, initial here _____ .

If this statement reflects your desires, initial here _____ .

Other or additional statements of desires, special provisions, or limitations.

_____

_____

_____

_____

_____

(You may attach additional pages if you need more space to complete your statement. If you attach additional pages, you must DATE and SIGN EACH PAGE.)

5. CONTRIBUTION OF ANATOMICAL GIFT

(You may choose to make a gift of all or part of your body to a hospital, physician, or medical school for scientific, educational, therapeutic or transplant purposes. Such a gift is allowed by California's Uniform Anatomical Gift Act. If you do not make such a gift, you may authorize your agent to do so, or a member of your family may make a gift unless you give them notice that you do not want a gift made. In the space below you may make a gift yourself or state that you do not want to make a gift. If you do not complete this section, your agent will have the authority to make a gift of all or a part of your body under the Uniform Anatomical Gift Act.)

If either statement reflects your desires, sign the box next to the statement. **You do not have to sign either statement.** If you do not sign either statement, your agent and your family will have the authority to make a gift of all or part of your body under the Uniform Anatomical Gift Act.

(_____)   Pursuant to the Uniform Anatomical Gift Act, I hereby give,
　　　　　　(signature)　　　　　　　　effective upon my death:

☐ Any needed organ or parts; or

☐ The parts or organs listed:

_____

_____

_____

(_____)   I do not want to make a gift under the Uniform Anatomical
　　　　　　(signature)　　　　　　　　Gift Act, nor do I want my agent or family to do so.

6. DESIGNATION OF ALTERNATE AGENTS.

(You are not required to designate any alternate agents but you may do so. Any alternate agent you designate will be able to make the same health care decisions as the agent designated in Paragraph 1, above, in the event that agent is unable or unwilling to act as your agent. Also, if the agent designated in Paragraph 1 is your spouse, his or her designation as your agent is automatically revoked by law if your marriage is dissolved.)

If the person designated in Paragraph 2 as my agent is not available and willing to make a health care decision for me, then I designate the following persons to serve as my agent to make health care decisions for me as authorized in this document, such persons to serve in the order listed below:

A. First Alternative Agent

Name: _____

Address: _____

Telephone Number: _____

B. Second Alternative Agent

Name: _____

Address: _____

Telephone Number: _____

7. DURATION.

I understand that this power of attorney will exist for seven years from the date I execute this document unless I establish a shorter time. If I am unable to make health care decisions for myself when this power of attorney expires, the authority I have granted my agent will continue to exist until the time when I become able to make health care decisions for myself.

(Optional) I wish to have this power of attorney end before seven years on the following date: _____.
(Fill in this space ONLY if you want the authority of your agent to end EARLIER than the seven year period described above.)

8. PRIOR DESIGNATIONS REVOKED.

I revoke any prior durable power of attorney for health care.

Date and Signature of Principal

(YOU MUST DATE AND SIGN THIS POWER OF ATTORNEY)

I sign my name to this Durable Power of Attorney for Health Care on _____ at
                                                                                  (Date)

_____ , _____
                        (City)   *(State)*

                                    _____
                                                 (Signature of Principal)

THIS POWER OF ATTORNEY WILL NOT BE VALID UNLESS IT IS EITHER: (1) ACKNOWLEDGED BEFORE A NOTARY PUBLIC IN CALIFORNIA OR (2) SIGNED BY AT LEAST TWO QUALIFIED WITNESSES WHO PERSONALLY KNOW YOU AND ARE PRESENT WHEN YOU SIGN OR ACKNOWLEDGE YOUR SIGNATURE.

CERTIFICATE OF ACKNOWLEDGEMENT OF NOTARY PUBLIC

(You may use acknowledgment before a notary public instead of the statement of witnesses.)

State of California   )

) ss.

County of _____)

     On this _____ day of _____, in the year _____,

before me, _____ ,
                                    (here insert name of notary public)

personally appeared _____ ,
                                    (here insert name of principal)

personally known to me (or proved to me on the basis of satisfactory evidence), to be the person whose name is subscribed to this instrument, and acknowledged that he or she executed it. I declare under penalty of perjury that the person whose name is subscribed to this instrument appears to be of sound mind and under no duress, fraud, or undue influence.

NOTARY SEAL

                                    _____
                                                 (Signature of Notary Public)

STATEMENT OF WITNESSES

(If you elect to use witnesses instead of having this document notarized, you must use two qualified adult witnesses. None of the following may be used as a witness: (1) a person you designate as your agent or alternate agent, (2) a health care provider, (3) an employee of a health care provider, (4) the operator of a community care facility, (5) an employee of an operator of a community care facility. At least one of the witnesses must make the additional declaration set out following the place where the witnesses sign.)

I declare under penalty of perjury under the laws of California that the principal is personally known to me, that the principal signed or acknowledged this durable power of attorney in my presence, that the principal appears to be of sound mind and under no duress, fraud, or undue influence, that I am not the person appointed as attorney-in-fact by this document, and that I am not a health care provider, an employee of a health care provider, the operator of a community care facility, nor an employee of an operator of a community care facility.

Signature: _____ Residence Address: _____

Print Name: _____ _____

Date: _____ _____

Signature: _____ Residence Address: _____

Print Name: _____ _____

Date: _____ _____

(AT LEAST ONE OF THE ABOVE WITNESSES MUST ALSO SIGN THE FOLLOWING DECLARATION.)

I declare under penalty of perjury under the laws of California that I am not related to the principal by blood, marriage, or adoption, and to the best of my knowledge I am not entitled to any part of the estate of the principal upon the death of the principal under a will now existing or by operation of law.

Signature: _____

(Optional Second Signature): _____

COPIES

YOUR AGENT MAY NEED THIS DOCUMENT IMMEDIATELY IN CASE OF AN EMERGENCY THAT REQUIRES A DECISION CONCERNING YOUR HEALTH CARE. YOU SHOULD KEEP THE EXECUTED ORIGINAL DOCUMENT AND GIVE A COPY OF THE EXECUTED ORIGINAL TO YOUR AGENT AND ANY ALTERNATE AGENTS. YOU MAY ALSO WISH TO GIVE A COPY TO YOUR DOCTOR OR TO MEMBERS OF YOUR FAMILY. PHOTOCOPIES OF THIS DOCUMENT CAN BE RELIED UPON AS THOUGH THEY WERE ORIGINALS.

SPECIAL REQUIREMENTS

(Special additional requirements must be satisfied for this document to be valid if (1) you are a patient in a skilled nursing facility or (2) you are a conservatee under the Lanterman-Petris-Short Act and you are appointing the conservator as your agent to make health care decisions for you. If you are not sure whether you are in a skilled nursing facility, which is a special type of nursing home, ask the facility staff.)

1. If you are a patient in a skilled nursing facility (as defined in Health and Safety Code Section 1250(c)) at least one of the witnesses must be a patient advocate or ombudsman. The patient advocate or ombudsman must sign the witness statement **and** must also sign the following declaration:

I further declare under penalty of perjury under the laws of California that I am a patient advocate or ombudsman as designated by the State Department of Aging and am serving as a witness as required by subdivision (f) of Section 2432 of the Civil Code.

Signature: _____   Address: _____

Print Name: _____   _____

Date: _____   _____

2. If you are a conservatee under the Lanterman-Petris-Short Act (of Division 5 of the Welfare and Institutions Code) and you wish to designate your conservator as your agent to make health care decisions, you must be represented by legal counsel. Your lawyer must also sign the following statement:

I have advised my client _____ concerning
                                                 (Name)

his or her rights in connection with this matter and the consequences of signing or not signing this durable power of attorney and my client, after being so advised, has executed this durable power of attorney.

Signature: _____   Address: _____

Print Name: _____   _____

Date: _____   _____

California Medical Association
44 Gough Street, San Francisco 94103

CMA 11/84

APPENDIX G
MEMORANDUM TO NEWLY APPOINTED CONSERVATOR

Superior Court of California
San Francisco

JOHN A. ERTOLA, JUDGE

Dear Conservator:

You have now been appointed a Conservator.

I hope that the following comments will help answer some of the questions that may arise regarding the duties you have just assumed. My remarks are only general in nature, however, and you should always remember that your attorney is the person best qualified to advise you.

The attached memorandum is divided into three sections. The first section applies to all conservatorships. The second section is directed to those of you who have been appointed Conservator of Person only; the third section is intended for those who have been appointed Conservator of Estate only.

If you have been appointed Conservator of Person and Estate you should read the attached memorandum in its entirety.

My remarks are intended to alert you to the general nature of the duties and obligations you have assumed and, even more importantly, to remind you that you are entering upon a very honorable undertaking, the purpose of which is to provide for the welfare of another person.

I wish to thank you for your willingness to assume that responsibility. I am confident that you will not only perform this task well but that you will receive great satisfaction from the performance of your duties.

With every good wish, I am,

Sincerely yours,

JOHN A. ERTOLA

Prepared by Catherine Gibbons, Court Investigator under the direction of Judge John A. Ertola. Reprinted by the permission of Catherine Gibbons and John A. Ertola. San Francisco, 1982.

295

PROBATE DEPARTMENT
SUPERIOR COURT
CITY AND COUNTY OF SAN FRANCISCO

GENERAL COMMENTS

(This section applies to all Conservators and to all conservatorships.)

1. The date stamped at the top of the form entitled Letters of Conservatorship is the date on which you have been appointed a Conservator. This document empowers you to act.

2. Another document of importance is the Order Appointing Conservator. Every Conservatee retains certain rights unless they are specifically taken away by this Order or by other order of court. These rights include the right to make a Will, the right to contract for the necessities of life, the right to accept or refuse medical treatment, and the right to marry. The Order, or the finding of a Court Investigator, can also disqualify a Conservatee from voting. You should be familiar with the terms of the Order Appointing Conservator.

3. Your attorney should always know your current address and telephone number. In the event your permanent address or the address of the Conservatee changes, it is your responsibility to see that the court is notified.

4. Approximately one year after issuance of the Letters of Conservatorship, and every second year thereafter, a Court Investigator will arrange to visit the Conservatee. The purpose of these visits, basically, is to determine how the conservatorship is working and to help resolve any problems before they develop into major difficulties. The Court Investigator will cooperate fully with you and your attorney.

5. The court has the responsibility of seeing that the Conservatee is protected. This fact should not intimidate you. We consider that part of the protection we owe the Conservatee is the smooth operation of the conservatorship. The personnel of the Probate Department will always be willing to listen to your problems and they will help you in any way they can. There are services and agencies which provide in-home nursing care, house cleaning, shopping, and the like. Court personnel can direct you to these services.

6. Please remember, however, that court personnel cannot give legal advice. Your attorney is the person best qualified for that.

7. As Conservator you are entitled to be reimbursed for your reasonable expenses and to receive compensation for the services you render to the Conservatee. Your attorney will advise you how to apply for such payments.

CONSERVATORSHIP OF PERSON

(If you have been appointed Conservator of Estate only, the following section does not apply to you.)

As Conservator of Person you are responsible for the physical needs of the Conservatee. That means you are charged with supplying food, clothing, shelter, medical care and, if appropriate, education. The Probate Code states that you have the care, custody, and control of the Conservatee.

The Order Appointing Conservator may limit your powers, depending on the ability of the Conservatee to care for some of his or her own personal needs, and, in some cases, you may be given additional duties which would not ordinarily be required of a Conservator. Additional duties will never be imposed upon you without your prior knowledge and consent.

The care you provide the Conservatee should be suitable, depending upon the circumstances of the individual conservatorship. You may find that you receive a great deal of conflicting advice from relatives, friends, the medical profession, and others. But you are the person in charge. Do not be afraid to follow your judgment and common sense in deciding what is best for the Conservatee. Two areas require special mention.

Fixing the residence of the Conservatee: Unless the Order specifically states that the Conservatee can determine his own residence, you have the power to determine where, within the State of California, the Conservatee shall live. This is a serious responsibility and you should keep in mind that the least restrictive living arrangements are usually the best. Depending, of course, upon the condition of the Conservatee, the Conservatee's own home is preferable to a board and care facility and a board and care facility is better than a convalescent hospital. Strict legal provisions protect any Conservatee from being placed in a locked mental health facility without due process of law.

If you wish to move the Conservatee to another state, you must first get the permission of the court.

Medical care: Conservatees are not automatically deprived of the right to decide on their own medical care. If the Order does not declare that the Conservatee lacks the capacity to give informed medical consent, then he can consent (or refuse to consent) to his own treatment and, in such case, you can require that the Conservatee receive medical treatment you consider to be necessary only by securing a court order or, in an emergency, you can order treatment when it is necessary to alleviate severe pain or when lack of treatment would lead to serious disability or death.

If the Order states that the Conservatee does lack the capacity to give informed medical consent, you have the authority to act on his behalf and you can consent to such medical treatment as you determine to be necessary, with certain prohibitions:

(a) If, prior to the conservatorship, the Conservatee was an adherent of a religion calling for prayer alone for healing, the treatment must be by an accredited practitioner of that religion; and,

(b) No Conservatee can be forced to accept sterilization or certain drug treatments.

CONSERVATORSHIP OF ESTATE

(If you have been appointed Conservator of Person only, the following section does not apply to you.)

As Conservator of Estate your duties are twofold. You are expected:

(a) To furnish comfortable and suitable support and maintenance for the Conservatee, keeping in mind the size of the estate and the condition of the Conservatee; and,

(b) To use ordinary care and diligence in managing, protecting, and controlling the assets of the estate.

In appointing you Conservator of Estate the court has placed you in charge of the financial affairs and assets of the Conservatee. There are a few exceptions to your complete control; namely, the Conservatee has control over any wages or over any allowance. Establishment of an allowance is subject to court approval.

The Probate Code sets forth certain requirements which you must obey:

Separation of the estate's assets: You must keep the money and property of the estate separate and not mix or combine them with your own or other property.

Inventory and Appraisement: You must determine what assets exist and then, within three months of your appointment, file an Inventory of all the money and other property belonging to the Conservatee's estate as of the date of your appointment.

Accountings: One year after your appointment, and at least every two years thereafter, you must file an Accounting which shows the value of the estate at the start of the accounting period, all property received during the accounting period, what has been spent, and what is left on hand. The court reviews these Accountings; therefore, you should be careful that all expenditures from estate funds are proper and reasonable. You should keep careful records and obtain vouchers or receipts for your expenditures. Under certain circumstances the Probate Code permits a Conservator to dispense with Accountings if the estate is very small and the income limited. Your attorney can advise you if the estate you manage qualifies.

To summarize what is required:

Inventory is due — — — — — — — —   90 days after issuance of the Letters of Conservatorship

First Accounting is due — — — — —   One year after issuance of the Letters of Conservatorship

Future Accountings are due — — —   At least every second year thereafter

Unless the Order specifies otherwise, your appointment as Conservator of Estate means that the Conservatee lacks the legal capacity to enter into any contracts, except for the necessities of life. But at the same time the law protects any person who in good faith purchases real property from a Conservatee, unless a notice of the establishment of the conservatorship has been recorded in the county where the property is located. For this reason you should consider the prompt recording of such notice in any county where real property of the estate is located.

You should also be aware that if you are a Conservator for your spouse or for any other married person, even if the community property is not made a part of the conservatorship estate, you still have certain duties in connection with that community property.

Prior court authorization is not required for many of your routine actions, but certain actions you may think desirable will require prior court authority—such as some investments, borrowing money, selling real estate. The Probate Code itself places limitations upon certain actions. And all transactions are subject to court review. It is important, therefore, that you consult and cooperate with your attorney at all times. Your attorney will be happy to assist you in carrying out your responsibilities.

The foregoing comments are not intended to alarm you. Remember that the court has already determined you to be the person most qualified to serve as Conservator. If you rely on your attorney and on your own intelligence and good will, I am confident you will encounter no serious difficulties in carrying out your duties to your own, and to the court's, satisfaction. The best of luck to you.

JOHN A. ERTOLA
Judge of the Superior Court

APPENDIX H
California Penal Code §368
Person Causing Pain to
or Suffering of Dependent Adult;
Theft or Embezzlement by Caretaker

(a) Any person who, under circumstances or conditions likely to produce great bodily harm or death, willfully causes or permits any dependent adult, with knowledge that he or she is a dependent adult, to suffer, or inflicts thereon unjustifiable physical pain or mental suffering, or having the care or custody of any dependent adult, willfully causes or permits the person or health of the dependent adult to be injured, or willfully causes or permits the dependent adult to be placed in a situation such that his or her person or health is endangered, is punishable by imprisonment in the county jail not exceeding one year, or in the state prison for two, three, or four years.

(b) Any person who, under circumstances or conditions other than those likely to produce great bodily harm or death, willfully causes or permits any dependent adult, with knowledge that he or she is a dependent adult, to suffer, or inflicts thereon unjustifiable physical pain or mental suffering, or having the care or custody of any dependent adult, willfully causes or permits the person or health of the dependent adult to be injured or willfully causes or permits the dependent adult to be placed in a situation such that his or her person or health may be endangered, is guilty of a misdemeanor.

(c) Any caretaker of a dependent adult who violates any provision of law proscribing theft or embezzlement, with respect to the property of that dependent adult, is punishable by imprisonment in the county jail not exceeding one year, or in the state prison for two, three, or four years when the money, labor, or real or personal property taken is of a value exceeding four hundred dollars ($400), and by fine not exceeding one thousand dollars ($1,000) or by imprisonment in the county jail not exceeding one year, or both, when the money, labor, or real or personal property taken is of value not exceeding four hundred dollars ($400).

(d) As used in this section, "dependent adult" means a person who, because of any mental disability due to birth defect, physical disorder, or advanced age, is unable to properly provide for his or her own personal needs with regard to his or her physical health, food, clothing, or shelter, or is substantially unable to manage his or her own financial resources or to resist fraud or undue influence.

(e) As used in this section, "caretaker" means any person who has the care, custody, or control of or who stands in a position of trust with, a dependent adult. Leg. H. 1983 ch. 968, 1984 ch. 144 (amended and renumbered from §367a).

Reprinted from Deering's Penal code of the state of California 1985 pocket supplement. San Francisco: Bancroft-Whitney Co., 1985.

References

Ackley, D. A brief overview of child abuse. *Social Casework*, 1977, 58(1), 21–24.

Advocate's guide to elder abuse, neglect, and exploitation. Seattle: Evergreen Legal Services, 1983.

Alliance/Elder Abuse Project. *An analysis of states mandatory reporting laws on elder abuse*. Syracuse, N.Y.: Author, 1983.

Anastasio, C. J. *Elder abuse: Identification and acute care intervention*. Paper presented at the National Conference on Abuse of Older Persons, Boston, March 1981.

Anderson, S. *Management of child abuse and neglect, overview and protocol*. Seattle: Harborview Medical Center, 1981.

Arlow, J. A. Psychoanalysis. In R. J. Corsini (Ed.), *Current psychotherapies* (2nd ed.). Itasca, IL: F. E. Peacock, 1979.

Aronson, M. K. Update of Alzheimer's: Introduction. *Generations, Quarterly Journal of the Western Gerontological Society*, 1984, 9(2), 5–6.

Attorney General's Task Force on Family Violence. *Final Report*, Washington, DC, 1984.

Ban, T. A. The treatment of depressed geriatric patients. *American Journal of Psychotherapy*, 1978, 32, 93–104.

Basch, M. F. *Doing psychotherapy*. New York: Basic Books, 1980.

Berger, L., & Berger, M. A holistic group approach to psychogeriatric outpatients. *International Journal of Group Psychotherapy*, 1973, 23(4), 432–445.

Blake, R. What disables the American elderly. *Generations, Quarterly Journal of the Western Gerontological Society*. 1984, 8(4), 6–9.

Blenkner, M. Social work and the family. In E. Shanas & G. Streib (Eds.), *Social structure and the family: Intergenerational relationships*. Englewood Cliffs, NJ: Prentice-Hall, 1965.

Blenkner, M. The normal dependencies of aging. In R. Kalish (Ed.), *The dependencies of old people*. Ann Arbor: University of Michigan Institute of Gerontology, 1969.

Blenkner, M., Bloom, M., & Nielson, M. A research and demonstration project of protective services. *Social Casework*, 1971, 52(8), 483–497.

Block, M. R., & Sinnott, J. D. (Eds.). *The battered elder syndrome: An exploratory study*. College Park, MD: University of Maryland Center on Aging, 1979.

Block, M. R. Special problems and vulnerability of elderly women. In J. Kosberg (Ed.), *Abuse and maltreatment of the elderly: Causes and interventions*. Littleton, MA: John Wright·PSG, 1983.

Blom, M. F. Dramatic decrease in decubitus ulcers. *Geriatric Nursing*, 1985, *6*(2), 84–87.

Bloom, M., & Nielson, M. The older person in need of protective services. *Social Casework*, 1971, *52*(8), 500–509.

Borup, J. H. Transfer trauma and the law. *Generations, Quarterly Journal of the Western Gerontological Society*, 1984, *8*(3), 17–20.

Brantley, P. J., & Sutker, P. B. Antisocial behavior disorders. In H. E. Adams & P. B. Sutker (Eds.), *Comprehensive handbook of psychopathology*. New York: Plenum Press, 1984.

Brody, E. M. "Women in the middle" and family help to older people. *The Gerontologist*, 1981, *21*(5), 471–479.

Brody, E. M. Parent care as a normative family stress. *The Gerontologist*, 1985, *25*(1), 19–29.

Brody, E. M., & Spark, G. Institutionalization of the aged: A family crisis. *Family Process*, 1966 5, 76–90.

Brotman, H. *Every ninth American*. U.S. House of Representatives Select Committee on Aging, 97th Congress (Comm. Pub. No. 97-332), Washington, DC: Government Printing Office, 1982.

Brown, S. *The second forty years. Coalition for the Medical Rights of Women*. Transcription of a speech to the Fifth Annual Conference of the California Psychiatric Association, San Francisco, Dec. 1978.

Burnside, I. M. Clocks and calendars. *American Journal of Nursing*, 1970, *70*(1), 117–119.

Burnside, I. M. Long-term group work with the hospitalized aged. *The Gerontologist*, 1971, *11*(3)1, 213–218.

Burnside, I. M. *Nursing and the aged*. New York: McGraw-Hill, 1976.

Burr, J. J. *Protective services for adults*. U.S. Department of Health and Human Services [Pub. No. (OHDS) 82-20505], Washington, DC: 1982.

Burston, G. R. Do your elderly parents live in fear of being battered? *Modern Geriatrics*, November 16, 1978.

Butler, P. E. *Talking to yourself*. New York: Stein and Day, 1981.

Butler, R. N. The life review: An interpretation of reminiscence in the aged. *Psychiatry*, 1963, *26*, 65–76.

Butler, R. N. *Why survive? Being old in America*. New York: Harper & Row, 1975.

Butler, R. N., & Lewis, M. I. *Aging and mental health: Positive psychosocial approaches*. St. Louis: C. V. Mosby, 1973.

Butler, R. N., & Lewis, M. I. *Aging and mental health: Positive psychosocial and biomedical approaches* (3rd ed.). St. Louis: C. V. Mosby, 1982.

Caffey, J. Multiple fractures in the long bones of children suffering from chronic subdural hematoma. *American Journal of Roentgenology*, 1946, *56*, 163.

Cantwell, H. B. *Standards of child neglect*. Denver: Department of Social Services, 1978.

Carkhuff, R. R., & Anthony, W. A. *The skills of helping*. Amherst, MA: Human Resource Development Press, 1979.

Carson, B. Children's observations of interparental violence. In A. Roberts (Ed.), *Battered women and their families*. New York, Springer, 1984.

Clark, N. M., & Rakowski, W. Family caregivers of older adults: Improving helping skills. *The Gerontologist*, 1983, 23(6), 637–642.

Collins, M., & La France, A. B. *Improving protective services of older Americans: Social worker role*. Portland, ME: Human Services Development Institute, Center for research and Advanced Study, University of Southern Maine, Sept. 1982.

Commission on the Status of Women (COSW). Facts about comparable worth. San Francisco, COSW Publication, 1984.

Consortium for Elder Abuse Prevention. *Protocols*. San Francisco: Mount Zion Hospital and Medical Center, 1983.

Cormier, W. H., & Cormier, S. L. *Interviewing strategies for helpers*. Monterey, CA: Brooks/Cole, 1985.

Crossman, L., London, C., & Barry, C. Older women caring for disabled spouses: A model for supportive services. *The Gerontologist*, 1981, 21(5), 464–470.

Cutler, L. Counseling caregivers. *Generations, Quarterly Journal of the American Society on Aging*. 1985, 10(1), 53–57.

Davidson, H. *Mandatory reporting of child abuse: History and recent developments*. Paper presented at the National Conference on Abuse of Older Persons. Boston and San Francisco, March and April 1981. Sponsored by Legal Research and Services for the Elderly.

Davoren, E. The role of the social worker. In R. E. Helfer & C. H. Kempe, *The battered child*. Chicago: The University of Chicago Press, 1968.

Douglass, R. L., Hickey, T., & Noel, C. *A study of maltreatment of the elderly and other vulnerable adults*. Ann Arbor: Institute of Gerontology, University of Michigan, 1980.

Douglass, R. L., & Hickey, T. Domestic neglect and abuse of the elderly: Research findings and systems perspective for service delivery planning. In J. I. Kosberg (Ed.), *Abuse and maltreatment of the elderly: Causes and interventions*. Littleton, MA: John Wright·PSG, 1983.

Dowd, J. J. Aging as exchange: A preface to theory. *Journal of Gerontology*, 1975, 30, 585–594.

Drabble, M. *The middle ground*. Toronto: Bantam Books, 1980.

Ebersole, P. From despair to integrity through group reminiscing with the aged. *ANA Clinical Sessions, 1974*. New York: Appleton-Century-Crofts, 1975.

Ebersole, P. Reminiscing and group psychotherapy with the aged. In I. M. Burnside (Ed.), *Nursing and the aged*. New York: McGraw-Hill, 1976.

Ebersole, P. A theoretical approach to the use of reminiscence. In I. M. Burnside (Ed.), *Working with the elderly: Group processes and techniques*. New York: Duxbury Press, 1978.

Ebersole, P., & Hess, P. A. *Toward healthy aging: Human needs and nursing response*. St. Louis: C. V. Mosby, 1981.

Elliot, C. Notes from talk given on domestic violence and rape in marriage to King's County Prosecutor's Office, Seattle, WA, Dec. 1983.

English, R. W. Combating stigma toward physically disabled persons. In R. P. Marinelli & A. E. Dell Orto (Eds.), *The psychological and social impact of physical disability*. New York: Springer, 1977.

English, R. W. *Elder Abuse*. Philadelphia: Franklin Research Center, 1980.

Finklehor, D. Common features of family abuse. In D. Finkelhor, R. J. Gelles, G. Hotaling, & M. Straus (Eds.), *The dark side of families: Current family violence research*. Beverly Hills, CA: Sage, 1983.

Fitting, M. D., Rabins, P. V., & Lucas, M. J. *Caregivers for dementia patients: A comparison of men and women*. Paper presented at the 37th Annual Scientific Meeting of the Gerontological Society of America, San Antonio, TX, Nov. 1984.

Fitting, M., & Rabins, P. Men and women: Do they give care differently? *Generations, Quarterly Journal of the American Society on Aging*, 1985, *10*(1), 23–26.

Folstein, M. F., Folstein, S. E., & McHugh, P. R. Mini-mental state. *Journal of Psychiatric Research*, 1975, *12*(3), 189–198.

Foster, J. R., & Foster, R. P. Group psychotherapy with the old and aged. In H. I. Kaplan (Ed.), *Comprehensive group psychotherapy*. Baltimore: Williams & Wilkins, 1983.

Fry, P. S. Structured and unstructured reminiscence training and depression among the elderly. *Clinical Gerontologist*, 1983, *1*(3), 15–37.

Galbraith, M. W., & Zdorkowski, T. Teaching the investigation of elder abuse. *Journal of Gerontological Nursing*, 1984, *10*(12), 21–25.

Gambrill, E. *Casework: A competency-based approach*. Englewood Cliffs, NJ: Prentice-Hall, 1983.

Ganley, A. L. *Court mandated counseling for men who batter: A 3-day workshop for mental health professionals*. Washington, DC: Center for Women Policy Studies, 1981.

Gesino, J. P., Smith, H. H., & Keckich, W. A. The battered woman grows old. *Clinical Gerontologist*, Fall 1982, *1*(1), 59–67.

Golan, N. *Treatment in crisis situations*. New York: Free Press, 1978.

Golan, N. Crisis theory. In F. J. Turner (Ed.), *Social work treatment: Interlocking theoretical approaches*, New York: Free Press, 1979.

Goldfarb, A. I., & Sheps, J. Psychotherapy of the aged. In S. Steury & M. L. Blank (Eds.), *Readings in psychotherapy of older people*. Washington, DC: National Institute on Mental Health, 1978.

Goodwin, D. W., & Guze, S. B. *Psychiatric Diagnosis* (3rd ed.). New York and Oxford: Oxford University Press, 1984.

Guide to protective services: Alternatives in assisting vulnerable older adults. Seattle, WA: Evergreen Legal Services, 1981.

Havemeyer, H. *Key points for adult services testimony*. Lakewood, CO: Jefferson County Department of Social Services, 1980.

Havemeyer, H. *Adult protective services: Overview*. Lakewood, CO: Jefferson County Department of Social Services, 1982a.

Havemeyer, H. *Legal and social work values in adult protection*. Lakewood, CO: Jefferson County Department of Social Services, 1982b.

Havemeyer, H. *Philosophy of adult protective services*. Lakewood, CO: Jefferson County Department of Social Services, 1982c.

Havighurst, R. J., & Glasser, R. An exploratory study of reminiscence. *Journal of Gerontology*, 1972, *27*, 245–253.

Hayes, C. L. *A manual for the development, implementation, and operation of family support groups for the relatives of functionally disabled elderly*. Richmond, VA: Commonwealth of Virginia Department for the Aging, 1984a.

Hayes, C. L. *Elder abuse and the utilization of support groups for the relatives of functionally disabled older adults*. Center on Aging, Catholic University of America, Unpublished manuscript, 1984b.

Headley, L. *Adults and their parents in family therapy*. New York: Plenum Press, 1977.

Hennesscy, M. J. Music and group work with the aged. In I. M. Burnside (Ed.), *Nursing and the aged*. New York: McGraw-Hill, 1976.

Herr, J. J. Psychology of aging: An overview. In I. M. Burnside (Ed.), *Nursing and the aged*. New York: McGraw-Hill, 1976.

Herr, J. J., & Weakland, J. H. *Counseling elders and their families*. New York: Springer, 1979.

Heston, L. L., & White, J. A. *Dementia: A practical guide to Alzheimer's disease and related illnesses*. New York and San Francisco: W. H. Freeman, 1983.

Hickey, T., & Douglass, R. L. Neglect and abuse of older family members: Professionals' perspectives and case experience. *The Gerontologist*, 1981, *21*(4), 171–176.

Hooyman, N., & Lustbader, W. *Taking care: Supporting older people and their families*. New York: Free Press, 1985.

Huber, K., & Miller, P. Reminisce with the elderly—do it. *Geriatric Nursing*, March–April 1984, pp. 84–87.

Hwalek, M., Sengstock, M. C., & Lawrence, R. *Assessing the probability of abuse of the elderly*. Presented at the Annual Meeting of the Gerontological Society of America, Nov. 1984.

Improving protective services for older Americans, a national guide series. University of Southern Maine, 1982.

Ireland, M. Starting reality orientation and remotivation. *Nursing Homes*, 1972, *21*, 10–11.

Jacobs, M. More than a million older Americans abused physically and mentally each year. *Perspectives on Aging*, 1984, *13*(6), 19–20, 30.

Jarrett, W. Caregiving within kinship systems: Is affection really necessary? *The Gerontologist*, 1985, *25*(1), 5–10.

Jarrik, L. F., & Kumar, V. Update on diagnosis: A complex problem. *Generations, Quarterly Journal of the Western Gerontological Society*, 1984, *9*(2), 7–9.

Jensen, G. D., & Oakley, F. B. Aged appearance and behavior: An evolutionary and ethnological perspective. *The Gerontologist*, 1980, *20*(5), 595–597.

Johnson, C. L., & Catalano, D. J. A longitudinal study of family supports to impaired elderly. *The Gerontologist*, 1983, *23*(6), 612–618.

Johnson, D. Abuse of the elderly. *Nurse Practitioner*, 1981, *6*, 29–34.

Johnson, R. A. Mobilizing the disabled. In J. Freeman (Ed.), *Social movements of the sixties and seventies*. New York: Longman, 1983.

Kahn, R. L., Goldfarb, A., Pollack, M., & Peck, A. Brief objective measures for the determination of mental status in the aged. *American Journal of Psychiatry*, 1960, *117*(4), 326–328.

Katz, S., Ford, A. B., Moskowitz, R. W., Jackson, B. A., & Jaffe, M. W. Studies of illness in the aged—The index of ADL: A standardized measure of biological and psychosocial function. *Journal of the American Medical Association*, 1963, *185*(12), 914–919.

Kempe, C. H., & Kempe, R. S. *Child abuse*. Cambridge, MA: Harvard University Press, 1978.

Kennedy, T., Graham, W., Miller, S., & Davis, T. Management and prevention of pressure ulcers. *American Family Physician*, 1977, *15*(6), 84–90.

Kenoyer, L., & Bateman, P. *Peace of mind: Senior citizen self-protection*. Seattle: Alternatives to Fear, 1982.

King Lear. In W. Wright (Ed.), *The complete works of Shakespeare*. Cambridge Edition, New York: Garden City, 1936.

Kirkpatrick, C. *The family as process and institution*. New York: Ronald Press, 1955.

Klingbeil, K. *Domestic abuse—battered woman syndrome: Medical and social work protocol*. Seattle: Harborview Medical Center, 1979.

Klingbeil, K. S., & Boyd, V. D. Emergency room intervention: Detection, assessment, and treatment. In A. R. Roberts, (Ed.), *Battered women and their families*. New York: Springer, 1984.

Langsley, D. G., & Kaplan, D. M. *The treatment of families in crisis*. New York: Grune & Stratton, 1968.

Lau, E. A., & Kosberg, J. I. *Abuse of the elderly by informal care providers: Practice and research issues*. Paper presented at the 31st Annual Meeting of the Gerontological Society, Dallas, Nov. 1978.

Lau, E. A., & Kosberg, J. I. Abuse of the elderly by informal care providers. *Aging*, 299–300, Sept.–Oct. 1979, pp. 10–15.

London, C. *Elder abuse and the family: A systems approach*, Unpublished manuscript, 1983.

London, C. Personal communication, 1985.

Lowry, F. The caseworker in short contact services. *Social Work*, 1957 *2*(1), 52–56.

Mace, N. L., & Rabins, P. V. *The 36 hour day*. Baltimore: Johns Hopkins University Press, 1981.

Manfreda, M. L., & Krampitz, S. D. *Psychiatric nursing* (10th ed.). Philadelphia: F. A. Davis, 1977.

Martin, D. *Battered wives*. New York: Pocket Books, 1976.

Maslach, C. *Burnout—The cost of caring*. Englewood Cliffs, NJ: Prentice-Hall, 1982.

Mitchell, A. M. The objects of our wisdom and our coercion: Involuntary guardianship for incompetents. *Southern California Law Review*, 1979, 52, 1405–1442.

Mitchell, W. Bargaining and public choice. In H. Leavitt & L. Pondy (Eds.), *Readings in managerial psychology* (2nd ed.). Chicago: University of Chicago Press, 1973.

Murdach, A. Bargaining and persuasion with nonvoluntary clients. *Social Work*, 1980, *25*(6), 458–461.

National Center for Health Statistics, Feller, B. Americans needing help to function at home. *Advance data from vital and health statistics*, No. 92. DHHS Pub. No. (PHS) 82-1250. Hyattsville, MD: Public Health Service, Sept. 1983.

Nuessel, F. H. The language of ageism. *The Gerontologist*, 1982, 22(3), 273–275.

O'Malley, H. C., Segars, H., Perez, R., Mitchell, V., & Knuepel, G. M. *Elder abuse in Massachusetts: A survey of professionals and paraprofessionals*. Boston: Legal Research and Services for the Elderly, 1979.

O'Malley, T. A., Everett, E. D., O'Malley, H. C., & Campion, E. W. Identifying and preventing family mediated abuse and neglect of elderly persons. *Annals of Internal Medicine*, 1983, 90(6), 998–1005.

Ory, M. G. The burden of care. *Generations, Quarterly Journal of the American Society on Aging*, 1985 10(1), 14–17.

Ostrovski (Quinn), M. J. Life review and depression in late life. Unpublished master's thesis, 1977.

Ostrovski (Quinn), M. J., Transition to adulthood. In I. M. Burnside, P. Ebersole, & H. E. Monea (Eds.). *Psychosocial caring throughout the life span*. New York: McGraw-Hill, 1979.

Ostrovski-Quinn, M. J. The frail vulnerable old. In P. Ebersole & P. Hess (Eds.), *Toward healthy aging: Human needs and nursing response* (2nd ed.). St. Louis: C. V. Mosby, 1985.

Parad, H. J. Crisis intervention. In *Encyclopedia of social work* (Vol. 1). Washington, DC: National Association of Social Workers, 1971.

Parad, H. J., Selby, L., & Quinlan, J. Crisis intervention with families and groups. In R. W. Roberts & H. Northern (Eds.), *Theories of social work with groups*. New York: Columbia University Press, 1976.

Pedrin, V., & Brown, S. Sexism and ageism: Obstacles to health care for women. *Generations, Quarterly Journal of the Western Gerontological Society*, 1980, 4(4), 20–21.

Pepper, C. *Opening statement: Elder abuse: A national disgrace*. Hearing before the U.S. House Select Committee on Aging, Subcommittee on Health and Long-term Care. May 10, 1985. Washington, DC.

Pfeiffer, E., & Busse, E. W. Mental disorders in later life—affective disorders: Paranoid, neurotic, and situational reaction. In E. W. Busse & E. Pfeiffer, *Mental illness in later life*. Washington, DC: American Psychiatric Association, 1973.

Phillips, L. R. Abuse and neglect of the frail elderly at home: An exploration of theoretical relationships. *Journal of Advanced Nursing*, 1983, 3, 379–392.

Pillemer, K. *Domestic violence against the elderly: A case-control study*. Unpublished doctoral dissertation, Department of Sociology, Brandeis University, 1985a.

Pillemer, K. *The dangers of dependency: New findings on domestic violence against the elderly*. Annual Meeting of the American Sociological Association, Aug. 1985b.

Pillemer, K., & Finkelhor, D. *Domestic violence against the elderly: A discussion paper*. A paper prepared for the Surgeon General's Workshop on Violence and Public Health, Leesburg, VA, Oct. 27–29, 1985.

Pizzey, E. *Scream quietly or the neighbors will hear*. Baltimore: Penguin Books, 1974.

Quinn, M. J. Elder abuse and neglect raise new dilemmas. *Generations, Quarterly Journal of the American Society on Aging*, 1985, *10*(2), 22–25.

Radbill, S. A history of child abuse and infanticide. In R. E. Helfer & C. H. Kempe (Eds.), *The battered child*. Chicago: The University of Chicago Press, 1968.

Rapoport, L. The state of crisis: Some theoretical considerations. *Social Service Review*, 1962, *36*(2), 211–217.

Rapoport, L. Crisis intervention as a mode of brief treatment. In R. W. Roberts & R. H. Nee (Eds.), *Theories of social casework*. Chicago: University of Chicago Press, 1970.

Rathbone-McCuan, E. *Inter-generational family violence and neglect: The aged as victims of reactivated and reverse neglect*. Presented at International Conference of Gerontology. Japan, Nov. 1978.

Rathbone-McCuan, E. Elderly victims of family violence and neglect. *Social Casework*, 1980, *61*(5), 296–304.

Rathbone-McCuan, E. Older women: Endangered but surviving species. *Generations, Quarterly Journal of the Western Gerontological Society*, 1982, *6*(3), 11–12, 59.

Rathbone-McCuan, E., & Voyles, B. Case detection of abused elderly parents. *American Journal of Psychiatry*, 1982, *139*, 189–192.

Rathbone-McCuan, E., Travis, A., & Voyles, B. Family intervention: Applying the task centered approach. In J. Kosberg (Ed.), *Abuse and maltreatment of the elderly: Causes and intervention*. Littleton: John Wright·PSG, 1983.

Roberts, A. R. Intervention with the abusive partner: In A. R. Roberts (Ed.), *Battered women and their families: Intervention strategies and treatment programs*. New York: Springer, 1984.

Romaniuk, M. The application of reminiscing to the clinical interview. *Clinical Gerontologist*, 1983, *1*(3), 39–43.

Roy, M. (Ed.), *The abusive partner: Analysis of domestic battering*. New York: Van Nostrand Reinhold, 1982.

Salend, E., Kane, R. A., Satz, M., & Pynoos, J. Elder abuse reporting: Limitations of statutes. *The Gerontologist*, 1984, *24*(1), 61–69.

Schmidt, G. L., & Keyes, B. Group psychotherapy with family caregivers of demented patients. *The Gerontologist*, 1985, *25*(4), 347–349.

Schmidt, M. G. Failing parents, aging children. *Journal of Gerontological Social Work*, 1980, *2*(3), 259–268.

Seligman, M. E. P. *Helplessness*. San Francisco: W. H. Freeman, 1975.

Sengstock, M. C., & Hwalek, M. *A critical analysis of measures for the identification of physical abuse and neglect of the elderly*. Presented at the Annual Meeting of the Gerontological Society of America, Nov. 1983(a).

Sengstock, M. C., & Hwalek, M. *Sources of information used in measures for the identification of elder abuse*. Presented at the Annual Meeting of the Gerontological Society of America, Nov. 1983b.

Shanas, E. *The health of older people: A social survey*. Cambridge: Harvard University Press, 1962.

Simon, B. K. Social casework theory: An overview. In R. W. Roberts, & R. H. Nee (Eds.), *Theories of social casework*. Chicago: University of Chicago Press, 1970.

Snyder, M. Self-fulfilling stereotypes. *Psychology Today*, 1982, *16*(7), 60–68.

Sommers, T. Untitled article. *The WGS Connection*. Newsletter published by the Western Gerontological Society, 1984, 5(1), 1.

Sommers, T. Caregiving: A woman's issue. *Generations, Quarterly Journal of the American Society on Aging*, 1985, *10*(1), 9–13.

Sonkin, D. J., & Durphy, M. *Learning to live without violence*. San Francisco: Volcano Press, 1982.

Sonkin, D. J., Martin, D., & Walker, L. E. A. *The male batterer*. New York: Springer, 1985.

Star, B. Treating the battered woman. In J. Hanks (Ed.), *Towards human dignity: Social work in practice*. Fifth NASW Symposium. Washington, DC: National Association of Social Workers, 1978

Steele, B. F., & Pollock, C. B. A psychiatric study of parents who abuse infants and small children. In R. E. Helfer & C. H. Kempe (Eds.), *The battered child*. Chicago: University of Chicago Press, 1968.

Steinmetz, S. K. Battered parents. *Society*, 1978, *15*(15), 54–55.

Steinmetz, S. K. *Prepared statement: Elder abuse: The hidden problem*. Briefing by the Select Committee on Aging. United States House of Representatives. 96th Congress, June 23, 1979. Boston, MA, Washington, DC. 1980, pp. 7–10.

Steinmetz, S. K. Elder abuse. *Aging*, 315–316, Jan.–Feb. 1981, pp. 6–10.

Steinmetz, S. K. Dependency, stress and violence between middle-aged caregivers and their elderly parents. In J. I. Kosberg (Ed.), *Abuse and maltreatment of the elderly*. Boston: John Wright·PSG, 1983.

Steuer, J. Caring for the caregiver. *Generations, Quarterly Journal of the Western Gerontological Society*, 1984, 9(2), 56–57.

Steuer, J., & Austin, E. Family abuse of the elderly. *Journal of American Geriatric Society*, 1980, *28*, 372–376.

Stone, G. Patient compliance and the role of the expert. *Journal of Social Issues*, 1979, *35*(1), 34–59.

Straus, M. A. *A sociological perspective on the causes of family violence*. Paper presented at American Association for the Advancement of Science, Houston, Tex., Jan. 1979.

Straus, M. A., Gelles, R., & Steinmetz, S. K. *Behind closed doors: Violence in the American family*. Garden City, NY: Anchor/Doubleday, 1980.

Streib, G. Older families and their troubles: Familial and social responses. *Family Coordinator*, 1972, *21*, 5–19.

Strickler, M., & Bonnefil, M. Crisis intervention and social casework: Similarities and differences in problem solving. *Clinical Social Work Journal*, 1974, 2(1), 36–44.

Szaz, T. S., & Hollander, M. H. A contribution to the philosophy of medicine: The basic models of the doctor–patient relationship. *Archives of Internal Medicine*, 1956, 97(5), 585–592.

Taulbee, L., & Folsom, J. C. Reality orientation for geriatric patients. *Hospital and Community Psychiatry*, 1966, *17*, 133–135.

Thobaben, M., & Anderson, L. Reporting elder abuse: It's the law. *American Journal of Nursing*, 1985, 85(4), 371–374.

Tomita, S., Clark, H., Williams, V., & Rabbitt, T. *Detection of elder abuse and neglect in a medical setting*. Paper presented at First National Conference on Abuse of Older Persons, San Francisco, 1981.

Tomita, S. Detection and treatment of elderly abuse and neglect: A protocol for health care professionals. *PT & OT in Geriatrics*, 1982, 2(2), 37–51.

Umana, R. F., Gross, S. J., & McConville, M. T. *Crisis in the family*. New York: Gardner Press, 1980.

U.S. Bureau of the Census, Current Population Reports, Series P-23, No. 128. *America in transition: An aging society*. Washington, DC: Government Printing Office, 1983.

U.S. Bureau of the Census, Current Population Reports, Series P-23, No. 138. *Demographic and socioeconomic aspects of aging in the United States*. Washington, DC: Government Printing Office, 1984.

U.S. Department of Health and Human Services. *Alzheimer's disease* [DHHS Publication No. (ADM) 84-1323]. Washington, DC: Government Printing Office, Sept. 1984.

U.S. House of Representatives Select Committee on Aging. *Elder abuse: An examination of a hidden problem*. 97th Congress (Comm. Pub. No. 97-277), Washington, DC: Government Printing Office, 1981.

U.S. Senate Special Committee on Aging in conjunction with the American Association of Retired Persons. *Aging America: Trends and projections* (2nd ed.). Washington, DC, 1984.

Villamore, E., & Bergman, J. (Eds.). *Elder abuse and neglect: A guide for practitioners and policy makers*. Manual prepared for the Oregon Office of Elder Affairs by the National Paralegal Institute, San Francisco, CA, and Legal Research & Services for the Elderly, Boston, MA, Feb. 1981.

Walker, L. E. *The battered woman*. New York: Harper & Row, 1979.

— Walker, L. E. *The battered woman syndrome*. New York: Springer, 1984.

Wasserman, S. L. Ego psychology. In J. F. Turner (Ed.), *Social work treatment: Interlocking theoretical approaches*. New York: Free Press, 1979.

Weston, J. T. The pathology of child abuse. In R. E. Helfer & C. H. Kempe, (Eds.), *The battered child*. Chicago: University of Chicago Press, 1968.

Williamson, J., Stokoe, I. H., Gray, S., Fisher, M., Smith, A., McGhee, A., & Stephenson, E. Old people at home: Their unreported needs. *Lancet*, 1964, 1(1743), 1117–1120.

Wolf, R., Strugnell, C. P., & Godkin, M. A. *Preliminary findings from three model projects on elderly abuse*. Worcester, MA: University of Massachusetts Medical Center, Center on Aging, Dec. 1982.

Wolf, R. S., Godkin, M. A., & Pillemer, K. A. *Elder abuse and neglect: Final report from three model projects*. Worcester, MA: University of Massachusetts Medical Center, Dec. 1984.

Wolf, R. S., & Pillemer, K. A. *Working with abused elders: Assessment, advocacy, and intervention*. Worcester, MA: University of Massachusetts Medical Center, 1984.

Women's Studies Program and Policy Center. Inequality of sacrifice: The impact of the Reagan budget on women. George Washington University, 1982.

Wurtman, R. J. Alzheimer's disease. *Scientific American,* 1985, *252*(1), 62–74.

Zarit, S. W., Reever, K. E., & Bach-Peterson, J. Relatives of impaired elderly: Correlates of feelings of burden. *The Gerontologist,* 1980, *10*(6), 649–655.

Zarit, S. W. New directions. *Generations, Quarterly Journal of the American Society on Aging,* 1985, *10*(1), 6–8.

Index